WEYERHAEUSER ENVIRONMENTAL BOOKS

William Cronon, Editor

Weyerhaeuser Environmental Books explore human relationships with natural environments in all their variety and complexity. They seek to cast new light on the ways that natural systems affect human communities, the ways that people affect the environments of which they are a part, and the ways that different cultural conceptions of nature profoundly shape our sense of the world around us. A complete list of the books in the series appears at the end of this book.

CHRISTOPHER W. WELLS

UNIVERSITY OF WASHINGTON PRESS
Seattle and London

CAR COUNTRY

AN ENVIRONMENTAL HISTORY

Foreword by William Cronon

Car Country: An Environmental History is published
with the assistance of a grant from the Weyerhaeuser
Environmental Books Endowment, established by the
Weyerhaeuser Company Foundation, members of the
Weyerhaeuser family, and Janet and Jack Creighton.

© 2012 by the University of Washington Press
Printed and bound in the United States of America
Design by Thomas Eykemans
Composed in Sorts Mill Goudy by Barry Schwartz
Display type set in Intro by Svetoslav Simov
17 16 15 14 13 12   5 4 3 2 1

UNIVERSITY OF WASHINGTON PRESS
PO Box 50096, Seattle, WA 98145, USA
www.washington.edu/uwpress

LIBRARY OF CONGRESS CATALOGING-IN-PUBLICATION DATA
Wells, Christopher W.
Car country : an environmental history / Christopher W. Wells.
    p. cm. — (Weyerhaeuser environmental books)
Includes bibliographical references and index.
ISBN 978-0-295-99215-0 (hbk. : alk. paper)
1. Automobiles—Environmental aspects—United States—History.
2. Automobiles—Social aspects—United States—History.
3. Transportation, Automotive—United States—History.
4. Urban transportation—United States—History.
5. City planning—United States—History.
6. Land use—United States—History.
1. Title.
HE5623.W45 2012   388.3′420973—dc23   2012026654

For Marianne

CONTENTS

FOREWORD
Far More Than Just a Machine

WILLIAM CRONON

If I were to ask my students who invented the automobile, I suspect their most likely response would be Henry Ford. That answer would be wrong, but wrong for the right reasons. Although there are a number of candidates for the first creator of a road vehicle powered not by animals but by steam or electricity or petroleum, no one person can be given credit for the transportation technology that ultimately changed the face of the planet over the course of the twentieth century. By the time Ford began adding gasoline engines to four-wheeled vehicles in the 1890s, he was one of a small legion of inventors all trying to do the same thing. He became famous in 1904 when one of his cars set a new land speed record of more than ninety miles per hour, but that is not why my students (and most of the rest of us) remember his name more than anyone else associated with the early history of the automobile. It was his invention of the wildly popular Model T in 1908 that assured his place in history and in our memories.

Ford's Model T may not have been the first automobile, but it was the first to make a compelling case that owning and operating a car might become a normative experience for most Americans. By embracing a robustly simple design that any reasonably competent mechanic could maintain, by using standard interchangeable parts, and by manufacturing the vehicles by arranging workflow along an assembly line (a technique he introduced in 1913), Ford was able to reduce his costs of production so much that he could repeatedly cut the price of these "Tin Lizzies," successfully marketing them to middle-class customers and even to his own workers. When his employees began quitting because of the grueling pace required by the assembly line, Ford doubled their wages by introducing the five-dollar workday, which had the indirect effect of making it more possible for these working-class Americans to purchase the cars they were building. Ford eschewed changes in style, famously remarking that his customers could have the car in any color they wanted as long as it was black, and this too held down costs even though it opened the door to the changing styles and brands that by the 1920s would characterize one of Ford's most successful competitors, General Motors. But that lay in the future. By the end of World War I, half the cars in the United States were Model T's.

That is why my students would not be entirely wrong if they guessed that Henry Ford invented the automobile, for that error hides a deeper truth. Although we tend to think of a car as a single object—that is, after all, the way we purchase it—it actually consists of myriad different parts, each of which has behind it a complex history of invention, development, and use. The internal combustion engine has quite a different history than the petroleum distillates that power it, the generator providing the sparks to ignite that fuel, the drive shaft that conveys rotational energy to the wheels, or the rubber with which the tires on those wheels are made—and this list only scratches the surface of all the different pieces that must be brought together if a car is ever to make it out of the garage and onto the road. Ford's genius was to figure out a way to assemble these parts in the cheapest possible way, which in turn enabled him to sell more than fifteen million Model T's by 1927.

But the car itself is hardly the end of the story. If most of us take utterly for granted the complex inner mechanisms beneath the hoods of our automobiles, the same is no less true of complex features of the highways and street systems on which we operate these vehicles and the landscapes through which we drive. Although a passing familiarity with the history of transportation technologies quickly leads one to conclude that the twentieth century was the age of the automobile just as the nineteenth century had been the age of the railroad, most of us rarely stop to think about what that actually means. In truth, the rise in the United States of a culture in which mass ownership of automobiles became typical constituted one of the most sweeping cultural and environmental revolutions in human history. What Ford and his fellow automobile manufacturers helped invent—with help from countless others—was essentially a technological ecosystem, an intricate set of interconnected inventions, institutions, and behaviors that by mid-century more or less defined the American way of life.

This is the great insight that organizes Christopher W. Wells's superb new book, *Car Country: An Environmental History*. Wells seeks in this lively, playful, and wonderfully accessible account to introduce readers to the transformations wrought upon the national landscape of the United States to make it fit for Americans and their cars. He tells us the stories not just of Ford and his Model T, but of highway engineers, street designers, real estate developers, policy-makers, and all the other people and professions who created the automobile infrastructures that became second nature to Americans during the twentieth century. Almost nothing about Car Country escapes Wells's eye: the gravel and asphalt with which highways are paved, the layout of streets designed for different speeds of travel past and through neighborhoods, the road signs and other navigational devices that enable strangers to make their way through communities they have never visited before, the retail institutions that were able to attract ever larger numbers of customers from ever greater distances—and, of course, the concomitant challenge of figuring out where all those customers could possibly park all those cars. Witness the emergence of this automobile-dependent landscape in the pages of this book, and you will never again see the world around you in quite the same way.

You can read this book purely for the pleasure of discovering the stories behind endless features of your own life and world that are probably so familiar that you barely even notice them. I know of no other book that explores in a single volume so many different aspects of our automobile-dependent culture: the design of cars, the paving of streets, the engineering of highways, the refining of gasoline, the taxing of fuel sales at the pump, the laying out of subdivisions, the marketing of real estate, the zoning of cities, the building of parking lots, the lobbying of legislatures, and so on and on and on. If any of these sound dry or technical, never fear: Chris Wells is an engaging storyteller, and the only thing dry about this book is his sardonic wit. Amid his many explanations of how and why Car Country works the way it does—and he is a master explainer—is a constant peppering of anecdotes and observations that make the book a delight to read.

But Wells also has a much larger purpose in mind. He opens the book by reflecting on his own youthful enthusiasm for the first vehicle he ever owned, a 1975 SR5 long-bed Toyota pickup truck that symbol-ized freedom and adulthood and that made his teenage comings and goings far easier than would otherwise have been the case. Then he went off to a small liberal arts college without a car and found to his surprise that he rarely missed it—except when he returned home to Atlanta and found himself in need of a vehicle to do almost anything. During extended travels in Europe, he again found himself missing his car almost not at all—until he came home to Atlanta and again felt his mobility and lifestyle severely cramped, because neither his bicycle nor the available mass transit options were sufficient to get him safely to where he needed to go. "With such poor options for getting around," he remembers, "I felt incapacitated without a car." Then he went off to graduate school in Madison, Wisconsin, where the university and its student neighborhoods are compactly laid out on an isthmus between two lakes, and suddenly the car again became as much an inconvenience as a benefit.

From this small autobiographical sketch, Wells draws a large and important conclusion. Once one recognizes that the automobile is not just a machine but a single element in a vast technical ecosystem in which every part is connected to every other and all human behaviors and institutions are shaped by its presence or absence, one is forced to recognize that any changes in this car-dependent landscape are almost inevitably trickier and more complicated than they first appear. It's not just that Americans love their automobiles; it's that the landscape we have created for them makes no other options available to us. We have no choice but to love them. John Muir once famously said of the natural world that "when we try to pick out anything by itself, we find it hitched to everything else in the universe." The same is equally true of the human world, for reasons that have as much to do with history and culture as they do with nature. It has taken more than a century to create the complex interconnections that have made Car Country second nature to us. The scale of our resulting dependence on the automobile is so vast—ranging fractally from the largest public works project in history (the interstate highway system) all the way to what we do when we feel the impulse to drink a well-made cup of coffee—that unwinding these dependencies is hard even to imagine. And yet we may have no choice in the matter, since some of the elements on which the system depends—cheap liquid fuel most of all—may prove less sustainable in the twenty-first century than they appeared to be in the twentieth. Sustainable or not, the challenge of imagining our transportation future will require a better understanding of our transportation past than most of us now possess. To grasp the complexities and fascinations and paradoxes of Car Country, I know of no better guide than this engaging book.

ACKNOWLEDGMENTS

When I first began to work on what ultimately became this book, now nearly a dozen years ago, I had little inkling of just how much its completion would rely on the stunning generosity, support, insight, and assistance of others. I can never hope to repay the debts that I have accrued, but I am more than happy to name names.

I owe particular thanks to my mentors at the University of Wisconsin–Madison, Bill Cronon and the late Paul Boyer, whose extraordinarily high standards for scholarship, teaching, advising, and engaging with a scholarly community were exceeded only by the understated grace and modesty with which they both modeled those standards. I am more grateful than I can say for their advice, rigor, generosity, and friendship. James Baughman, Rudy Koshar, Eric Schatzberg, and Stanley Schultz also lent their critical eyes and ears to my research in its early phase, improving it in ways large and small. Chuck Cohen, Linda Gordon, Bill Reese, Anne Firor Scott, and Joel Wolfe had nothing directly to do with this project, but all are fine scholars and teachers who went out of their way to help me learn what it means to be a historian.

At the University of Washington Press, acquiring editor Marianne Keddington-Lang provided constant advice, encouragement, and support through the long process of transforming my research into a book. Together with Bill Cronon, she has helped make the Weyerhaeuser Environmental Books series at the University of Washington Press into a real community of authors, not just a list of books. Were I to have tried to dream up a better editor, I would have fallen well short of the mark that Marianne establishes. I am indebted as well to Julie Van Pelt, who read the final manuscript with an incredible combination of precision and artistic sensibility.

Many others have read drafts, offered advice, and helped me with the process of transforming crude ideas into a more polished form. Peter Norton and one anonymous reviewer read the entire manuscript with critical eyes, offering suggestions and insights that measurably improved the final product. Ellen Arnold and Tom Robertson read and critiqued most of the manuscript, much of it in prose so raw that none but true friends would willingly subject themselves to the task. Greg Bond, David Hertzberg, Hiroshi Kitamura, and Michael Rawson all read and commented on the lion's share of my dissertation, and Jeff Allred, Thomas Andrews, Will Barnett, Katie Benton-Cohen, Tracey Deutsch, Jim Feldman, Jeff Filipiak, and Alexander Shashko also read, commented on, and improved various portions of the book. Thanks as well to J. Brooks Flippen, Mathieu Flonneau, Libbie Freed, Jordan Kleiman, Timothy Lecain, Tom McCarthy, Clay McShane, Martin Melosi, Federico Paolini, Pamela Pennock, Paul Sutter, and Thomas Zeller, and the audiences of panels at various conferences where I presented pieces of the research in this book. Thanks for their help and insights to Brian Black, Ed Linenthal, Karen Merrill, Ty Priest, and the anonymous readers at the *Journal of American History*; Pamela Laird, John Staudenmaier, and the anonymous readers at *Technology and Culture*; and Claire Strom at *Agricultural History*. And finally, a heartfelt thanks to the students in several iterations of the research seminar that I have taught on the subject of this book at Macalester College, Davidson College, and Northland College. In addition to giving me a platform to think out loud about its subjects and issues, these students contributed their own perceptive ideas and provided a critical audience, helping me weed out some of my less useful approaches to the material.

Before I could write a word, I benefited from the labors of what feels like a countless number of librarians, reference specialists, and archivists, who helped me navigate collections and track down elusive materials while offering the sort of moral support that keeps isolated researchers going even when they encounter an inevitable rough patch. At The Henry Ford, where I spent four months in the archives, thanks to Judith Endelman, Mark Greene, Cathy Latendresse, Andy Schornick, and Linda Skolarus. I also owe a substantial debt to the staff of the Library of Congress, who filled my steady stream of book orders and shared their magnificent reading room, which served as my daily office for six months. Jeffrey Stine and Roger White at the Smithsonian showed me their collections, answered my questions, and helped make my time in Washington a pleasant experience. I would also like to express gratitude to the many librarians and archivists at the National Archives II, the Bentley Historical Library, the Detroit Public Library, the State Historical Society of Wisconsin, and the Minnesota Historical Society. The interlibrary loan staffs at both the University of Wisconsin–Madison and Macalester College secured a multitude of sources ranging from the important to the obscure, without which I simply could not have written this book. Last but not least, Terri Fishel and her staff provided a sabbatical office in the Macalester College library, offering a quiet place to work as well as help and collegiality whenever I descended from the garret.

A remarkable range of people contributed to my research along the way. Maggie Hughes helped me get organized as I pivoted from working on research to working on a book, and Ben Poupard confirmed a hunch by tracking down important evidence in the Ford archives. Trent Boggess, Lendol Calder, Bob Casey, and David Louter generously shared their knowledge and materials at key points in the process. Aaron Isaacs shared his vast expertise about railroads and streetcars at a crucial point and provided the commuter rail timetables for St. Paul Park that became the basis for one of the maps in this book. I owe an eternal debt to Ross Donihue, Sarah Horowitz, and Birgit Muehlenhaus, who applied their GIS savvy to help me transform a motley mix of timetable information, railroad and streetcar maps, road construction maps, oil pipeline maps, and my own nascent ideas into elegant cartographic renderings.

Even more people provided intangible support along the way as friends, colleagues, students, and intellectual sparring mates. Special thanks to Shelby Balik, Karen Benjamin, Jonathan Berkey, Ann MacLaughlin Berres, Dawn Biehler, Louisa Bradtmiller, Scott Breuninger, Thea Browder, Ernie Capello, Chris Capozzola, Adrienne Christiansen, the late Judy Cochran, Hal Cohen, Alison Craig, Vivien Dietz, Jerald Dosch, Ann Esson, Ted and Abby Frantz, Tony Gaughan, Aram Goudsouzian, John Gripentrog, Suzanne Savanick Hansen, Paul Hass, Sandy Heitzkey, Dave Holmes, Jack Holzheuter, Dan Hornbach, Lynn Hudson, Mary and Toni Karlsson, Tina Kruse, David Levinson, Jane Mangan, Christie Manning, Sarah Marcus, Tom McGrath, Sally McMillen, Ray Mohl, Alicia Muñoz, Lara Nielsen, Nancy O'Brien Wagner, Roopali Phadke, Bill Philpott, Peter Rachleff,

Andy Rieser, Mark Rose, Honor Sachs, Jim Schlender, Zach Schrag, Matt Semanoff, David Sheffler, Tony Shugaar, Deb Smith, Kendra Smith-Howard, Chris Taylor, Trish Tilburg, Dan Trudeau, George Vrtis, and Kristen Walton.

Generous financial support also helped bring this book to fruition. At the University of Wisconsin–Madison, various grants and travel fellowships helped launch the early stages of research. A Henry Austin Clark Fellowship from The Henry Ford made possible my extended time in Dearborn. Several awards from the Mellon-funded Three Rivers Center at Macalester helped extend my sabbatical, buying much-needed time to dedicate myself to full-time writing. I am particularly grateful for the investments that Macalester College makes in its junior faculty. Without its generous junior sabbatical and family leave policies, completing this book would have been a very different—and much more difficult—process.

Last, but certainly not least, I owe a tremendous personal debt to the members of my family. Their love, support, and unstinting belief in the path I have chosen mean more to me than I can put into words. My wife, Marianne Milligan, has talked through every idea and read every word in this book—and then some. Only she knows just how much it has taken to write this book, particularly after Jack, Annie, and Meg joined our family. I dedicate this book to her.

A Car of One's Own

A good transportation system minimizes unnecessary transportation.
—Lewis Mumford (1958)[1]

Like many of my friends, I was ecstatic when the long vigil leading up to my sixteenth birthday ended, and I finally—finally!—got my driver's license. Driving opened a new world of freedom and mobility, particularly after my father bought a new car and gave me his old one: a yellow 1977 Toyota long-bed pickup truck. Despite its flashy white racing stripe, my new truck was in sad shape. Parts of the bed were rusting through, torn bits of foam protruded from gaping holes in its vinyl seats, and the passenger-side door, which was crumpled from a previous accident, could only be opened by observing a careful sequence of steps that flummoxed all but a select group of initiates. I was utterly blind to its problems: the truck was a piece of junk, but it was *my* piece of junk.

My truck made everything about high-school life easier. Now that I was finally free of the complicated process of arranging rides home after my various practices and after-school activities, it also became infinitely easier to get to friends' houses, to soccer games and debate tournaments, and to movies and parties. Best of all, the costs of my newfound mobility were negligible: I had only to make an occasional emergency run to the grocery store for my mother, to give my younger sister a ride when she needed one, and to use my own money to keep the truck's tank full.[2] My previously well-used bicycle went into storage, and for the rest of high school came out only for recreational rides with friends.

When I left home for college in the mountains of western Massachusetts, first-year students were barred from owning vehicles—a policy designed to prevent the town's picturesque streets from becoming a parking lot. Full of regret, I left my truck behind. I still vividly remember the phone call, several months later, when I asked about my truck and got silence in return. After some prodding, my parents

1977 Toyota sr5 long-bed pickup truck (with racing stripe).
Ben Piff, courtesy of oldparkedcars.com

explained that it had been totaled—the victim of a fallen tree during a storm. The insurance company proclaimed it a worthless hunk of metal, but I knew better: its loss meant forfeiting the easy mobility that I had enjoyed through my last years of high school. I spent my remaining college breaks in Atlanta hitching rides with friends or negotiating the use of one of my parents' cars.

Somewhat to my surprise, though, I seldom missed my truck at college. The campus itself was less than one square mile in extent and contained everything a student could need: dormitories, dining halls, classrooms, athletic fields, museums, a variety of shops and restaurants on main street, and a profusion of public gathering spaces that hosted a diverse mix of activities, including lectures, musical and theatrical performances, and whatever else two thousand college students living in an isolated town could dream up. When I moved off campus as a senior, two of my housemates had cars—although most of the time they sat parked outside the house, unused, until one of us needed to run to the nearest grocery store in the next town over.

After graduation, I took a job teaching high-school history in

Switzerland, and like many Americans living in Europe I marveled at how easy it was to get around by foot, bus, and train. Even without a car, it was easy (and affordable, even on my small salary) to spend my free weekends traveling. By contrast, on the occasions when I had to drive a school van, driving seemed downright cumbersome. Narrow streets, low speed limits, what struck me as outrageously high gasoline prices, and exceedingly scarce parking—not to mention the boisterous teenagers I was carting around—undercut much of driving's appeal. Rather than embodying freedom and mobility, driving in Switzerland seemed more like an expensive, inconvenient, and at times even harrowing chore.

Yet almost immediately upon returning to Atlanta for the summer, the familiar yearning for a car of my own came flooding back. Even something as simple as meeting friends during their lunch breaks presented significant obstacles. Infrequent, inconveniently located bus service in my neighborhood made buses unappealing, and the nearest stop on the city's pleasant, rail-based rapid-transit system (whose tracks did not run anywhere I wanted to go) was nearly three miles away from my parents' house. Cycling, the preferred transportation of my youth, was fine in my neighborhood but felt dangerous beyond it, where a crush of traffic had enveloped the city in the 1980s.[3] With such poor options for getting around, I felt incapacitated without a car.

Interestingly, my intense desire for a car quickly dissipated after I moved to Madison—the capital of Wisconsin and a bustling university town—to attend graduate school. Madison's main commercial street downtown, State Street, which connects the university campus on one end with the state capitol on the other, is lined with enough bookstores, coffee shops, restaurants, bars, and small specialty shops to keep the university's forty-thousand-plus students happy. I rented an apartment within a short walk of my classes and the library, dropping my vague plan to buy a car upon learning that off-street parking would add 50 percent to my monthly rent. I worried about getting groceries until discovering a store—half a mile away—that offered free delivery. With most of what I needed located within a reasonable walk, I never really missed having a car.

By this point my interest in the differing transportation systems of Europe and the United States had captured my academic interest as well—but popular works on the subject seemed to raise more questions than they answered. The most prevalent explanation for the remark-able success of the automobile in the United States—the ubiquitous "love-affair" thesis—suggests that Americans fell in love with automo-biles and, once enamored, did whatever was necessary to accommodate them. "It is, at base, quite simple," one popular history of automobiles declares: "Americans have a fervent, intense, enduring love affair with their cars."[4] Most of those who adhere to this explanation see automo-biles as basically good—as a technology that is ultimately liberating, enabling, empowering, and democratic, all qualities that accord well with American values. To be sure, proponents of the love-affair thesis concede that the country's dependence on automobiles has its nega-tive side, including environmental damage, steep infrastructure costs, the frustrations of jammed traffic, and dependence on foreign oil, but these problems are simply the unfortunate trade-offs that Americans must make to ensure universal access to an otherwise useful and bene-ficial technology. Deep down, advocates of the love-affair thesis argue, Americans love their cars, whatever their flaws, and this more than anything else explains the country's relationship with automobiles.[5]

A second popular explanation—call it the "conspiracy" thesis—attributes the privileged position of automobiles in American life to powerful interests foisting automobiles on an unwary public. A cabal of automakers and various affiliated conspirators used underhanded means to deprive the country of effective public transportation, according to this argument, and powerful road builders have used their clout to secure public financing for huge construction projects at the expense of other social needs. Proponents of the conspiracy thesis sometimes grudgingly concede that cars have certain positive qualities, but on balance they see the country's car culture as a nega-tive, damaging force. Given free choice and a level playing field, they argue, Americans would certainly choose a less automobile-dependent lifestyle.[6]

Neither of these explanations for the dominance of cars in the United States squares particularly well with my own experience, in which my desire (and need) for a car has varied dramatically from place to place. In Atlanta, I nearly always felt confined and helpless without a car because what I wanted to do was spread out over a large area, making driving the only practical way to get around. Both in Switzerland and in two very different college towns, however, not having a car proved at worst a minor inconvenience. Because most of what I needed in a normal day was located in easy walking or bicycling distance from where I lived, having a car was more a convenience than a necessity. To put it another way, the physical arrangement of the built environment, in which housing, retail, and businesses intermingled in relatively close quarters—a condition that planners refer to as "mixed-use landscapes"—meant that my opportunities per square mile in all three places were much higher than in Atlanta. Significantly, the prevailing patterns of land use limited my options for conducting my everyday affairs as much or more than the quality of public transportation, which varied from excellent in Switzerland to nonexistent in western Massachusetts. How I felt about cars had little bearing on whether or not I needed one.[7] I did not want a car so much as I wanted to be able to *do* things quickly and easily: get groceries, get to work, see my friends.[8] In Atlanta I needed a car; in the other places I have lived since I left home for college, having a car did not factor as much into the equation.

As I thought through these relationships, it became increasingly clear that most public discourse about the role of automobiles in American life erects a false boundary between *how Americans feel* about transportation technologies and *why Americans drive* so much more than people elsewhere in the world. In endlessly debating the merits of particular technologies—Priuses versus SUVs, buses versus light rail—we lose sight of the social and environmental context in which those technologies operate. This oversight has implications both for how we live our lives and for the environmental effects of the technologies we use. The language of the love affair, and the often moralistic approach of critics who condemn the automobile, privileges a tight focus on the relative vices and virtues of individual behaviors and technologies at the expense of coming to grips with either the genuine advantages and freedoms that cars create or the social and environmental costs of the nearly universal automobile use that car-dependent landscapes foster.[9]

Focusing on feelings about transportation technologies rather than the conditions in which they operate can have nefarious consequences, as the case of Atlanta's transit system illustrates. The system's trains function well as machines: when installed, they were quiet, smooth, comfortable, clean, and fast and could efficiently move large numbers of people over long distances. Judged on these merits alone, they should have been a resounding success, but in the real world their success has been mixed, at best. How can we explain this? Among the residents of Atlanta I have talked to, the most popular explanation directly mirrors the logic of the love-affair thesis: "I guess people here just don't like to ride trains." Pressed to elaborate, people tout the relative virtues of cars (deemed convenient, flexible, inexpensive, and fast) and the relative vices of the trains (deemed awkward, rigid, expensive, and slow).

Yet focusing on people's predilections ("people here just don't like to ride trains") suggests that their attitudes are somehow timeless and innate rather than informed reactions to a changing world. In the case of Atlanta's rail-based transit, for example, nearly all of its stations until recently have connected the city's airport with four main things: giant parking lots for commuters, office space, convention-oriented facilities, and sports venues. The opportunities per square mile surrounding each rail stop, in other words, cater almost entirely to out-of-town visitors, office workers, mall-goers, and sports fans. Why should anyone else ever ride the trains? The land uses within easy walking distance of each station send strong signals about who is supposed to use the trains—large parking lots scream "I am for drivers," just as rail stops surrounded by office buildings and hotels declare "I am for office workers and conventioneers." As a result, the rail-based transit system *is* awkward, rigid, expensive, and slow for most Atlantans, although this is not because the trains are technologically deficient: it is because most of the city's residents are neither conventioneers nor employees of a company located near a rail stop. From its inception, the system's engineers did not design it to help most city residents do the things they need and want to do as part of their everyday lives.[10]

To understand how powerful the relationship between successful mass transit systems and land-use decisions is, compare Atlanta's system to one of any number of successful European systems. Why would the latter enjoy much heavier ridership than Atlanta's, even in cases when they employ older, slower, less comfortable technology? Following the love-affair thesis, we might conclude that Europeans have a stronger affinity for trains or, alternatively, that Europeans just do not love cars as much as Americans. Paying attention to land-use patterns, however, suggests that transit prospers in places where stops grant access to many opportunities per square mile and are within easy walking distance of housing. The relationship is not hard to grasp: if just about anyone can leave home and take a short walk to a transit stop, and if nearly every stop along the line offers a diverse mix of incentives to exit and spend time and money in nearby businesses, then people are likely to use the system heavily—even if they own cars. When transit conveniently connects housing to the innumerable opportunities of dense, mixed-use landscapes, transit seems to thrive. This appears to be particularly true when the opportunities near rail stops are not limited to major attractions like ball fields and museums but also feature businesses that cater to more mundane everyday needs, like drug stores, hardware stores, and supermarkets.[11]

Anecdotal evidence suggests that rail systems traversing landscapes that are rich in opportunities per square mile seem to appeal as much to substantial numbers of Americans as to Europeans. For example, consider American cities like New York, Boston, and Chicago, where subway and elevated train systems still attract heavy ridership. The transit stops in these places are frequently within walking distance of residential areas and offer numerous attractive opportunities within a short walk. Consider also the attitudes of even resolutely car-loving Americans who encounter robust rail-based transit systems when traveling abroad. Many are pleasantly surprised to be able to get around without a rental car and describe their experiences by saying things like, "Streetcar systems would never work in the United States because Americans don't like public transportation, but the streetcars in Europe are very pleasant and convenient." In truth, streetcar systems *would* stand little chance of succeeding in the United States without radically different land-use patterns—but the point is that land-use patterns, not attitudes toward rail, are the best determinant of likely success or failure.

What is true of light rail is also true of cars: when we design landscapes that are easily navigated only by personal vehicles, people tend to drive everywhere they need to go. In this book, I try to move past the language of the love affair to focus on the built landscape. I do so in part because the love-affair framework so poorly explains my own changing relationships with cars and in part because thinking in terms of love and hate is conceptually limiting. However one feels about cars—whether you love them, hate them, or are filled with ambivalence—you will not find much about those emotions in the pages that follow. Instead, this book will ask you to think about landscapes: the everyday world around us, from the mundane to the magisterial, and especially the various principles that guide its physical organization. Sometimes I employ the language of ecology to describe its organization, particularly in order to explore the environmental implications of near-universal automobile use in the United States. Yet I will also have occasion to describe changes in very different terms: more often than not, the people who rearranged the American landscape in the ways I describe did not think much about the effects of their actions on "nature" or "the environment" as part of their decision-making processes, even though the environmental consequences of their decisions have been profound.

Understanding the landscape's physical arrangement is crucial to understanding why Americans drive so much. In addition to shaping the fortunes of transportation systems like light rail, land-use patterns also govern *how far* car-dependent Americans must drive to conduct their everyday affairs. The easiest way to illustrate this point is to examine how the physical layouts of two very different residential areas in the St. Paul metropolitan region—one urban, the other suburban—affect the transportation needs of their residents. The first of these two residential areas is a collection of subdivisions located off an interstate exit ramp roughly fourteen miles south of downtown St. Paul in Eagan, Minnesota, a suburban community of more than sixty thousand people spread out over 34.5 square miles. Its land-use patterns were established primarily in the 1970s and 1980s in direct relationship to the newly constructed interstate.[12] The layout of one of Eagan's neighborhoods, grouped around an interstate exit ramp (fig. 1), reflects the approach that suburban developers have honed to a science in the interstate era. Eagan's general land-use practices differ little from those of innumerable suburban communities around the country.

In order to understand the organization of this exit-ramp neighborhood, which covers roughly 5.5 square miles, one must first appreciate

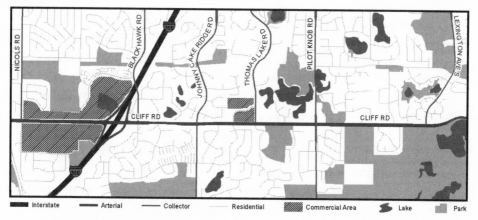

1.1 Exit-ramp neighborhood, Eagan, Minnesota. Cartography by Birgit Mühlenhaus, 2011.

how city planners in the last four decades or so have understood different kinds of roads, which they have sorted into clear hierarchical categories based on intended use. Planners divide roads into two broad categories—high-speed highways and lower-speed roads—and then make further distinctions within each category. In the lower-speed road category, for example, planners distinguish between arterial roads, collector roads, and residential streets and rely on each to serve a different transportation purpose. *Arterial roads* are the most heavily traveled of the three and typically connect important central locations with one another and with the interstate. They tend to be zoned for large developments like shopping centers, strip malls, office parks, and townhouses rather than for single-family housing. In Eagan, as in most interstate-oriented suburbs, the highway's entrance and exit ramps are located on a major arterial road. By comparison, suburban *collector roads* have a lower capacity than arterials, and as their name implies they are designed to "collect" traffic from adjacent subdivisions and funnel it to arterials. The zoning regulations along collectors tend to permit only a few small commercial and community-oriented developments; they are usually easy to identify by the many subdivision entrances along their length. *Residential streets*, the final road type, are contained entirely within individual subdivisions—thus discouraging through traffic—and the land adjacent to them tends to be zoned exclusively for residential land uses.

By manipulating the arrangement of these different road types, planners and developers create a rational transportation system that is easy to navigate (by those with cars), ensures the relatively efficient distribution of utilities like sewers and water mains through low-density areas, keeps heavy traffic concentrated on major routes (and out of neighborhoods), and locates most everyday essentials within a short drive of residential areas. Because zoning bars commercial activities from residential areas, shopping trips typically begin at home, move through curving residential streets to a collector, follow the collector to the arterial, and take the arterial toward the businesses clustered around the interstate ramp. In well-developed suburbs like Eagan, exit-ramp commercial clusters typically boast a variety of establishments, including restaurants, grocery stores, barber shops and hair salons, real estate agencies, financial services companies, various professional offices, and perhaps even a movie theater or hardware store—enough to satisfy a typical family's everyday needs. Whenever something is not available locally, the interstate provides a direct link to the larger resources of the metropolitan region.

The second sample residential area, whose physical organization differs markedly from Eagan, is Macalester-Groveland, an urban neighborhood in St. Paul with twenty thousand residents spread over roughly 2.25 square miles, located roughly 4 miles west of downtown. As with Eagan, the key to understanding the neighborhood's spatial organization is to understand how its developers designed it in relationship to the dominant transportation system of the time. The streetcars around which the neighborhood was developed from 1910 through the 1920s have been defunct for five decades, but the land-use patterns established during the streetcar era still have a profound and continuing impact on the everyday transportation demands of the neighborhood's residents today.

A map showing the relationship between the neighborhood's commercial infrastructure and its old streetcar lines demonstrates why this is true (fig. 2). Unlike Eagan, whose developers sorted various highways and roads into an elaborate, multilevel hierarchy, Macalester-Groveland's developers distinguished only two road types: residential streets and streetcar streets. Three east–west streetcar lines, spaced every half mile, ran through the neighborhood, putting all residents within four

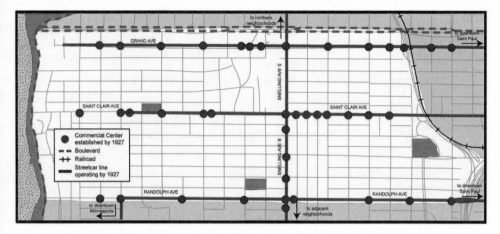

1.2 Streetcar neighborhood, Macalester-Groveland, St. Paul, Minnesota.
Cartography by Birgit Mühlenhaus, 2011.

blocks of a streetcar stop. East–west and north–south streetcar lines
gave residents access to the rest of the city as well as to downtown Minneapolis, seven miles to the northwest.

Of more lasting importance than the streetcars, however, are the
small commercial nodes, located every half mile—and sometimes
every quarter mile—that sprang up along their routes.[13] In contrast
to Eagan, where the interstate ramp provides the center of gravity for
nearly all nonresidential activities, all three east–west streetcar lines
in Macalester-Groveland attracted businesses to the regularly spaced
clusters of storefronts along their length. As a result, commercial
establishments spread somewhat evenly throughout the neighborhood, putting nearly all residents within six blocks or less of multiple shopping areas by the late 1920s. For those who required goods
or services unavailable in the many nearby stores, streetcars provided
a direct link to all of the small commercial sites along any particular
route and, ultimately, to the resources of downtown St. Paul.

The very different land-use patterns established during the initial
development of Eagan and Macalester-Groveland continue to shape
the mobility options of their residents today. The developers of both
neighborhoods carefully separated residential and commercial areas
but balanced separation against easy access to everyday goods and
services. In a key difference between the two areas, entrepreneurs

from 1910 through the 1920s defined "easy access" in relationship to the slow speeds of pedestrians and streetcars. As a result, Macalester-Groveland's commercial establishments spread thickly and fairly evenly through the neighborhood along the old streetcar routes—with the result that even today, without streetcars, large numbers of stores exist within a short distance of all neighborhood homes. Because distances are short, walking and bicycling remain practical options. In Eagan, on the other hand, where planners defined "easy access" in relationship to cars, the distances between residences and commercial establishments are much longer. The distance a person can walk in five minutes is much shorter than one can drive in five minutes, and in Eagan (as in most post–World War II suburbs), short walks seldom give residents access to any shopping opportunities at all. In addition, since most commerce is concentrated on highly trafficked arterial roads, few cyclists feel safe making even reasonably short shopping trips unless a special, separate infrastructure is provided for them. The only quick, safe option is to drive.

All of this has implications, not only for how easily people can walk or bicycle in Eagan and Macalester-Groveland, but also for the distances that residents must travel to conduct their everyday affairs. Measured in time and convenience rather than distance, there is little appreciable difference between the commercial options in Eagan and Macalester-Groveland—in both places, most of what people need is a short trip away. Measured in *distance* rather than time, however, the differences have the potential to add up quickly (fig. 3).[14] As figure 3 suggests, Macalester-Groveland residents typically have smaller distances to travel for these everyday needs than Eagan residents. Each neighborhood design, in other words, imposes very different minimum "mobility requirements" on its residents—and those designed into Eagan's landscape (as measured in mileage) are notably greater than those designed into Macalester-Groveland's. These requirements exist independent of what type of transportation residents use—but because distances tend to be shorter in Macalester-Groveland, both walking and bicycling require less effort than in Eagan and thus are more likely to be part of the mobility mix for larger numbers of residents.

Eagan represents what I call Car Country, a shorthand label for places where car dependence is woven into the basic fabric of the

Business Type	Eagan	Macalester-Groveland
Grocery store	2.4	0.9
Nursery school	2	0.8
Hardware store	1	0.4
Regional mall	7.9	6.8
Doctor's office	2	0.6
Haircut	1	0.5
Movie theater	2.4 (16 screens)	0.9 (2 screens)
		1.6 (2 screens)
		6.8 (14 screens)
Gas station	1	0.5
Restaurant A	1.0 (nearest)	0.3 (nearest)
Restaurant B	2.5 (5+ choices)	0.5 (5+ choices)

1.3 One-way distance, in miles, from home to nearest business.

landscape.[15] In the second half of the twentieth century, such places have become ubiquitous in the United States, and during that same period cars have become integral parts of the daily lives of most adult Americans. It is a mistake, I believe, to explain this state of affairs either as the simple product of an ardent love affair with automobiles or as the result of a conspiracy to foist cars on an unwary public. Instead, the nation's dependence on cars stems from a reality at once more prosaic and more profound: Americans drive because in most places the built environment all but requires them to do so. Landscapes in the United States that are easily navigable without personal vehicles have become rare—small islands in the vast sea of Car Country.

Despite their ubiquity, today's car-dependent landscapes are a relatively new historical development. As recently as the early twentieth century, the nation's social, political, and economic institutions were oriented entirely around foot-, rail-, and water-based transportation systems. Rural roads were decrepit—the casualty of a half century's investment in railroads at the expense of highways—and turn-of-the-century streets in big American cities were in crisis. Few resources existed to change this state of affairs. In 1900, for example, the total annual budget for the sole federal agency involved in road improvement was just $8,000, and its staff faced a strict ban on direct involvement in road construction. Most states had sizable road-building budgets, but funding sources were unreliable and almost none of the countless local officials charged with road construction and maintenance had any training in engineering. Few of the car-oriented features that are integral to the modern American landscape, from limited-access motor highways to parking lots, existed yet even as ideas. Further complicating the picture, early motor vehicles were ostentatiously expensive and notoriously unreliable, making it a laughable idea that the country's leaders would ever devote themselves to the complex and forbiddingly expensive task of remaking the nation's transportation system around cars.

Yet, in relatively short order, this is exactly what happened. Politicians at every level of government funneled unprecedented sums into developing and expanding the nation's automotive infrastructure in the first half of the twentieth century. Initially, these changes focused on accommodating the flood of automobiles pouring onto American roads and streets, as engineers wrestled to design both cars and roads that could overcome difficult environmental conditions. Then in the interwar years, after a series of significant technological and fiscal breakthroughs, powerful cars and expanding networks of smooth roads finally began to give motorists the ability to reliably overcome older environmental limits on private transportation. Only then did planners and engineers begin to make serious plans for completely car-centered landscapes that were designed not just to make driving easier but to unlock the full transportation potential of automobiles; only then did significant numbers of people begin to reorganize their everyday activities and landscapes around automobiles. After World War II, with the profitability, practicality, and political attractiveness of car-centered activities well established, governments at all levels supplemented existing car-oriented transportation policies with new rules and incentives governing land-use practices that redefined "development" as "car-oriented development." By 1956, when Congress funded construction of the interstate highway system, nearly all of the basic patterns underpinning the creation of car-centered landscapes— as well as nearly all of the most significant environmental problems related to heavy car use—were firmly in place. With these changes, the United States became Car Country.

This transformation required two equally profound changes: first, the development of a well-funded, car-oriented transportation infrastructure; and second, a complex set of regulations, incentives, and practices regarding land uses that helped create a new, car-dependent economic geography. As a car-friendly transportation infrastructure became a normal part of the American landscape—think stop signs and centerlines, traffic lights and limited-access highways—car use became significantly *easier*. In addition, as car-friendly land-use practices became a normal part of the American landscape—think ample parking lots and convenient drive-through windows, vast subdivisions of single-family housing and regional malls rivaling the size of downtown—car use became more *necessary*. As the different sectors of the American economy dispersed more thinly across the landscape, even the most mundane of everyday tasks moved out of easy reach of most people traveling on foot or by public transportation. Car use became not just easy but—for most people and in most places—almost mandatory.

As car-dependent landscapes became the norm, they locked in the significant environmental consequences of nearly universal car use in a large, affluent nation. Born, as it was, from the desire to overcome environmental limits on personal mobility, Car Country profoundly altered how people interacted with nature. People developed new ways of thinking about and interacting with the environments in which they lived—and particularly with the roads and streets that ran through their communities—as federal, state, and local governments reshaped them based on the needs of wheeled traffic rather than the needs and desires of people living along them. More subtly, cars transformed how people understood their place in the world and their ability to move around within it, redefining "local" space and prompting new ideas about how to array everyday activities and enterprises across the landscape. In addition to changing people's interactions with the environment, building Car Country required tumultuous, large-scale transformations of the natural world. Dramatic increases in automobile use spurred the growth of the oil industry and its related environmental problems, for example, which became necessary and significant adjuncts to Car Country's continuing successes. The momentous industrial effort required to put the nation on wheels had profound environmental consequences, as did the equally momentous road-construction program that provided the vast networks of streets and highways that made driving so convenient. By introducing these changes, Car Country put more people than ever before within an easy drive of places where they could find ample greenery, recreational opportunities, and a sense of reconnection with the natural world. In short, Car Country refashioned, on a grand scale, both the basic patterns of interaction between people and the environment and the fundamental structure and composition of the nation's ecosystems.

Almost from the beginning, these changes inspired a legion of vociferous critics.[16] By the time full-blown discontent with America's car culture and its destructive environmental effects finally percolated up into national politics in the 1960s and 1970s, however, patterns of sprawling, low-density development had already become thoroughly ingrained in the American political economy. Moreover, Car Country's critics too often focused on particular problems—factory pollution, tailpipe emissions, roadside eyesores, suburban "boxes made of ticky tacky,"[17] the loss of public "open space" and "pristine wilderness"—without understanding the broader, interconnected forces at work that continued to roll out new car-dependent communities year after year. Environmentalists secured new regulations that limited some of low-density sprawl's more damaging environmental effects, but they failed to stop sprawl itself or the engines driving its expansion. The overwhelming tendency among critics, with a few important exceptions, has been to focus on cars rather than roads and on the behavior of drivers rather than the powerful forces shaping American land-use patterns.[18]

Without effective critics—and with car-oriented facilities incorporated as a basic feature of the nation's political, social, and economic approach to both transportation and land-use practices—car-dependent landscapes have multiplied, older ways of moving around have steadily disappeared as practical options for most Americans, and more and more people have begun to drive longer and longer distances, whether they have wanted to or not. In Car Country, driving and sprawl have become essential, interlocking components of American lives, landscapes, and relationships with the natural world.

Car Country

PART I

Before the Automobile, 1880–1905

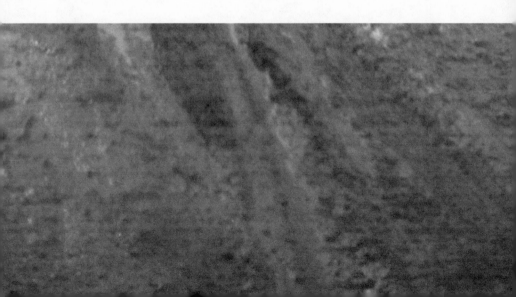

UNDRAGGED ROAD IN SAC COUNTY. MARCH 28. 1905,

DRAGGED ROAD IN SAC COUNTY, MARCH 28. 1905.
Maintenance on this road costs $2.50 per mile per year.

ONE

ROADS AND REFORMERS

ISAAC POTTER WAS A MAN ON A MISSION. BY 1891, HE AND A SMALL but growing group of like-minded reformers had been agitating for a decade to improve what they saw as the deplorable state of American country roads. Their efforts had run into staunch resistance from American farmers, however, who generally regarded the prosperous city dwellers who dominated the road-improvement crowd as unwelcome interlopers into rural affairs. Potter, who was trained as an engineer and whose zeal for better roads had grown by the early 1890s to an almost fevered pitch, had finally had enough. He agreed to edit a new magazine, *Good Roads*, which began publication in January 1892. In advance of its first issue, he sat down to pen an essay titled "The Gospel of Good Roads: A Letter to the American Farmer," which, in addition to running as the lead article in the new magazine, was also widely distributed as a stand-alone pamphlet. "In these years, when the voice of your complaint is loud in the land, and a thousand partisans are declaiming a thousand theories to account for the 'decline of agriculture,'" he began, "I will try to write you a letter, in which, I

Roads before and after dragging, Sac County, Iowa, March 1905. From Iowa State Highway Commission, *The Good Roads Problem in Iowa*, Bulletin No. 6 (Iowa State Highway Commission, June 1905), 14.

believe, I can make it appear that the greatest remedy for the cure of unprofitable farming lies in your own hands."[1] This greatest of remedies, of course, was better roads.

George E. Waring was also a man on a mission, though of a slightly different sort. Stepping into the grandly named position of commissioner of the Department of Street-Cleaning of New York City on January 15, 1895, he assumed leadership of a thoroughly embattled branch of municipal government. The city's newspapers had for decades offered routine reports on the city's wretched street conditions, in general, and on the failures of its street-cleaning department, in particular, especially during the winter when snow piled high on top of heavy accumulations of refuse. Describing the conditions in front of one block of tenements, the New York Times spared no condemning detail, declaring that the street "from curb to curb looks like a well-patronized dumping ground. Ash heaps, kitchen refuse, decayed vegetables, and straw, chips, old crockery, cans, &c., are spread all over the street, mixed with the dirty snow."[2] Residents were "loud in their complaints of the negligence shown by the Street-cleaning Department," another article reported.[3] In March 1893, fed-up members of the City Club had launched a campaign to document the problem, collecting affidavits and taking photographs of appalling street conditions all over the city, with the aim of having the street-cleaning commissioner, Thomas Brennan, removed from office for dereliction of duty. Waring was the second reform-minded commissioner to follow Brennan, and he was determined to succeed. "It is utterly hopeless," his wife told him after seeing the city's streets for the first time, imploring him to step down. "You will only disgrace yourself by trying to do it." Ignoring his wife's plea, and with an enthusiasm for clean streets that matched Potter's zeal for good roads, Waring reorganized his beleaguered department, outfitted his street sweepers in bright white uniforms, and sent them forth to do battle with the city's piles of garbage.[4]

Potter and Waring were but two amid a legion of American reformers during the 1880s and 1890s aspiring to completely remake the roads and streets of the United States. These late-nineteenth-century campaigns displayed a number of key characteristics of the forces that remade the United States into Car Country over the first half of the twentieth century. In particular, they reflected a strong willingness to use government resources to completely reengineer landscapes to solve environmental problems and to advance various social and economic goals. Far from being a response to automobiles, however, these diverse reform efforts arose *before* automobiles appeared in the United States. The first American automaker, for example, opened its doors for business in 1895, and as late as 1900 there were a meager eight thousand automobiles nationwide—many of them frail prototypes or foreign imports. The story of Car Country thus begins with a riddle: Road and street improvements were expensive, disruptive, and broke with long-standing political traditions favoring local road and street administration. Why, then, did the push for road and street improvements begin *before* legions of motorists began clamoring for good roads? Why did so many people suddenly begin to care so passionately about road and street improvements in the last part of the nineteenth century?

The answers to these questions turn out to have nothing to do with automobiles and everything to do with the urbanization, industrialization, and rapid technological development that remade the United States with lightning speed in the decades after the Civil War. The forces driving the country's rise to prominence had an unruly, volatile, disorganized quality, prompting the nation to oscillate wildly between boom and bust. The desire to impose some sort of order onto this chaos—to harness the era's creative energies while mitigating its disruptive, damaging by-products—consequently drove the political agenda of an entire generation.[5]

It was in this context, and before motor vehicles began to exert a significant presence in the United States, that reformers launched their ambitious, wide-ranging road- and street-improvement efforts. Significantly, and despite varying goals that sometimes caused different groups to work at cross-purposes, a set of core beliefs about nature and nature's proper role in the modern world drove most of the era's reformers. First, these reformers believed that the dark underbelly of the natural world—in the form of wind and rain, fire and disease, befouled air and poisoned water—presented, if left uncontrolled, a powerful obstacle to national progress. In big cities, reformers condemned filthy, crowded streets as proxies for larger threats of disease and disorder, and in rural areas they indicted muddy, rutted roads as barriers to full participation in the modern economy and modern social life. Second, both urban and rural reformers gradually began to perceive roads and streets not as part of the environment but as technologies that government agencies—staffed by experts—could use to overcome what earlier generations had always seen as fundamental environmental limits on private transportation. An opportunity existed, the era's reformers believed, to remake roads and streets in ways that would fundamentally transform travel possibilities, promote economic growth, and create a healthier, more moral, less chaotic society. The practical results of their campaigns varied widely, but together they set changes in motion that slowly but permanently transformed the relationships that Americans had with their roads and streets, with one another, and with the natural world. Unwittingly, these changes set the stage onto which the automobile would ultimately roll at the end of the nineteenth century.

NATURE RUN AMOK

During the late nineteenth century, urbanization, industrialization, and rapid population growth generated substantial chaos in American cities, creating the impression that some of the more ominous forms of nature were running amok on big-city streets. During the same period, the mechanization of farm work and the powerful new ties developing between cities and the countryside transformed rural life, fostering a belief that rural Americans—for all their advances—were somehow being left behind in the rush to modernization.

The effects of these changes on cities were particularly profound. The Industrial Revolution, with its new factory system of manufacturing, had begun to reshape the spatial arrangements of American cities beginning in the 1830s. Before the Industrial Revolution, when the craft apprentice system dominated American manufacturing, few cities had distinct areas devoted exclusively to residential use. The system had fostered close ties between home and workplace, with apprentices and sometimes even journeymen living as members of the master craftsman's household, which itself was typically located above or behind the shop. As a result, residences tended to intermix with workshops, churches, warehouses, businesses, boardinghouses, and places of entertainment, all of which coexisted in close proximity to one another. Few people commuted, in the modern sense of the word, because little, if any, physical separation existed between the home and the workplace. Those with the greatest wealth and highest social standing tended to occupy prime real estate in the city's center, but they still lived cheek by jowl with poorer neighbors who crowded into nearby alleys and courtyards. Suburbs occupied the least desirable land on the urban periphery, where noisy and otherwise undesirable enterprises like tanneries, glue factories, and slaughterhouses predominated.[6]

In the new factory system, however, factory owners had little incentive to house their wage laborers—and even less to welcome them as members of their own households. Moreover, growing numbers of factories began to shift from the traditional reliance among craftsmen on muscle power toward utilizing coal-fired machinery in the manufacturing process—a shift that made dirty air a staple of big cities. Greater production also generated more factory wastes, creating disposal problems that were often solved by creating impromptu dump sites on vacant lots or by disposing wastes in local waterways. Factory pollution affected immediately adjacent areas most acutely, prompting those who had the means—mainly salaried managers and factory owners—to move away, making room for hourly laborers to crowd in. Distinct residential neighborhoods thus formed along class lines as homes and workplaces separated.[7]

As the century progressed and the factory system spread, affluent urbanites took advantage of new transportation technologies, such as the steam ferry, horse-drawn streetcar, and commuter railroad, to live farther away from their workplaces than it was practical to walk. Some of the resulting residential neighborhoods extended in radial lines adjacent to horsecar routes; others, such as Philadelphia's famous "Main Line" suburbs, took shape in new developments that grew within walking distance of steam-railroad stations like pearls along a necklace. The resulting depopulation of the urban center and the movement of wealthy residents towards the urban edge created, as one eminent historian of the subject has put it, "the most fundamental realignment of urban structure in the 4,500-year past of cities on this planet."[8]

Cities exploded after 1870, accelerating the rate of spatial transformation. In 1869, just nine American cities had over 100,000 residents; three decades later, thirty-two did.[9] Among the ten largest cities in the country in 1900, all had at least doubled their populations since 1870, and nine of the ten exceeded 250,000 inhabitants.[10] Compared to preindustrial cities, these numbers were staggering in both total and relative terms. Whereas the urban population in 1790 comprised just 3 percent of all Americans and only fifteen cities had more than 5,000 residents, by 1900 nearly 40 percent of all Americans lived in cities and about 140 cities boasted populations of 30,000 or more.[11] Meanwhile, cities expanded geographically, too, especially in the 1890s after the advent of new electric trolley systems—which roughly doubled the six-miles-per-hour average speed of horsecars—greatly increased the amount of land within a half-hour commute of urban central business districts.[12] In a wave of annexations, city after city brought this newly accessible territory under municipal control, with the most prominent example occurring in 1889 when Chicago annexed a 120-square-mile territory.[13]

To many people of the era, these changes reflected an urban nature that seemed to be under near-constant assault. Many of the challenges seemed downright elemental: billowing smoke turned city air gray, rivers ran black with factory wastes, refuse piled high in the streets, and the threat of fire, punctuated at both ends of the period by major conflagrations in Chicago (1871) and San Francisco (1906), hovered constantly over the wooden-framed buildings that enabled urban America's rapid growth. Meanwhile, poor foreign immigrants, the major engine driving population growth, found housing only by packing into expanding slum districts, where tall tenement buildings lining dirty, narrow streets created dark canyons without direct sunlight, fresh air, or open space. Congested traffic packed big-city streets, contributing to the sense of overcrowding and hinting at a barely controlled chaos lurking beneath the excitement and vitality of urban America. "The tendency of congested city life," one reformer declared, "is to banish nature and children." Yet nature was everywhere present on city streets—albeit in a state of profound upheaval—in the form of epidemic diseases, rotting garbage, piles of manure, smoky skies, polluted waterways, and occasional fires.[14]

Meanwhile, industrialization and rapid technological advancements drove equally profound changes in the American countryside, reinforcing the idea that new technologies were empowering farmers to surmount long-standing environmental limits. Perhaps most importantly, new farm machinery began to replace traditional agricultural labor in the decades after the Civil War. Moldboard plows, designed to be pulled by a draft animal and steered by someone walking behind, evolved quickly as steel replaced wood and iron. Riding plows soon gave farmers a place to sit and steer, and gang plows enabled farmers to plow multiple furrows at once. Grain drills gave farmers precise control over the depth and location of seeds, replacing seeding by hand or by mechanical broadcasters. Large horse-drawn machines automatically mowed, raked, and loaded hay, while others cut, sheafed, and bound wheat. Horse-powered grain separators gave way to steam-powered threshing machines—and then to enormous smoke-belching combines that in a single pass converted a wide swath of waving grain into sacks ready for market. This new machinery—combined with corporate management and seasonal migrant labor—underwrote the vast bonanza farms of the Red River Valley of North Dakota and Minnesota and in the Central Valley of California, where the single-largest farm measured sixty-six thousand acres and produced over a million bushels of wheat annually. But the new technologies also transformed countless household farms as their average investment in machinery skyrocketed, aided by equipment manufacturers who began to extend short-term credit. On bonanza farms and small family farms alike, machines dramatically increased worker productivity, enabling farmers to cultivate many more acres per laborer—and thus to produce much bigger surpluses for market.[15]

The nation's expanding railroad network also transformed rural life, guiding settlement and forging powerful new links between the country and the city. Railroads sped and shaped settlement patterns by targeting fertile land with good farming potential for development. Doing so clearly served the railroads' best interests, for in attracting farmers—who would subsequently need to ship their crops to market—railroads guaranteed future business for themselves. Not surprisingly, then, railroads spread thickly across areas with good soils and less so in areas without them.[16] As a result, the pioneering farmers who established new farms west of the Mississippi River in the late 1800s depended on railroads in profound ways. Before railroads, when most heavy freight moved long distances by water, the combination of good farmland and proximity to rivers had structured settlement decisions, just as the course of rivers had determined farmers' trade options. As railroads fanned out across the great fertile grasslands of the American West after the Civil War, however, farmers could cultivate land that in an earlier era would have been hopelessly isolated from the marketplace. Railroads also made it possible for corporate executives, rather than water's tendency to follow the path of least resistance, to determine the routes and rate structures that determined which marketplaces were most favorable for trade.[17]

The same railways that enabled farmers to sell their produce in distant big-city markets also gave them better and more direct access to the wares of urban merchants. Beginning in the 1850s, for example, sales of new agricultural machinery like the McCormick reaper steadily followed the railroads as they opened new agricultural areas.[18] Railroads also gave farmers access to the consumer goods flowing out of urban factories. Because railroads dramatically reduced the cost of shipping goods, rural merchants could sell items that once had been quite expensive at significantly lower prices. Moreover, because railroads increased shipping speeds, rural merchants could offer a wider range of goods, with less capital investment in stock, than in the prerailroad era.[19] Railroads also allowed mail-order retailers like the Chicago-based Montgomery Ward, founded in 1872, to give rural consumers an experience akin to that of urbanites wandering through the lavish displays of big-city department stores. Offering merchandise that catered to rural tastes and needs, mail-order catalogs gave farm families access to a wider range of products than general stores could ever stock. By the late 1880s, for example, Ward's catalogs numbered better than five hundred pages and offered more than twenty-four thousand products.[20]

As the world changed around them, farmers began to organize. Two contradictory impulses—on one hand to defend traditional agricultural life from the influences of industrialization, and on the other to organize farmers to ensure that they would reap maximum benefits from the new industrial-capitalist order—manifested themselves in the rise of organizations like the Patrons of Husbandry, also known as the Grange. Founded in 1867 as a social organization designed to combat rural isolation by bringing together rural Americans to socialize with their neighbors, by the mid-1870s its membership had swelled to 775,000 members organized in twenty thousand local chapters. The Grange soon adopted an economic agenda, launching a full-scale assault against people they called "middlemen." Their campaigns against what they saw as abusive rate-setting practices by railroads had national implications, as did their numerous cooperative endeavors, which included stores, grain elevators, banks, mutual insurance companies, and even utilities and farm-equipment manufactories.[21] In this context, improving the quality of rural roads soon became one of the organization's many projects.

REFORMING ROADS AND STREETS

In many ways, roads and streets came to epitomize the sense of crisis that both urbanites and rural residents were beginning to feel by the 1880s and 1890s. On big-city streets in particular, the combination of rapid urbanization, industrialization, and population growth radically transformed city streets, putting them at the center of pressing problems of pollution, disease, fire, and social order. By contrast to today, American cities of the time were heavily built up, with very little open space. Moreover, the multifamily tenement and apartment buildings that dominated big-city housing in the late nineteenth century often left much to be desired: buildings had few public spaces aside from hallways and shared toilets, most spaces were small and cramped, rooms often lacked access to light and fresh air, and the ratio of people per room was much higher than today. In New York's infamous "dumbbell" tenements, for example, the typical four-room apartment, which frequently housed multiple families, had a ten-by-eleven-foot kitchen, a ten-by-eleven-foot living room, and two seven-by-eight-foot bedrooms.[22] Streets consequently provided the main form of public space that all urban residents could easily access—and as a result they served a multitude of purposes, including socializing, doing business, and finding amusement. In important ways, streets *were* the city—or at least were the primary way that people experienced and understood it.

Streets varied considerably from one part of a city to another and tended to reflect the major uses of abutting land. In warehouse districts and areas around railroad terminals, for example, streets paved with sturdy granite blocks carried a dense traffic of horse-drawn wagons carrying heavy freight. In expensive residential areas, where wide and well-paved streets reflected the neighborhood's prestige and exclusivity, tightly compacted crushed-stone surfaces known as macadam gained popularity for their clean appearance and smooth surface, which allowed wealthy residents to parade horse-drawn carriages with ease and comfort. In working- and middle-class residential neighborhoods, streets off the main transportation corridors were often unpaved or paved with inexpensive gravel or cobblestone. These streets accommodated a broad mix of uses, from peddlers hawking milk, meat, and vegetables to providing space for people to congregate, transact business, socialize, and entertain themselves. In the slum districts, the streets and alleys reflected the squalor and overcrowding besetting their inhabitants, while the streets and sidewalks of the central business district carried a chaotic mix of pedestrians, horse-drawn streetcars, carts, hacks, local and through traffic, vendors, and even construction crews, all vying for space in and along the crowded thoroughfares.[23]

The transportation functions of big-city streets became much more important during the 1880s and 1890s as traffic grew thicker, faster, and more dangerous, especially along major thoroughfares. Purveyors of public transportation—known at the time as "traction" companies—extended their track mileage in the 1870s and 1880s with great success in major cities; in New York, for example, the five major lines carried 103,978,554 passengers in 1884 alone.[24] The effects of these conveyances on urban thoroughfares intensified in the 1890s as traction companies replaced horses with electric motors. The switchover was swift and dramatic. In just six years after the introduction of the first successful electrified streetcar system in Richmond, Virginia, in 1887, traction companies electrified more than seven thousand miles of urban streetcar lines, roughly 60 percent of the country's total mileage. The system continued to expand and electrify at a rapid pace, and by the end of 1903 the nation had approximately thirty thousand miles of streetcar routes, 98 percent of them electrified.[25]

Electric streetcars changed the basic character of the streets that carried them. Before the advent of the trolley, street traffic moved only as fast as the fastest horse, and transportation uses had to compete with the many social and commercial functions of city streets. Yet for electric streetcars to achieve their major promise—dispersing residences over a broader area without lengthening the duration of the commute downtown—they had to be able to travel at rapid, previously unheard-of speeds over public streets. As they began to do so in growing numbers during the 1890s, electric streetcars transformed the thoroughfares over which they ran. Major streets became, in the words of one historian, high-speed "arteries for traffic" that began to undercut the more traditional (but incompatible) social functions of city streets.[26]

This change provoked a mixed response. Some urbanites protested, complaining about ugly overhead wires, denouncing the monopolistic practices of streetcar companies, and seeking legislation to protect quiet streets from the incursion of new rail lines. Others pushed to *expand* streetcar networks—even when they agreed with the critiques leveled against them—because of the perceived social benefits of urban residential dispersal.[27] "The municipality must . . . understand that on good rapid transit facilities depend in a large measure the expansion and development of the city," one group of reformers argued in a typical example of this position. "A corporation which is disposed to give good accommodations and quick transit is a public benefactor, and should be given every encouragement and facility for improving its service."[28]

Yet the very success of urban streetcar networks limited their potential as reformers usually defined it. In 1890, for example, as the mileage of electrified lines began its upward climb, roughly eight hundred streetcar companies already carried approximately two billion passengers nationwide.[29] Because nearly all streetcar lines converged on the central business district, they fostered an exaggerated dependence among riders on downtown establishments, generating an ever-increasing volume of traffic and ushering in the heyday of the downtown department store and the skyscraper.[30] With increased traffic came congestion, particularly downtown, where big-city streetcars discharged passengers into a frenzied mix of delivery wagons, hacks, carts, carriages, streetcars, and pedestrians competing for scarce street space. Given the sheer numbers of people and vehicles on big-city streets, especially during the morning and evening rush hours, streetcars often crawled through traffic at a snail's pace. As congestion increased, commuting times lengthened and frustration with streetcar companies grew for failing to provide bigger cars, faster and more frequent service, and more comfortable accommodations.[31]

The growth of street traffic had other significant implications for the urban street environment. Horse droppings, to take just one particularly odious example, created serious problems as the number of urban horses swelled to over three million by the turn of the century.[32] With New York City's horses alone producing between 800,000 and 1.3 million pounds of manure daily, the streets became "filled with filth, refuse, and carrion," in the words of one contemporary, "abounding in sources of disease and pestilence."[33] In dry weather, it turned to dust and blew around, irritating lungs and noses; in wet weather, it stuck to clothing and shoes. "A person upon arriving at home, after a day's business," complained the New York Times in 1874, "finds himself rich in landed property clinging tenaciously to his clothing, boots, and sometimes to his hands and face."[34] Conditions only seemed to worsen. "In the middle of the street and on both sides stagnant pools of typhoid fever germs mingled with little rivers of mud and filth, breeding the microbes of a dozen contagions," an observer reported of Brooklyn's streets in the spring of 1890. "The gutters, long since unaccustomed to the cleansing processes of sewer drains, became thicker and more offensive as the rain percolated through the Winter's accumulations of blackened snow, garbage, manure, ashes, and mud."[35]

Manure was not the only objectionable thing to accumulate in the streets. Because most big cities lacked effective administrative systems to keep up with rapid expansion, problems mounted, especially in the densest and poorest sections of the cities. The advent of municipal waterworks during this period, for example, caused urban water consumption rates to rise—especially as urbanites embraced indoor bathrooms—but most cities initially lacked effective sewers. As a result, wastewater overwhelmed the older system of cesspools and privy vaults designed to accommodate human wastes, causing untreated sewage to spill over into streets and basements, contaminating groundwater supplies and creating particularly bad problems in areas with poor natural drainage.[36] Meanwhile, piles of refuse accumulated in the streets, waiting for trash collectors who arrived at all-too-infrequent intervals (if they came at all). "There are many places on both the East and West Sides which apparently have received no attention whatever from the street-cleaning authorities," reported the New York Times in 1882. "On some of the streets may be seen rows of overflowing ash barrels and boxes and huge mounds of refuse, extending for blocks, and which represent the accumulation of weeks."[37]

The inability of urban governments to control growing street pollution created a grave environmental threat to the health of city dwellers, particularly for residents of overcrowded slums. Major epidemics of cholera, yellow fever, and typhoid, among many other diseases, wreaked havoc on American cities throughout the nineteenth century, striking fear into urbanites of all incomes and backgrounds and prompting growing attention to sanitation and hygiene.[38] "There cannot," editorialized the New York Times in 1890, "exist in any great city a breeding place of disease that does not constitute a menace to the health of everybody in that city."[39]

In the face of these problems, urban reformers initially targeted patronage politics. In particular, they worried that the patronage system—in which elected officials distributed nonelected government jobs, such as those in the street-cleaning and public works departments, to active members of their party—hindered the ability of public agencies to operate efficiently or effectively. "To the victor go the spoils," the saying went, and on this principle newly elected officials sometimes laid off entire agency staffs, including their most experienced and talented members, to make room for political supporters. This robbed agencies of both experience and administrative continuity. In addition, reformers complained that appointees frequently lacked relevant experience and sometimes devoted more effort to party organization and campaigning than to their government jobs. "If we would ever have a reform in City government, if we would enjoy clean streets and unimpeded traffic and healthy conditions in this City," editorialized the New York Times in a typical statement of the problem, "if we would have . . . all the thousand blessings that a well-governed metropolis ought to have, we must begin at the bottom and do away with this vicious system of patronage. There can be no good municipal organization while offices are given as party rewards."[40] Putting disinterested "experts" in positions of power and charging them to efficiently administer various aspects of city streets, reformers argued, would translate into safer, more orderly, and less problem-ridden cities.[41]

Unlike city streets, whose problems seemed to stem from too rapid an embrace of industrialization and growth, reformers saw poor rural roads as barriers to modernizing the countryside, where residents seemed to be falling ever farther behind their city cousins. The reformers had a case, at least as far as the decrepit condition of the nation's country roads went: as railroads spread their networks across the country following the Civil War, making long-distance transportation much faster and more reliable, investments in rural road maintenance shriveled, and even formerly well-traveled rural highways lost nearly all but their local traffic. As a result, most rural roads devolved in the second half of the nineteenth century to serve strictly local functions, with even formerly well-maintained roads generally falling into a state of disrepair.[42] The stark contrast between the cutting-edge transportation of railroads and the frequently impassable condition of rural highways—characterized by dust in dry weather, mud in wet weather, and rutted, treacherous surfaces year-round—highlighted what reformers saw as the backwardness and isolation of rural farm communities. "It is a blot upon our civilization," one such critic proclaimed, "a scourge upon the industry of the farmer and upon every town surrounded by a farming population."[43]

Early rural road reformers thus singled out rural road administration practices as their initial target of reform. Much as urban reformers blamed the serious problems with city streets on the inefficiencies of patronage politics, rural reformers identified rural road administration as the root cause of poor road conditions. Although practices differed from place to place, most states relied on the custom known as "statute labor," which allowed farmers to pay their road taxes by devoting a certain number of days to road work. Others financed roads through poll and property taxes, which farmers could pay either in cash or (more frequently) in labor.[44] Typically overseen by local officials without any engineering training, performed with tools designed for farming rather than road work, and conducted during slack periods in the agricultural calendar rather than when roads most needed attention, this system provoked reformers' ire both for its inefficiencies and for the flawed roads that it produced. With expert, centralized administration, reformers argued, they could solve the worst problems with rural roads.[45]

In addition to seeking administrative changes, early rural road reformers also championed wider use of new construction techniques, better road-making equipment, and hard surfaces. A relatively small percentage of rural road mileage in the United States in the late nineteenth century could accurately be called "highways"—roads slightly elevated above the surrounding topography and flanked by drainage ditches to prevent water's most damaging effects on road surfaces.[46] Given the substantial labor, expense, and technical knowledge required to build durable highways—and the clear superiority of railroads as a rapid, economical form of long-distance overland transportation—this was hardly surprising. Yet improved technical knowledge and new labor-saving construction equipment, reformers argued, made it possible to produce markedly better rural highways if properly utilized. Moreover, new pavements and surfacing methods made it much easier and more affordable to build "all-weather" highways with smooth, hard pavements. Why should farm communities continue to flounder in the mud, reformers asked, if the possibility of good roads was within their grasp? By the late 1880s, the number of reformers asking this question began to swell rapidly, pushing the question into the realm of national debate.

REBUILDING CITY STREETS

Like their rural counterparts, groups championing street reforms also gained support and momentum through the 1880s and 1890s as problems mounted and new demands outstripped the existing infrastructure's effective capacity to deal with them. In big cities, especially, streets attracted growing public attention as they devolved into increasingly noxious, chaotic environments. Reformers focused most of their attention on developing problem-specific solutions—focusing, say, on street cleaning, or traffic congestion, or sewer construction—rather than confronting the full range of issues, and their widely varying interests sometimes made them adversaries. Despite this lack of common cause, most urban reformers agreed that the success of their individual agendas hinged on thoroughly remaking the urban street environment. "The control of the streets," one prominent reformer intoned, "means the control of the city"—and most of his fellow reformers would have agreed.[47]

In their efforts to control the streets, reformers advanced fully three-dimensional changes—on, under, and over the streets—that together steadily expanded their capacity to control nature run amok. It was under the streets that they laid the systems of pipes, conduits, and sewers that supplied cities with freshwater, natural gas, and electricity while evacuating their wastes and protecting them from fire. It was above the streets that they installed lights and wires and ran elevated tracks for high-speed trains. And it was upon the streets themselves that they sent brigades of street cleaners into battle, installed streetcar rails, and experimented with new pavements. By pouring their energies into remaking city streets, late-nineteenth-century reformers helped bring the era's environmental crisis to heel.[48]

Removing untreated sewage from the streets was a top priority. As a result, sewer construction proceeded rapidly in the last two decades of the nineteenth century, with the nation's three largest cities nearly tripling their mileages between 1890 and 1902.[49] Financing for the new sewers came from many sources, including city treasuries, special assessments, and the pocketbooks of private developers, but construction generally proceeded under the supervision of municipal governments—and often at the instigation of city officials rather than the owners of abutting property.[50] The most dramatic example of transforming city streets to install sewers came in Chicago, where the engineer Ellis S. Chesbrough designed a sewer system that accommodated the city's high water table by raising the entire level of the city—buildings, streets, and all—to a new grade that in places stood twelve feet higher than before. It took a decade for workers to build the new sewers, cover them with fill, construct new streets on top of them, and, with the help of large hydraulic jacks, raise buildings up to the new grade.[51]

As with sewers, reformers systematically seized control over perhaps the most visible aspect of the urban street crisis: street cleaning. Once the responsibility of individual property owners, 140 of 199 municipalities surveyed for the 1880 census provided street-cleaning services.[52] In a few cities, like Boston, the new street-cleaning systems responded tolerably well to the increasing volumes of refuse.[53] In other cities, like Milwaukee, physicians and sanitarians successfully directed street-cleaning efforts in the name of public health.[54] In most large cities, however, reformers fought losing battles against the outdated methods of city street departments, the role of patronage in selecting street cleaners, and the unequal treatment of streets in poor and wealthy neighborhoods.[55]

Not until the 1890s and the early twentieth century did most reform battles for effective street-cleaning programs begin to achieve some success, with New York City providing the best-publicized example of dramatic improvement. New York's turning point came in 1895 when the city's new reform mayor, William L. Strong, put George Waring in charge of the task. A committed sanitarian with a national reputation, Waring had a penchant for self-promotion and a flair for the dramatic, qualities that served him well in his new post. In his three years as street commissioner, Waring increased the number of street sweepers to more than two thousand, removed political appointees who failed to meet his standards, and reformed his department's administration. In a master stroke of public relations, Waring theatrically outfitted his street sweepers in white uniforms that resembled those of health-care workers, dubbed them "White Wings," and vigorously promoted their effectiveness. By all accounts, Waring's reforms brought remarkable cleanliness to New York's roughly paved streets, which had long been judged among the dirtiest in the country.[56]

Whereas Waring's success depended on a combination of bluster, publicity, and the visibility of his ubiquitous White Wings, other cities turned to new technologies, including street-cleaning machinery and street-flushing devices, both of which followed closely on the heels of growing mileages of smooth pavements, particularly asphalt, in downtown areas.[57] By 1905, nearly 85 percent of U.S. cities larger than twenty-five thousand people—and over half of the nation's smaller cities—had replaced hand-broom methods with machine sweepers. Although the particular machines and flushing systems varied widely from city to city, the results were cleaner streets and fewer obstructions in urban areas around the nation.[58] Even so, reformers found it no easy task to create a culture of cleanliness among citizens long accustomed to seeing urban streets as "catch-alls" for their trash. "The fact remains that [you can] surface your streets with the most modern paving, and place your patrol sweepers where you will," complained Boston's street commissioner in 1903, but "if the public persist in throwing papers, fruit parings, store sweepings, etc., into the streets, the surface cannot be kept in a clean condition."[59]

Corporations selling a range of new amenities also significantly reshaped the urban street environment so that they could deliver their products—which included natural gas, steam heat, electricity, and telephone service—to their customers. Like municipal sewers, these utilities required extensive systems of pipes and wires above and below urban thoroughfares; unlike sewers, private corporations typically developed these utilities as profit-generating enterprises with minimal government oversight.[60] Installing and then maintaining these elaborate technological systems often required digging up and then repaving the streets—a disruptive and often damaging process—and city dwellers objected both to the unsightliness of overhead wires and to the alarming number of fires and occasional electrocutions that they caused.

The rapid expansion of utilities provoked intense discussions about exactly who had control—and who ought to have control—over the urban street environment. "The rights and wishes of the people are wholly disregarded by the corporations, which act as if they owned not only the streets of the City but the roofs of all its buildings," the *New York Times* editorialized in December 1883. "The outrage has grown to such dimensions in this City that it is plain that something will have to be done or violent hands may be laid on the offending poles and wires."[61] Prodded in part by this public outcry, and in part by insurance underwriters who saw aboveground wires as serious fire risks, cities began requiring utilities to relocate wires into conduits below city streets. Companies balked at the additional cost and trouble, but it resolved abutters' aesthetic and safety concerns while preserving easy access for repairs and inspection.[62]

For many reformers, the most appealing solution to big-city problems was to invest in new transportation technologies that could spread overcrowded urban populations over a broader area. Well before the arrival of the automobile, new transportation technology seemed the perfect panacea for urban problems of filth, disease, and overcrowding. Reformers championed the horsecar and commuter railroads in the 1870s and 1880s, and then electric streetcars in the 1890s, primarily on the grounds that they could eradicate slums by dispersing urban populations—without sacrificing easy access to downtown.[63]

Although horsecars and streetcars helped most American cities, traffic congestion in the biggest cities negated the advantages of speed and convenience that smaller cities enjoyed. If only the streetcars could soar above the traffic-choked streets, some big-city reformers and businessmen began to think, they could solve the entrenched problems of congestion. Beginning in the 1870s and 1880s in New York, Brooklyn, Chicago, and Kansas City, and followed later in Boston and Philadelphia, city governments granted exclusive franchises for the construction of elevated railways to serve their cities.[64] The hulking structures necessary to carry elevated trains, however, so significantly altered the street environments below them—the novelist Stephen Crane likened them to "some monstrous kind of crab squatting over the street"—that they engendered fierce protests and court challenges, leading most would-be imitators elsewhere to drop their plans.[65] The trains operated profitably where they existed, with the Manhattan Elevated alone carrying 196.7 million passengers in 1891, but even reformers who valued the capacity of elevated lines to disperse residential settlement saw their drawbacks.[66] "For several decades the elevated roads have borne their millions of passengers up and down the city," wrote one prominent reformer in 1904, "making three or four of the great north and south thoroughfares hideous with darkness, noise, and obstruction."[67] Even in cities with elevated systems, businessmen continued to clamor for easier access to downtown, commuters to call for better and faster service, and reformers to seek transportation alternatives that would alleviate residential overcrowding.

With the advent of electric trains in the 1890s, American attitudes began to warm toward the possibility of subways, which unlike steam railroads could operate underground in relative comfort—insulated from the weather and without the major disruptions to the street environment that elevated railways caused. Boston acted first, gaining authorization in 1894 for a 1.5-mile-long subway under Tremont Street in the heart of the city's retail district. Completed in 1898, it immediately generated tens of millions of riders each year, disproving the older conventional wisdom that Americans would not patronize underground transit facilities. Building on this success, a second tunnel to East Boston opened in 1904. New York City soon followed Boston's example, starting construction on its own subway line in 1900. It opened in 1904 to the first of what quickly became hundreds of millions of passengers annually, and the success of New York's extensive subway inspired strong support for similar proposals in other cities among reformers and downtown business interests alike.[68]

In the midst of all these changes below, above, and upon city streets, street surfaces themselves underwent a minor revolution in the late nineteenth century as engineers made a series of breakthroughs with new pavements and paving techniques. Before the Civil War, cobblestone and gravel had accounted for the vast majority of paved urban streets. After the war, cities introduced a host of new pavements—including macadam, vitrified brick, sheet asphalt, and paving blocks made of stone, wood, and asphalt—and greatly improved the quality of street foundations by using Portland cement.[69] In many large cities, the move away from older pavements was dramatic. In Philadelphia, for example, 93 percent of the city's paved streets in 1884 had a cobblestone surface; two decades later, following a successful campaign to repave the city—which, it is worth noting, had nothing to do with automobiles—cobblestone accounted for a mere 6 percent of Philadelphia's total pavements.[70]

Eventually these new pavements would thoroughly remake city streets across the country, particularly as automobile ownership exploded in the 1910s, but late-nineteenth- and early twentieth-century street pavements suffered a series of almost continuous disruptions as utilities fitted the streets of downtown areas with new technologies. "No pavement, no matter how well laid, can be kept in proper order if it is constantly disturbed for the purpose of laying or repairing underground pipes," the Philadelphia Board of Experts on Street Paving reported in 1884. "In order to avoid this as far as possible, all drains, gas, water and other pipes, should be laid, or if already laid, should be thoroughly repaired, before the pavement is put down."[71] Yet in a period of chaotic change, this sensible recommendation proved little more than a fond dream. New York, for example, reported 19,371 street openings in 1889 for utility repairs and new installations; in 1892, Boston issued 10,696 permits for similar openings.[72] Urbanites grumbled that utility companies rarely resurfaced their openings adequately, and the battle for control over the streets intensified as city after city passed ordinances in the 1880s and 1890s requiring utilities to receive permits before tearing up pavements for repairs.[73] In 1892, for example, the city engineer of St. Joseph, Missouri, went so far as to have representatives of the St. Joseph Gas and Fuel Company arrested and brought to trial for tearing up a street pavement without a permit. "The contest," reported the *Engineering Record*, called into question "the extent of the rights of a municipality in and over its own highways."[74]

GETTING FARMERS OUT OF THE MUD

In contrast to the uncoordinated campaigns to remake big-city streets, rural road reformers launched a cohesive national movement that came to be known simply as the "good-roads movement."[75] Although it focused exclusively on improving the condition of rural roads, the movement originated, somewhat counterintuitively, among city dwellers who had to work hard to convince rural Americans to join their cause. Only after building a vigorous national movement that promoted a host of new ideas about the characteristics, appropriate uses, and proper administration of country roads, were good-roads reformers slowly able to overcome a series of entrenched rural objections and obstacles. When the new ideas at the heart of the good-roads movement finally began to make headway, however—both among rural Americans and in the halls of Congress—they ushered in a profoundly new era for the nation's country roads.

Although various engineers, equipment manufacturers, and reformers had begun to point out the possibilities of building better rural roads in the 1860s and 1870s, good roads first emerged as a national political issue in the 1880s. Bicycle ownership provided the initial impetus, exploding from roughly 100,000 to 2.5 million between the mid-1880s and mid-1890s. As the ranks of cyclists grew, urban bicycle clubs led frequent excursions into the countryside—where they confronted a reality of muddy, dusty, and rutted roads that belied their romantic visions of cycling as leisurely, pleasant recreation.[76] "Farmers have been content to have for alleged highways strips of mud, sometimes frozen, sometimes dried, sometimes liquid," one cyclist complained, "and the rest of the world would never disturb this serenity of farmers if the farmer alone were abused and injured."[77] By the late 1880s, after nearly a decade of suffering the "abuse and injury" of ill-maintained country roads, cyclists had seized leadership of the campaign for good roads. Among the various good-roads organizations to spring up, the League of American Wheelman (LAW), a national organization comprised mainly of urban cyclists from the East and Midwest, played a particularly important role. In addition to coordinating a sizable network of lobbyists to pursue favorable legislation at all levels of government, LAW also funded a massive public-relations campaign, issuing more than five million pamphlets promoting the good-roads cause in the decade after 1889 and launching Isaac Potter's magazine, *Good Roads*, in 1892.[78]

The efforts of cyclists slowly began to attract new adherents. Railroad executives, especially, began to see better farm-to-market roads as a way to boost the volume of agricultural commodities on their lines by increasing the distance from each station that farmers could profitably transport their products. Compared to the high costs of developing and operating spur lines—the traditional strategy for connecting new agricultural land to markets—even relatively small investments in good-roads propaganda had potentially significant implications for railroad company profits.[79] Cyclists achieved another major goal in 1893 when LAW's longstanding campaign to gain a toehold in the federal government finally resulted in the creation of the Office of Road Inquiry (ORI) within the Department of Agriculture. Directed by Roy Stone, a dynamic former lumberman, brigadier general, and LAW activist, the ORI published a wide variety of good-roads pamphlets and closely coordinated its activities with LAW. Martin Dodge, a lawyer and former president of the Ohio State Highway Commission, took over the newly renamed Office of Public Road Inquiries (OPRI) in 1899. In his six years as director, Dodge expanded the federal agency's working relationships with good-roads organizations such as the National Good Roads Association (founded 1901). He also helped secure sizable railroad company donations to various projects, causing railroads to leapfrog the bicycle industry as the largest contributor to good-roads causes.[80]

Even as the good-roads movement expanded its coalition, it encountered substantial obstacles in its efforts to win over rural Americans themselves, a vital constituency for the movement's success. Among the various objections that good-roads reformers encountered, perhaps the most significant was the idea that the condition of rural roads did not actually represent a problem—that mud, dust, and ruts were expected and even natural characteristics of country roads. According to this worldview, roads were just one element of a carefully maintained agricultural landscape in which farmers labored to raise crops and to support their families in the face of variable weather and regular seasonal change. Farm implements were perfectly suitable tools—and farmers themselves were the logical and appropriate group to provide the labor—for whatever maintenance roads required.[81] "Mud does not give back anything to anybody. There is nothing reciprocal about it," railed one frustrated reformer in 1893. "Mud knows neither friend nor foe. In the natural organization of matter mud may have a place, but that place is not in the road."[82] Yet many farmers disagreed. What was unusual, farmers wondered, about a dirt road turning to mud in the rain? Rural roads lacked the hard pavements of big-city streets, but this hardly made them deficient as long as they adequately served local needs—and most farmers concluded that they did so. "The road over which I travel," one farmer explained in an article rejecting the good-roads agenda, "is good enough for me."[83]

In addition to disagreeing with reformers that country roads were a serious problem, many farmers embraced an ideology of republican self-government that clashed with another key reform prescription: improving the efficiency of road administration by centralizing it under expert control. Where reformers saw an inefficient system that routinely placed a technically demanding task in untrained hands, farmers were more inclined to see a system that protected them from the capricious decisions of distant experts who had few incentives to consider local interests.[84] The attempts of reformers to centralize and professionalize road administration thus ran into sometimes fierce resistance. "The liberty of localities to perform their own functions in road building and road working is in danger," one advocate of local control warned in 1894, "and if people do not exercise this liberty it will be wrested from them."[85] Moreover, the fact that the early charge for good roads was led by wealthy urban cyclists, whose interests clearly diverged from those of rural dwellers, gave farmers pause. "We don't want any eastern bicycle fellers or one-hoss lawyers with patent leather boots, to tell us how to fix the roads that we use," resolved an 1893 Iowa farmers' convention, summing up this strand of thinking.[86] Farmers knew what sort of roads they needed better than outsiders—especially fancy urban cyclists!—went the argument, and so farmers should remain in charge of their own roads.

If farmers cared about local control because of republican principles and the long-established tradition of home rule, they also cared because the sort of hard-surfaced, all-weather roads that good-roads reformers advocated were quite expensive. The high costs of road improvements prompted farmers to meet good-roads entreaties with three significant objections, all of which related to traditional methods of financing rural roads. First was a problem of equity: The financing for rural road improvements typically came entirely from local government revenue, especially property taxes levied on the owners of abutting property. Urban cyclists and other nonlocal travelers would derive clear benefit from hard-surfaced roads, but farmers alone were expected to foot the bill. Second was the problem of cash payments: Most good-roads proposals would not only increase the size of road taxes but they would also eliminate the traditional option of paying them in labor rather than cash. For cash-starved agricultural communities, the combination of cash payments and higher taxes represented an untenable double burden. Third, many farmers regarded with skepticism good-roads claims that hard-surfaced roads represented a one-time investment—many enthusiasts referred to them as "permanent" roads—that would eventually pay itself back in reduced transportation costs.

By the late 1880s and early 1890s, reformers began to increase their efforts across a broad front to recruit more farmers to the good-roads cause. Rather than assuming, as many early reformers had, that poor road conditions presented a self-evident problem, good-roads advocates began to pay more attention to enumerating the ways that maintaining the status quo hurt farmers and to stress the specific advantages that improved roads would bring. In particular, reformers stressed the idea that ungraded, unsurfaced, poorly sited, heavily rutted, and frequently muddy country roads had the effect of isolating farmers in economically and socially detrimental ways. "You have produce to sell, purchases to make, grain to grind, timber to haul, bills to collect and obligations to meet," wrote Potter in his famous pamphlet, *The Gospel of Good Roads* (1891), "but all these must wait because your only avenue of travel is taking its annual soak."[87] Arguing that farmers should think of their wagons and roads as equivalents to railroad engines and rails—and should judge their efficiency in similar terms—good-roads advocates drew a direct analogy between investing in modern farm equipment and investing in good roads.[88] Both required significant up-front investments in new technologies, but both justified those investments by reducing unit costs, boosting operating efficiency, and increasing profits.

Advocates also trumpeted the social advantages that better roads would bring, arguing that they would make it easier to visit neighbors, go to town, and attend church or school. "The American farmer has nerve, vigor, ambition, industry, good soil, good climate and every natural facility for the successful pursuit of agriculture, but the average American farm is a lonely institution," Potter proclaimed. "Its owner is separated from his neighbors, [and] largely denied the many social advantages which belong to people who are able to mingle with each other from day to day."[89] If poor roads were the ultimate cause of farmers' isolation, reformers argued, then it stood to reason that good roads would create immense social advantages.

In response to the fierce defense of local control over road administration, good-roads advocates emphasized the efficiencies of centralized administration and publicized testimonials from those who had replaced taxes paid in labor with cash taxes. Centralized administration had the advantages of skilled leadership, the ability to coordinate action over a broad area, and efficiencies of scale; cash taxes allowed administrators to hire workers to perform road maintenance at times when farmers were occupied with agricultural work, to purchase advanced construction machinery, and to buy high-quality surfacing materials that were not locally available. In response to continuing skepticism, reformers solicited testimonials on behalf of cash taxes from those who had adopted them. Between 1894 and 1896, for example, the ORI surveyed citizens from New York, Wisconsin, Iowa, and Indiana who lived in districts that had "experimented with the money system of taxation in place of the ancient labor system." Although many respondents expressed continuing reservations with particular policies and the centralization of power, the vast majority supported cash taxes. "In reference to the change from the labor tax to the money system, I would say that I prefer the latter, not only for the sake of economy, but also for the sake of having better roads," wrote one respondent. "Under the old system in some cases it is simply a question of putting in the allotted time without any view of improving the road." Others agreed. "We are about entering upon the second year of working roads by tax levied upon taxpayers instead of the old system," wrote another respondent. "Under the new system I think we can get better roads, properly managed. . . . I believe the new method is an improvement upon the old way."[90]

In response to farmers' strident objections to the high expense of road improvements, reformers adopted a mix of strategies. First, supporters emphasized the high cost of hauling goods over poor roads. By crunching data on agricultural production, farm profits, railroad haulage rates, horse maintenance costs, and so forth, they calculated the average per-ton costs of hauling farm products over typical American country roads. They then compared these costs to the (much lower) estimated hauling costs of farmers in various European countries with advanced rural road-building programs.[91] Labeling the jaw-dropping difference a "mud tax"—an unproductive expense that, reformers argued, would be much better spent on improving roads—good-roads advocates developed a new rallying cry: American farmers paid for good roads whether they had them or not. Second, good-roads advocates argued that properly designed cash-financing systems would be more equitable than the old labor system. Farmers were not the sole road users, reformers noted, which meant that responsibility for financing them ought to be shared at the township, county, or even state level. In addition, by issuing bonds, these higher levels of government could gather the significant up-front costs of large-scale improvement programs but still spread out the costs to taxpayers over time. "We must find out all the parties to be benefited," one supporter of this approach argued in 1894, "and see that each bears his proper share of the cost, whether or not he belongs to the immediate locality, or even to the present generation of men."[92] Finally, reformers stressed the idea that state governments routinely supported public works projects that primarily benefited nonfarm groups—such as canal, harbor, and even prison improvements—and that farmers *deserved* similar support.[93]

Good-roads advocates used a variety of techniques to advance these arguments. Numerous good-roads organizations, operating from the local to the national level, brought good-roads advocates together. Taken as a whole, they generated a tremendous volume of printed materials, sponsored speeches and conventions, lobbied politicians, and collected and disseminated technical information about road building. In addition, the OPRI popularized two hands-on publicity techniques that exposed farmers directly to good-roads ideas. The first, known as the "object-lesson road program," involved building short lengths of paved roads so that skeptical farmers could try them for themselves. "People who have once had the benefit of good roads are always in favor of extending the same to other communities," Dodge explained in 1903, "and people who have not been blessed with these advantages seldom appreciate their value until they have been brought into contact in some way with such roads, or at least samples of them."[94] The second, which the OPRI developed in cooperation with the National Good Roads Association and various railroads beginning in 1901, was to sponsor traveling good-roads demonstrations known as "Good Roads Trains." Traveling from one town to the next in a well-publicized tour, the trains sponsored speeches, exhibited new construction equipment, and distributed literature along their routes. At some stops, they staged good-roads conventions and even built short stretches of object-lesson roads.[95]

By the late 1890s and early 1900s, as growing numbers of farmers became more interested in the issue of good roads, a handful of political and technological developments further augmented the appeal of good-roads arguments. First, two significant political trends reduced local government responsibility for financing road improvements, especially in wealthier industrialized states. These included the slow spread of "state aid," in which state legislatures contributed a fixed percentage of the costs of improving important state routes, and a wave of new enabling legislation that allowed townships and counties to issue voter-approved bonds for road work.[96] Second, a potent new incentive for road improvement emerged with the U.S. Post Office's new Rural Free Delivery (RFD) program. Launched in 1896, RFD delivered mail directly to rural homes—rather than to the nearest post office—but only, after 1899, if communities maintained "passable" roads year-round.[97] Third, a simple new tool known as the "split-log drag" dramatically decreased the costs (and increased the convenience) of basic road maintenance. Easy to construct from a single log split lengthwise, farmers could use road drags after a rain to compact the soil, smooth ruts, and create water-shedding crowns on dirt roads. When used consistently, road drags empowered even poor communities to maintain local roads in decent condition at relatively small cost.[98]

By 1905, the point after which motorists finally began to inject steadily growing enthusiasm into the cause, the good-roads movement had achieved mixed results. After more than two decades of agitation, the actual mileage of improved roads in the United States remained pitifully small: the OPRI's 1904 road census counted just over 7 percent of the nation's vast rural road mileage as "improved," including many roads in this number that fell well short of the standards that good-roads reformers advocated.[99] Similarly, the key economic and administrative reforms that good-roads leaders championed remained the exception rather than the rule in most states, although this was starting to change. On the other hand, and in some ways most importantly, large numbers of American farmers had begun to advocate for better roads. Increasingly swayed by the arguments that poorly maintained rural roads created social and economic barriers to full participation in the modern, rapidly industrializing world—and that road improvements offered a feasible way to reengineer the rural landscape to foster better social and economic connections to the outside world—the cause took on new life and political force.

CONCLUSION

The physical changes that late-nineteenth-century reform movements secured placed Americans in complicated new relationships both with their roads and streets and with the natural world. In rural areas, the greatest accomplishment of the good-roads movement grew from its efforts to convince farmers to see their roads in a new light. Roads, they argued, ought to be seen—just like any other technology—as man-made instruments for achieving social and economic goals. This view clashed directly with the traditional view of roads as organic entities governed by wind and water, muscle and wagon wheels, soil and stone, but had nevertheless gained increasing sway by the dawn of the twentieth century. The idea that roads naturally expressed local conditions and values slowly yielded to new ideas that increasingly gave outside interests—including those of the centralized agencies that oversaw road improvements, the engineers who designed them, and the wheeled traffic that took advantage of them—the power to determine the shape of rural environments.

In urban areas, changes were equally profound. Indoor bathrooms that sent wastes into state-of-the-art sewer systems, subways that comfortably whisked riders to their destinations whatever the weather or the traffic conditions, and dramatic reductions in epidemic diseases all signaled clear victories over nature run amok. Reformers believed, with some evidence, that problems like bodily wastes, refuse, overcrowding, disease, and street congestion could be engineered away, while clean water, electricity, telephones, subways, and smooth street pavements could be engineered into the basic fabric of the landscape, thus creating a new and better urban nature.[100] Yet such changes were not always quite as straightforward as they seemed. Clean streets solved some problems and undoubtedly made urban life more pleasant, yet when scows full of urban garbage dumped their contents into lakes and oceans, or when rendering plants processed urban garbage into new forms, the results were polluted water, refuse-speckled beaches, and noxious air. "Tidying up the metropolis," as one historian has noted, "meant compromising life in other quarters."[101]

The physical changes to roads and streets that reformers secured also necessitated sweeping changes in administration and finance.

Reformers insisted that political bosses—and the graft and patronage politics they represented—had to go; so, too, should the various local road officials whose road-building expertise revolved around the use of agricultural implements like hoes, shovels, and plows. By the early years of the twentieth century, these arguments had gained substantial currency, and governmental structures were beginning to change accordingly.

Also significant was the degree to which these late-nineteenth-century movements introduced reforms that privileged the needs of travelers on roads and streets over those of the residents who lived along them. In big cities, as streets became ever more thoroughly enmeshed in new technological networks, new urban services, new administrative systems, and growing volumes of traffic, nonlocal interests began to exert significant new claims over street landscapes. These changes left residents with less and less control over the shape of streets in front of their homes. Even in quiet and seemingly isolated neighborhoods, each vehicle—as well as each pipe, wire, rail, tube, or conduit built into the landscape—connected urban residents in powerful new ways to the larger world beyond their individual streets. Similarly, the needs of people like urban bicyclists, long-distance travelers, and mail carriers began to exert a great deal of influence over formerly isolated rural spaces once shaped strictly according to local needs.

Although these late-nineteenth-century campaigns had nothing to do with catering to automobiles, the underlying values that drove the road-improvement agenda—such as the emphasis on economy and efficiency, the faith in administrative expertise, and the willingness to engineer the landscape to achieve social and economic goals—were entirely consistent with enthusiasm for the automobile (and the willingness to remake the landscape around it). And so, both in the values that they reflected and the physical changes that they sought, the road- and street-reform efforts of the late nineteenth century effectively set the stage for the rapid diffusion of automobiles in American life in the first two decades of the twentieth century.

PART II

Dawn of the Motor Age, 1895–1919

TWO

AUTOMOTIVE PIONEERS

THE MOTOR-VEHICLE INDUSTRY IN THE UNITED STATES ROSE SO quickly into prominence, overcoming such formidable obstacles along the way, that in retrospect its success seems almost to have been fore-ordained.[1] On Thanksgiving Day, 1895, when the *Chicago Times-Herald* sponsored the country's first widely publicized motor-vehicle race, only six contestants made it to the starting line; of those, only two managed to finish over the snow-covered course. From these shaky beginnings, however, the U.S. industry grew rapidly. Europeans scoffed at the comparative crudity of early American vehicles, but in just more than a decade the United States had overtaken France as the world's leading producer. From the relatively paltry total production in 1900 of 5,000 motor vehicles, for example, American factories boosted their output by 1910 to a total of 187,000.[2]

Although passenger cars remained expensive, ownership continued to grow rapidly, reaching 194,400 in 1908, 618,727 in 1911, 2.3 million in 1915, and an eye-popping 8.1 million in 1920 (fig. 2.1).[3] Viewed from another angle, the automobile's popularity was also evident in the ratio between numbers of motor vehicles

A pioneering motorist in the automotive equivalent of battle armor. Detail from the collections of The Henry Ford, THF25029.

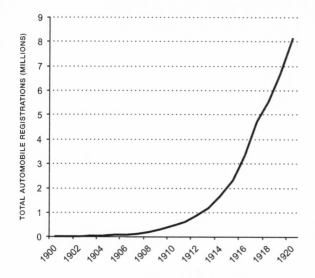

2.1 Total registered automobiles in the United States, 1900–1920. Federal Highway Administration, *Highway Statistics to 1985*, 25.

and Americans old enough to drive, which plummeted from one automobile for every 6,255 adults in 1900, to one for every 133 adults in 1910, and finally to one for every 7.8 adults by 1920 (fig. 2.2).[4] The quality of the industry's products also grew as their popularity swelled. By 1908, the watershed year in which Henry Ford introduced his revolutionary Model T and William Durant founded General Motors, the typical American motor vehicle had achieved a level of technological sophistication and everyday acceptance that would have astounded observers a decade earlier. From very early on, the United States embraced the role of the world's leading nation on wheels.

From the introduction of the Model T in 1908 until the United States entered World War I in 1917, the American automotive industry underwent a complicated but significant process of realignment as a single company (Ford) and a single car (the Model T) challenged prevailing orthodoxy on such fundamental issues as basic automotive design, manufacturing processes, and the demographics of automobile ownership. Ford's Model T played such a dominant role during these years that the entire pioneering period can be viewed, with little distortion, through its lens. Unlike any other car before or since, the Model T became a ubiquitous and celebrated feature of everyday American life—the benchmark against which all automobiles were compared—prompting one contemporary to dub it "the first log cabin of the Motor Age."[5]

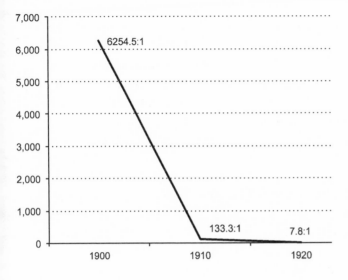

2.2 Ratio of population aged fifteen years and over to total registered motor vehicles, 1900–1920. Federal Highway Administration, *Highway Statistics to 1985*, 39.

As the auto industry began its spectacular rise, however, automakers and motorists alike confronted a series of substantial environmental obstacles. Unlike later years, when cars and roads worked together almost seamlessly as mutually complementary parts of a larger, coordinated transportation system, wretched road conditions in the early twentieth century threatened both the viability and popular appeal of automobiles. Early automakers struggled to design cars with the power and durability to handle the mud and ruts of typical country roads, and they experimented with a variety of approaches and adaptations before Ford's dramatic success with the Model T. Early motorists, too, braved various hardships in traveling by car and increasingly enlisted the aid of a wide range of accessories to pad the bumps and bruises of driving and to seal out the harsher effects of inclement weather. In many ways, the pioneering period before World War I is best understood in terms of the constant efforts of automakers and motorists to adapt to—and prevail over—challenging environmental conditions.

OVERCOMING BAD ROADS

Although the year 1895 marked something of a beginning for the American automobile industry, by then the self-propelled road vehicle already had a long lineage on both sides of the Atlantic. The earliest motor vehicles on record, for example, date back to huge, lumbering steam wagons built in the late eighteenth century, although the pace of innovation did not accelerate until the 1870s, when lightweight, high-pressure steam engines opened new opportunities for overland travel. By the 1880s and 1890s, a growing number of inventors were beginning to achieve some success in adapting electric and gasoline engines to road vehicles as well.[6]

In many respects, the new machines shared little but the ability to travel under their own power. Steam, electric, and internal-combustion engines powered vehicles ranging from bicycles and adult-sized tricycles to small single-seat carriages and enormous multiseat coaches. As the liabilities of slight bicycle and tricycle frames for carrying heavy motors became clear, most development in the United States turned to adapting motors to a dizzying array of carriage designs, including phaetons, runabouts, stanhopes, surreys, victorias, hansoms, and more. By 1899, when thirty American manufacturers produced 2,500 vehicles, a large segment of the market had stabilized around the small, four-wheeled, tiller-driven, surrey-style vehicle widely known as the "horseless carriage."[7] Many of those who were or later became important forces in the industry got their start in the 1890s building vehicles of this type.[8]

As inventors tackled the persistent mechanical problems that made their early prototypes unreliable, they labored in the shadow of another large and seemingly intractable problem: the sorry state of American country roads. Challenging road conditions subjected early motor vehicles to incredible stresses, highlighting their various weaknesses and contributing to the notoriously frequent, costly, and inconvenient breakdowns that typified the early years of automotive development. "The American who buys an automobile finds himself confronted with this great difficulty. He has nowhere to use it," wrote Albert Pope, who, as the nation's largest bicycle manufacturer in the late 1880s, was often called the father of the American good-roads movement. "He must pick and choose between bad roads and worse."[9]

The experiences of Hiram Percy Maxim, an early inventor and one of Pope's employees, were typical. "Late in March, 1897," Maxim explained, "it seemed to me that the frost had come out of the ground enough to permit [his prototype gasoline] tricycle to venture upon the country roads. I had detected a dry spot in the macadam in front of the factory, and it sang the song of the open road to me." Convincing his trusted assistant, Lobdell, to join him, Maxim made his way out of the city. "At the city line the street lights ended along with the macadam," he wrote, and the two adventurers promptly plunged into the mud of an unpaved country road. It "was nothing less than a quagmire," Maxim recalled. "We advanced about a hundred yards, wallowing and slithering sidewise in the dark, Lobdell pushing and pulling, and everything else jangling, clattering, and rattling as the poor little engine struggled under the heavy load." With the engine overheating after only meager progress, the two men called it quits and returned to the factory.[10]

Not everyone agreed with Pope that the best interests of motorists lay in making common cause with the well-established good-roads movement. Most early motorists had the financial resources to get good roads in other ways, and many wondered why they should wait for good roads when they could transport their cars by rail or ship to a locale that already had them. This logic produced the motoring vacation, a popular pastime among elite motorists of the era. Many manufacturers, too, transported their vehicles great distances in search of good roads, especially when high-speed races beckoned with their promises of favorable publicity. The naturally smooth, level surfaces of frozen lakes, salt flats, and hard-packed beaches were favorite sites for early races, though specially surfaced oval racetracks also began to appear. The most extreme example of the lengths to which some aficionados would go to secure a well-paved road, however, is provided by William K. Vanderbilt, great-grandson of Commodore Cornelius Vanderbilt and heir to the Vanderbilt fortune, who in 1908 constructed a private, twenty-mile-long toll road on Long Island. The new tollway allowed Vanderbilt to operate his high-powered automobiles, which boasted names like "The White Ghost" and "The Red Devil," without fear of being ticketed by local police for speeding. It also provided a venue for the Vanderbilt Cup, one of the premier early American automobile races.[11] Expensive trips in search of smooth surfaces were at best a stop-gap solution, however, and expensive private highways were obviously a nonstarter for those without Vanderbilt's enormous resources.

As the solutions of the elite, the impatient, and the speed-obsessed, these strategies for overcoming poor road conditions did little to resolve the basic threat that they posed for the nascent auto industry, whose machines continued to rattle apart when faced with even the relatively "normal" condition of American country roads. Many manufacturers chose to downplay the threat, arguing that with sufficient time and effort they would eventually figure out how to design cars that could handle even the worst roads. "Don't preach that motor vehicles depend on roads. They don't," one *Motor Age* writer argued in 1899. "They depend on good, suitable construction to negotiate any kind of road surface, and on perfectly reliable motors."[12]

The possibility of designing vehicles that could "negotiate any kind of road surface" grew exponentially with the introduction of the 1901 Mercedes, which marked a quantum leap forward for automotive design in the realms of power, speed, and reliability. The key breakthroughs came when a wealthy enthusiast and Daimler board member, Emile Jellinek, asked a Daimler engineer to develop a vehicle based on his ideas. Named after Jellinek's daughter Mercédès, the resulting vehicle combined a number of advances—including mechanically operated inlet valves, a honeycomb radiator, an improved gearbox, a front-mounted four-cylinder engine, and a pressed-steel chassis—that marked a significant break with earlier motor-vehicle designs. Despite its German origin, Americans described this novel tonneau-style body as "French style," equating it with the front-mounted engines that were then popular in France.[13]

The bruising conditions on American country roads, however, initially limited the utility—and thus the market share—of these fast, powerful new machines. "Those Americans who have imported French or German racing or road vehicles are finding them excellent for very high speeds, and stanch in their wagon work," ran one typical critique in the popular press, "but hard to take care of, delicate in motor mechanism, inconvenient to repair, and generally to be classed as 'white elephants.'" The *Nation* concurred, explaining that "many foreign cars built for European conditions are unfitted for use in America, where the roads are of a kind wholly undreamed of in Europe."[14]

Such complaints were clearly based in reality. From an American perspective, the main problem with imported Mercedes-style vehicles

Dressed for a ride. Pioneering motorists encountered the elements in visceral ways and could expect the full range of experiences that came with exposure to the weather. From the collections of The Henry Ford, THF25029.

grew from the European practice of placing the chassis low and near the road, a practice that increased stability during rapid cornering. This worked for Europeans on their smooth roads and for racers on beaches and frozen lakes but was a liability on typical American country roads. As one auto tourist explained, "You must be prepared for 'roads' that are simply two deep ruts, with a stony ridge in the middle on which the car bottom will drag." Further illustrating this point, an author in 1905 explained the differences in European and American motor-vehicle design by telling the story of a Turkish man who traveled to the United States to purchase an automobile. The author asked the man why he did not make his purchase in France and thus reduce his shipping costs to Turkey. "His answer was that a car made for use on American roads would be far more serviceable in his own country, than a French car built chiefly for speed, as the latter sets too low to the ground for satisfactory use on ordinary and sometimes very bad roads."[15]

The American environment—and especially poor American roads—thus had a direct and profound impact on how automotive technology evolved in the United States.[16] In particular, American manufacturers adapted Mercedes-style automobiles to poor country roads by raising the chassis to provide greater road clearance. They also specified thicker and stronger materials to ensure durability; outfitted automobiles with extra-strong axles, frames, and suspension systems; and, in contrast to European manufacturers, adopted larger engines that gave drivers enough power to escape from treacherous spots in the road while reducing the need for frequent gear changes. The result was the American touring car, a versatile modification of the Mercedes-style automobile carefully designed to negotiate even the worst of roads. "The one great essential of a touring motor car is power of endurance over roads good or execrable, whether the floods come or the sun shines," editorialized *Outing*.[17] "The automobile . . . must force its way over stony places," agreed *Munsey's*, "must plunge through slough, and climb steep gradients, must take the luck of the road, and, at its home coming, must be content with the rough and ready cleansing of an ignorant attendant." Manufacturers thus "Americanized" French technology by accommodating their designs to the poor roads that dominated the American landscape, transforming a natural-born racer into a powerful back-roads "touring car."[18]

The emergence of a distinctly American touring car based on French gasoline-engine technology caused the average cost of automobiles in the United States to rise significantly. In 1903, two-thirds of the country's new motor vehicles sold for $1,375 or less; by 1907, two-thirds of sales exceeded that amount. Rising prices reflected new trends, such as the growing number of cylinders and the higher average weight of heavy touring automobiles. As the *Independent* put it in 1908, the "infancy of spindly, fragile 'horseless carriages' has grown to a youth of mighty road engines continually increasing in size, in power, in cost of purchase and maintenance, and, naturally, in excellence of construction."[19]

Although experts quickly agreed that the modified Mercedes touring car represented the American state of the art, consumers gave two very different styles of motor vehicle a sizable—and expanding—segment of the marketplace. Although each of these vehicle types differed from the other in substantial ways, they shared two vital characteristics: both were significantly less expensive than the new touring cars, and both were capable of operating on challenging American country roads.

The first of these new vehicles—the "runabout" or "gas buggy"—was an inexpensive, one- or two-cylinder gasoline-powered vehicle with a rear-mounted motor and seating for two. The wildly popular curved-dash Oldsmobile, which captured 36 percent of the American market in 1902 with four thousand sales, was the most popular early runabout. It also illustrated what in 1904 *Outing* called a "distinctly American" trend toward building vehicles "in very large numbers for a ready sale at prices well below the thousand-dollar mark." Some of the more important manufacturers to follow Oldsmobile in runabout production between 1903 and 1910 included the Thomas B. Jeffery Company, the Cadillac Motor Car Company, and the Ford Motor Company, all of which used economies of scale to help them incorporate the high-quality materials and craftsmanship of French-style automobiles into low-priced vehicles.[20]

The second new type of gasoline carriage—the "high-wheeler"—was basically a motorized wagon designed for farmers, with large-diameter, solid-tired wheels, low horsepower, high road clearance, a rear-mounted engine, and prices ranging from $250 to $950. Among the more important high-wheeler manufacturers, whose production concentrated heavily in the Midwest, were the W. H. McIntyre Company in Auburn, Indiana; the Schacht Company in Cincinnati; and Chicago's International Harvester, H. K. Holsman Company, and Sears, Roebuck and Company.[21]

With one eye on the potential profitability of the low-priced market and another on the strengths of the Americanized Mercedes, some other manufacturers also began to develop stripped-down touring cars. Recognizing this trend as early as 1904, *Outing* magazine noted a "possible third type" of motor vehicle that would combine low weight, moderate cost, and simple design—a hybrid mix of heavy touring car and low-priced runabout that it dubbed the "lightweight automobile." "It is simply impossible that the average French touring car carrying four persons can be equaled in all-round qualities by any mere amplification of the light American runabout," the article explained, "but it is not impossible that a system of construction may be perfected to a point where it will give a four-passenger car of reasonable efficiency and moderate speed at a cost of not very much over one thousand dollars." Such a hybrid would certainly compromise the power and amenities of expensive touring cars, the article continued, but would nonetheless find a market among consumers who were "content to dispense with some of the more sensational features of motoring so long as they can travel safely and surely."[22]

Although the prospect of an inexpensive, powerful, lightweight, full-sized automobile that could handle rough American roads had wide appeal, automakers struggled to design such vehicles in the half decade before 1908. Building powerful engines was not the problem, for as engineering expertise grew a number of techniques developed to produce them, such as adding cylinders, improving machining toler-ances, and reducing the weight of reciprocating parts. Adding horse-power created other problems, however. Bigger engines weighed more, required stronger frames and, in combination with rough American roads, subjected vehicles to increased stress and fatigue. In an era of soft steels, engineers could accommodate more powerful engines only by increasing the thickness, and thus the weight, of frames and com-ponents. In short, building a more powerful engine required a heavier, more substantial vehicle to carry it—with the added weight offsetting the power advantages of the bigger engine.

Because increased power necessitated a heavier frame and thicker, stronger parts, weight-to-power ratios—a rough measure of perfor-mance in which lower ratios indicate better performance—stabilized among better-quality vehicles in the neighborhood of 80:1. The small, 22-horsepower engine of the popular 1908 Buick Model 10, for exam-ple, powered a relatively light 1,750-pound vehicle and had a weight-to-power ratio of 80:1. The more powerful 28-horsepower engine of the 1906 Olds Model S, on the other hand, propelled a heavier 2,300-pound vehicle, giving it a ratio of 82:1. The even more powerful 1906 Pierce Great Arrow had a 32-horsepower engine, but its 2,700 pounds pushed its ratio to 84:1. In the simplest possible terms, no one could seem to figure out how to give full-sized automobiles more power with-out also increasing their weight—and thus effectively offsetting the advantages of more power.[23]

It was in this context that Henry Ford joined the chase to produce a powerful lightweight automobile. After winning a power struggle within his company, Ford devoted his resources to the high-volume production of his Model N, a small, premium runabout with a front-mounted, 15-horsepower engine that debuted in 1906 for $500. Though the price rose to $600 in 1907, the Model N—along with its cousins, the Model R and Model S (essentially Model Ns with some cosmetic upgrades)—generated sales of 8,243 vehicles between October 1906 and September 1907, vaulting the company into first place among the nation's automakers.[24]

For all its success, however, the Model N was still a two-passenger runabout with a small engine, and Ford believed his company's future lay in its ability to solve the seemingly intractable problem of building a lightweight, full-sized, amply powered automobile. As he wrote in *The Automobile* in January 1906,

The greatest need to-day is a light, low-priced car with an up-to-date engine of ample horsepower, and built of the very best material. One that will go anywhere a car of double the horsepower will; that is in every way an automobile and not a toy; and, most important of all, one that will not be a wrecker of tires and a spoiler of the owner's disposition. It must be powerful enough for American roads and capable of carrying its passengers anywhere that a horse-drawn vehicle will go without the driver being afraid of ruining his car.[25]

This list of characteristics—light, low-priced, amply powered, versatile, reliable, and sturdy enough for poor roads—defined precisely the sort of automobile that Henry Ford hoped to bring to market.

Ford's confidence that he could do so grew partly from his belief that a workable solution to the weight-to-power dilemma lay in vanadium steel, a tough and light new alloy then commercially unavailable in the United States.[26] After commissioning a steel company in Ohio to produce a small amount of the material, Ford gathered a team to design a vehicle that would capitalize on the new alloy's strength and low weight.[27] One of the most important members of that team, Joseph Galamb, recalled years later that the entire design process had aimed "to make the car light. That's what Mr. Ford's idea was always, to make the car light."[28] As Ford himself put it, "Automobiles have been built too heavy in the past . . . and the key-word for getting cars down to a rational weight is, without doubt, 'Simplicity.'"[29] After much trial and error, Ford's team developed a design—dubbed the "Model T" when it went into production—that finally seemed to thwart the circular curse of weight and power.

The resulting innovation transformed the auto industry. Coupling strong, lightweight materials with a four-cylinder, 20-horsepower engine, the Model T had a 100-inch wheelbase—a good deal shorter than that of other Americanized touring automobiles—and weighed only 1,200 pounds. This gave it a weight-to-power ratio of just 60:1, similar to the 64:1 achieved by the excellent 1906 Thomas Flyer, which won a well-publicized race from New York to Paris in 1908. But where the 1906 Thomas Flyer sold for $3,500 and featured a 50-horsepower engine, the Model T debuted with less than half the horsepower at just $850 in October 1908. "No car under $2,000 offers more, and no car over $2,000 offers more except the trimmings," crowed a Ford advertisement, with justifiable pride.[30] Spindly, even grasshopper-like, in appearance, the Model T sat high above the road like a high-wheeler, had significantly more power than the best runabout, and provided the performance (if not the amenities) of Americanized touring cars. It thus became the first example of the "lightweight automobile" that *Outing* had called for in 1904—an inexpensive hybrid that combined the strengths of other motor-vehicle types while avoiding their most significant weaknesses.

One of the Model T's more important features—and crucial to its ability to handle poor roads—was its suspension system. Unlike most of its competitors, which featured beefy, heavy chassis designed to take a pounding, the Model T combined transverse leaf springs with a light chassis that twisted, bent, and flexed with the contours of the road. Because it provided ample road clearance and kept the vehicle's wheels in constant contact with even the most irregular terrain, the suspension reduced stress on the chassis while providing excellent performance on rough and rutted roads. That it sometimes pitched and rolled like a ship at sea when driven at high speeds on smooth roads seemed beside the point to most drivers.[31]

With its excellent weight-to-power ratio and resilient suspension, the Model T represented the first high-performance Mercedes-style option for consumers in the low-cost market, albeit at the upper end of that category.[32] In stark contrast to the runabouts and high-wheelers that dominated the low-cost market, which had small engines and poor weight-to-power ratios, the Model T proved itself able to keep up with more expensive machines under even the most challenging conditions. In the summer of 1909, for example, a Model T defeated a stable of heavier, pricier touring automobiles in a 4,100-mile race from New York to Seattle sponsored by the Alaska-Yukon-Pacific Exposition. From the outset, public commentary focused on the diminutive stature of the two Model Ts entered in the race, with the *New York Post-Standard* declaring that they "look like pygmies beside the other cars as they sport along through the dust." The driver of the race's pace car, itself a big six-cylinder Ford Model K, called the Model Ts "midgets."[33]

Once the race pushed west past St. Louis, challenging road conditions became the major theme of the contest. "Through Kansas, . . . owing to unusually heavy rains, we encountered about twelve inches of mud almost every mile of the state," remarked one of the drivers of the Shawmut to the *Seattle Daily Times*. "Conditions were worse in Colorado when the rains, added to gumbo and quicksand, made traveling terrible. Then, too, there were no bridges in many places, and we were obliged to ford rivers and streams swollen to twice their normal size."[34] The Ford drivers also found the conditions difficult. "There were just no roads—just mud," said C. J. Smith, one of the drivers of Ford car No. 2. "Of course, if it was dry it wasn't so bad. Lots of times we had to push the car along when it was wet. . . . Out west, there were just sand beds. When it rained, it flooded up about a foot and a half or two feet deep. We'd wade through it first and then pull the car through. We'd dry the coils out and go on."[35]

Twenty-two days after the race began, when a Model T crossed the finish line in first place, observers had begun to understand its combination of durability, power, and size as an asset. "One thing—and a very important one—that was not taken into consideration by those who prophesied defeat for the Fords, was the fact that the little cars had more horse power to comparative weight than the larger and racier looking machines," explained the *New York Times*. "Had it been merely a question of speed over smooth and unobstructed roads the larger cars would have triumphed."[36]

In addition to this new appreciation of the Model T's light weight, the race also generated substantial publicity for its durability and performance on poor roads. In its advertising celebrating the New York-to-Seattle race, for example, Ford stressed the Model T's practicality as much as the adventure of cross-country racing. "The Ford won in a contest where the roads were just like those on which you want a car to run," one advertisement declared. "That's the reason winning the race means so much to the car-buying public."[37] Continuing this theme, the company cycled through a number of utility-oriented slogans in its national advertising, including "the family car at an honest price," "the farmer's car," and "the merchant's car," before finally settling on the "Universal Car."[38]

To label the Model T the "Universal Car" was grandiose marketing hype, and yet, as a description of the first automobile to appeal to adventure seekers and those who wanted practical everyday transportation, it contained more than a little truth. American farmers in particular bought Model Ts in large numbers during the 1910s, a decade when they enjoyed above-average prosperity. And why not? It was big enough for a family, it had the support of the industry's most extensive network of dealers, and its inexpensive replacement parts and simple design made repairs cheap and easy.[39] Moreover, the Model T displayed extraordinary flexibility as ingenious farmers adapted it as a portable power plant for such varied uses as grinding, sawing, pumping, shelling, plowing, and even running washing machines.[40] "These farmers want touring cars, not roadsters. They all have families, hence, a rational five-passenger car," explained *Motor Age* in 1915. "In general the farmer wants a tonneau type as he can carry his produce to market, [and] bring home his flour, groceries and binder twine."[41]

The Model T's unique synthesis of utility, reliability, and high quality, which made it so well adapted to rough American country roads, was no accident. More than anything else, it reflected the specific goals and desires of Henry Ford, who had aimed to produce a "universal car" from an early point in his career. "From the day the first motor car appeared on the streets it had appeared to me to be a necessity," Ford explained. "It was this knowledge and assurance that led me to build to the one end—a car that would meet the wants of the multitudes."

As its sales began to climb, it increasingly seemed that the Model T could become just such a car.[42]

SEALING OUT THE WEATHER

Although the Model T's innovative design dealt admirably with poor road conditions, numerous problems remained for anyone driving a Model T, ranging in severity from minor nuisances to major aggravations. Nearly all of these stemmed from the variability of the weather, and most revolved around a single fact: the vast majority of early automobiles, including the Model T, were open to the elements. Closed-body cars existed before World War I, but as late as 1917 they accounted for just 4 percent of all new-car sales in the United States.[43] Most of these were high-end makes designed explicitly to provide chauffeured transportation for urban elites, and they rarely ventured off well-paved city streets. This was true for the simple reason that they could not withstand the pounding forces of uneven roads, which could wrench apart their elegantly appointed enclosures and crack their expansive windows. Most cars, then, were open to the elements, save for those outfitted with waterproof cloth tops.[44]

Like the drivers in the 1909 New York-to-Seattle race, pioneering motorists experienced the elements in visceral ways that are almost completely foreign to today's drivers. In addition to the exhilarations of high-speed travel on roads that permitted it—and the near-constant jostling caused by roads that did not—early motorists could expect the full range of experiences that came with exposure to the weather: blistering heat and bone-chilling cold, glaring sun and pelting rain, nose-tickling dust and spattering mud, the putt-putt-putting of the engine and the relentless howling of the wind.

For early motorists in all but the mildest of climates, variable weather directly shaped the possibilities of driving. In colder climates, snow and ice prompted motorists to take their cars out of service by putting them "up on blocks" through the winter—a practice that helped preserve tires through long periods without use. Even in milder climates, many motorists limited their driving during colder weather as well as through long stretches of wet weather that turned unpaved roads to mush and made driving considerably less pleasant.

Even during favorable seasons when the weather was generally good, the travel narratives of early motorists often seemed little more than compilations of weather-induced encounters with undrivable roads. "We had not travelled more than about thirty miles out of Gotherburg when we were treated to a heavy downpour of rain," reported one cross-country motorist in 1910, "with the result that what we had so often been told was soon to be demonstrated, namely: 'The roads are fine when it does not rain.' It did not require much rain to make the roads too slippery for safe travelling."[45] Not surprisingly, pioneering motorists ventured forth with ropes, tire chains, and block and tackle, in case the weather took an unexpected turn that caused the roads to deteriorate. Most motorists were also careful to bring cash—if for no other reason so they could hire a farmer with a horse team to extricate stuck vehicles from the mud.[46]

Early motorists dealt with other effects of the weather by donning the automotive equivalent of battle armor. An array of specialty clothing quickly appeared and found a ready market: waterproof driving coats for the rain, goggles for the eyes, long overcoats aptly named "dusters" to protect clothing from blowing dirt, blankets and muffs to shield from the cold, and a variety of hats, gloves, shoes, scarves, and other protective gear. It did not take long, however, for motorists (and manufacturers) to realize that relatively simple modifications to their automobiles could provide even greater comfort than protective clothing.

No car proved more amenable to after-market modifications than the Model T, and by the 1910s a burgeoning market for Model T accessories empowered owners to adapt their cars in apparently limitless permutations. As inexpensive Model T accessories proliferated, owners personalized and modified their automobiles so that no two cars were ever quite the same. "There was this about the Model T: the purchaser never regarded his purchase as a complete, finished product," explained the author E. B. White in his elegiac essay on the car. "When you bought a Ford, you figured you had a start—a vibrant, spirited framework to which could be screwed an almost limitless assortment of decorative and functional hardware. Driving away from the agency, hugging the new wheel between your knees, you were already full of creative worry."[47]

Consumers eager to channel their "creative worry" into concrete change could find Model T accessories almost anywhere by the late 1910s, from the counters of large department stores like Marshall Field's to the pages of mail-order catalogs like Sears and Western Auto.[48] Many add-on features, such as steering-column braces and antirattle devices, smoothed over the Model T's rough edges. Other mechanisms, such as fan-belt guides, leak-proof seals, and a wide array of tools, allowed owners to remedy small defects in its performance. Still other elements, such as hood ornaments, gracefully curved fenders, and streamlined radiators, allowed style-conscious owners to add a touch of panache to their otherwise plain vehicles. Self-starters eliminated the labor and danger of kickback that accompanied hand-cranking the Model T, allowing drivers to start the vehicle from the comfort of the front seat rather than from the mud of the road. "When you begin buying gadgets it is like eating water cress or smoking opium," wrote an author in *Motor*. "The more you get the more you want."[49]

Perhaps the most telling accessories, however, reflected motorists' clear desire to overcome the limitations that poor weather imposed on car use and to incrementally improve their ability to do so. Some equipment that enabled owners to drive in inclement weather, such as windshields and weatherproof tops, was available early in the Model T's production run as optional equipment and later became standard. Accessory manufacturers were usually ahead of the factory in helping drivers overcome the elements, however, offering equipment such as foldable ventilating windshields, windshield wipers, and drop-down "rainproof" side curtains with cellulose windows. [50] "When rain threatened," the novelist William Faulkner noted wryly, "five or six people could readily put up the top and curtains in ten or fifteen minutes."[51] Increasingly powerful headlights and brighter reflectors made it safer to drive at night; snow chains and heaters aided owners wishing to drive through the winter; and rearview mirrors, horns, and speedometers allowed drivers to negotiate growing traffic with greater safety. "Some years ago owners of automobiles seemed to think it necessary to put their cars away for the winter and not have use of them during the cold weather months," an enthusiast explained in 1912. "Nowadays the people who keep their cars in commission throughout the snow months are far in the majority."[52]

Although many manufacturers rushed to incorporate standard equipment that protected drivers from the weather and otherwise made driving more comfortable, the Ford Motor Company—and especially its founder and chief executive, Henry Ford—resisted the trend toward incorporating too many "improvements" into the Model T. Ford himself expressed a dislike for a number of the era's key innovations, such as the electric starter, refusing to offer it on the Model T until 1919—and even then only as optional equipment on the touring model.[53] In stark contrast, by 1914, just two years after the electric starter's introduction, fully 92 percent of all touring-automobile manufacturers offered the feature.[54] "He [Ford] believed that people should hand crank their cars as he did his," explained H. L. Maher, who designed the starter that Ford eventually offered. "He also was against the installation of what he termed knickknacks on his Model T. He tried hard to eliminate them."[55]

In some ways Ford's resistance to accessorizing the Model T reflected his eccentricities, but in others it reflected the core philosophy behind his commitment to the Model T as a "universal car." "It is strange how, just as soon as an article becomes successful, somebody starts to think that it would be more successful if only it were different," Ford grumbled in 1922, just before the Model T's popularity reached its peak. "There is a tendency to keep monkeying with styles and to spoil a good thing by changing it."[56] Most of his critics, Ford believed, simply failed to understand a core truth about the Model T: the same stripped-down, utilitarian, knickknack-free design that made it such an attractive platform for the creative energy of accessory manufacturers was also an essential part of his company's strategy to resolve major problems in the manufacturing process.

MANUFACTURING THE "UNIVERSAL CAR"

To produce a truly universal car, Ford needed two things: a car with broad appeal and the ability to sell it in massive quantities. With the Model T, Ford clearly had designed an appealing car. For a variety of compelling reasons, however, most automobiles before the Model T tended to be manufactured in relatively small numbers and at very high cost. First, cars required large quantities of expensive, high-quality materials. It was possible, as the example of the high-wheeler demonstrated, to produce low-cost motor vehicles by skimping on materials and taking design shortcuts, but the results, as the high-wheeler also demonstrated, sacrificed both performance and durability. Second, the complexity of motor vehicles meant that automakers had to hire large numbers of skilled laborers to assemble them. Before the advent of interchangeable parts, for example, skilled machinists had to carefully file and fit all moving parts by hand as they assembled each automobile. Complex designs also required skilled workers in a variety of nonmechanical areas: seats needed upholsterers; early auto bodies, which were made of wood, required carpenters and painters; and so on. Third, early car designs changed rapidly at a time when the automotive state of the art was advancing quickly. Most early automakers thus offered a variety of models and changed them annually, introducing new mechanical improvements and design alterations during the slack winter sales period. Although this ensured product diversity and encouraged mechanical innovation, it also kept the price of vehicles high because each design change potentially required a heavy investment in new dies, jigs, and machine tools. The high prices of automobiles reflected these realities.

Well before Ford began its first experiments with assembly lines, and even before it began to manufacture the Model T, Henry Ford had championed economies of scale as a way to reduce his company's per-unit manufacturing costs—and thus to lower its prices. "Look here!" he told a *Motor World* writer who questioned the wisdom of his company's low price for the Model N. "Look at what we saved yesterday on one contract alone. On one part the cost of dies was $1400. To build one hundred machines would be $14 each. On the 10,000 we will build it will be 14 cents each. Work the same thing through the whole car and you can get some idea of how we are able to do it."[57] The decision to fix the Model T's initial annual production run at 10,000 vehicles per year—the same target as for the Model N—thus factored prominently in the Model T's relatively low $850 introductory price. Although $850 significantly exceeded the price of most runabouts and high-wheelers then available to American buyers, it represented an excellent deal given the Model T's design, performance, and use of high-quality materials. Sensing its value—"We have rubbed our eyes several times to make sure we were not dreaming," one agent wrote upon seeing the first Model T announcement—dealers flooded the factory with so many orders that the company had to cease accepting new ones between May and July of 1909.[58] Ever optimistic, Ford planned to expand production from 10,000 cars during 1908–1909 to a projected 25,000 for 1909–1910.[59]

To meet the deluge of orders, the company adopted a suite of policies designed to radically simplify some of the major complications in the automaking process. Early in the Model T's production run, for example, the company departed from traditional industry practice by focusing on a single model with a largely unchanging design. This policy allowed minor alterations to the Model T's design whenever doing so presented a production or sales advantage, while also avoiding the costly and disruptive problems associated with major annual design changes.[60] A second important policy was the company's insistence on truly interchangeable parts—an old idea, particularly among New England machinists, but not yet widespread in the auto industry. By investing in a variety of expensive jigs, fixtures, and gauges that Ford's plant superintendent referred to as "farmer's tools," since they allowed unskilled workers to produce work with an accuracy equivalent to that of highly skilled mechanics, the company dramatically reduced the need for skilled labor (and its associated costs) during manufacture and assembly. In a third related policy, the company capitalized on the Model T's relatively static design by acquiring highly specialized machine tools. These tools—such as milling machines that enabled an unskilled operator to mill thirty cylinder heads at a time—were significantly more efficient than those of competitors, who needed more flexible tools to build multiple models. Heavy use of specialized machine tools steadily shrank the company's per-unit manufacturing costs by cutting labor costs while boosting productivity.[61] Finally, on January 1, 1910, the company opened a massive new plant in Highland Park, located on the edge of Detroit, which in a single stroke increased the company's factory space from 2.65 to 32 acres.

With a new high-capacity factory, a commitment to large-scale production, and a single-minded focus on the Model T, by late 1910 Ford was able to inaugurate a policy of annual price cuts by slicing the Model T touring car's price nearly 18 percent from $950 to $780.

The next year, when production reached 54,000 Model Ts—up from over 20,000 in 1910—the company reduced the price to $690. In 1912 production reached 108,000, and the price dropped to $600.[62] The 1912 price denoted a turning point both for the company and for the country's car culture as a whole, marking as it did the first time the Model T's price dropped below the average annual wage in the United States.[63] It also indicates the extent to which motor-vehicle ownership remained a privilege of the wealthy and the well-off, even in the early Model T era. In 1910, for example, there were still 131 adult Americans for every motor vehicle in the country.[64]

With Model T production soaring, Ford stood poised to help reduce that ratio. Based on all outward appearances, in fact, by the end of 1912 the company had already solved what only two years earlier *Harper's Weekly* called the "knotty question" of producing an automobile "that will be entirely sufficient mechanically, and whose price will be within the reach of the million who cannot yet afford automobiles."[65] Even experts like Fred Colvin, a technical journalist whose series of articles in *American Machinist* in 1913 described Ford factory operations in great detail, had difficulty finding words to capture the remarkable scale and efficiency of Ford's manufacturing practices. Noting that the company had much lower costs per vehicle in early 1913, when its annual production goal stood at 200,000 Model Ts, than it had in 1907–1908, when its sales barely exceeded 6,000 vehicles, Colvin suggested that Ford had pushed the logic of economies of scale to its outer extremes. "What more could the greatest high priest of efficiency expect?" he asked.[66]

What Colvin did not know—indeed could not have known—was that, even as he wrote, the company had already begun to experiment with assembly lines, an epoch-making innovation that would soon make its 1912 operations look outdated at best and inefficient at worst. Assembly lines pushed Ford's attempts to simplify manufacturing operations to an extreme by subdividing assembly processes into discrete steps, assigning each step to a different worker at a stationary post, and using conveyors to move assemblies from one worker to the next in a predetermined sequence. Although a conflicting documentary record makes it impossible to date the evolution of assembly lines at Highland Park precisely, it is clear that experimentation began in the early spring of 1913. In just over a year, assembly lines had swept throughout the factory, beginning with various subassemblies and then spreading to the assembly of the chassis. Most of the components of mass production had been utilized before in American industry—indeed, the eagle-eyed manager with a stopwatch and a penchant for efficiency had been a standard fixture in most big American factories for decades—but Ford's production engineers had developed a new combination of techniques and methods that constituted an entirely new way to manufacture a product as technologically intricate as an automobile.[67]

The new methods transformed labor productivity. The average time per worker required to assemble a magneto, for example, fell from 20 to 5 minutes, and the time per worker to assemble an engine from 594 to 226 minutes. Most dramatically, nine months of experimentation with chassis assembly reduced the required assembly time per worker from just under twelve and a half hours—a performance that industry experts had lauded in early 1913 as the height of efficiency—to a mere 93 minutes by April 1914.[68] Coupled with the other techniques that had already evolved at the company—the standardization and interchangeability of parts; the careful sequencing of machine tools

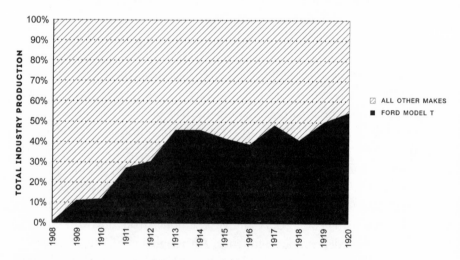

2.3 Model T production as a percentage of total automobile industry production, 1908–1920. McCalley, *Model T Ford*, 502–536; National Automobile Chamber of Commerce, *Facts and Figures* (1928), 6.

in the order of their manufacture; and meticulously timed systems automating the flow of materials, parts, and assemblies within the factory—the result was an astonishingly efficient system that has come to be called mass production but that, at the time, observers simply called "Fordism."[69]

Production figures leaped forward, rising from 211,447 in 1913 to 586,203 by 1916, during which time the Model T's price plummeted from $550 to $360.[70] Between January 1910 and December 1919, Ford produced a total of 3,645,810 Model Ts, a remarkable 42.9 percent of the American industry's total output (fig. 2.3).[71] As manufacturing methods climbed previously unscaled peaks of efficiency, booming production and progressive price cuts slowly dropped the Model T's price into reach of "the multitudes," transforming it year by year from merely another well-designed vehicle into the affordable, widely available universal car that Henry Ford had envisioned all along.

Ford's production engineers quickly discovered that, although the new assembly-line techniques dramatically increased worker productivity, they also created serious labor problems. Assembly-line work was both demanding—the lines moved at a steady, relentless pace over which workers had no control—and endlessly repetitive. From the company's perspective, this created two problems. First, the turnover rate among workers spiked as large numbers of workers quit, preferring to take their chances in Detroit's booming labor market than to suffer the rigorous monotony of working at Ford. Second, upon introducing assembly lines, worker productivity initially failed to increase as dramatically as test runs suggested it should. In a diagnosis of the problem that mirrored widespread biases and attitudes of the time, Ford executives decided that it was immigrant laborers themselves—or, more specifically, their foreign customs and culture—that hampered the expected productivity gains.

The company took a two-pronged approach to solving its "labor problem," beginning by rationalizing its pay scale and arranging its jobs into a clear hierarchy, thus giving workers the sense that they could move up through the company's ranks. Next, in early 1914—as assembly lines were spreading steadily through the factory—Ford introduced the Five Dollar Day. Nominally a "profit-sharing" plan, it guaranteed a minimum daily wage that roughly doubled the industry's prevailing rate while reducing the length of the workday from nine to eight hours. To qualify, however, workers had to allow members of the company's new Sociological Department into their homes to study their habits and home life—and to change any practices that Ford representatives found objectionable. Despite the intrusiveness of the policy, the lure of a doubled wage proved enough to achieve the results that managers desired: absenteeism and turnover fell among employees, and productivity rose to expected levels.[72]

As an integral part of Fordism, in which high wages were as important as mechanization and high-volume production, the Five Dollar Day was an industrial watershed. Not least, it made Henry Ford a business celebrity, attracting significant attention to the Model T in the process. Writing in 1929, Ford biographer Charles Merz pointed out that the entire popular-press coverage of Henry Ford before the five-dollar-wage announcement consisted of a single article: a 1907 *Harper's Weekly* piece on the metallurgical significance of Ford's experiments with vanadium steel. When the Ford Motor Company announced the Five Dollar Day, however, the press embraced Henry Ford as an iconoclastic corporate renegade—an image that Ford thereafter fostered with apparent relish. "It was a good story for a news-hungry press, and a good story especially for one reason," Merz wrote. "Out of a clear sky and on a lavish scale a successful business man had chosen suddenly to experiment with the divine law of supply and demand by paying double the market value for his labor."[73]

As an integral part of Fordism, the Five Dollar Day was also an *environmental* watershed, presaging a broader shift in the American economy whose implications are difficult to overstate. On the production side of the equation, the success of the Five Dollar Day suggested to other manufacturers that higher wages could cement the exponential increases in worker productivity that came with mass-production techniques, despite the undesirable working conditions that they created.[74] With automakers leading the way in the quest for high-volume, low-cost manufacturing, one industry after another launched experiments with assembly lines, specialized production machinery, precision manufacturing, shorter workdays, and higher salaries. On the consumption side of the equation, the Five Dollar Day created a template that included both higher wages and a shorter workday. As both spread to other industries, manufacturers gained legions of new buyers from among their own employees. Meanwhile, industrial workers gained a combination of higher wages, lower prices, and access to a growing variety of consumer goods. Not surprisingly, the automobile quickly became a potent symbol of the blossoming American consumer economy, which rested on the twin premises of material abundance and the widespread affordability of even the most expensive and luxurious consumer goods. In light of this seductive vision, the environmental implications of mass production—including its intensive resource and energy consumption, its pollution, and its waste—attracted little comment.[75]

CONCLUSION

Before wartime shortages reduced the auto industry's output in the last two years of the decade, sales of new passenger automobiles peaked in 1917 at 1,740,792.[76] Of this total, 834,663, or 48 percent, were Model Ts.[77] The remainder were accounted for by 137 American manufacturers offering 643 distinct models.[78] The motor-vehicle market in the United States thus had two very different halves as the United States entered World War I. On one side stood the Ford Motor Company, whose universal car continued to be an excellent value despite having little real competition in its price range. Thoroughly controlled by Henry Ford, who steadfastly hewed to the principle of minimizing design changes, the Ford Motor Company devoted itself to improving manufacturing efficiency. On the other side stood a large group of manufacturers producing a diverse array of vehicles. In search of a competitive advantage, these automakers scrambled not only to emulate Ford's methods of mass production but also maintained their practice of introducing technical and stylistic improvements into their designs every year. As each side pursued its own agenda in the last years of the decade, a wide and expanding gulf began to grow between the appearance, performance, and features of Ford's universal car and the automobiles that the rest of the industry offered.

After the war, the industry recovered quickly, with production bouncing back to 1,657,652 passenger cars in 1919, just shy of prewar levels. The industry managed to escape direct experience with the widespread industrial labor strife of 1919, but strikes in the steel and coal industries did hamper automotive production, and postwar inflation and materials shortages suppressed sales in 1919 to lower-than-expected levels. Inflation also pushed passenger-car prices much higher by the end of 1919 than they had been before the war, with the Model T touring car's increase from $360 in late 1916 to $525 by the end of the decade serving as a bellwether for trends in the rest of the industry.[79]

As 1919 came to an end, American automobile manufacturers bore very little resemblance to the nascent industry struggling into existence only two decades earlier. Motor vehicles had gained markedly in speed, power, and reliability, even as the industry's scale of production had increased exponentially, rising from a mere 5,000 passenger vehicles in 1900 to over 1.6 million in 1919 alone. Motor-vehicle ownership had shifted decisively from the exclusive province of wealthy urbanites to a much broader middle- and upper-middle-class market, with agricultural regions accounting for the largest and most significant proportion of new owners. By pioneering and then refining the techniques of mass production, the industry had unleashed a powerful new force with deep implications not only for manufacturers of automobiles but for the culture, economy, and environment of the entire nation.

As growing numbers of motorists took to the nation's country roads, these roads' deficiencies came into sharper focus. Among automakers and motorists, the situation highlighted the question of whether automobiles like the Model T should continue to be designed to overcome poor roads or whether the nation should invest in improving its roads to serve growing numbers of motorists. For established good-roads reformers, on the other hand, who had been fighting for more than two decades to improve rural road conditions on behalf of farmers, swelling automotive traffic and intensifying interest among motorists in good-roads issues challenged the good-roads movement's established priorities. Further complicating the picture, at about the same time that the Model T began its spectacular rise, the first generation of good-roads reformers was quickly giving way to a new generation of leaders, whose preoccupations, training, and temperamental inclinations differed markedly from those of their elders. As this second generation of leaders assumed administrative control over the nation's roads and streets, they benefited from the enthusiasm and support that earlier reformers had generated, but they also faced a variety of significant new problems. Somewhat unexpectedly, one of the biggest of these was the automobile itself—and more particularly the new traffic problems that swelling numbers of motorists created.

THREE

BUILDING FOR TRAFFIC

IN NINETEENTH-CENTURY AMERICA, THE NAME JOHN L. MCADAM
was synonymous with the idea of hard-surfaced roads, so much so that
improved roads were said to be "macadamized" and roads with stone
surfaces were said to be made of "macadam." The Scottish road expert
had gained fame early in the century for building smooth-surfaced
highways in the area around Bristol, England, using construction
methods that eschewed the heavy stone foundations used by older road
engineers in favor of well-drained soil foundations covered with multiple layers of small crushed stones. Held together by a clay or stone-dust
binder and tightly packed with heavy horse-drawn rollers, his stone-
surfaced roads seemed to defy the destructive effects of the weather,
creating the standard to which early good-roads reformers aspired.

"Roads must be built to accommodate the traffic," wrote McAdam,
laying out a basic principle of road building, "not the traffic regulated
to preserve the roads."[1] As the good-roads cause entered the motor
age, this seemingly simple axiom took on
a host of new meanings—many of them
unanticipated by McAdam himself—as
automobiles proliferated on the nation's
roads and streets. In rural America, where

Trying to cross Fifth Avenue,
New York City. From Dosch,
"The Science of Street Traf-
fic" (1914): 402.

the good-roads gospel had taken root, many communities made significant progress after 1905 toward overcoming long-standing environmental barriers to easy overland movement by ditching, draining, and dragging their earth roads, thus creating smoother, drier routes between their fields and the local railroad stations that connected them to the larger world. In this work they enlisted the aid of state and federal road-building experts, whose skill and specialized knowledge helped rural communities maximize meager local resources while building technically sound roads.

As improved roads began to spread across the countryside, growing crowds of motorists began to follow, creating a range of problems for farmers and road builders alike. Motorists joined the good-roads cause in large numbers, giving it new vitality and political power—but their growing presence also sparked a contentious new debate over the relative importance of the farm-to-market roads that had long been the movement's focus and the continuous, long-distance tourist roads that urban motorists favored. By 1916, when Congress passed the Federal Aid Road Act—thus committing federal money to building rural roads for the first time—the competition between farm-to-market advocates and tourist-road advocates had created tensions that thoroughly divided the good-roads movement. Were the new federally funded roads supposed to accommodate the needs of farmers or motor tourists?

Meanwhile, in large American cities that had already taken great strides toward securing cleaner, smoother streets, rising volumes of traffic posed a variety of pressing new questions. With a dense and diverse mix of pedestrians and vehicles threatening to choke all movement on downtown streets in big cities, a broad consensus emerged that something had to be done. Yet just what ought to change, and how, was a subject of intense disagreement. Pedestrians, horse-drawn wagons, streetcars, and abutting property owners held competing interests, and decisions that helped one almost invariably hurt another. By the time automobile use began its spectacular rise in the 1910s, making already poor conditions worse, two main approaches to dealing with the onslaught of traffic had congealed. One focused on changing people's behavior, hoping that if everyone would only follow a simple set of new rules, the problems and perils of heavy traffic could be resolved. Others focused on altering the streets themselves, hoping that physical changes might ease the flow of traffic and make streets safer for everyone. Following McAdam's simple-sounding command to accommodate traffic, it turned out, was not quite so simple.

In both rural and urban America, the contentious disagreements over how best to accommodate traffic were resolved as much on cultural terms as on technical ones. McAdam's argument that roads "must" be built for traffic was itself open to challenge, and both farmers and urbanites who disliked the effects of growing traffic—and especially automobile traffic—rebelled against the changes. Yet McAdam's maxim ultimately carried the day because the values and priorities of American road activists shifted, especially among those who exercised administrative control over roads. Whereas road reformers in the late nineteenth century had crusaded for better roads and streets as a way to build a healthier, more moral, less chaotic society, early twentieth-century road administrators championed the very different values of efficiency, scientific scrutiny, and expertise, particularly as roads became more reliable as technologies for overcoming natural limits.

As growing traffic problems helped propel engineers and administrators into positions of power, these experts made accommodating traffic their top priority. Even after they discovered that building roads capable of withstanding heavy automobile use presented significantly greater technical challenges than building roads capable of withstanding the weather, they continued to adopt traffic accommodation as their guiding principle. In the context of rising automobile use, the solutions they championed had an unanticipated effect on how people interacted with the environment. In particular, their new approach changed the basic relationship between roads and the communities through which they ran by giving the upper hand to traffic—rather than the needs of the places that traffic traversed—when priorities inevitably conflicted.

FARMERS, MOTORISTS, AND THE PATH TO FEDERAL AID

The Office of Public Roads (OPR), the Office of Public Road Inquiry's new name following a major reorganization in 1905, played a decisive role in shaping the changing rural roads of the United States before 1920.[2] How it did so owed much to the OPR's new director, Logan W. Page, who had led the office's materials testing laboratory during Martin Dodge's tenure as director. Upon ascending to OPR leadership, Page abandoned many of the older promotional techniques that his two predecessors, Dodge and Roy Stone, had employed, steering the good-roads movement in a decidedly more scientific direction.[3]

Advocating a distinctive brand of what might be labeled "scientific localism," Page believed that the large-scale improvement of rural roads had to begin with attention to the unique details of individual roads and the landscapes they crossed. "It is necessary," he wrote in 1910, "to study the needs of the road by actual observation rather than to endeavor to learn them from printed rules. Local conditions must be studied and overcome on their own ground."[4] In part, Page's emphasis on local conditions reflected his conviction that earlier reformers had erred in encouraging every community, regardless of its needs and resources, to aspire to the ideal of expensive macadamized roads. John McAdam may have developed one of the best road surfaces available, but Page believed that McAdam's more important innovation was the axiom that roads should be built to accommodate traffic. Adhering to that principle, Page concluded that most rural roads lacked sufficient traffic to justify expensive macadamized surfaces.

In Page's view, emphasizing expensive surfaces rather than cheaper improvements like grading and proper drainage had too often led to a misallocation of the scarce capital available for rural road improvements. The OPR under Page's command thus focused on teaching local road officials simple techniques, such as using split-log drags, that allowed them to use local materials and resources more efficiently. In the process, Page hoped to maximize practical improvements that would help rural communities meet growing demands on their roads. Preferring technical instruction to the exhortation of the good-roads gospel, Page gathered a staff of engineers with a penchant for experimentation, careful procedure, and attention to detail. Together they shifted the good-roads movement's focus away from mobilizing rural support and toward developing practical, inexpensive techniques for rural road improvement.

Page's changes to the object-lesson road program highlight the OPR's new approach. Before 1905, the object-lesson road program used state-of-the-art machinery to build short stretches of expensive roads in isolated communities, hoping to prompt locals to invest in their roads and to support road-reform legislation. As devoted preachers of the gospel of good roads, both Stone and Dodge used the term "object lesson" in the sense meaning "a tangible illustration of a moral principle," and they used the object-lesson road program in an evangelical fashion to win converts to their cause. Page, on the other hand, used the term "object lesson" in the sense meaning "a lesson taught by using a physical object." Rather than converting nonbelievers, Page's OPR used object-lesson roads to teach local road supervisors the practical knowledge they needed to sustain effective road-improvement programs after OPR experts left town.[5]

Page's goals required much closer attention to local variables than had been the case under Stone or Dodge, who had favored a whirlwind of convention speeches and object-lesson construction projects in small communities that they treated more or less interchangeably. In stark contrast, Page's OPR refused to undertake any object-lesson project until the petitioning community completed a standardized application that required a good deal of legwork and planning by local road officials. OPR agents then inspected the area, familiarizing themselves with, among other things, the road's traffic patterns, favorable seasons for road work, locally available surfacing materials, the roadbed's soil composition, the roadway's grades and drainage, and local labor costs.[6] In the process, OPR engineers modeled the "scientific" planning of road-building projects by walking local officials through the steps involved, including drafting "plans, profiles, cross sections, and estimates" during the planning stages and strict record-keeping during construction. "In short," Page wrote, his teams spared "no effort . . . to place the field construction work on a thoroughly systematic and businesslike basis."[7]

In accord with the principle that rural road improvements should be both affordable and practical, the OPR shifted its preferred road surface away from macadam, the darling of the early good-roads movement, toward carefully graded and maintained earth roads, including entirely unsurfaced roads and roads with sand-clay surfaces. "The mileage of roads in the United States is so immense and the improvement so slight that no matter how great our progress in the building of hard roads, earth roads will continue for many years to constitute by far the largest percentage of our highways," Page announced in his 1907 director's report. "It is clear, therefore, that the maintenance and improvement of earth roads is of vital importance."[8] By 1908, the OPR's new emphasis had begun to translate into change at the state level, with Page reporting "a decided increase in the mileage of earth roads built, which illustrates the policy of the Office in advocating the form of construction best suited to local conditions and local means."[9]

Page launched an array of initiatives that similarly stressed teaching local road officials how to work within the constraints of tight budgets, available materials, labor costs, and local political realities. The OPR tested all road materials free of charge, for example, and reported on the strengths and weaknesses of each sample for use as a road surface, thus encouraging the use of local materials. A second OPR program trained civil engineers in road-building techniques. A third dispatched OPR engineers to help local officials with matters as diverse as "proper methods of quarrying, excavating, the location and grade of roads, the selection of materials, the organization of working forces, systems of reporting work, or . . . actual construction of roads."[10] A fourth program, officially called Model Systems of Road Construction, Maintenance, and Administration, assigned an OPR engineer on a long-term basis to work with county road officials to develop new administrative systems adapted to local realities.

The OPR's work on sand-clay road surfaces epitomized Page's commitment to road improvement through scientific study and careful attention to local conditions. In their object-lesson road work, OPR engineers had noted that many soils prevailing in the Northeast and Midwest responded well to road drags—forming smooth, hard surfaces when dry—but that even well-crowned roads quickly returned to their "original plastic and sticky condition" during rains, which made them highly susceptible to rutting.[11] Armed with technical data from soil analyses, however, OPR engineers noticed that clay soils with higher sand contents, which prevailed in parts of the South, remained firm when wet. Better yet, dry sand-clay soils formed hard, smooth surfaces almost on par with expensive mac-adamized pavements. Soil analysis revealed why: whereas clay soils contracted when dry and expanded when wet, sandy soils contracted when wet and expanded when dry. "By a careful study," an OPR analyst reported, "a correct theory may be established. This theory is that there is a point between the gumbo limit on one side and the clean sand limit on the other where the opposite characteristics of each are neutralized and the resulting composition is a better road material than either alone."[12]

As a result, the OPR began to encourage communities to submit samples of local soils for analysis. After studying them, OPR engineers concocted a mixture of locally available clays and sands to form a surfacing material with optimal characteristics—using local ingredients to create a recipe for a cheap "all-weather" surface. By combining careful attention to local conditions with scientific methods, the OPR helped communities develop durable yet inexpensive road surfaces with qualities that rivaled those of significantly more expensive macadam. But unlike macadam, which typically required purchasing crushed rock from a commercial supplier and paying to have it imported by rail, sand-clay roads could almost always be built entirely from cheap local materials.

Under Page's guidance, the OPR's emphasis on systematic procedure and full knowledge of local conditions had important implications. It meant relying on locally available tools rather than showcasing expensive machines on temporary loan. It meant working within local budgets rather than encouraging communities to spend more than they felt they could afford. It meant fostering local, county, and state administrative structures and cultivating a systematic approach to road engineering rather than relying on the emotional appeal of the good-roads gospel. And, most portentously, it meant encouraging communities to make incremental road improvements based on the needs of existing traffic—a policy known as "stage construction"—rather than pushing communities to spend heavily on expensive road surfaces. The policy of stage construction, most evident in the object-lesson program's shift toward earth roads in communities with little traffic, became a cornerstone principle for the OPR in decades to come. With it, the OPR developed the argument that the demands of traffic—even when that traffic was light—provided the best way to establish road-improvement priorities.

Unlike some of the early preachers of the good-roads gospel, whose urban biases had alienated rural audiences, Page's scientific localism at least appeared to emphasize local needs and priorities over those of outsiders. This helped build rural support for the OPR. In the principle of stage construction, for example, rural communities found an argument that deflected the voluble demands of outsiders clamoring for expensive improvements in isolated areas. Because most rural traffic was still predominantly local, with Rural Free Delivery mail carriers and tourists being the major exceptions, communities could minimize expenditures by focusing on easy and inexpensive improvements, such as grading, ditching, and dragging, or perhaps adding a sand-clay surface. Thus the OPR helped rural communities make affordable improvements that met local needs. Yet the principle of stage construction was in some ways a Trojan horse for maintaining local control over road-improvement decisions, for if traffic—not local desires—was indeed the most impartial and "scientific" way to establish priorities, then what would happen to local needs and preferences if nonlocal traffic should grow dramatically? In 1905, few foresaw the forcefulness with which the nation's large-scale adoption of the automobile would soon drive home this question.

As it turned out, the rapid diffusion of automobiles into American society, which began around 1905 and accelerated after 1910, greatly complicated the rural road-improvement agenda in the years before World War I as the automobile's presence on the national stage expanded. On one hand, as motorists joined the good-roads cause in growing numbers, they injected a newfound vigor into the movement and added a powerful new political rationale for road improvements. On the other hand—and to the great annoyance of the rural Americans, road engineers, and preachers of the good-roads gospel who had been advocating road improvements for decades—the new needs and values of motorists acted as a fly in the ointment to the cause's long-established agenda and hard-won consensus, splitting the movement's fragile urban-rural coalition and prompting a fierce new debate over road-improvement priorities.

Early motorists proved particularly vexing to rural Americans, prompting a short but intense flare-up of anti-automobile sentiment in the rural United States during the first decade of the century. "In the backwoods and out-of-the-way districts," reported one observer in 1904, "the harmless automobile has been looked upon as the creation of the Evil One."[13] Rural resistance to automobiles resembled the hostility earlier directed at cyclists, but because motor vehicles were larger, faster, noisier, and generally more disruptive than bicycles, farmers often reacted more vehemently and with even more of a sense that motorists were invading rural turf. "The public seems to have lost sight of the fact that [the automobilist] has rights," wrote John Farson, president of the Automobile Association of America (AAA), in 1906, "and in some quarters he is openly treated as a trespasser."[14] Farmers plowed roads and sprinkled them with glass, hindering automobile traffic without affecting horses or pedestrians. Small towns enforced registration and speed-limit laws with an enthusiasm that motorists denounced as ignorant and arbitrary. In some cases, resistance even took more dangerous forms, as in the case of angry farmers who stretched barbed wire across roads, threw stones, or threatened speeding motorists with firearms.[15] Such palpable anger inspired much concern and commentary, most famously Woodrow Wilson's often-quoted declaration that automobiles incited class envy. "Nothing has spread Socialistic feeling in this country more than the use of automobiles," Wilson said in a 1906 speech. "To the countryman they are a picture of [the] arrogance of wealth with all its independence and carelessness."[16]

Motorists responded by forming automobile organizations like the AAA to fight the new restrictions. Some denounced the growing regulations aimed at automobiles as "class legislation." Others appealed to the character of motorists, asking them to behave well so that laws (and their unwelcome enforcement) would be unnecessary.[17] Still others objected less to the principle of regulation than to the frustrating variety of local, county, and state requirements that they encountered during their travels. "There seems to be evinced by each state legislature a desire to diverge as far as possible from the automobile laws of every other state, even though the states adjoin, the topography is identical and the class of residents the same," wrote one frustrated motorist. "In fact, the nearer the conditions of two states conform, the greater the difference in their laws and ordinances—or better yet, restrictions—is to be found."[18]

Rural anti-automobile sentiment peaked somewhere in the middle of the first decade of the century and by the mid-1910s existed mainly in more isolated locales. Most observers explain its evaporation as a result of the exponential growth of automobile ownership during these years from eight thousand in 1900 to more than one million by 1913.[19] As motorists on rural roads became just as likely to be local residents as to be "outsiders," the logic goes, farmers dropped their opposition to automobile use.

Although this explanation contains some truth, it obscures an equally significant factor behind declining rural anticar sentiment: a growing consensus on the appropriate and inappropriate uses of automobiles in rural areas. The period's conflicts represented at heart a struggle for the power to define the uses and social meanings of rural landscapes during a period of flux, not class-based clashes between wealthy urbanites and poor farmers over automobiles. As rural communities passed laws restricting the activities of motorists, and as motorists banded together to resist what they saw as unjust rules, their heated arguments gradually produced a set of compromises to govern their interactions. In the end, *all* automobile owners—urban and rural—agreed to follow rules that minimized disruption of rural life, and in exchange farmers ceased treating motorists as pariahs with no right to drive on rural roads.

These compromises had important implications, for by carving out a place for automobiles in rural areas they transformed the ways that *all* Americans—rural and urban, motorist and nonmotorist— understood the rural landscape in general and rural roads in particular. Making a place for automobiles on rural roads was not a one-way process: farmers agreed to adapt to certain demands of outsiders, and urban motorists agreed to obey laws that stipulated how they could and could not use rural roads. Such mutual accommodation altered customary uses of rural roads but did so in ways farmers could tolerate. Even after large numbers of farmers became motorists themselves in the 1910s, laws regulating car use on rural roads remained, a clear indication that the point of legislation was not simply to antagonize motorists. Ultimately, motorists as a group—not wealthy urban

Americans as a class—had to obey regulations like speed limits, licensing, and registration. The real significance of the anticar battles of the period, then, resided less in people's feelings about automobiles themselves than in the contentious renegotiation of the uses and meanings of rural roads and rural landscapes that motorists' growing presence ignited.[20]

Like rural Americans, road engineers found that swelling automotive traffic created serious new problems. In the pre-automotive era, the effects of water on roads had been the road engineers' major concern. "Ordinary country roads do not wear out," Roy Stone had declared in 1897. "They wash out and freeze out. Water is the great road-destroying element."[21] Road reformers consequently focused on improving roads by draining, ditching, crowning, and grading them, techniques that protected roads primarily from the weather and only secondarily from traffic. (Reformers concerned about traffic focused on requiring heavy wagons to use wider tires, which protected road surfaces by dispersing the weight of the heaviest, most damaging vehicles over a broader surface.) It was precisely this logic that allowed the OPR to adopt the stance that only rural roads with relatively heavy traffic required expensive surfacing.

Automobiles challenged the logic of this approach, however, underscoring the degree to which early road and automobile technologies often conflicted with one another—in stark contrast to later years, when roads and cars operated almost seamlessly as two complementary parts of a vast, unified technological system. Initially, the automobile's basic problem appeared to be that it raised dust, prompting both the specialized attire of begoggled motorists and a chorus of complaining farmers. The automobile "hurls clouds of dust over the houses and crops by the roadside," reported the *Independent* in 1908, "causing annoyance and at times seriously impairing rental values."[22] To the dismay of rural communities with sizable investments in macadam roads—and countless I-told-you-so's from the naysayers who had opposed them—it gradually became clear that automobiles caused bigger problems than dust alone. As the *New York Press* reported, "The old macadam roads for horse and wagon use go to pieces in no time under even moderately heavy motor traffic"—a particularly grave problem since macadam roads seemed to attract automobiles like magnets, inspiring recreational motorists to travel well out of their way for the chance to use well-surfaced roads.[23]

Two technical explanations for the automobile's destructive effects on macadam soon emerged. First, the dust thrown in the air turned out to be important to macadam's structural integrity. Just as sand-clay roads needed the proper proportions of sand and clay to make a durable surface, macadam required both crushed rock and the fine dust that automobiles kicked up, for the dust bound the crushed rocks together, keeping roads smooth and flat. Whereas the friction of iron horseshoes and steel-tired wagons on rock surfaces had generated enough new dust to replace what wind and rain carried away, fast-spinning automobile wheels removed huge quantities without replenishing the supply. Second, the rubber tires of heavy automobiles exerted a shearing force that caused even tightly packed crushed-rock surfaces to unravel and break down when they lacked a strong binder.[24] Significantly, one of the earliest mentions of motor vehicles in the annual director's reports of the OPR was not to praise them for bringing in a new good-roads constituency—a major theme of the post–World War I period—but to address the problems they caused. "The necessity for the treatment of macadam roads so as to enable them to resist the destructive action caused by the general use of motor vehicles," Page wrote in 1907, "has become increasingly apparent within the last few years."[25]

With automobiles wreaking havoc, good-roads advocates scrambled to find ways to protect expensive macadam roads. Reflecting the evolving technical understanding of the problem, the OPR's first experiments focused on the "dust nuisance" rather than on preventing damage, beginning with a 1905 experiment that applied petroleum mixtures and tars to macadam surfaces (hence the neologism "tarmac," a combination of "tar" and "macadam").[26] The agency began a more elaborate set of experiments with tar and asphalt in 1907, reflecting a new emphasis on road preservation.[27] The OPR's experiments produced a number of innovations, including new mixing and penetration methods for tar and asphalt binders and new, uniform specifications for bituminous materials.[28] The first major impact of motorists on the good-roads cause was thus negative, forcing engineers to invent new ways to protect roads from their destructive effects.

The resulting "dustless road" technologies were slow to spread. Of the 2.4 million miles of rural roads in the United States in 1914, according to that year's road census, roughly 10.5 percent, or 257,291 miles, qualified as "improved" mileage, a substantial increase from the 190,476 miles of such roads in 1909. Yet only 32,180 of these miles—12.5 percent of all surfaced roads in 1914 and a mere 1.3 percent of the total mileage of rural roads—had dustless surfaces of brick, concrete, or bitumen. Moreover, over three-fourths of the asphalt-paved rural highways in the United States in 1913 were in New York, Massachusetts, Ohio, and Maryland.[29] In all but the most heavily settled states of the East Coast, "dustless" roads in the 1910s remained a research project and did not become a widespread building method until new administrative and funding structures made large-scale construction possible in the 1920s.

Although roads designed specifically for automobiles still lay well in the future in most parts of the country, improved administration and routine dragging operations on earth-surfaced roads significantly improved the condition of heavily traveled routes, particularly in wealthier agricultural states.[30] "In the Middle West, automobile associations and highway commissioners do magnificent work. Roads are splendidly signposted, and in the dragged road districts, the rain no sooner stops than the big four- and six-horse drags are out," wrote Emily Post, the author best known for her writing on etiquette, in a book about the cross-country automobile journey that she undertook with her son in 1916. "Follow a rainstorm in a few hours, and you will find every road ahead of you as smooth as a new-swept floor. Hence for the patient motorist, who can spare the time, there is always an eventual moment when there are good roads."[31]

One reason that automobile-specific pavements spread so slowly may be that it took years for motorists to become an active force in the good-roads cause. Although some early motorists did join the reform cause, the links between automobile groups and the good-roads movement were more imagined than real before 1905, a period when most automobile clubs focused on fighting restrictions, building repair facilities, hosting automobile exhibitions, and opening driving schools.[32] At the 1903 National Good Roads Convention in St. Louis, for example, which drew addresses from such well-known politicians as William Jennings Bryan and President Theodore Roosevelt, only one speaker even mentioned automobiles.[33] Three years later, delivering an address at a Good Roads Conference in Denver, the representative of the local automobile club downplayed the importance of motorists within the good-roads movement. "While it goes without saying that any owner of an automobile desires good roads and will do his best to procure them," he told his audience, "he really is but a small factor in this enterprise of building highways. . . . The old horse and mule still holds the road and are of really more importance than the automobile."[34] Not until 1907, when the AAA held its first good-roads convention, or more significantly in 1908, when it sponsored its first National Roads Convention, did a major automotive group devote sustained attention to road improvements.[35] Even then, however, the AAA initially did little in its sponsoring role to change the movement's traditional emphases, and speakers representing state highway departments, the OPR, and the Grange continued to dominate the proceedings.[36]

The commitment among motorists to the good-roads cause—and to automobile-specific pavements—reached a turning point in 1912, when Carl Graham Fisher, a promoter of the Indianapolis Speedway and founder of the Prest-O-Lite Company, proposed his idea for the Lincoln Highway: a "coast-to-coast rock highway" for motor tourists stretching from New York to San Francisco.[37] The idea caught on quickly, and in 1913 the Lincoln Highway Association—which included the prominent automobile executives Henry B. Joy (Packard) and Roy D. Chapin (Hudson) among its leaders—filed formal papers of incorporation. Rival associations promoting other tourist routes soon emerged, including the Dixie Highway, the Ocean-to-Ocean Highway, the Southern National Highway, the Robert E. Lee Highway, and the Grant Highway, among others. Many later joined forces in the National Highways Association, which was founded in 1912 to act as an umbrella organization for the good-roads movement.[38]

The Lincoln Highway and its imitators sparked a heated debate over priorities within the good-roads movement. For adherents of the good-roads gospel—primarily farmers and railroads interested in better farm-to-market roads—the emphasis that motorists placed on long-distance tourist roads clearly conflicted with the long-standing commitment to lifting the farmer out of the mud.[39] For advocates of the good-roads gospel, diverting scarce money from farm-to-market roads for expensive motor roads represented the worst possible priority—an approach that would leave local roads mired in mud while ushering growing numbers of sightseeing motorists into rural territory. Not all rural Americans objected to the tourist-road plans, however. Schemes like the Lincoln Highway, for example, found ready allies among rural merchants and small-town boosters hoping to coax tourist traffic to their towns. One reason for the profusion of Lincoln Highway imitators, in fact, was that boosters excluded from one promising tourist-highway project often responded by proposing yet another through their town. The pursuit by boosters of motor roads thus recapitulated in some ways nineteenth-century campaigns to attract railroad lines through isolated rural towns.[40]

As motor-road advocates became louder and more insistent, good-roads rhetoric shifted in subtle but significant ways. Whereas good-roads gospelers emphasized the perspective of farmers, advocates of long-distance roads stressed that of long-distance travelers. "The automobile manufacturer," wrote one such advocate, "is interested in getting a *traveler* out of the mud; in providing highways which are *travelable* in wet weather. He is equally interested in getting the *traveler* out of the dust in dry weather."[41] Thus did automotive interests adapt traditional-sounding out-of-the-mud rhetoric that had once been applied exclusively to farmers, co-opting it to serve the very different, and in many ways contradictory, road-improvement agenda of long-distance motor tourists.

For the OPR, the debates that the Lincoln Highway ignited over priorities created an inconvenient distraction from its attempts to get states to focus on administrative reforms and making basic, low-cost road improvements to extensive rural highway mileages. Moreover, from the OPR's perspective, other automobile-related issues—such as safety and traffic regulations, better signage, and developing dust-free surfaces—outranked expensive tourist roads as spending priorities.[42] Page thus responded to those soliciting his agency's support for various tourist-road schemes by downplaying their chances of success. In response to a letter inquiring about one ocean-to-ocean highway, for example, Page replied that "there are so many different roads of this nature proposed, that it is impossible to keep up with them all. As a rule, nothing much results from agitation over roads of this nature."[43]

Despite the OPR's attempts to deflect attention from them, the era's debates over long-distance tourist roads had important implications. First, they reflected both the growing clout of motorists and their subordinate newcomer status within the good-roads movement. Second, motorists' enthusiasm for long-distance roads challenged the social-reform premises of the good-roads gospel, setting the stage for Page's OPR to promote its conviction that traffic ought to be the final arbiter in such debates: accommodating travelers—including both urban tourists and farmers—should be the focus of planning. Because cross-country motorists comprised such a tiny proportion of total traffic, this meant ignoring calls for an expensive cross-country road system and focusing instead on improving country roads in ways that would serve the actual traffic that they carried.

Finally, and perhaps most importantly, these disputes reinforced the growing belief after 1910 that the federal government should have more than an advisory role in road construction. This significant shift is captured in Woodrow Wilson's evolving positions on automobiles and roads as he moved from college administration into politics. By 1912, serving as governor of New Jersey and running for president, Wilson had backed away from his 1906 denunciation of cars as symbols of the "arrogance of wealth." In a campaign speech describing his newfound "enthusiasm for good roads," Wilson made clear that his support went beyond the interests of either farmers or motorists. "I tell you frankly my interest in good roads is not merely an interest in the pleasure of riding in automobiles," he declared. "It is not merely an interest in the much more important matter of affording farmers of this country and residents in villages [the] means of ready access to such neighboring markets as they need for economic benefit." Rather, he said, he supported road improvements because he believed that "the United States should think in big pieces, should think together, should think ultimately as a whole."[44]

Wilson's changing attitudes toward roads as he rose through the political ranks reflected the evolving political consensus of the time. The effort to commit federal money to state road-building projects ultimately culminated in the passage of the Federal Aid Road Act of

1916, which President Wilson signed into law, but only after a long and difficult battle. Rep. Walter T. Brownlow, a Republican from Tennessee, launched the fight in 1903 when he proposed a $20 million federal subsidy for post roads. For over a decade thereafter, every congressional session featured bills supporting some form of federal aid for rural roads, although none reached the floor until 1912, the same year that the AAA and the American Highway Association cosponsored a large convention in favor of federal aid for road construction.[45] Later that year, Congress allocated $500,000 to evaluate links between better roads and Rural Free Delivery costs. Congress also created a Joint Committee on Federal Aid in the Construction of Post Roads and instructed it to hold hearings on the subject.[46] Although the money set aside for post roads proved more of an irritant than a salve for the OPR, the congressional hearings provided a framework for the fierce debates that ultimately produced the successful 1916 legislation.[47]

Even before the joint committee reported to Congress early in 1914, legislators began jockeying for advantage. After much debate, the House passed Rep. Dorsey Shackleford's "ABC Rental Plan," which proposed subsidies for rural road construction in amounts that varied according to their type. The bill faced stiff Senate opposition, however, largely because Shackleford, a Democrat from Missouri, unabashedly favored what he called the "business-roads class," which supported farm-to-market priorities, over what he called the "touring-roads class," which wanted, he claimed, to "limit [national] road activities to the construction and maintenance of a few 'ocean to ocean' and 'across-country' highways of great perfection and then leave the rest of the people to build their own roads or do without, as they may choose."[48] Shackleford's plan drew the ire of automotive groups like the AAA, which backed exactly the sort of highway system that Shackleford denounced.[49] With automotive interests calling for "roads which lead from somewhere to somewhere" and decrying "the construction of dis-connecting miles of good roads here and there"—as one critic voiced a common judgment against farm-to-market roads—the Shackleford bill failed in the Senate.[50]

In the face of strong opposition, Shackleford drafted a compromise measure with extensive input from Page.[51] After some wrangling, it passed as the Federal Aid Road Act of 1916, which Wilson signed into law in June. It limited federal aid to "post roads"—political language that refused to privilege either farm-to-market or long-distance roads while finessing constitutional objections to federal involvement in road building. States thus continued to set their own priorities, subject only to approval by the Office of Public Roads and Rural Engineering (OPRRE), the OPR's new name after 1915. The act allocated $75 million of federal aid to the states, spread over five years in increments that rose from $5 million in 1916 to $25 million in 1921, to be distributed on a fifty-fifty matching basis according to a formula based equally on population, area, and post-road mileage.[52] Because the OPR had found it difficult during its post-road experiments to deal with county and local governments, the 1916 legislation limited the disbursal of federal money to states with operating state highway departments that agreed to the act's terms, prompting each of the seven remaining states with no state highway organization to form one by 1917. A final key provision limited federal aid to communities with less than twenty-five hundred people—a size that in 1916 still accounted for the majority of Americans—underlining the federal-aid road program's rural orientation.[53]

With the OPRRE in charge of administering the new program, Page made two decisions. First, he invited the heads of state highway departments to help him finalize the regulations governing the new program's implementation. Such federal-state collaboration soon became a hallmark of the federal-aid highway system's administration.[54] Second, Page clarified an important ambiguity in the new law, which limited federal aid to roads that were "substantial in character." To alleviate fears that the OPRRE would exclude inexpensive earth roads from funding, the agency declared that it had "placed absolutely no restrictions, either direct or implied, upon the kinds of highways to be constructed." States could seek funding for "any kind of road, even an earth road, and approval will be given if the construction be substantial in character, suitable for traffic needs, and meets the terms of the Federal act."[55] Thus did the OPRRE push the debates over farm-to-market roads versus long-distance tourist roads—at least temporarily—out of national politics and back down to the state level. Both types qualified for federal aid, and state highway departments would have to decide for themselves which ones to build.

Although the Federal Aid Road Act of 1916 marked the start of a new era in American road building, getting a vast new bureaucracy up and running presented formidable challenges. Complicating efforts was the country's growing involvement in the war that had broken out in Europe. As American manufacturers scrambled to mobilize for war in 1917, state highway departments faced materials shortages, wage hikes, and rising shipping costs that seriously hampered road construction. But the blow that brought road construction to a virtual halt came in November, when the Council of National Defense's Priority Board banned shipments of road materials by rail.[56]

An equally serious problem—the growing use of heavy motor trucks on rural roads—came from the same transportation crunch that limited road builders' access to construction materials. Banned from shipping nonessential goods by rail, businesses began using motor trucks—and discovered that, for some short hauls, trucks actually had lower door-to-door delivery costs than the traditional combination of railroads and express companies. In addition, trucks performed better than anticipated in long-distance operations, albeit with exceedingly high per-mile costs, as demonstrated by the well-publicized military truck convoys from Detroit to Maryland organized by Roy Chapin, who in December 1917 left his post at the Hudson Motor Car Company to direct the Council of National Defense's Highway Transport Committee.[57]

Heavy wartime use of motor trucks came at a huge cost to improved rural roads, however, particularly when expensively surfaced midwestern highways that had withstood heavy truck traffic through the winter—when they were frozen solid—began to break apart during the spring thaw of 1918. "Congestion on our railways . . . has put upon our roads a transportation burden never expected and consequently not provided for," explained *Public Roads*, the OPRRE's new monthly journal. "From horse-drawn vehicles with concentrated load of probably 3 tons at most, traveling at a rate of 4 miles an hour, sprung almost overnight the heavy motor truck with a concentrated load of from 8 to 12 tons, thundering along at a speed of 20 miles an hour."[58] Motor trucks thus played an important dual role during the war years, dramatizing the economic potential of good roads even as they pulverized some of the prewar period's most advanced rural highways, pushing the country's highways into a state of crisis. The need to develop surfaces that could withstand heavy truck traffic—a project significantly more challenging and expensive than developing dustless roads for automobiles—further complicated the postwar road-building agenda.

Meanwhile, arguments over farm-to-market roads versus tourist roads raged on. Rural Americans, fearful that the 1916 legislation would fail to protect their interests, vigorously pushed their agenda. "Powerful organizations," warned one member of the National Letter Carriers' Association, "with big Capital behind them, are seeking to capture this appropriation for good roads from the Rural People who were to be benefited by this Federal expenditure."[59] The charge had more than a kernel of truth, for many supporters of long-distance highways had become convinced that it was necessary to replace the federal-aid system with a national road-building commission empowered to construct a comprehensive national highway system. When Page died of a heart attack in December 1918 in the middle of a Highway Industries Association meeting, hope for a quick compromise between the two contending factions all but disappeared.[60]

In February 1919, Congress addressed some of the 1916 legislation's most obvious shortcomings. One sticking point for opponents of the federal-aid system was its language limiting expenditures to post roads. Especially in sparsely settled areas, including much of the West, this limitation hampered the construction of the kind of interconnecting system of highways that motoring groups favored. Congress thus expanded its definition to include "connecting roads" between post roads up to ten miles long. Congress also doubled the maximum federal contribution to $20,000 per-mile in order to address wartime inflation's erosive effects on purchasing power. Attempts to increase the overall appropriation and to renew the federal-aid system through 1924, however, met stiff resistance from those who wished to replace the federal-aid system with a national road-building commission. These forces blocked the extension of the federal-aid system beyond 1921 but acquiesced to a $200 million increase during the system's remaining three years.[61] "We should get this additional money for the Federal Aid Road Act," wrote one motor group's lobbyist, who favored replacing the federal-aid system with a national highway commission, "for if we oppose it, we would appear to abandon our own child before it had grown up and was able to take care of itself."[62]

The decade thus ended in a state of semicrisis. Far from resolving the role of the federal government in road-building efforts, the Federal Aid Road Act of 1916 now struck many of its initial supporters as a poor compromise between the incompatible goals of farmers and proponents of a national system of motorist-friendly long-distance highways. With urban and rural interests at odds, the untimely death of the good-roads movement's recognized leader, the damaging effects of war-related traffic, runaway inflation, and materials shortages, things looked bleak for the good-roads cause.

Despite the gloomy outlook, the changes of the two preceding decades were profound. In 1904, only nine states had highway departments, the country's mileage of surfaced roads totaled 153,662 miles, and national road expenditures amounted to just under $80 million.[63] In 1919, on the other hand, every state had an operating highway department, the country's mileage of surfaced roads had more than doubled to 350,000 miles, and combined state and federal funds available for rural road construction had soared more than sixfold to well above $500 million.[64]

In addition, federal engineers and administrators had considerably increased their influence within the good-roads cause. Congress elevated the OPRRE to the level of a bureau within the Department of Agriculture on July 1, 1918, renaming it the Bureau of Public Roads (BPR). Its new status reflected both its changing bureaucratic fortunes and its expanding influence. By melding the gospel of good roads with Logan Page's scientific localism, federal engineers had helped establish the idea that roads formed important links between rural Americans and the outside world. Whether those links would ultimately be farm-to-market roads or long-distance tourist roads remained an open question, but John McAdam's conviction that roads ought to be built to accommodate the needs of traffic was firmly entrenched as a basic principle. It had become the starting point from which all other decisions flowed.

LEARNING TO LOOK BEFORE CROSSING

Developments in big American cities during the first two decades of the twentieth century mirrored the major trends that transformed the rural good-roads movement during the same years. As in rural America, administrators and engineers seeking the most efficient, science-based approach to resolving problems seized control of street administration from the first generation of reformers. As one student of public administration in the United States put it, the decades after 1900 saw a decided shift "from an era of crusade to an era of technique."[65] As advocates of centralized administration, attention to local conditions, and expert leadership, the era's new wave of urban street administrators shared much with their rural counterparts. Yet urban administrators faced one very important difference that made their efforts to improve city streets an urgent necessity: an unprecedented increase in traffic.

As the new century dawned, the most prominent forms of vehicular traffic—horse-drawn wagons and streetcars—plied the streets of downtown America in large and growing numbers. Horse-drawn traffic had increased sharply in the late decades of the nineteenth century, and it continued to rise in the new century, with New York City alone home to over 130,000 horses.[66] Joining these horse-drawn vehicles was a large and growing army of electric streetcars, whose ridership expanded exponentially in the early twentieth century.[67] It was pedestrians, however—not horses or streetcars—that comprised the largest percentage of downtown street traffic in the early twentieth century. During a ten-hour period in early November 1915, for example, pedestrians outnumbered all types of vehicles combined at Fulton Street and Broadway in Manhattan by 223,000 to 10,300.[68] Hardest pressed were the central business districts of big cities, where streetcar after streetcar discharged passengers into already crowded streets. On a typical Tuesday afternoon in November 1912, for example, two Boston retailers, A. Shuman & Company and the Jordan Marsh Company, each drew over 100,000 customers. At noon, crowds outside the stores grew so thick that pedestrians overflowed into the street. During that evening's rush hour, with heavy vehicular traffic confining pedestrians to the sidewalks, conditions became so crowded that pedestrians and vehicles alike could barely move.[69] Rush-hour conditions in other big cities were much the same.

The surge in street traffic can be attributed to the centralization of American cities that began in the nineteenth century and accelerated in the early twentieth. Railroad and streetcar lines converged downtown, bringing freight and passengers. Moreover, urban retailers, office buildings, factories, warehouses, and entertainment providers all congregated close to city centers. Such centralization guaranteed streets full of shoppers, delivery wagons, streetcars, and thrill seekers, and created twice-daily rush hours as commuters made their way to and from work. Rising building heights aggravated conditions, with the towering steel-framed behemoths of the turn of the century, such as the thirty-story Aetna Building in New York, dwarfing the tallest ten- and fifteen-story masonry buildings of the early 1890s. Even taller structures followed, led by the fifty-three-story Woolworth Building in Manhattan, completed in 1913.[70] By 1910, experts dubbed the congestion wracking major cities a "crisis," blaming high buildings, narrow streets, centralized factories, and concentrated retail districts as causes.[71]

During the 1910s, automobiles added significantly to the congestion. Automobile registrations grew quickly—from 77,400 in 1905 to more than 8 million by 1920.[72] Equally important, improved reliability made automobiles practical for commuting and running errands, adding new possibilities to their earlier, more recreational uses. As a result, automotive traffic swelled even faster than automobile registrations.[73] Initially, enthusiasts predicted that growing car use would *reduce* city traffic. "Its introduction lessens street congestion," ran a typical explanation in 1907, "because the car occupies less space than horse machines, carries double and treble their loads, and moves . . . twice as fast."[74] But the crush of motor vehicles soon belied these rosy predictions. In Chicago, the number of automobiles crossing the Rush Street Bridge into the Loop jumped from 1,421 in a twelve-hour period in October 1907 to 10,158 in an eight-hour period in July 1915; in St. Paul, Minnesota, motor-vehicle registrations more than quadrupled between 1911 and 1915.[75] "The traffic problem of New York . . . is the problem of all our cities," wrote one traffic expert in early 1916. "Los Angeles feels it; it is an acute issue in Chicago; both are simply representative of dozens of other cities in which congestion, narrow streets, and automobiles have created a situation that requires a drastic remedy."[76]

This geometric growth in traffic created a deadly competition for street space among parties competing on very unequal terms.[77] For motorists and streetcar commuters, congestion's main effect was delays. In 1916, for example, the New York Railway Company estimated that its streetcars were blocked once every eight minutes.[78] For pedestrians, however, heavy traffic threatened injury or death. New York City's traffic fatalities doubled between 1902 and 1907, with horse-drawn vehicles and streetcars the main culprits. As late as 1907, motor vehicles accounted for under one-sixth of the city's traffic fatalities, but as automobile use grew, so did pedestrian deaths.[79] In New York, whose traffic paced the nation in density and danger, car-related fatalities rose steeply after 1910, killing 112 New Yorkers, making them the third-deadliest vehicles behind streetcars (148) and horse-drawn wagons (201). In 1911, automobiles killed 142 people, overtaking streetcars (109) but not horse-drawn wagons (172). In 1912, automobiles killed 221 people, exceeding both wagons (176) and streetcars (135). Forty-two percent of the victims from 1910 to 1912 were children under sixteen years old, and all but 13 of the 473 people killed were pedestrians.[80] By 1915, street accidents killed over two and a half times as many New Yorkers (659) as murder (260).[81] According to the National Workmen's Compensation Service Bureau, car-related deaths nationwide totaled 5,928 in 1915 and grew steadily to 9,827 by 1919.[82]

Downtown traffic became more deadly for many reasons. Horses bit, kicked, and bolted, and teamsters had trouble stopping, starting, and maneuvering heavy wagons in noisy, congested conditions. Fast, multiton vehicles also introduced new dangers. "Where a few years ago pedestrians heard the warning clatter of slow-moving, horse-drawn vehicles," wrote one author in 1916, "now a new type of wagon, shod in noiseless rubber, rushes down upon them with no warning save the honk of a horn, and this too often drowned in the roar and rattle of trucks, trolley cars, and delivery carts."[83] The easy maneuverability and acceleration of cars may also have encouraged risky driving. "Many, if not most, of the automobile accidents are due to the fact that the drivers do not know or do not realize the relation which speed bears to danger," wrote one reader to *Scientific American*. "A person struck by an automobile going twenty-five miles an hour," he explained, "receives the same fall as though he himself had fallen from a height of twenty-one feet, or say from a second-story window."[84]

As in rural areas, many of those who reviled changing conditions focused their wrath on motorists, particularly before automobile ownership became common. Between 1901 and 1906, for example, the *New York Times* reported at least thirty-four incidents as urbanites responded to the intrusive, and sometimes deadly, presence of motor vehicles. Some confrontations involved children throwing rocks or firecrackers; others, particularly those involving pedestrian deaths, provoked shootings—and even one murder, committed by the grief-stricken father of an accident victim.[85] The *Chicago Tribune* reported similar altercations, from stonings to shots fired at cars, during the same period.[86] "I think the time when motor vehicles are desirable assets to society at large is yet to come," wrote one author in the *Independent*, "and that at present a certain excess must be charged to them in the debit column. They have endangered a reckless personal extravagance that must bring remorse and suffering to many some day."[87] Even John Farson, the president of the AAA and a vigorous defender of motorists, denounced what he saw as "much ignorant, reckless and even criminal operation of automobiles upon the public streets."[88]

Early motorists aggravated tensions by blaming the problems they created on others. Some insisted that hired chauffeurs, not their employers, were responsible for accidents. "Chauffeurs are notoriously reckless," reported *Literary Digest*. "Owners driving their own cars are in the main careful. Drivers of their own cars are often put at the mercy of reckless chauffeurs, who are driving other cars, which owner-drivers are compelled to pass or avoid on the road."[89] Others blamed incompetence and irresponsibility. "Of course automobile accidents cannot be attributed to any one thing, but certain it is that the long-suffering and much-abused term 'recklessness' is not by any means the chief offender, as generally is charged," editorialized *Outing* in 1906. "If one will substitute inability, the truth more nearly will be reached."[90] Others blamed pedestrians. "No matter how you drive, the pedestrian will get you," wrote one motorist in 1911, after describing a series of close encounters with erratic pedestrians. "While you are figuring out what he is going to do another vehicle rams you. If people would only cross on the regular crossings and nowhere else it would be simply great."[91]

Observers of the time and present-day historians have both interpreted the clash between automobiles and pedestrians as a class issue.[92] Given the class tensions then roiling urban America and class-based differences in motor-vehicle ownership, with prohibitive prices restricting ownership to the wealthy, such an interpretation has merit. Yet class was but one element at work on the congested streets of large cities, just as it was but one element at work on rural highways. Speeding motorists struck pedestrians of all backgrounds and classes. Chauffeurs and owner-drivers both caused accidents. Congestion and danger affected everyone on downtown streets, whether they were on foot, in streetcars, at the reins, or behind the wheel. And much anticar activity, especially stone throwing, was the work of rowdy children staking a claim to their turf.[93]

As was the case in rural America, the primary impetus for restrictions on how automobiles could be used on city streets came not from unequally distributed income and privilege but from the changing uses of streets—in this case, the congestion, danger, and vehicular traffic that were eroding the traditional street culture of downtown America. Growing traffic and its dangers challenged older ideas about how streets should and should not be used, even as it made older uses impossible except on isolated side streets away from transportation corridors.[94] Automobiles were only one element in the changing composition and speed of urban traffic—although as automobile use exploded in the 1910s, motor vehicles became a central concern among city officials seeking solutions to traffic congestion. The automobile did not create the predicament so much as it exacerbated preexisting problems, but during the 1910s it almost single-handedly transformed a difficult situation into something almost intolerable.

With congestion, noise, and danger invading downtown America, urbanites invented new conventions to govern behavior in heavy, fast-moving traffic. Long-standing "rules of the road," which only required vehicles to stay to the right and proceed at a reasonable and prudent pace, proved ineffective as traffic volume swelled and vehicles attained unprecedented speeds. The elaborate regulatory regime governing modern street life—speed limits, lined roads, crosswalks, traffic police, designated parking spaces, ubiquitous signposts, and timed traffic signals—had yet to be invented. And at the heart of its invention lay a struggle for power over who would control the streets of urban America and on what terms, at what cost, and for whose benefit.

As a deluge of traffic descended upon downtown streets, various groups competed to impose order on the growing chaos. City police, auto clubs, urban planners, reformers, municipal engineers, streetcar companies, pedestrians—all had legitimate interests in resolving the new problems of congestion and safety, though their perspectives and concerns diverged widely. Some focused on changing people's behavior, seeking to build a new street culture in place of the one that growing traffic was destroying. Others preferred to alter the streets physically, engineering their various components to work in better unison. Whatever their interests, all desired new rules to choreograph the chaotic movement overtaking the streets of downtown America—even when they had conflicting ideas about just what form those rules should take.

As the arm of government responsible for public order, police departments responded first to the traffic tangle, which they initially saw as a series of isolated incidents to control and resolve. Although officers had occasionally directed big-city traffic as early as the 1860s, the practice did not become widespread until the early twentieth century. By 1910 most large cities stationed officers at important intersections, and during the 1910s many formed specialized "traffic squads."[95] Supplementing officers who directed traffic at intersections were mounted officers who unknotted snarls and cleared streetcar tracks of obstructions.[96] The police presence was strongest in the most congested cities—by 1909, New York's traffic squad numbered 743 officers, 138 of them on horseback—but size did not guarantee effectiveness.[97] In Boston, for example, a 1914 investigation found that crossing guards could at best impose a thin veneer of order on rush-hour traffic. "The police gave most of their attention to keeping the streams of traffic moving as rapidly as possible," the report said. "So far as observed the police halted no vehicles during the period of observation, either for violation of traffic rules or for any other reason except for that of passing pedestrians over the crossings."[98]

Early traffic-control advocates quickly recognized that their efforts hinged on the willingness of urbanites to internalize new rules and make them routine. As a result, their initial proposals focused as much on educational campaigns as on police enforcement. The work of William Phelps Eno, a wealthy New Yorker with an avid interest in traffic control, illustrates this point. Eno's traffic-control career began in 1903 when he convinced the New York City police commissioner to issue seventy thousand copies of a short booklet titled *Rules for Driving*, which required vehicles to stay to the right of the street, standardized hand signals for turning, preserved the right-of-way for streetcars along their tracks, and instructed vehicles to obey municipal speed limits.[99] When these and other regulations met with protests and outright disregard over the next several years, Eno made public relations the keynote of his approach. "It is very important to have the police trained for traffic duties, but infinitely more important that drivers should know what is expected of them," Eno wrote in his first full-length book, *Street Traffic Regulation* (1909), the country's first traffic-control manual. "When the drivers know, they usually not only comply themselves, but protest when others do not, and thus themselves become regulators of traffic."[100] He repeatedly stressed this theme, and he inscribed the title page of his next book, *The Science of Highway Traffic Regulation* (1920), with this "traffic axiom": "It is easy to control a trained army, but next to impossible to regulate a mob."[101]

Most traffic-enforcement officials adopted this principle in the 1910s, emphasizing "education" while downplaying the coercive element of new street regulations. In Chicago, for example, Joseph Sabath presided over more than twenty thousand cases while sitting on the nation's first traffic court. In a 1917 article titled "What a Traffic Court Can Do," Sabath explained that he made a "systematic course of education" the heart of his job. "It is my experience that the man who is fined and compelled to pay the penalty usually leaves the court room defiant," Sabath wrote. "But if he finds a judge who patiently and earnestly points out to him the seriousness of his offense, his better self responds." Sabath thus waived fines against those who promised not to repeat their mistakes. He also gave traffic-safety talks around the city and touted the city's Safety First Commission, which had persuaded thousands of motorists to pledge to obey and promote traffic regulations.[102] Although this faith in education and motorists' "better selves" might today appear naïve, during the 1910s it reflected a realization on the part of overwhelmed traffic-enforcement officials that the changes they hoped to bring about depended less on enforcement than on changing behavior. The changes they sought were as much cultural as legal.

No group recognized the potential benefits of fostering new street behaviors more than automobile clubs, which complained loudly about pedestrians' unwillingness to concede street surfaces to vehicles. Why pedestrians ought to do so, however, was at issue, for pedestrians had traditionally held the same rights to roadways as any vehicle.[103] In the nineteenth century, many cities had maintained street-corner "crossings," often paved with flagstones and swept clean for the convenience of pedestrians, but regulations against what would soon be called "jaywalking" did not exist in most cities before the 1920s.[104] As a result, pedestrians crossed streets when and where they wished, often with what today would appear to be a cavalier disregard for precautions like looking both ways before crossing. Complicating matters further, the same street-cleaning campaigns and pavements that smoothed the way for high-speed traffic in the early twentieth century also made it easier—and cleaner—for pedestrians to cross streets anywhere. New pavements also eliminated the visual contrast between flagstones and cobblestones that had once marked pedestrian crossings. The only incentive for crossing at corners was thus to get the assistance of a police officer directing traffic.[105]

In an effort to convince pedestrians to cross only at corner crossings, big-city auto clubs launched "pedestrian safety" campaigns during the mid-1910s that combined public-spirited reform with two self-serving premises. The first was that pedestrians—not motorists—were responsible for their own safety when they ventured into the street. The second was that the proper function of streets was high-speed movement, not pedestrian use. Most such campaigns targeted children, who were both the most vulnerable and the most malleable of all pedestrians. The National Highways Protective Society, for example, formed a Junior Branch in 1912 that required its members to pledge, among other things, to "cross the streets only by crosswalks," never to "play ball or any game where a missile is thrown in the streets," and not to "jump at, throw stones, or stand in front of automobiles, wagons and trolley cars."[106] Similarly, the Automobile Club of Hartford launched a "Safety First" campaign in 1914, during which its members fanned out into the city's schools, giving lectures, posting signs, and distributing instructional cards, all with the message that children should cross streets only at the corners and should avoid playing street games.[107] Thus did motorists attempt to teach the first generation of motor-age American children to look both ways before crossing the street.

Though motorists were quick to educate pedestrians on "proper" street etiquette, they bristled at instruction from others—particularly on the subject of speed regulations. A frequent claim was that because automobiles enjoyed superior maneuverability and control compared to horse-drawn vehicles, they were safe traveling at faster speeds. Arguing for the "reasonable and prudent" standard, motorists believed drivers should trust their own best judgment when setting a pace. The issue ought to be safety, they argued, not some arbitrary speed limit. "The fatal fault underlying the legislation of most countries is found in the designation of a specific speed limit as a means of insuring safety to other road-users," one such motorist wrote. "'Speed' and 'danger' are not equivalent terms, any more than 'slowness' and 'safety'; and the use of discretion by the driver is a better guarantee of safety to the public than the mere limitation of miles per hour."[108] That automobiles were difficult to operate safely amid crowds of people on foot was seldom acknowledged, and then only to encourage greater care on the part of pedestrians. "It is hard to say that one rate of miles an hour is dangerous whereas another is not," began one such typical statement. "Much depends upon the driver, much depends upon the mechanical condition of the car, and, more perhaps than these, much depends upon the movement and carefulness of persons crossing the streets."[109]

Pedestrians were not the only group to come under attack, nor were motorists the only group to seek new restrictions. Trades that had done a brisk business on downtown streets in the late nineteenth century, for example, such as street musicians, express delivery drivers, news boys, bootblacks, and peddlers, became the focus of various reform efforts in the early twentieth century as "improper" uses of streets. In Hartford, Connecticut, for example, farmers and peddlers had unofficially created an early morning produce market along Main Street, but in the early twentieth century merchants began to complain that it blocked traffic and littered the street. City officials decided in 1912 to banish this street-based wholesale market from downtown, requiring it to relocate to an official "Hucksters' Market" on the city's East Side, where they could regulate it more easily. Officials similarly heeded the calls of reformers to remove or curtail the activities of express delivery drivers, newsboys, and even playing children from downtown Hartford, a process similar to that playing itself out in cities across the nation. The results were more regulated and less diverse uses of downtown streets—which served not only the intended purpose of bringing order and decorum but also the secondary, largely unintended purpose of speeding up the flow of traffic through downtown.[110]

As police departments, auto clubs, and "safety first" organizations worked to change America's culture of street use, others sought to transform the streets themselves, hoping that physical refinements might make traffic safer, more orderly, and less congested. Although some visionaries proposed ambitious plans to remake American cities, small city budgets (and the fact that municipalities did not qualify for the era's state and federal highway aid programs) limited the funds available to pursue them.[111] As a result, the most significant physical changes to city streets during the 1910s tended to be small and local, with effects that were more incremental and accretive than extensive or dramatic. The most common changes—smoother pavements, wider roadbeds, and a profusion of painted lines, signposts, and mechanical traffic-control devices—both capitalized on and reinforced the behavioral changes slowly taking hold of the urban citizenry. In the process, administrative control over streets became more centralized, and the balance of power between the desires of abutters and the needs of traffic swung decisively toward the latter.

Perhaps the grandest hopes for remaking downtown streets came from proponents of the "city beautiful" movement, which had advocated broad boulevards, civic centers, and municipal monuments in the late nineteenth century. This school of thought reached its apotheosis in 1909 with Daniel Burnham's *Plan of Chicago*, an ambitious, wide-ranging, and broadly publicized document that moved well beyond older city beautiful schemes and toward a more comprehensive view of Chicago. In this vision, solving the traffic crisis—not merely beautifying the city—was a key element. "Chicago has now reached the point in its growth when the congestion within the city demands new and enlarged channels of circulation," wrote Burnham, "in order to accommodate the increasing throngs that choke the narrow and inadequate thoroughfares."[112] This could be achieved, he believed, by remaking Chicago's street system, which he divided into boulevards ("a combination of park and driveway"), avenues ("on which tides of traffic and travel surge back and forth"), and streets ("the general type of artery").[113] Burnham also distinguished "residence streets" from "traffic streets," arguing that good planning could protect the former from becoming the latter, and pushed for a system of circumferential highways to act as "collectors" and "distributors" of incoming traffic.[114] "Liberality in road building now will be repaid many fold in the future," Burnham prophesied. "The aim should be to adopt the best routes, the best curves and turns, and the most perfect construction known at the present day."[115]

Although Burnham's Chicago plan enjoyed an extraordinary public relations success, its implementation bogged down in politics, financial constraints, and sundry disagreements, forcing its supporters to focus on its more feasible aspects.[116] In this, events in Chicago reflected a broader shift in the city-planning profession from city beautiful ideas toward a newer vision of the "city efficient." Proponents of this viewpoint, which gained widespread notice in 1909 at the first National Conference on City Planning, often saw Burnham as an impractical dreamer, too much guided by aesthetic and moral concerns and too little aware of how cities actually functioned—but largely agreed with his ideas about the functional differences among various types of streets. Focusing on issues such as traffic flow, street widths, difficult intersections, and the virtues of different street pavements, city efficient planners adopted a rhetoric of efficiency, scientific analysis, and utility that diverged sharply from earlier planners' emphasis on good citizenship, civic harmony, and aesthetic unity. In a review of Pittsburgh's 1911 city plan, for example, which had been drafted by the firm headed by Frederick Law Olmsted Jr., *Outlook* commended its "quest for convenience, economy, comfort, practicality." Noting that the planners involved had studied local conditions "not by rule of thumb, but scientifically," the reviewer especially praised its careful survey of traffic conditions and the "thoroughgoing way in which these studies were made."[117]

In shunning the majestic vision of planners like Burnham in favor of scrutinizing local conditions, city efficient planners mirrored the concurrent shift in rural road policy away from the good-roads gospel and toward Page's brand of scientific localism. Both focused on small-scale, local projects rather than large-scale, all-encompassing schemes. Olmsted Jr.—whose father had designed New York's Central Park—had by the 1910s emerged as an influential city planner in his own right. As head of the American Society of Landscape Architects, the American Institute of Planners, *and* the National Conference on City Planning, Olmsted played an important role in developing city efficient thinking and its emphasis on poring over local conditions.[118] His 1913 article "How to Organize a City Planning Campaign" stressed the need to approach city plans on a city-by-city basis, arguing that each presented unique problems and thus required individualized solutions. Proper planning, he wrote, required a veritable army of specialists, whose careful study of local conditions would maintain "that correspondence with the hard facts of the situation which distinguishes real planning from dreams." Good city planning demanded "such an enormous diversity of technical training and experience," Olmsted argued, "that it is wholly impracticable for any one man, or even for any small group of men, to assume with success the sole authorship of a complete plan."[119]

Municipal engineers took the lead in translating centralized administration into small physical changes in city streets, solving localized problems on a case-by-case basis. As with their counterparts in the Office of Public Roads, municipal engineers established construction priorities based on traffic needs and often collected reams of statistical evidence on existing street uses before launching their projects. They conducted traffic counts, street censuses, and transit studies, all with an eye toward identifying projects—some large, most small—that might relieve congestion or speed traffic.[120] "This method of work, systematized, standardized, 'Taylorized,' as it is, has most decidedly proved its worth," editorialized *American City* in 1913, just weeks before Ford Motor Company engineers translated these same values into the auto industry's first moving assembly lines. "It appeals strongly to the business man, the man who has to pay the bills, and convinces everyone that the experts have real knowledge on which to base their recommendations, and are not presenting mere dreams, pretty but impracticable."[121]

Most of the changes engineers advocated fell into two categories. One approach was to modify the streets themselves to improve their safety and speed up traffic, as when cities laid smooth pavements, eliminated at-grade railroad crossings, widened streets, and cut back the radius of curbs at intersections to make turns easier for vehicles. A second approach was to impose new rules on street users. Cities created one-way streets and erected traffic signs, for example, and used painted lines to delineate crosswalks, driving lanes, and "safety zones" for loading streetcars. Methodical and meticulous, municipal engineers implemented seemingly minor changes that forever changed city streets.

Laying new pavement was perhaps the era's most common physical change. In 1902, for example, eleven of the nation's largest cities had paved, on average, just over half of their streets; by the early 1920s, only streets carrying little traffic, such as alleys and quiet residential streets, remained unpaved. In addition, the wide range of pavements that characterized the 1880s and 1890s quickly gave way to automobile-friendly sheet asphalt, which grew as a percentage of all street pavements in the same eleven cities from 17 percent in 1902 to 47 percent in 1924.[122] In many cities, paving became almost synonymous with city planning. In Chicago, for example, the Chicago Plan Commission abandoned the more expensive and politically contentious aspects of Burnham's 1909 city plan, choosing instead to focus on the city's streets and parks.[123]

Street-widening projects could change streets as significantly as new pavements. In the nineteenth century, in an era of less traffic, most cities laid very narrow pavements, especially outside of the central business district. "Excessive width delays or prevents the getting of any pavement at all," explained one street-construction textbook, noting that wide streets ate into tiny street-improvement budgets. "Hence one help toward securing a pavement is to make the pavement only wide enough to accommodate the traffic."[124] The remaining area between the curb and the buildings featured sidewalks and strips of greenery called "parking." In the 1910s, when cities widened pavements to create additional lanes, they simply moved the curbs toward the buildings. This meant reducing the width of the sidewalks, the parking, or both. In places where pedestrian traffic was heavy enough that sidewalks could not be reduced, cities either abandoned their projects or paid dearly to condemn property to widen the roadway.[125]

New York City's street-widening efforts between 1908 and 1912 illustrate the detail-oriented, cost-conscious approach that guided municipal engineers, as well as their conviction that streets ought to privilege traffic needs over those of abutters. The project began with a series of traffic studies to identify which city thoroughfares most needed widening. For most of these streets, such as Fifth Avenue, cutting back the sidewalks would have left them, in the words of one journalist, "reduced to a negligible quantity," and high property costs ruled out condemnation. The city's surveys, however, revealed that few buildings observed the city's legal setback requirements.[126] Over the vigorous objections of property owners, the president of New York City's Board of Aldermen, George McAneny, ordered all encroachments removed at their owners' expense. The powerful Fifth Avenue Association interceded, securing a small variance of two and a half feet. "By forcing back these encroachments," *American City* reported, the city "added more space to the sidewalks, which, in turn, made it possible to move in the curbs and add from five to fifteen feet to the width of streets."[127] Financed by a de facto assessment on some abutters, the city's street-widening project captured the degree to which the needs of traffic—vehicular *and* pedestrian—trumped those of property owners, including even the powerful business owners along Fifth Avenue.

On narrow, congested streets where street widening was impossible or impractical, cities turned to one-way regulations to untangle traffic. Traffic experts like William Phelps Eno recommended their broad application. "One-way traffic should be the rule at all hours in streets not wide enough for two vehicles, and during congested hours in those not wide enough for four vehicles," Eno wrote in 1913. "Where streets are practically parallel and near together 'one-way traffic' is especially desirable, as it moves in one direction in one street and in the opposite in the next."[128] Philadelphia became the first American city to convert its narrowest downtown routes into one-way streets, and by 1914 both Boston and Pittsburgh had followed suit.[129] Because most early one-way streets were narrow and highly congested, few abutters objected to the plans.[130]

As the use of one-way streets spread, however, they exposed tensions between the desires of property owners and the needs of traffic. In New York, for example, city leaders first considered one-way streets in 1914, when the Committee on Public Thoroughfares began investigating the city's traffic problems. "The clearing of encroachments from the sidewalks, with the widening of the roadways, has helped a great deal," wrote Ernest P. Goodrich, a consulting engineer, "but in spite of this the congestion still exists. It can be relieved only by thoroughly scientific regulation."[131] To general public acclaim, the city converted twenty-seven cramped downtown streets to one-way traffic in 1915 and 1916.[132] By the end of the decade, however, congestion threatened even main thoroughfares with "complete paralysis." "For the first time . . . since the great diminution of horse-drawn traffic," reported the *New York Times* in January 1920, "there have been impassable jams along Fifth Avenue this Winter because of the great increase in the number of motor cars."[133] Fifth Avenue merchants initially approved a new plan for one-way regulations, but a loud minority objected, claiming merchants would lose customers.[134] When the city began operating a series of five traffic-control towers between Thirty-Fourth and Fifty-Seventh Streets—among the first red-yellow-green traffic lights in the country—it "postponed indefinitely" the one-way rule. But officials stood ready to implement it, despite abutter protests, should traffic conditions again demand.[135]

Cities also began to make simple mechanical changes to downtown streets with the explicit intention of reshaping how people used them. Big cities had been building "isles of safety"—raised islands in the middle of broad, heavily traveled streets—as places for pedestrians to take refuge from traffic since early in the century, and nineteenth-century boulevards had used similar raised curbs to delineate separate driving lanes. By the 1910s, however, cities began to substitute painted lines for permanent raised obstructions. Officials soon found a cornucopia of uses for painted lines: to mark off "safety zones" for unloading and loading streetcars, to identify pedestrian crosswalks, to divide vehicular traffic into distinct lanes, and even to designate parking spots. The result was a cheap, easy, and flexible method of dividing street space into multiple zones of use.[136] A similarly effective and inexpensive technique was to post signs that warned drivers of danger, indicated crosswalks and no-parking zones, and marked one-way streets.[137] Although not everyone observed traffic signs or the distinctions that painted lines tried to create, particularly when cities were slow to repaint lines that had grown faint, together they marked an important step toward physically segregating different street users from one another—a key both for safety and for the smooth movement of traffic.

Cities embraced new traffic-control technologies as well. By the mid-1910s, the locus of innovation shifted from the biggest cities, such as New York and Chicago, to rapidly growing metropolises like Detroit and Cleveland, where expanding automobile use created big-city problems almost overnight. In 1913, the Detroit police department introduced mechanical semaphores—tall poles crowned by four blades, alternately marked "Stop" and "Go"—which traffic officers rotated a quarter turn each time they wished to change the direction of traffic. The practice, with some variations, spread quickly to other cities.[138] In Cleveland, the police introduced a system of red and green traffic lights at the corner of Euclid Avenue and East 105th Street in 1914, operated by an officer in an elevated booth on the corner. "I have found to my great satisfaction that the system has in a great measure succeeded in doing what the traffic officer stationed in the street was unable to do," a Cleveland official reported, "educate pedestrian traffic to follow vehicular traffic."[139] Other cities experimented with traffic-control towers at busy intersections, which gave officers a better view of the traffic they were directing.[140]

Despite the contentious relationship between pedestrians and automobiles, few objected to the new traffic-control technologies that promised better pedestrian safety even as they sped up vehicles. This helps explain, perhaps, why pedestrians failed to form lobbying groups to protect their traditional rights in the same way that auto clubs lobbied for the interests of motorists. Crosswalks and zones of safety appealed to pedestrians because they established spaces where pedestrians did not have to fear for their security. Faced with the reality of dangerous city streets, most pedestrians seemed disinclined to assert their rights vis-à-vis vehicles. "It is a matter of daily observation in walking about the streets of New York," wrote one perturbed citizen, "that whatever rights the law may give the pedestrian he gets none de facto."[141] On the other hand, the era's innovations began to eliminate the diverse mix of downtown traffic by enacting rules that segregated traffic types, especially vehicles and pedestrians, in increasingly sophisticated ways.

Although seemingly mundane, these changes reflected a profound transformation of street use that dwarfed the effects of much bolder contemporary proposals to remake American cities. Amateur would-be city builders addressed the era's traffic crisis with a fertile imagination, and schemes for the ambitious reconstruction of American cities were frequently discussed in the press.[142] Plans abounded for double- and triple-decked streets, arcaded sidewalks, and vast tunnel systems for moving freight and streetcars.[143] Most of these were little more than castles in the air, but as the case of urban subways illustrates, quite serious plans for the expensive reconstruction of urban infrastructures failed during the 1910s—despite the backing of some of urban America's wealthiest and most influential denizens.[144] For every fantasy plan that went unbuilt, cities made a hundred small changes to their streets, from erecting signs to painting lines, that hastened the flow of downtown traffic and reinforced the behavioral changes city leaders hoped to nurture. These changes may appear relatively minor when viewed outside the context of the traffic crisis that produced them. By the early 1920s, however, a significant new culture of regulation had begun to assert itself on the streets of American cities, large and small.

CONCLUSION

Although superficially very different, the changes to rural roads and city streets in the first two decades of the century shared much in common. In both cases, the moralistic reformers who had led the nineteenth-century good-roads cause gave way in the twentieth century to engineers and administrators guided by faith in the power of science and efficiency. In both cases, road administration became more centralized at higher levels of government. In both cases, growing numbers of automobiles created problems that demanded creative approaches and new courses of action. And in both cases, McAdam's belief that roads always ought to be built for traffic became firmly entrenched as a guiding principle among road and street administrators, who translated it into infrastructural improvements and regulatory changes that made it much easier and more pleasant to drive.

Nevertheless, the strikingly dissimilar contexts in which these trends played out produced some significant differences. In rural areas, for example, farmers invoked the principle that roads ought to be built to accommodate traffic as a way to stave off outsiders' demands for expensive projects that exceeded their financial means. Because the prevailing traffic in most rural areas was light, improved earth roads most often proved adequate. In large cities, on the other hand, surging traffic posed immediate threats to pedestrian safety, mass transit, and economic efficiency and prompted fierce debates about the different rights of various street users. As a result, the impulse to accommodate traffic went well beyond providing wide, durable street surfaces and moved into the realm of creating an entirely new culture of street use.

The realization that "traffic" comprised competing interest groups also developed differently in rural and urban places. The major debate between farmers and long-distance motor tourists, for example, revolved around how to connect rural areas to the outside world. Farmers favored short radial routes extending from railroad stations into surrounding farmland, while tourists favored continuous, long-distance recreational routes with expensive pavements. In cities, on the other hand, engineers and street administrators searched for an equitable balance among the competing (and frequently incompatible) claims of diverse street users. Pedestrians, streetcar operators, teamsters, and motorists all had their say—but property owners, once central to such discussions, became increasingly marginalized.

After World War I, with its pioneering period behind it, the auto industry entered an era of vibrant growth and rapid technological improvement. Over the next two decades—one of sustained boom, the other of sustained bust—cars became a widespread fixture of American life. The ratio of driving-age Americans to registered automobiles, which had already fallen to 7.8:1 by 1920, continued to plummet through the interwar years, despite the severe economic downturn of the 1930s, reaching just 3:1 by 1940.[145] As Americans of all stripes wrestled to adapt to the automobile's sudden ubiquity, the first major building blocks of Car Country began to fall into place, setting in motion a cascading series of changes with major ecological consequences.

Photo Gallery One

The Newburgh Steel Works darkens the skies over Cleveland, 1893. Riotous growth and industrialization pushed cities into a state of environmental crisis toward the end of the nineteenth century, creating the ominous feeling that nature had run amok on the streets of big American cities. Western Reserve Historical Society, courtesy of Library of Congress Prints and Photographs Division, HAER OHIO, 18-CLEV,32—6.

Downtown Philadelphia traffic, ca. late 1890s. The transportation functions of big-city streets became much more important during the 1880s and 1890s as traffic grew thicker, faster, and more dangerous. U.S. Bureau of Public Roads.

Horse droppings and refuse bury the pavement of Morton Street, New York City, March 1893. In big cities, especially, streets attracted growing public attention as they devolved into increasingly noxious, chaotic environments, prompting aggressive reform campaigns to place disinterested "experts" in positions of power over street cleaning and administration. From Waring, *Street-Cleaning*, 8.

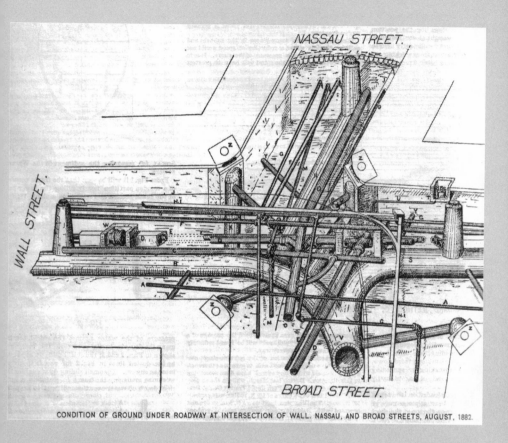

CONDITION OF GROUND UNDER ROADWAY AT INTERSECTION OF WALL. NASSAU, AND BROAD STREETS, AUGUST, 1882.

An engineering sketch of the various systems running underneath the intersection of Wall, Nassau, and Broad Streets, New York City, 1882. In the late nineteenth century, streets became conduits for the spread of a cacophony of new underground technological systems designed to solve urban environmental problems, beginning with sewers and then expanding to a host of systems delivering amenities such as natural gas, steam heat, electricity, and telephone service. From *Engineering News* 1 (Nov. 1890): 402.

Overhead wires in New York City after the great blizzard of 1888. City dwellers objected both to the unsightliness of overhead wires and to the alarming number of fires and occasional electrocutions that they caused, provoking intense discussions about exactly who had control—and who ought to have control—over decisions that shaped the urban street environment. New York Historical Society.

A giant horse-drawn combine makes its way through an Oregon farm field, 1903. Industrialization and rapid technological advances sparked changes in the American countryside that were every bit as profound as those in big cities. Courtesy of Library of Congress Prints and Photographs Division, LC-USZ62-88985.

A typical turn-of-the-nineteenth-century rural road. The poor condition of rural highways—characterized by dust in dry weather, mud in wet weather, and rutted, treacherous surfaces year-round—highlighted what reformers saw as the backwardness and isolation of rural farm communities, despite their increasingly sophisticated farm equipment and ready access to urban markets via railroad. From Bureau of Public Roads, *Bulletin No. 27*, pl. I, fig. 1.

Mercedes touring car, 1901. The possibility of designing vehicles that could handle rough rural roads—and transform rural transportation in the process—grew exponentially with the introduction of this vehicle, which marked a quantum leap forward for automotive design in the realms of power, speed, and reliability. This Mercedes departed substantially from the "horseless carriage"–style designs that had prevailed before its introduction, but it had to be adapted to American road conditions before enjoying wide success in the United States. From *Horseless Age* 21 (Aug. 1901): 431.

The Leader of the Holsman Line, a Serviceable Runabout for Rough Roads

Along with two-seat runabouts, high-wheelers like this 1910 Holsman offered a low-priced alternative to much more sophisticated (and expensive) Mercedes-style automobiles. High-wheelers served reasonably well as a substitute for horse-drawn carriages over poor rural roads, and they enjoyed their greatest popularity in the rural Midwest as well-to-do farmers and townsfolk moved into the ranks of motor-vehicle owners. From *Automobile* 9 (Sept. 1909): 450.

A Model T shows off its simple but extraordinarily effective suspension, which reduced stress on the chassis while providing excellent performance on rough, rutted roads. By combining the strengths of other motor-vehicle types while avoiding their most significant weaknesses—all in a remarkably affordable package—the Model T design helped Ford make good on its grandiose marketing description of the Model T as the "Universal Car." From the collections of The Henry Ford, THF32262.

**'GOLD RUSH'
IS STARTED
BY FORD'S
$5 OFFER**

Thousands of Men Seek Employment in Detroit Factory.

Will Distribute $10,000,000 in Semi-Monthly Bonuses.

No Employe to Receive Less Than Five Dollars a Day.

When workers responded to the rigor and monotony of new assembly-line methods by quitting in droves, Ford responded with the Five Dollar Day—roughly doubling the industry's prevailing wage rate. Its widespread adoption as a basic part of Fordism marked an industrial *and* environmental watershed. *Cincinnati Times-Star*, 7 January 1914, p. 1.

THE FIRST AUTOMOBILE IN BUNGTOWN

A cartoon from October 1900 captures both the novelty of early horseless carriages and what rural residents often characterized as urban
motorists' haughty disregard for established customs of rural road
and street use. In the years before large numbers of rural Americans
themselves became car owners, conflicts such as this prompted a short
but intense flare-up of anti-automobile sentiment in the rural United
States. From *Motor Age* 3, 4 (4 Oct. 1900): 159.

A road crew applies a tar-based binder to a macadam road in an effort to improve its durability under growing automotive traffic, late 1910s or early 1920s. In addition to disrupting established patterns of rural life, early automobiles wreaked havoc on expensive macadamized rural highways, challenging the established priorities of the good-roads movement and prompting a concerted research-and-development effort to protect improved rural roads from their destructive effects. From Chatburn, *Highways and Highway Transportation*, 254.

MAYOR HARRISON OF CHICAGO—"These wild autos must be suppressed."—Chicago Record-Herald.

"These wild autos must be suppressed," 1902. As in rural areas, motorists took to city streets in ways that clashed with the traditional street culture of downtown America, prompting a contentious, high-stakes struggle to redefine proper street uses in motor-age cities. From *Motor Age* 1, 22 (29 May 1902): 32.

A sign instructs pedestrians to observe an important new motor-age behavior: "Look Before Crossing," 1916. Police departments initially responded to the traffic tangle as a series of isolated incidents to control and resolve, forming "traffic squads" to direct traffic, unknot snarls, and "educate" pedestrians to observe new traffic regulations. From Woods, "Keeping City Traffic Moving," 623.

"How Children Are Killed and Injured," 1916. Motorists launched (frequently self-serving) "pedestrian safety campaigns" that both implicitly and explicitly elevated the rights of high-speed traffic to street space over those of other users. Early efforts focused particularly on educating children, who suffered disproportionately in early auto-related pedestrian deaths. From Woods, "Keeping City Traffic Moving," 626.

Traffic tower on Fifth Avenue, New York City. As part of their effort to unsnarl traffic, some cities experimented with traffic-control towers at busy intersections, which gave officers a better view of the traffic they were directing. From Chatburn, *Highways and Highway Transportation*, 446.

PART III

Creating Car Country, 1919–1941

FOUR

MOTOR-AGE GEOGRAPHY

SOARING AUTOMOBILE OWNERSHIP DURING THE 1920S PLACED
stiff new demands on American roads and streets. Some of those
demands challenged basic road technology, prompting road engineers
to devise safer, more durable roads. Others challenged the traditional
purposes of roads and streets, triggering a host of new ideas about how
to adapt the country's social and economic life to widespread automobile ownership. Faced with exploding numbers of motor vehicles, the
engineers and administrators who had steadily gathered road-making
authority into their hands during the 1910s shifted their attention during the 1920s toward transforming the country's mismatched jumble
of roads and streets into coordinated systems. Unlike their predecessors, who tended to see cars as a damaging new form of traffic that
threatened the durability of improved roads, interwar engineers and
administrators tended to see road and street

Park and Shop, Washington,
D.C., ca. early 1930s. Theodor
Horydczak, courtesy of
Library of Congress Prints
and Photographs Division,
LC-H814-1049.

systems as powerful tools for systematically
overcoming environmental constraints
on transportation and fostering economic
development.

Despite an almost exponential increase
in resources at every level of government,

however, and despite the growing tendency to see cars and roads as complementary elements of a coordinated transportation system, concerted system-building efforts failed to keep pace with either the expanding quantity or the changing uses of automobiles. As the number of motorists grew in every part of the country—from the broad, crowded avenues of big-city commercial districts to the dirt roads of remote national forests—the flood of automobiles began to dominate all other forms of traffic. Faced with this deluge, urban builders fought to accommodate automobiles as best they could simply to keep street systems functioning, while rural highway builders presided over a construction boom designed to make extensive improvements as quickly as possible.

Although administrators and engineers spent tens of billions of dollars during the interwar period addressing the new realities of large-scale car use, they focused overwhelmingly on adapting the existing infrastructure to meet the demands of traffic, *not* on ambitious attempts to remake the built environment in ways that would unlock the full potential of automobiles to enhance personal mobility. Rural projects, for example, focused on ditching, draining, paving, and widening highways along existing alignments; similarly, cities focused on widening existing streets, imposing new traffic-control regulations, and addressing parking problems. Such projects made life significantly easier for motorists and adapted roads and streets to growing car use, but their purpose remained accommodation, not transformation.

Motorists, on the other hand, embraced the new possibilities for personal mobility that automobiles and incremental improvements to the automotive infrastructure created. As networks of smooth roads and streets spread across the country and as cars achieved ever-greater speeds and reliability, motorists gained the confidence to make decisions about everyday automobile use that were largely independent of the environmental constraints that had loomed so large in earlier years. In this context, motorists began to develop a new understanding of the relationship between time and distance—and, by extension, began to envision new relationships with the larger world premised on flexible, reliable mobility. As motorists acted on their new ideas, a cadre of real estate developers, retailers, and various other groups searched for ways to capitalize on growing car-based mobility. Well before engineers and policy makers fully appreciated the implications of new mobility patterns for the nation's highways, a new geography for the motor age began to emerge—and the seeds of car dependence slowly began to sprout.

CATCHING UP TO CARS

The vast road- and street-improvement efforts in the United States between the two world wars revolved around a single fact: the demands of traffic grew much faster than road builders could respond, forcing them into a frantic race to catch up to cars. Three interrelated problems thwarted road and street administrators at every turn. First, car ownership, which jumped from less than half a million to 8.1 million between 1910 and 1920, continued its explosive growth through the 1920s, peaking at 23.1 million in 1929. Car registrations initially declined with the onset of the Great Depression, falling 10.7 percent from their 1929 high to 20.7 million in 1933—but then resumed their steady upward climb, reaching 29.6 million in 1941 (fig. 4.1).[1] Aside from the initial dip, new-car sales closely paralleled population growth during the 1930s, with the ratio of driving-age Americans to registered vehicles falling slightly from 3.2:1 in 1930 to 3:1 in 1940 (fig. 4.2).[2] Second, traffic volume grew much faster than car ownership as motorists took more trips and drove greater distances. In 1920, for example, 8.1 million vehicles each traveled an average of 5,152 miles; in 1930, 23.1 million automobiles each drove 7,713 miles; and in 1940, 27.5 million cars each drove 9,312 miles.[3] Third, the average speed of traffic rose steadily during the interwar years, revealing safety problems of highways that had not been designed with large numbers of fast-moving vehicles in mind.

These rapid changes, combined with strong political pressure to maximize road improvements within available budgets, pushed administrators to rush to adapt existing highways to growing traffic. They accomplished this mainly by cobbling together a national highway system from existing routes, typically by identifying the most important, most traveled highways and improving them as rapidly as possible. Conditions changed so quickly, however, that administrators had trouble anticipating problems; worse, solutions to one set

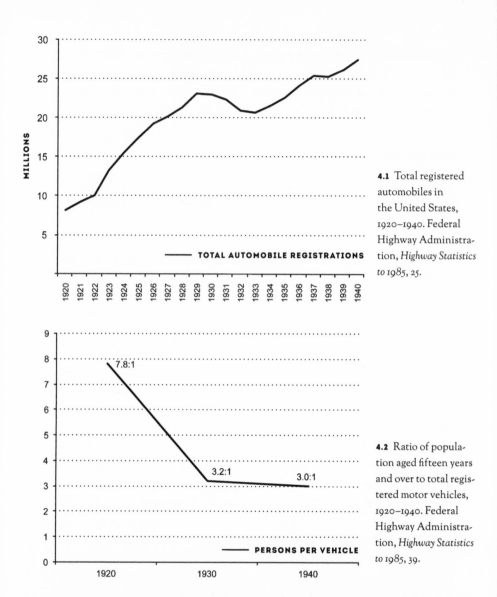

4.1 Total registered automobiles in the United States, 1920–1940. Federal Highway Administration, *Highway Statistics to 1985*, 25.

TOTAL AUTOMOBILE REGISTRATIONS

4.2 Ratio of population aged fifteen years and over to total registered motor vehicles, 1920–1940. Federal Highway Administration, *Highway Statistics to 1985*, 39.

PERSONS PER VEHICLE

of problems frequently exposed other, more significant problems. In addition, the vast size of road and street systems made it impossible to implement changes quickly on a systemwide scale. As a result, a perpetual sense of crisis prevailed, and even massive, nationwide changes appeared inadequate and insubstantial in light of traffic's growing demands. Thus did an era marked by the expenditure of tens of billions of dollars to adapt the nation's infrastructure of roads and streets to automobiles—an era one historian has described as "the golden age of highway building"—begin and end with very much the same problem: confronting a crushing burden of traffic that rendered the nation's roads and streets increasingly outdated and obsolete.[4]

The interwar road construction boom began with the passage of the Federal Highway Act of 1921. Designed to address a variety of problems that had plagued the pioneering Federal Aid Road Act of 1916, the 1921 law also reflected a crucial concession to the motoring wing of the good-roads movement, which had aggressively argued that the federal-aid system was producing, in the words of the new chief of the federal Bureau of Public Roads (BPR), Thomas MacDonald, "little pieces of road."[5] The 1921 legislation's key provision required state highway departments to designate 7 percent of their states' total highway mileage to be included in a comprehensive federal-aid system, with 3 percent forming a connected system of interstate "primary" routes and the remaining 4 percent forming a connected system of intercounty "secondary" routes. Only highways within this system would qualify for federal aid. The act also stipulated that all federal-aid roads were to have "only such durable types of surface and kinds of materials . . . as will adequately meet the existing and probable future traffic needs," cementing the traffic-service vision that administrators had long championed.[6]

In many ways, the Federal Highway Act of 1921 was an unparalleled success, launching a sustained construction boom and creating a coordinated national highway system that, by the end of the 1920s, put an improved federal-aid road within ten miles of roughly nine of every ten Americans.[7] In addition, the boom survived—indeed thrived—during the Great Depression, because road construction was a politically attractive place for federal work-relief funds, particularly after a 1932 study showed that each new job in road work created roughly seven jobs in supporting industries.[8] Measured in mileage of improved roads and dollars spent, the interwar construction program achieved substantial results. Between 1921 and 1941, for example, the surfaced mileage of American highways rose from 387,000 to 1.38 million miles. Meanwhile, total rural highway expenditures totaled $36.3 billion during the same period, making road construction the second-largest object of government spending behind education.[9]

Despite these impressive numbers, much of the era's new construction became obsolete soon after its completion, sparking a vicious cycle of iterative, incremental improvements in which solutions to one set of problems begat further problems as traffic grew thicker. In the northern and eastern states, for example, which during the 1920s had comparatively large highway budgets and substantial numbers of motorists, previous experience with cars suggested the desirability of dustless, all-weather pavements, and experience with trucks suggested those pavements must be durable under heavy loads. With support from BPR researchers who helped clarify the basic engineering principles involved, these states launched aggressive (and expensive) paving campaigns. Yet thickening traffic soon revealed new problems. One holdover of road design from the horse-drawn era, for example, was the practice of giving pavements a pronounced crown to shed water quickly. To avoid the unpleasant tipping sensation that accompanied driving toward the edge, where the slope of the crown was most pronounced, most drivers sought the center of the road. This practice had been fine on lightly traveled roads, but as traffic increased it resulted in cars hurtling toward one another down the center of paved roads and then swerving onto the steep outer halves as they converged. Highway departments addressed this early game of automotive chicken by reducing crowns and painting centerlines on highways—only to find that motorists felt cramped on half a road, particularly when big trucks approached. Slightly wider highways and broader shoulders helped, but as heavy trucks moved into the designated lanes and off the thick center portion of the road, they caused its thinner edges to break up—necessitating new slab designs with thickened edges.[10]

By the late 1920s, particularly as more accurate traffic-forecasting methods evolved, the rising speed of traffic sparked a new problem-solution-problem cycle that shaped much of the 1930s agenda. The basic issue was road alignments, most of which had been determined with horse-drawn traffic in mind. Horses had particular trouble with steep grades, especially when hauling heavy loads over poorly maintained earth roads. As a result, the desire to maintain reasonable grades in hillier regions—while avoiding labor-intensive earthwork operations—had produced notoriously crooked alignments. Horses and motorists, of course, could both handle even sharp turns easily when they were moving slowly. Where poor brakes, blowout-prone tires, rough and muddy roads, sight-obscuring dust, and frequent encounters with horse-drawn vehicles had once kept most motorists to relatively low average speeds, however, by the end of the 1920s conditions were changing. Cars had gotten faster, more reliable, and easier to stop; horse-drawn traffic had thinned; and more highways featured smooth, dust-free pavements.

Speeds rose as a result, creating significant new dangers on crooked roads. In 1918, for example, only three states had speed limits above the national average of 25 miles per hour. By 1929, however, the national average had risen to 35 miles per hour—and one researcher estimated that "the average speed on the open road to-day is fully 20 miles per hour greater than it was 10 years ago."[11] At these higher speeds, the poor sight lines and sharp turns of existing roads created serious dangers. The result was a bloodbath, with annual deaths from automobile accidents rising steadily from 12,155 deaths in 1920 to 32,914 in 1940.[12]

Unfortunately for highway departments, these safety problems did not appear until after many roads had been expensively paved, in part because smooth pavements made motorists feel more comfortable driving at high speeds. Facing the dilemma of designed-in dangers on one hand and expensive alterations to highways carefully engineered for long-term durability on the other, many highway departments initially opted for site-specific fixes—cutting the corners of an exceptionally sharp turn here, realigning a short stretch of particularly crooked road there.[13] By the early 1930s, though, as the speed and volume of traffic rose and deaths mounted, it became clear that piecemeal solutions fell well short. The BPR began approving "reconstruction" projects in 1929, and in the 1930s states turned over thousands of miles of expensively paved (but poorly aligned) roads to local authorities, replacing them with new roads along straighter alignments. For these new roads, engineers capitalized on automobiles' greater power than horses, opting for steeper grades—as much as 9 percent in places—where earlier road builders would have put sharp turns. The resulting highways had a distinctive roller-coaster character that discouraged horse-drawn vehicles. At 35 or 45 miles per hour, the limited sight distance of such roads did not create problems, but speeds kept creeping upward, and by the late 1930s new design-related safety problems were again becoming apparent.

The lag between developing design solutions and translating them widely into road-building practice frustrated engineer-administrators, who pushed to standardize and codify "best practices" as a way to hasten the speed and consistency of their implementation. Reflecting the shifting concerns of highway builders, much of the effort in the 1920s had focused on standardizing materials and construction specifications.[14] By the second half of the 1930s, though, efforts shifted toward safer "geometric design," which included attention to such elements as grade, sight distance, and the radius and superelevation of curves. The first important development occurred in 1935, when Joseph Barnett coined the term "assumed design speed" to describe a new goal: improving safety by coordinating all of a highway's geometric design features so that no aspect of its design would require a motorist to slow down to less than the assumed speed.[15] This idea required a remarkable shift in the perspective of engineers, asking them to exchange the bird's-eye view of traffic moving through a system—a view that had dominated highway circles since at least 1916—for an explicitly motorist's-eye view of the road.

This new perspective marked a crucial turning point in the competition between motorists' needs and those of the communities through which highways ran. The American Association of State Highway Officials' Committee on Planning and Design Policies quickly adopted the idea of design speed, incorporating it into a series of pamphlets between 1937 and 1944 that standardized highway industry practices well into the postwar period.[16]

As administrators prepared new design standards, traffic woes continued to mount, fostering a continuing sense of crisis. "It is a patchwork of pieces of road having little or no continuity," declared a 1936 *Fortune* exposé on problems with the American highway system, "leaping without rhyme or reason from dirt to macadam and concrete; from two-lane to three-lane to four-, five-, and six-lane breadth; from well-calculated curves to slithering turns having not the slightest respect for centrifugal force."[17] Even the BPR agreed. "Many of the existing highways are not equal to the burden now placed upon them by the modern motor vehicle," concluded a 1937 BPR report on highway

safety and traffic conditions. "Many are not built to standards necessary to accommodate the traffic of today at the speeds now considered
reasonable with the maximum degree of convenience and safety."[18] By
the time the United States entered World War II, highway engineers
had codified new design principles that over time would completely
remake the nation's highways around the motorist's perspective—yet
after two decades and $36.3 billion invested during the unprecedented
interwar highway construction boom, the nation's highways still
lagged well behind the demands of overwhelming numbers of faster
and faster cars.

The efforts of city leaders struggling to catch up to cars mirrored
the travails of rural highway engineers in some crucial respects but in
others reflected very different problems. Traffic volumes that urban
engineers considered low, rural highway officials considered high—
and distances that urban engineers considered long, rural highway
officials considered short. Moreover, heavily built-up urban land
with dense populations gave city engineers little space to maneuver.
Merely widening a street, for example, could pose intractable political
problems and cost astronomical sums if abutting land had to be condemned to make room. This translated into a relatively narrow range
of improvements that planners could realistically consider, making it
virtually impossible to extensively revise the existing shape of urban
street networks, particularly after city budgets fell precipitously during the economic crisis of the 1930s.

Those tasked with adapting American cities to the automobile,
however, did share at least two traits with their rural counterparts:
both initially approached traffic problems from a bird's-eye perspective, and both wanted to create a comprehensive network of arteries
whose individual parts could be engineered to work together toward
larger traffic-service goals. Taken together, these two tendencies
guided interwar efforts to untangle urban traffic. Following the advice
of two new professions—city planning and traffic engineering—urban
leaders created comprehensive city plans and conducted citywide traffic surveys, both of which inspired new policies that treated streets as
rational systems designed to move traffic (which increasingly meant
automotive traffic) quickly and safely around the city. Significantly, the
two professions approached their work from different angles. Where

city planners began their work from a land-use perspective, traffic engineers began from a transportation perspective. Understanding the similarities and differences in their complementary approaches highlights the ways that land-use changes and new transportation policies fused together in support of a new motor-age geography.

As early as 1915, a vanguard of "city efficient" planners had embraced what they called "comprehensive" city plans. Although such plans theoretically dealt with every aspect of urban life, from transportation and housing to leisure and high culture, in practice they privileged zoning, subdivision regulations, and street planning over other issues.[19] Among the foremost practitioners of this brand of city planning was Harland Bartholomew, who in 1913 became the nation's first director of city planning in Newark, New Jersey, where he developed an early comprehensive plan. In 1916 he moved to St. Louis, where he served as the city planning commission's engineer. In that capacity, he tried to integrate the city's disparate neighborhoods by creating a comprehensive, citywide street system.[20] At the same time, his consulting firm, Harland Bartholomew and Associates, spread his ideas by producing nearly a quarter of all comprehensive city plans in the United States between 1920 and 1925—thirty-two altogether during the 1920s.[21]

A key theme running through Bartholomew's work, which he shared with both the "city beautiful" and "city efficient" traditions, was the idea that not all streets were (or should be) created equal. Just as state engineers categorized rural roads according to their volume and character of traffic, Bartholomew organized streets into a complementary, hierarchically organized mix of "main arterial thoroughfares" to carry the heaviest traffic burden; "secondary (crosstown) thoroughfares" to collect local traffic and direct it to arterials; and "minor streets" to serve predominantly local traffic.[22]

These distinctions served several purposes. They allowed cities to concentrate expenditures, for example, on a limited number of major routes. The distinctions also had functional advantages. Minor streets with light traffic, for example, did not require expensive pavements, and excluding them from the circulatory system insulated their residents from heavy traffic. Secondary crosstown routes, which typically appeared every half mile in the urban grid, connected major radials and gave access to residential enclaves. Primary thoroughfares connected the various parts of the city to the downtown business district, which remained the privileged area of the city. When they worked in concert, Bartholomew wrote in 1924, carefully designed street systems had a tendency "to promote order, facilitate movement, improve values and promote public safety."[23]

The second major component of comprehensive city plans was zoning, which planners touted as a powerful new tool for reducing traffic congestion, rationalizing land-use patterns, and decentralizing dense urban development. Zoning began to gain popularity after New York City adopted the nation's first comprehensive zoning ordinance in 1916.[24] As a tool for traffic control in built-up areas, and especially in densely settled cities, zoning's power was more theoretical than actual. Zoning's key insight regarding traffic was that large, frequently used buildings like downtown department stores and office buildings attracted far greater street traffic to their vicinity than less-used buildings like single-family homes. Zoning's promise as a tool for traffic control, then, was to give planners a means to regulate the relationship between street space and the traffic that particular buildings could be expected to generate.[25] As a tool for controlling traffic in crowded downtown areas, however, zoning laws had virtually no effect, primarily because interwar ordinances quite reasonably reflected existing land-use patterns—including the concentration of major traffic generators in central business districts—because to do otherwise would require the complete reconstruction of big cities. "Zoning is of inestimable value as a stabilizer and corrective," one engineer explained in 1924. "But, until the controls can be materially tightened, there will result little aid to traffic and transportation in reasonable time."[26]

In addition to rationalizing street systems and passing zoning ordinances, some cities undertook elaborate (and very expensive) projects that city planners devised to solve city-specific traffic problems. Chicago, for example, built two major double-decked streets along the Chicago River, including the famous Wacker Drive, to alleviate key bottlenecks in the central business district. Both projects separated slower-moving trucks from faster-moving automobiles by putting trucks on a separate belowground deck.[27] Atlanta, meanwhile, erected three large viaducts over its infamous "railroad gulch," thus making it easy to move between the formerly isolated halves of its business district.[28]

Given the massive expense and disruption of construction in densely developed areas, traffic regulation remained a popular (and cheaper) alternative for dealing with urban traffic, particularly after traffic engineering emerged as a profession in the early 1920s. In contrast to the 1910s, when police departments and self-styled "traffic experts" like William Phelps Eno made the key advances, traffic engineering grew out of the larger engineering profession, and its practitioners found homes in city engineering departments. Using techniques akin to those of hydraulic engineers, traffic engineers created citywide systems to channel and divert traffic's ebb and flow and to eliminate eddies and turbulence as traffic circulated through streets invariably described as arteries and conduits. "Traffic is much like water," wrote one engineer. "It flows where there is a natural attraction."[29] Using techniques to attract and repel traffic, they tried to engineer solutions to urban congestion by controlling the flow of people's movements on city streets.

Throughout the interwar years, Miller McClintock was to traffic engineering what Harland Bartholomew was to comprehensive city planning. In 1924, the Los Angeles Traffic Commission hired McClintock, then a young professor of municipal government, to study the city's traffic ordinances. He then helped rewrite the city's traffic code, which when implemented in January 1925 dramatically sped vehicular movement downtown, in part by banning horse-drawn vehicles during business hours and in part by requiring pedestrians to obey the traffic signals governing the movement of motor vehicles.[30] Later that year McClintock published Street Traffic Control, the nation's first textbook on the subject, and in 1926 he became the director of the Albert Russel Erskine Bureau for Street Traffic Research at Harvard University, where he established himself as the nation's most influential traffic engineer. In that capacity he wrote extensively on traffic problems for national publications and either authored or oversaw major street-traffic studies in Chicago (1926), San Francisco (1927), New Orleans (1928), Boston (1928), Providence (1928), Kansas City (1930), and Chicago again (1932), which together set the standard for municipal traffic research in the United States and spawned imitations in cities like New York, Buffalo, Detroit, Pittsburgh, St. Louis, and Washington, D.C.[31]

The key tool distinguishing interwar traffic engineers from the traffic experts of the 1910s was the citywide traffic survey, an elaborate system for recording and organizing data on city street uses. "The opinions of casual observers have often been helpful in assisting a city with its street problems, but more frequently plans and methods based upon such information have been found useless or worse than useless," McClintock explained. "The traffic system of a great city is of such magnitude and of such complexity that even the trained observer finds that he has need for exhaustive study before he can advance proposals of a satisfactory nature."[32] The surveys covered an exhaustive list of topics, each designed, in McClintock's words, to "substitute accurate facts of an engineering character for guesswork." These typically included the volume, character, and speed of street traffic on major and minor streets; the origins and destinations of vehicles; the total available curb space for parking and the average time that drivers parked; the shopping practices of curbside parkers; the volume, character, and speed of pedestrian traffic; the frequency of jaywalking; the locations and causes of traffic accidents; and the city's administrative structure for enforcing traffic regulations.[33]

After tabulating their data, traffic engineers created traffic-flow maps to identify the city's most heavily trafficked thoroughfares and intersections. The results resembled the street-classification schemes of city planners like Bartholomew, for they tended to divide into routes with high, medium, and low levels of traffic. These maps enabled engineers to see the citywide patterns of traffic movement whose efficiency they hoped to improve. During the 1920s, they did not see their job as manipulating land uses to *create* new major thoroughfares, as did city planners; instead, they saw it as *identifying* existing major thoroughfares and devising ways to improve the speed and safety of the traffic they carried.[34]

Traffic engineers were also more systematic than their predecessors in applying the traffic-control techniques that had developed prior to 1920. For example, stop signs, one-way streets, left-turn bans, and painted lines to delineate traffic lanes all continued to function in basically the same way as they had before 1920. Where administrators of the 1910s had used these tools to resolve localized traffic blockages, however, interwar traffic engineers used them to create coordinated systems for traffic circulation across entire metropolitan regions. Rather than just designating the narrowest, most congested downtown streets as one-way, for example, as was common in the 1910s, traffic engineers created entire systems of one-way streets that flanked major thoroughfares, substantially improving the flow of traffic. They also devoted considerable effort—with increasing input from automotive interests—to standardizing traffic laws and the various traffic signs, signals, and markings in use on city streets.[35]

One iconic advance in interwar traffic control came with the introduction of standardized, automatic traffic lights, which traffic engineers carefully timed to coordinate the flow of traffic not only through busy intersections but from intersection to intersection along major urban thoroughfares. The number of traffic lights rose quickly—from about one thousand in 1924 to eight thousand by 1927—and efforts to create coordinated systems proceeded rapidly. The earliest synchronized systems in New York, Detroit, Chicago, and Houston used a central control tower or operator to change all lights at the same time, but these systems encouraged motorists to race at dangerous speeds through as many lights as possible before they all turned red.[36] In the early 1920s, Los Angeles and Lancaster, Pennsylvania, introduced systems of progressively timed traffic lights that fostered continuous movement at a constant speed along major arteries. By the late 1920s, engineers had refined the process enough to interweave continuously moving "waves" of traffic from east–west and north–south streets without forcing either to stop at intersections as long as they stuck to the prescribed speed—an urban counterpart to the idea of "assumed design speed." In Chicago's Loop, accidents fell 23 percent and speeds increased 10 percent after the installation of progressively timed lights. Detroit, Los Angeles, Cleveland, and Erie, Pennsylvania, all reported faster traffic and fewer fatalities after introducing similar systems. In Washington, D.C., traffic on Sixteenth Street sped from a crawl to speeds approximating the legal speed limit of 22 miles per hour.[37]

The era's second iconic achievement was the elevation of the lowly stop sign into a means of creating major new automotive thoroughfares at very little cost. The key developments came in Chicago, where since the 1860s vehicles had been required to stop before crossing or turning onto the city's boulevards. Because vehicles on boulevards had the right-of-way through all intersections, they could travel much faster and with greater safety. In addition, boulevards further boosted their average speeds by barring slow-moving streetcars, horse-drawn wagons, and heavy trucks. They drew cars like a powerful magnet, and by the early 1920s motorists were clamoring for new automotive boulevards. The expense of constructing entirely new boulevards proved prohibitive, but in 1922 the city created its first automobile-only "instant boulevard" by applying a boulevard's rules of use to a route along preexisting streets. By forcing traffic on intersecting cross streets to stop at stop signs, the new system gave the right-of-way to vehicles on the instant boulevard. This very simple technique gave traffic engineers a way to create the sort of hierarchical distinctions among streets that factored so prominently in city plans without requiring any physical changes more dramatic than erecting new stop signs. In the instant boulevard, engineers found a technique that did nothing less than allow them to transform run-of-the-mill streets into custom-made, high-speed automotive routes.[38] The idea circulated rapidly, spreading by 1925 to Detroit, New Orleans, and Los Angeles, and by the 1930s full systems of instant boulevards interlaced most cities.[39]

Like state highway departments, however, city planners and traffic engineers always seemed to lag behind the escalating demands of surging traffic, creating the same sort of problem-solution-problem cycle that vexed rural administrators. No sooner did a city finish a major street-widening project, implement a carefully designed system of progressively timed traffic lights, or open a new instant boulevard than the improved facilities were swamped by sudden, substantial increases in traffic. Frederick Law Olmsted Jr. described the situation as a perpetual state of "almost but not quite intolerable congestion."[40] The central dynamic at work—improved facilities enabling more motorists to make use of them—only underscored the fact that there were more urban car owners than the street infrastructure could handle at once, and that for all the motorists already on the road there were others poised to join them should traffic speed up and driving become more convenient. Rather than relieving congestion by attracting drivers from other thoroughfares, wider, faster streets seemed to generate *new* traffic.[41]

By the early 1930s, as their most creative and expensive efforts to alleviate congestion failed, cities began to commission elaborate engineering studies to help guide them out of the traffic morass. In study after study, engineers responded with a radical—and radically expensive—solution: dramatically increasing the amount of urban land devoted to automotive transportation by building new networks of high-speed, multilane, limited-access highways connecting down-town with outlying residential areas.[42] McClintock, who oversaw many of these studies and whose proposal for a system of "limited ways" in Chicago established the template that others followed, became an outspoken supporter of the approach.[43] "Since the character of their physical design eliminates practically all of the sources of friction and delay to be found in surface routes," McClintock argued, "it may be said that the speed potentials of limited ways are practically bound-less."[44] Buoyed by this inspiring vision of greater speed and safety, cit-ies across the nation began planning freeway systems, though their prohibitive costs ensured that virtually all would remain unbuilt until after World War II. Before the war only a handful of places—including New York, New Jersey, Detroit, and Los Angeles—had completed any noteworthy high-speed urban roads designed specifically for automo-biles. Perhaps the most important of these was the Arroyo Seco Park-way, which was dedicated in late 1940 as the first link in what became Los Angeles's extensive postwar freeway system.[45]

As road and street administrators struggled to adapt the nation's infrastructure to the crushing new traffic burden, they consolidated the transformation of what were then widely called "public roads" into *motor* roads.[46] This transformation played itself out on numer-ous, mutually reinforcing levels. In finance and administration, local contributions to road budgets fell dramatically, particularly during the Great Depression, amplifying the waning influence of local govern-ments in road administration. This shift fostered traffic-service poli-cies that gave motorists priority over other road users and owners of abutting land. Horse-drawn wagons retreated from country highways, pedestrians retreated to sidewalks, and even streetcars and buses found themselves outnumbered—physically and politically—as motorists swamped the streets. "Our suburban and country highways are con-stantly being improved for motorists. Most of these are now unfitted for other users," complained William Phelps Eno in 1936, toward the end of his long traffic-control career. "It is no longer safe to walk, ride or cycle on public roads, especially at night when the peril is greatly increased."[47] Finally, engineers increasingly championed the idea that roads and streets existed primarily to move motor vehicles. This idea manifested itself most explicitly in the late 1930s and early 1940s, both in the motorist's-eye view of highway design guiding new geometric design standards and in the urban embrace of plans for limited-access automotive freeway systems, which barred nonmotorized vehicles and did not grant abutting landowners their traditional right of access.[48]

Despite this thoroughgoing shift toward adapting roads and streets to automobiles, and despite the increasing tendency of road and street administrators to view highways as parts of an abstract transportation system rather than in terms of their direct physical relationships with the particular environments they occupied, the interwar construction boom did surprisingly little to create car-dependent landscapes. The federal-aid highway system, for example, did not reshape the nation's basic geography. Compared to railroads, which had wrought the nation's essential development patterns in the second half of the nineteenth century, the interwar national highway system reinforced rather than challenged existing geographical patterns. State highway departments created the new 7 percent system by selecting routes from among existing highways, ensuring that the system connected all substantial cities and towns. Moreover, cities—which were excluded from federal aid for highways until 1934—designated all highway routes within city limits. In practice, this meant that most highways initially traveled down Main Street in every town on their path.[49] The degree to which this reinforced older geographical patterns—rather than establishing new ones oriented around motor vehicles—is perhaps best symbolized by the fact that, during the 1920s, nearly all Main Streets were oriented in relation to a railroad depot.

Even in cities, where cars dominated streets even more thoroughly than rural highways, no large-scale projects began—until the first experimental mileage of McClintock-style "limited ways"—with the premise that city landscapes should be completely redesigned to unleash the automobile's full potential. Surging interwar traffic was simply too overwhelming, and the infrastructure simply too far behind, to indulge such fantasies. Moreover, although cities made driving much easier during the interwar years, the combination of well-developed central business districts, streetcar systems, and walkable neighborhoods ensured that most urbanites could still get around without a car. Cars profoundly influenced and expanded Americans' mobility, but the interwar era's herculean efforts to adapt the nation's infrastructure to automobiles did not make Americans dependent on cars. Much more important in this regard was how motorists themselves understood and capitalized on the new possibilities for mobility that the combination of fast, reliable cars and smooth, hard-surfaced roads created. Initially, at least, automobiles had a much bigger impact on people's *mental* geographies than they did on the nation's physical geography.

MOTOR-AGE MOBILITY

As engineers and planners rushed to adapt road and street systems to growing traffic, nearly everyone else focused on cars—and especially their ever-growing capacity for speed, comfort, and flexible mobility. Although these characteristics did not translate into immediate, sweeping changes in the basic structure of the American landscape, they did have major implications for how growing numbers of motorists saw the world—and for their ability to move around within it. Because they made it so easy to overcome the limitations on travel that geography and difficult environmental conditions imposed, fast, reliable cars and smooth, carefully engineered roads together created an easy mobility for a rapidly expanding group of motorists that slowly but fundamentally altered how they understood the relationship between time and distance.[50] In short, cars created radically different "timesheds" for travel than competing rail-based transportation technologies, making frequent local travel fast and convenient while elevating the importance of places that were physically nearby but unconnected by rail.

When the first automobiles appeared at the end of the nineteenth century, they rolled into a world in which rail-based transportation systems had already launched a transportation revolution—a revolution that had *already* created unprecedented forms of personal mobility by overcoming environmental limits on travel and had *already* transformed basic, long-held ideas about the relationship between time and distance. Understanding the revolutionary aspects of auto-mobile-based personal mobility, then, requires an equal understanding of how rail-based systems like trains and streetcars structured late-nineteenth-century mobility patterns.[51]

Compared to traveling by foot or horse, the other major forms of over-land transportation through the nineteenth century, train travel was exponentially faster. Moreover, train travel empowered travelers to escape arduous road conditions, inclement weather, difficult topography, and the logistical challenges of feeding, resting, and stabling involved in horse travel. Train travel's comparative speed and ease prompted many paeans from travelers, who described the changes that trains introduced as bordering on the magical. They also prompted serious intellectual descriptions of their significance, such as Karl Marx's famous claim that railroads had ushered in "the annihilation of space by time."[52]

Yet if railroads annihilated space, they did not annihilate all space on equal terms: trains moved at unparalleled speeds over long distances but only along routes fixed in steel and maintained at huge expense. As a result, railroads compressed time's relationship with distance in highly *linear* ways. Given equivalent distances between any two points, in other words, direct connections were faster than indirect ones, especially when indirect routes involved long layovers. Moreover, because railroad corporations distinguished between competitive, high-traffic "trunk" lines and less competitive, lower-traffic "branch" and "feeder" lines, railroads compressed time's relationship with distance in markedly *hierarchical* ways. Railroad companies ran numerous daily passenger trains between major cities, for example, some as "express" trains with fewer stops and higher speeds than normal trains. Branch and feeder lines, on the other hand, often ran trains just once or twice a day that typically stopped at every small station along their routes, a practice that translated into lower overall speeds.[53]

Because of these linear and hierarchical characteristics, the most important thing that turn-of-the-century travelers needed to plan long-distance trips was not a map—for by then railroads enmeshed most states in a thick network of rails—but a timetable. Distributed freely in railroad stations across the nation, timetables listed each train traveling the line, along with their scheduled departure and arrival times. This information allowed passengers to figure out their time of departure, time of arrival, and duration of their travel. Those transferring from one train to another needed multiple schedules to make their calculations, including the duration of layovers.

Because of these factors, people's location relative to railroad lines profoundly shaped their everyday mobility options—particularly for travel over shorter distances.[54] In small rural towns served by a handful of trains each day, local travelers had limited options. Sometimes, and to some nearby places, departure and arrival times were convenient and did not require layovers; other times, and to other nearby places, schedules were significantly less favorable. For residents of big cities, on the other hand, railroads paled in significance to streetcars for travel over short distances. By the turn of the century, streetcar systems in every city of consequence connected downtown to outlying residential areas, ensuring short travel times from downtown to other parts of the city for those who could afford the standard nickel fare. Finally, for residents of affluent railroad suburbs around most major American cities, commuter-rail lines offered quick and convenient access to downtown and all points in between. Although the particulars necessarily varied from place to place, case studies of three typical places—a small town, a midsize city, and a commuter-rail suburb— illustrate the major ways that the linear, hierarchical structure of rail-based transportation systems shaped the everyday mobility options of turn-of-the-century Americans.

For residents of Blooming Prairie, Minnesota, a typical small rural town (population 1,655) located eighty-five miles south of St. Paul, railroads imposed a characteristically linear, hierarchical pattern on local travel options that encouraged people to measure the "closeness" of nearby towns in time rather than in distance. A time-distance map of Blooming Prairie based on timetable information from March 1900 (fig. 4.3) depicts the time requirements for travel within a three-hour radius, traveling first by rail and then transferring to a horse upon disembarking from the train.[55] Four major points stand out. First, railroads drastically reduced the amount of time required for residents to travel to the two biggest nearby towns, Austin (population 6,489) and Owatonna (population 5,561), both of which were within 35 minutes by train. Traveling by horse-drawn wagon and highway over

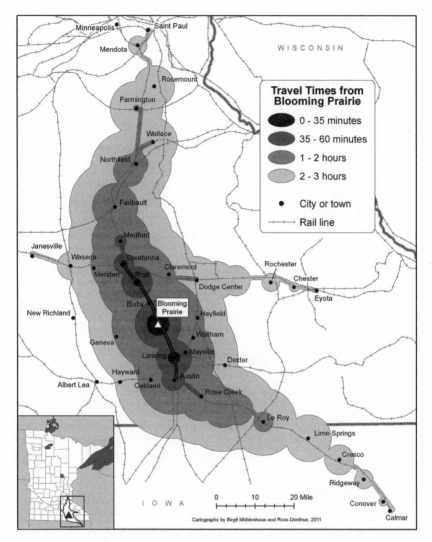

4.3 Time-distance map of travel options, traveling first by train and then transferring to a horse upon disembarking, beginning in downtown Blooming Prairie, Minnesota, 1900. Based on *Railroad Commissioners' Map of Minnesota* (1900) and data from American Association of General Passenger and Ticket Agents, *Travelers' Official Railway Guide* (March 1900). Cartography by Birgit Mühlenhaus and Ross Donihue, 2011.

well-maintained roads, the same trip would have taken roughly 2.5 hours to Austin (15 miles away) and roughly 3 hours to Owatonna (18 miles away). The railroad thus transformed travel to both towns from a lengthy, multiple-hour journey into an easy half-hour trip. Second, the railroad put the state capital, St. Paul, within just less than 3 hours away (2 hours 54 minutes)—replacing an arduous, multiple-day trip by horse with a train ride requiring the same time as a horse-and-buggy trip to Owatonna. Third, although Hayfield (less than 12 miles) and Geneva (13 miles) were slightly closer to Blooming Prairie in distance than either Austin or Owatonna, neither town had a direct rail connection. As a result, getting from Blooming Prairie to Hayfield took 5 hours 57 minutes by train—including a layover in Austin of 4 hours 5 minutes—versus a 2-hour trip by horse. Geneva, on the other hand, had no rail connection, leaving horse travel the only viable option. Fourth, although travelers from Blooming Prairie could transfer to east–west lines at both Owatonna and Austin, long layovers in Austin meant that travelers transferring there could not even get to the first stop in either direction within 3 hours—unless they took the train to Austin and finished the trip by horse. Shorter, more favorable layovers in Owatonna, on the other hand, made it possible to travel 24 miles to the west, and more than 60 miles to the east, within 3 hours.

For city dwellers, such as residents of St. Paul, Minnesota (population 153,063), turn-of-the-century rail travel compressed distance in very different ways. For long-distance travel, residents benefited from regular service to other big cities. City dwellers could also expect to spend less money and encounter fewer logistical challenges: prices along trunk lines were lower per mile than on branch and feeder lines, and big-city depot districts offered diverse, affordable, and readily available accommodations and transportation. For local travel, St. Paul's electric streetcar system allowed residents to cover a significantly larger area than any small-town resident could in a similar amount of time. A time-distance map for St. Paul in 1900 (fig. 4.4) reveals several important points.[56] First, the combination of streetcars and walking enabled people to get to any point in or near downtown within 15 minutes, to most of the city's settled areas within 30 minutes, and into the areas of neighboring Minneapolis that were closest to St. Paul within 45 minutes. Getting to downtown Minneapolis—10 miles to

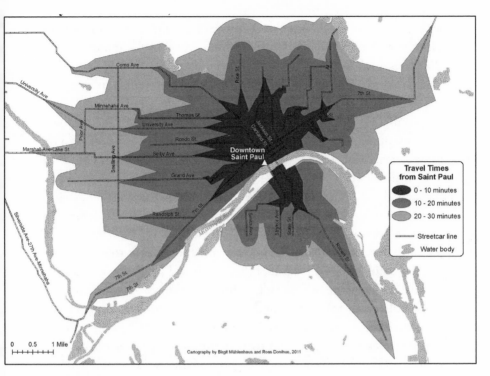

4.4 Time-distance map of travel by streetcar and foot from downtown St. Paul, Minnesota, 1900. Based on map in *The Twin Cities 1914: Where to Go, How to Go, How Much Will It Cost* (St. Paul: Twin City Lines, 1914) and data from *Free Pocket Directory: Names of Streets and Nearest Electric Lines* (St. Paul: Ramaley Print Co., 1899). Cartography by Birgit Mühlenhaus and Ross Donihue, 2011.

the west—required nearly an hour by streetcar. Second, the streetcar lines were dense enough and ran frequently enough during the day (a median of 10 minutes, with most lines every 5–15 minutes), that people could get everywhere in the city via streetcar and a short walk. In this sense, the streetcar *system* offset the linear characteristics of individual streetcar *lines*, enabling easy travel within all areas of the city where streetcars ran. Third, the tight relationship between streetcar lines and the city's settlement patterns is clear: streetcars linked all outlying residential areas to downtown.

For residents of St. Paul Park (population 1,200), a typical commuter-rail suburb 11 miles southeast of St. Paul, the picture differed yet again. Trains ran on average every 1.5 hours between 6:00 a.m. and

10:30 p.m., giving residents direct, convenient, speedy (27-minute) service to St. Paul. Most such railroads offered special commuter prices that were high enough to keep away "undesirables" while still being affordable to affluent suburbanites.[57] Again, a time-distance map of the community (fig. 4.5) underscores several important points.[58] First, the commuter line gave residents easy, direct access to downtown. Second, upon disembarking in St. Paul, commuters had access to the same streetcar system as everyone else to move around the city. Third, within the suburb of St. Paul Park itself, local mobility more closely resembled that of small-town residents than big-city residents, since no streetcars operated there. The major difference was that fewer suburban residents had easy access to horse-drawn transportation compared to residents of small rural towns, which meant that in the era before motor vehicles local mobility consisted primarily of walking, or perhaps bicycling. As a result, although residents of commuter suburbs could easily travel back and forth between home and downtown, and could move easily around downtown once they were there, there was no quick way to get from their homes to adjacent suburbs. "You have friends living five miles away by road," one author explained. "To visit them by rail you must go half a mile to the station, ride ten miles to a junction, wait an hour, and travel a dozen miles more to a station half a mile from their home. How often do you see your friends?"[59]

In stark contrast to the linear, hierarchical patterns characterizing turn-of-the-century rail travel, the automobile's great promise was its potential to compress time and distance relatively uniformly. Big-city congestion and impassable country roads initially circumscribed the automobile's ability to deliver on this promise, but by the middle of the interwar period the combination of improved roads and faster cars had created new options for personal mobility. Because motorists could escape what one contemporary described as "waits for trains, changes at inconvenient hours and out-of-the-way places, [and] the multifarious inconveniences of baggage," they enjoyed greater flexibility and control over routes and schedules than travelers by rail.[60] Increasingly, motorists could start and stop as they wished, whatever the weather, and pick from numerous routes in at least passable condition across almost any terrain. The resulting sense of power, freedom, and independence intoxicated legions of motorists.[61] Cars still could

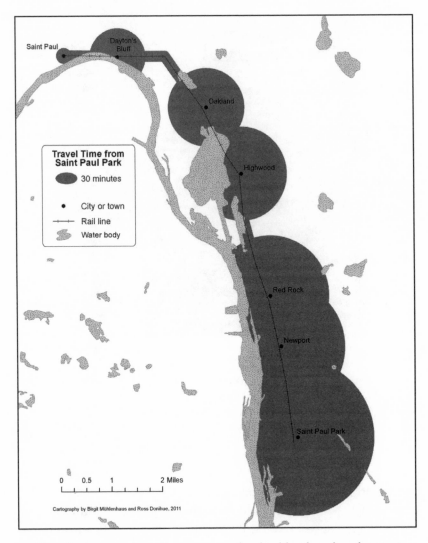

4.5 Time-distance map of travel by commuter railroad and foot from the rail station in St. Paul Park, Minnesota, 1900. "Chicago, Burlington, and Northern Railroad: Suburban Trains" (timetable), courtesy Aaron Isaacs. Cartography by Birgit Mühlenhaus and Ross Donihue, 2011.

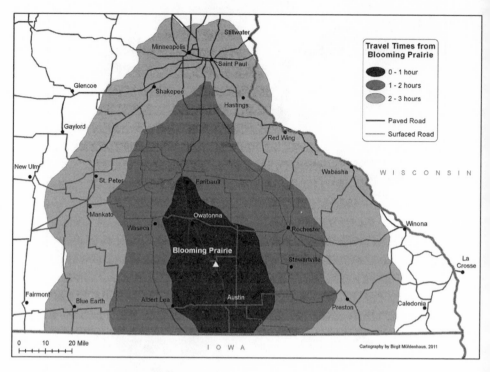

4.6 Time-distance map of travel by automobile from downtown Blooming Prairie, Minnesota, 1930. Based on Minnesota Department of Highway, *1930 Condition Map of Minnesota Trunk Highways.* Cartography by Birgit Mühlenhaus, 2011.

not approximate the speed or comfort of railroads over long distances, particularly along routes that lacked state-of-the-art highways, but compared to horses they could go farther, at less cost, and with fewer logistical challenges. (And unlike a horse, they could be maintained without a barn or the complications of feeding and caring for an animal.) As a result, by 1930 automobiles were helping create much less linear and hierarchical timesheds for local travel.

For rural motorists living in or near small towns, the new relationships between time and distance were particularly profound (fig. 4.6).[62] Because automobiles could travel wherever there were roads, and because roads were almost everywhere, they compressed space relatively uniformly, making distance a relatively straightforward function of time. The resulting time-distance patterns resembled concentric circles that created, in the words of the sociologist Amos Hawley, a "new scale of local distance."[63] In the case of Blooming Prairie, traveling by automobile eliminated the layovers in Austin that made it impractical to travel by rail to larger towns like Albert Lea. At 28 miles away, Albert Lea was located at the outer limits of a one-day, one-way trip by horse; by contrast, traveling by car required roughly an hour for a one-way trip.

In cities like St. Paul (fig. 4.7), traffic congestion and scarce parking facilities meant that cars changed mobility patterns somewhat less than in small rural towns, though it would be easy to overstate this point.[64] In 1930, most urban residents made regular, frequent trips downtown, resulting in large crowds in a confined space.[65] In St. Paul, whose population grew from 234,698 in 1920 to 271,606 in 1930, vehicular traffic entering and leaving downtown during a typical day nearly doubled in the first half of the decade, jumping from 52,000 in 1921 to 96,800 in 1926. More than 60 percent of commuters in 1926 still arrived by streetcar, as compared to 30 percent arriving by car—although automobiles greatly outnumbered streetcars as a percentage of traffic, ranging from a low ratio of 15:1 during the morning rush hour to an average ratio of 23:1 over the course of the day.[66] In addition, as more people turned to automobiles, streetcar ridership in St. Paul declined steadily, dropping from a peak of 89 million rides in 1920 to 51.8 million rides in 1930. By 1930, traffic congestion had substantially slowed all movement on the downtown streets of St. Paul, but people could still get most places in the city by streetcar and foot. Ridership nevertheless continued to drop—from 44.6 million rides in 1931 to 34.2 million rides in 1941.[67] Car ownership, by contrast, continued to rise, opening a host of new options for those who had them, including recreational drives into the countryside.

In commuter-rail suburbs like St. Paul Park, automobiles had perhaps their greatest effects—and created the most new opportunities (fig. 4.8).[68] Much as in small rural towns, cars enabled suburbanites to circumvent the linear, hierarchical patterns of rail-based transportation. Cars created easy access to parts of the metropolitan region that lacked direct rail service, including adjacent suburbs. So, too, did they create a "new scale of local distance" within suburban settlements, putting neighbors and local businesses in easy minutes' reach of each

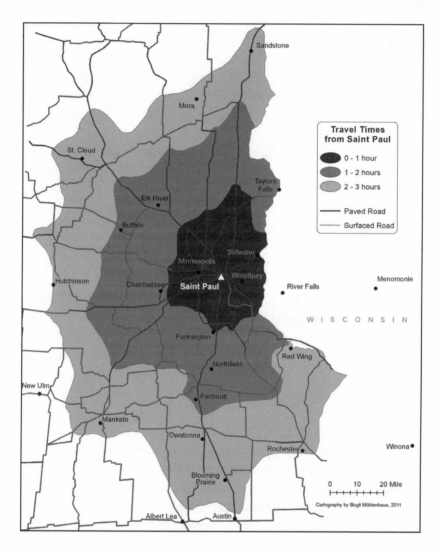

4.7 Time-distance map of travel by automobile from downtown St. Paul, Minnesota, 1930. Based on Minnesota Department of Highway, *1930 Condition Map of Minnesota Trunk Highways*. Cartography by Birgit Mühlenhaus, 2011.

other and opening land for development beyond easy walking distance of the railroad station. The same held true for the relationship between suburbs and the surrounding countryside, creating opportunities for recreation and travel independent of railroad routes and timetables. In

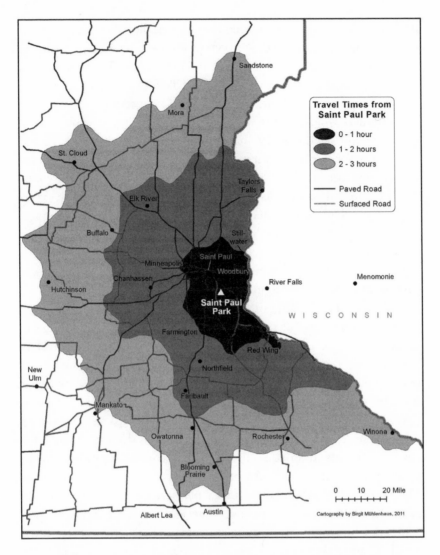

4.8 Time-distance map of travel by automobile from downtown St. Paul Park, Minnesota, 1930. Based on Minnesota Department of Highway, *1930 Condition Map of Minnesota Trunk Highways*. Cartography by Birgit Mühlenhaus, 2011.

addition, suburban motorists shared the opportunities that cars created for St. Paul's downtown residents. Automobile owners in St. Paul Park, for example, could choose between driving downtown *or* commuting by train (as long as the line remained in business). And finally, though suburban motorists faced the same traffic congestion and limited parking that plagued downtown residents, they were nevertheless well served by the disproportional attention that city planners and traffic engineers devoted to speeding the flow of arterial connections leading from the suburbs into central business districts.

Although where motorists lived and where they wanted to go greatly conditioned the new mobility options of the interwar period, several points stand out. First, motor-age mobility offered flexibility and convenience that rail-based alternatives, with their fixed routes and timetables, had trouble matching. Larger cities provided an exception, since downtown's dense development made walking practical, frequent streetcar service created high levels of mobility over a broad region, and traffic congestion and limited downtown parking compromised the automobile's speed and flexibility. Second, as cars became faster and more reliable, and as smooth road networks spread more thickly across the country, earlier environmental limits on travel in the form of inclement weather, steep hills, and long distances shrank in relative significance as major concerns for travelers. Third, since the automobile's speed and convenience transformed places that were nearby in distance into places that were also nearby in time, they tempted motorists to consider trips they would otherwise have skipped. Whether by taking more frequent trips to nearby small towns, venturing forth from the city for a Sunday drive, or having dinner with friends in an adjacent suburb, motorists everywhere began to imagine—and to take advantage of—new ways to move around. "The automobile not only provides a pleasant alternative to what are generally regarded as the inconveniences of necessity travel by rail," concluded one study of the subject in 1933; "it actually induces travel which would otherwise not be contemplated. An attitude of 'Let's go places and do things' follows naturally from extensive car ownership."[69] As a consequence of this attitude, motorists began to develop a new sense of their potential connections to the outside world.

Somewhat ironically, new automobile-inspired mobility patterns created tension with the work of those who were frantically trying to adapt the nation's infrastructure to growing automotive traffic. When rural highway administrators invested huge sums to improve roads only to find that new usage patterns were making them obsolete, for example, or when city traffic engineers sped the flow of downtown traffic only to find that the number of vehicles on downtown streets had doubled in five years, they responded by amplifying their efforts to expand and modify the existing infrastructure. Not until the end of the interwar years did they begin to seriously entertain proposals to radically alter landscapes by building new, entirely car-centered systems, such as limited-access freeways. In the meantime, however, as motorists reimagined their sense of place and how car use fit into their lives, they inspired a variety of groups hoping to capitalize on new motor-age mobility patterns to pioneer new spatial arrangements and consciously car-oriented land uses—most of them on a small scale and at the local level—that took automobile-based mobility for granted.

CENTRALIZATION, DECENTRALIZATION, AND THE SPATIAL LOGIC OF THE MOTOR AGE

As motorists created new patterns of everyday mobility, a growing variety of institutions, both public and private, began to experiment with new ways to adjust to—and profit from—growing numbers of motorists. As they did so, the logic behind the spatial organization of the American landscape began to change. In rural areas, where isolation had long been the bane of rural reformers, dispersed institutions consolidated their activities and relocated to more centralized locations. As a result, everyday life in agricultural communities increasingly reoriented itself around towns rather than rural neighborhoods, a shift that significantly increased the mobility requirements of large numbers of rural Americans. In urban areas, on the other hand, the pronounced trend was toward decentralization. Reformers had long blamed overcrowding and congestion as the main causes of urban strife, and real estate entrepreneurs eagerly promoted new suburban developments as a solution. Meanwhile, as downtown traffic congestion and parking woes became more pronounced, businesses experimented with new locations outside the city center. At the same time, businesses catering directly to swelling automotive traffic sprouted along highways across the country. In all cases, as institutions redistributed themselves to take advantage of growing numbers of motorists, older geographical patterns—including those oriented around less mobile parts of the population—began to break down or disappear entirely. As a result, automobiles became increasingly necessary, especially in rural and suburban America, to maintain easy access to important institutions and services.

As automobiles and hard roads dispersed into all but the most isolated rural areas during the interwar period, rural geography began to change.[70] Open-country rural neighborhoods—knitted together by their affiliation with loosely clustered local institutions—suffered terribly as crossroads general stores lost business and closed, one-room schoolhouses died out, and the number of rural churches dropped precipitously. As institutions that had once provided cohesion to open-country rural neighborhoods began to vanish, new patterns of social organization appeared. Rural neighborhoods near villages, for example, often became absorbed entirely into village life, whereas smaller villages and hamlets, particularly those with five hundred or fewer residents, lost their central role in community life to larger nearby towns. As a result, bigger rural towns grew in size and standing but also lost some of their traditional business functions to larger towns and cities.[71] "In those instances in which better facilities for motor-car transportation have come to isolated villages, the result has been materially to enlarge the size of the trade areas, and also to encourage their residents to come to the village more frequently," concluded a 1937 study. "With respect to villages near larger centers, improved transportation has caused some gain in size of trade areas, but has also caused the residents to shift some of their trade to the attractive stores of towns and cities."[72]

Greater rural mobility lay at the heart of these changes. Because fast cars and hard roads allowed rural residents to travel greater distances in less time, institutions could effectively attract more people from a larger area. This had several implications. First, it meant that centrally located institutions tended to grow by absorbing the functions of smaller, peripheral institutions. When rural one-room schoolhouses closed, for example, it was not because local children ceased needing schools—it was because improved mobility gave school reformers, who had long championed the idea of school consolidation, a practical and affordable means to implement their ideas. "Where it was necessary to have eight one-room schools in the past, there is now a single eight-room school," wrote one enthusiastic proponent. "The children are grouped together according to age and ability and they are taught by a teacher who is experienced in handling their particular problems and who has the time to specialize on difficult children."[73] Similarly, church closings indicated consolidation and shifting patterns of attendance, not a sudden loss of rural religiosity. According to one study, for example, the percentage of open-country members in village church congregations rose from 22.6 percent in 1920 to 39.3 percent in 1930, and in town church congregations rose from 6 percent to 22.6 percent.[74]

Second, the ability to attract people from a greater geographical area meant institutions could grow and offer a greater variety of activities or services. Because consolidated schools allowed the pooling of resources, for example, they were typically better equipped—and more varied in their programming and extracurricular activities—than the many small schools they replaced. Similarly, centrally located merchants, including a growing number of chain stores, could offer both a greater selection of merchandise and lower prices than smaller crossroads general stores. As a result, many village merchants expanded their trade area substantially in the interwar period—even as the Great Depression sliced their sales volume, on average, by half. On the other hand, improved mobility gave rural motorists access to services that had previously been beyond practical reach. Poor roads, for example, had once forced sick rural patients to wait for a home visit from a general practitioner with limited equipment and no facilities, whereas smooth roads and fast vehicles gave growing numbers of people safe, practical access to modern, well-equipped hospitals employing various specialists. "Today this town hasn't even a doctor," wrote an ambivalent E. B. White in a 1938 essay ruminating on these changes. "It doesn't have to have a doctor. If you chop off your toe with an ax you get into somebody's car and he drives you ten miles to the next town where there is a doctor. For movies you drive twenty-five miles. For a railroad junction, fifty."[75]

Third, greater rural mobility eroded the powerful influences of kinship, nationality, religion, and especially locality on rural institutions. Before the arrival of automobiles, rural residents made do with the limited array of institutions and neighbors within easy reach.

With cars and improved roads, on the other hand, motorists could meet easily and regularly with others to pursue common interests. As a result, sociological studies showed that the membership of rural social organizations became more voluntary and interest-based during the interwar years as distance became less of a barrier to social interaction. Group activities often changed to reflect this new reality.[76]

Although improved mobility ultimately had profound implications for rural spatial arrangements, the effects could be subtle and difficult to trace. In many ways rural spatial arrangements did not change. Towns stayed put. Farmland remained where it was. Highways gained hard surfaces but aside from an occasional realignment usually did not change course. The spatial distribution of institutions, on the other hand, changed significantly. One-room schoolhouses, small country churches, and crossroads general stores shut down in droves, while town-based schools, churches, and merchants became much more important in the everyday lives of open-country residents. By the end of the interwar period, as the once-ubiquitous small, local institutions of rural America disappeared, one study concluded that "the village or town center has become the capital of rural America. The crossroads neighborhood is no longer the chief integrating social factor in rural life."[77]

As small rural institutions closed, open-country residents found themselves increasingly dependent on the easy mobility that cars conferred. When a nearby one-room school, church, or general store closed, residents either went without the services of those institutions or, more frequently, bussed to a new consolidated school, traveled to a more distant place of worship, or went to town to shop. Cars made doing so both possible and convenient, making life easier and less isolating for legions of rural Americans in the process. For many, after all, motoring a longer distance (in a fast, reliable car over a smooth, well-maintained road) actually required less time and effort than going a shorter distance to a nearby institution by foot or horse. The rural sociological studies of the period are rife with evidence that rural Americans, and especially those in more isolated areas, enjoyed an explosion of social contacts after acquiring cars. They made more trips to town, visited more often with neighbors, and participated more frequently in planned social activities. "*Contacts within the community are multiplied out of proportion to contacts at a distance*," concluded two researchers in 1933. "Figuratively, while he meets with the stranger at a distance ten times to his father's once, his encounters with his neighbors are multiplied a hundred-fold."[78] Yet this benefit existed only for car owners and came at the cost of heightening the isolation of the carless.

The combination of fast cars and smooth roads, in other words, helped rural residents overcome the limitations of distance, geography, and the weather as serious obstacles to social interaction—for those who had cars. The closure of small open-country institutions raised the stakes for car ownership, making easy mobility a prerequisite for access to key goods, services, and social opportunities. The disappearance of open-country institutions—no matter how meager compared to those of nearby villages—meant that residents of such areas had little choice but to significantly expand the distances they traveled to conduct their everyday affairs. As a result, it became increasingly impractical for growing numbers of rural Americans to conduct their lives without access to a car. Not surprisingly, rural automobile ownership increased dramatically during the 1920s, with the number of farm families owning an automobile expanding from 30.7 percent in 1920 to 58 percent in 1930.[79] In 1935, a survey of thirty thousand New York Farm Bureau members showed that 98 percent owned at least one automobile or truck.[80] "Everything in life is somewhere else," concluded E. B. White, "and you get there in a car."[81]

In American cities, the new mobility options that improved cars and roads created manifested themselves in the opposite direction, enabling *decentralization* rather than the centralization sweeping rural America. This proved true in large part because, where contemporaries regarded the key rural problem as isolation, they regarded the key urban problem as congestion.

With hundreds of thousands of vehicles and pedestrians jamming narrow downtown streets and intersections every day by the early 1920s, many city leaders embraced decentralization as the key to counteracting worsening congestion. "Cities become so crowded that they cannot use their advantages," wrote one student of the problem in 1925, "exactly as an army jammed into a narrow space cannot maneuver systematically and becomes a mob."[82] Ironically, concerted efforts to decentralize urban housing along streetcar lines had helped create the problem by producing an exaggerated dependence among outlying residents on the central business district, making it *the* place to go: to work, to transact business, to shop, to find entertainment. Contemporaries called their frequent use of streetcars to get downtown "the riding habit," the significance of which is best illustrated by comparing the rate of population growth and streetcar use before 1920. Between 1890 and 1920, the nation's urban population boomed impressively, rising by approximately two and a half times. During that same period, however, urban streetcar ridership nearly octupled from 2 billion rides per year to roughly 15.5 billion rides per year.[83] Where population grew arithmetically, streetcar ridership grew geometrically.[84]

In this context, the flood of automobiles that began in the 1910s and accelerated in the 1920s dramatically worsened urban congestion. Downtown districts, already starved for space, became even more so as cars poured onto narrow downtown streets. "In the congested districts of some cities thousands of vehicles are forced to stand idle as much as half of their working time. The loss in gasoline alone is almost unbelievable," one contemporary observed. "Added to this must be the loss of time of drivers of commercial vehicles and persons in passenger cars and streetcars. Congestion slows the business of the city, and in making business more costly, it adds greatly to the cost of living."[85] A veritable Gordian knot of parking problems exacerbated the situation. "Politics," declared the comedian Will Rogers in 1924, "ain't worrying this Country one tenth as much as Parking Space."[86] Complaints about "parking hogs" and "the all-day parker" abounded, but legal time limits proved impossible to enforce.[87] Traffic engineers initially favored parking bans, in part because traffic surveys produced a comprehensive catalog of how parked cars interfered with traffic: robbing vehicles of traffic lanes, slowing streetcars, and hindering traffic as cars moved in and out of curbside parking spots.[88] Yet leaders feared parking bans would discourage motorists from shopping downtown, a position that Los Angeles's disastrous—and short-lived—parking ban in April 1920 helped solidify.[89] In most cities, parking bans were a political nonstarter. Proposals for multistory parking garages also went nowhere, since they were expensive and yielded lower returns than other uses of downtown real estate.[90]

But if automobiles aggravated congestion downtown, they also made it easier for automobile owners to live in decentralized locations. "We shall solve the City Problem by leaving the City," declared Henry Ford in one of his oft-quoted aphorisms. "Get the people into the country, get them into communities where a man knows his neighbor, where there is a commonality of interest, where life is not artificial, and you have solved the City Problem. You have solved it by eliminating the City."[91] As downtown interests struggled with snarled traffic and inadequate parking, real estate developers seized on Ford's logic—not to eliminate the city, as Ford suggested, but to expand it in a radically new car-dependent form on the city's outer fringe.[92]

Before World War I most cities had developed in a star-shaped pattern, with development radiating outward from downtown within walking distance of rail lines. By the 1920s, however, real estate speculators began marketing areas beyond the streetcar system to car owners.[93] Some such developments were unplanned and chaotic, comprised of self-built homes from mail-order kits, while others resembled streetcar suburbs aside from their obvious lack of streetcar access.[94] Still others, especially at the upper end of the market, resembled exclusive commuter-rail suburbs. "This type of suburb is usually carefully planned from the beginning, restricted, and landscaped," one contemporary observed. "There is here an absence of congestion, high buildings, or other indications of the city. Nearly the whole area consists of private dwellings on spacious grounds."[95]

Suburban growth of all types proceeded rapidly after World War I. In the eighty-five American cities with 100,000 residents or more during the 1920s, for example, the growth rate of suburban areas (39.2 percent) more than doubled the urban growth rate (19.4 percent).[96] Much of this occurred in car-dependent locations, prompting the President's Research Committee on Social Trends to conclude in 1933 that the old star-shaped pattern of growth had been rendered obsolete by metropolitan regions characterized by "a cluster or constellation of communities—villages, towns, and cities—with varying degrees of dependency upon the central city."[97] The Great Depression substantially slowed but did not stop such growth, and by 1940 an estimated 13 million Americans lived in suburban areas that lacked access to public transportation.[98]

The low-density development of new rail-free suburbs had important implications for the daily mobility requirements of their residents.
Because the average car suburb's building lot during this period was
roughly five thousand square feet, as compared to three thousand
square feet for streetcar suburbs, car suburbs had much lower population densities.[99] This translated into less support for local institutions
and retail establishments, which in turn meant longer distances for residents to travel to access everyday goods and services—many of which
lay outside their own suburb. Long distances and the lack of public
transportation meant that most (if not all) travel occurred by car.

Perhaps the most famous interwar car-based suburb, J. C. Nichols's
Country Club District outside of Kansas City, was notable in three
significant ways. First, Nichols used self-perpetuating deed restrictions—enforced by homeowners associations—to dictate the type,
minimum size, minimum price, and setback distance of houses as
well as to control the size and location of outbuildings and garages.[100]
Second, a particularly noteworthy deed restriction banned sales to or
occupancy by African Americans, emphasizing the degree to which
the new mobility that cars created did not extend equally or without
complication to all motorists. Although the Supreme Court had effectively barred the use of zoning as a tool for racial discrimination when
it struck down Louisville, Kentucky's racially exclusive zoning ordinance in 1917, the restrictive covenants that Nichols helped to popular-
ize remained a powerful tool for racial and religious discrimination in
real estate until 1948, when the Supreme Court finally made discrimi-
natory deed restrictions unenforceable.[101] Third, in 1922 Nichols began
construction on the Country Club Plaza, the nation's first decentralized, large-scale, car-centered shopping center. Many of Nichols's ideas
about suburban development were borrowed and synthesized from
others, but the Country Club Plaza was genuinely new—an amenity-
rich, car-oriented retail center catering to the Country Club District's
affluent residents. Comprising a mix of high-end specialty goods and
everyday convenience goods and services, Country Club Plaza became
a popular retail center that attracted customers from both within and
beyond the neighborhood.[102]

The Country Club Plaza heralded a second major development of
the 1920s: the rapid decentralization of urban retail. Several interrelated

factors fostered the trend. First, decentralization reflected the decision by some retailers to escape downtown's growing problems—including high rents, traffic congestion, and parking shortages—by relocating to outlying locations. Second, it demonstrated a growing willingness among retailers to risk their survival on their ability to attract motorist-consumers. Third, it reflected a growing understanding of how new retail practices were transforming the relationships between retailers and the trade area that they served. Finally, as outlying retailers became more dependent on shoppers arriving by car, they began to devise more car-friendly site layouts and to pay closer attention to ensuring ample parking for their customers.

Although these trends played out across the country, they are most easily seen in Los Angeles, where numerous car-oriented innovations originated.[103] Between the 1880s and the 1910s, Los Angeles had cemented its distinctive form as a sprawling city of detached single-family residences—not in response to the automobile, as is widely but mistakenly believed, but because of close ties between real estate development and the city's vast streetcar system, which at its peak operated 1,164 miles of track across the Greater Los Angeles area.[104] Like other big cities, Los Angeles's streetcar lines converged downtown in a compact, pedestrian-oriented retail district featuring both large department stores and a wide range of smaller specialty shops. Also like other big cities, during the 1910s a flood of automobiles began to push downtown traffic congestion in Los Angeles to the breaking point—prompting a series of changes that began Los Angeles's transformation into the famously car-dependent city that it is today.

Downtown retailers experimented with a variety of responses to the city's mounting problems. Some, especially large department stores, tried to resolve parking shortages by contracting with nearby private parking lots to provide parking for their customers. Others took the more radical approach of changing their location. Some new department stores, for example, opened along major streetcar routes on the edge of downtown in the direction of affluent settlement, while some smaller specialty retailers fled the core's high rents by forming a new shopping district on Flower Street, just beyond downtown's edge.[105] Many more small retailers, especially hardware stores, laundries, grocers, barbershops, branch banks, and chain stores, ventured significantly farther afield, clustering at streetcar stops in established outlying neighborhoods. Most commonly these formed small aggregations of two to ten businesses in basic storefront buildings called "taxpayer blocks," but some major arteries boasted multiblock, linear developments with as many as one hundred stores.[106] Between 1918 and 1922, for example, the number of stores in the "Wonder Street" section of Western Avenue (once the western boundary of the city) jumped from seven to around eighty, drawing customers by foot, streetcar, and automobile from as much as a three-mile radius.[107]

Buoyed by these experiments and inspired by growing numbers of car owners, by the mid-1920s Los Angeles retailers began opening in outlying locations not served by streetcars. By the end of the decade, for example, a corridor of small stores stretched some twenty-three blocks westward from downtown Los Angeles along Wilshire Boulevard, a major automotive approach into the city. Lacking a streetcar line, this new retail district relied on motorist-consumers, who were attracted to its location on a broad artery with fast-moving traffic and ample curbside parking.[108] Larger retailers, too, relocated outside of downtown. The most notable example was Bullock's, a high-end downtown department store, which opened a large branch store on Wilshire in 1928—two and a half miles west of downtown. Its orientation toward cars was unmistakable, both in its location and its unusual large, on-site parking lot.[109] A similarly ambitious car-oriented development was the "Miracle Mile," a vast linear retail corridor on Wilshire that began three and a half miles beyond Bullock's, six miles from downtown. Conceived in the early 1920s, it grew explosively after 1928, attracting a diverse mix that ranged from branch-store operations of downtown retailers to modest storefronts specializing in everyday convenience goods and services. The strip quickly rivaled downtown for the patronage of motorists in the western part of the city. Unlike downtown, which had little new construction during the Great Depression, the Miracle Mile successfully attracted new stores—especially chain stores and branch department stores—during the second half of the 1930s.[110]

If the willingness to experiment with decentralized locations was partly a reaction to the problems of downtown, it also reflected the period's sweeping changes in retail practice, as illustrated by the rise of the supermarket. In the early twentieth century, urban food shoppers typically patronized a variety of specialized vendors, including butchers for meat, vegetable dealers and farmers' markets for produce, milkmen for dairy, and grocers for foods from boxes, bins, barrels, cans, and vats. Haggling determined most prices, and clerks retrieved, by request, goods from tall shelves and glass display counters—out of customers' reach. Storekeepers cultivated loyalty by providing personal services like free delivery and liberal credit. In the interwar period, though, retailers began to eliminate many of the personal interactions and services that characterized earlier retail.

Policies like self-service (which put goods out for customers to peruse), fixed prices (which eliminated haggling), and cash-and-carry (which eliminated credit and home delivery), along with larger stocks of prepackaged, advertised, name-brand goods, transformed both the bottom-line logic of storekeepers and the shopping experiences of customers.[111] Early in the Great Depression, when food surpluses created fierce price competition and tight profit margins for food retailers, a new type of grocery store, the "supermarket," began to thrive. Offering all types of food, supermarkets kept prices low by combining earlier innovations with bulk purchasing, careful management, and high-volume sales and by seeking large, low-rent spaces in outlying locations. This location strategy hinged on both the ability—and the willingness—of customers to drive several extra miles in order to save a few dollars on their grocery bill. It succeeded wildly, and by the end of the interwar period a dramatic shift toward supermarkets had transformed food retailing.[112]

As other retailers undertook similar transformations, they planted some of the most significant seeds of Car Country. When retailers adopted a business model premised on low prices and high-volume trade, for example, they committed to attracting large numbers of daily customers to earn profits. Because outlying areas had lower densities than older urban neighborhoods, residents within walking distance could not provide a sufficient volume of business. Moreover, unlike downtown retailers they could not count on streetcars to deliver large crowds to their doors. In short, they had to draw customers from a relatively large geographical area—which meant attracting people arriving in cars.

As car-oriented retailers proliferated, congestion and parking shortages spread to some outlying business districts, prompting experiments with site layouts that would better accommodate cars. In Los Angeles, for example, gas stations and food markets pioneered what evolved into an L-shaped arrangement, with vendors arrayed around a common forecourt used for parking. The layout spread during the 1930s to planned neighborhood shopping centers, which usually had between eight and twenty small businesses catering to the everyday needs of nearby residents. Developed and managed as a unit, and sharing a common parking lot, they were almost always anchored by a supermarket, typically included a drug store, and often featured chain-store tenants.[113]

As these various changes accumulated, Los Angeles led the nation by the late 1930s as a city remaking itself around cars. "Los Angeles is a city built on the automobile as Boston was built on the sailing ship," observed an author in *Architectural Record* in 1937. "[It] appears to the casual view as a series of parking lots interspersed with buildings."[114] Other cities did not follow as thoroughly or as quickly—at least not yet—but many smaller stores failed under the dual pressures of low-priced competition and the economic hardships of the Great Depression. As they disappeared, so did some of the walkable retail options in many neighborhoods, ratcheting up the distances that residents had to travel to perform the same activities.

Few turned to streetcars to meet their heightened need for mobility. With car-oriented retailers proliferating, in fact, streetcar systems entered a period of crisis. Not only did cars free millions of Americans from their dependence on streetcars to get downtown, but the trend toward decentralized retail also reduced their dependence on downtown businesses, especially for everyday goods and services. Not surprisingly, streetcar ridership declined in city after city during the 1920s: between 10 and 20 percent in the biggest cities with the largest riderships, such as Boston, Philadelphia, and Chicago, and a more dramatic 40 to 50 percent in cities like Buffalo, Cleveland, and Los Angeles. The dismal declines continued in the 1930s, with streetcar ridership plummeting from 12 billion trips per year nationally in 1928 to 7.2 billion in 1937.[115]

Politically, streetcar companies garnered little sympathy for their plight. Long-standing resentments lingered over monopoly management, spotty service, and overcrowded cars. Many believed—despite evidence to the contrary—that only mismanagement could explain their failure to make money. As a result, political support for heavy regulation and fixed fares remained entrenched, and opposition to subsidizing streetcars remained strong. In stark contrast, the exhilarating freedom of driving, coupled with the idea that streets were public spaces that ought to be improved at public expense, generated substantial political support for large public investments in expensive public works projects for the benefit of motorists. As a result, streetcar companies hemorrhaged money even as public investments in roads and streets soared to unprecedented heights. [116]

Meanwhile, downtown businesses struggled. Parking shortages improved somewhat in the 1930s, when the owners of vacant or otherwise unprofitable buildings razed existing structures to reduce tax valuations and opened parking lots to generate cash flow.[117] The late 1930s also saw the proliferation of parking meters—the first of which were installed in Kansas City in 1935—which effectively discouraged all-day street parking while generating reliable municipal revenue.[118] As off-street parking spaces multiplied and parking meters increased the turnover of on-street spots, many cities began to get a handle on their parking problems for the first time since the rapid growth of automotive traffic began. Downtown's accessibility, on the other hand, remained a thorny issue, prompting cities across the country to draft plans for hugely expensive expressways as a way to facilitate the movement of cars to and from downtown. In the face of growing competition from outlying business districts, downtown was no longer *the* business district, but rather the largest and most central of many competing districts scattered across the city.[119] And though downtown remained accessible by streetcar, many of the new competing business districts were entirely car-dependent—in their location, in their site plans, and in their business practices.

In the same years that rural institutions centralized and urban institutions decentralized, a third distinctive trend took shape along what the writer and critic James Agee dubbed "the Great American Roadside."[120] Especially on highways with growing automotive traffic, entrepreneurs created an astonishing array of businesses—including gas stations, restaurants, bars, roadhouses, and overnight accommodations—that specifically catered to motorists. In addition, other car-oriented businesses appeared along the many "miracle miles" that cropped up on the edges of cities across the nation in emulation of the Los Angeles original, including auto showrooms, repair shops, supermarkets, mini–golf courses, and even drive-in movie theaters.[121]

In the early interwar years, small entrepreneurs with little capital launched most of these establishments. Restaurants proliferated, and many thrived. Truck stops offered meals and a full tank of gasoline; roadside stands hawked everything from farm produce to sandwiches and lemonade; small shacks offered hot dogs, barbecue, ice cream, doughnuts, fried chicken, hamburgers, coffee, and every regional specialty imaginable. For the more refined tastes of middle-class motorists, "tearooms" appeared—often in quaint abandoned buildings carefully decorated to evoke nostalgic associations—as did family restaurants.[122] When roadside commerce remained profitable during the Great Depression, roadside offerings became even more numerous as those unable to find work opened low-overhead retail operations like restaurants and gasoline filling stations.[123]

Growing competition spurred investment, and many roadside operations grew bigger, fancier, and more amenity-rich. Roadside accommodations, for example, evolved rapidly. In the early 1920s, small-town chambers of commerce began to finance free municipal campgrounds with communal sanitary facilities in order to attract tourists to Main Street businesses. In the mid-1920s, free camps gave way to camps charging a nominal fee to discourage vagrants and "undesirables." Private camps soon entered the fray, and escalating competition produced a steady accretion of new amenities. By the late 1920s and early 1930s, entire "cabin camps" of multiple small cabins appeared, each unit with its own bathroom and furnishings. By the late 1930s, the modern motel was born.[124] A similar story played out in other roadside industries, with those catering to the profitable middle-class market often attracting significant investment and attention from chains.

At the heart of the steadily expanding Great American Roadside, however, resided a paradox: where roadside entrepreneurs wanted motorists to stop and spend time and money, motorists more often had the goal of *going*, often as fast as possible.[125] Roadside vendors combated motorists' inclinations in a variety of ways. Signs sprouted like color-ful roadside weeds in an inharmonious cacophony of hand-painted placards, billboards, and neon lights, creating a country cousin to the elaborate visual displays of big-city venues like New York City's Times Square.[126] Architecture, too, provided a blank canvas for the fecund imaginations of roadside proprietors. During the 1920s, especially, it became popular to fashion buildings in eye-catching ways. Hot dog–shaped hot dog carts, pot-shaped coffeehouses, and keg-shaped root beer stands joined tourist cabins mimicking tepees, Dutch wind-mills, and rustic log cabins.[127] Architecture could signal "middle-class respectability" as well, as it did for the Howard Johnson's chain of fam-ily restaurants, which paired neoclassical features like shuttered win-dows and porticoed entrances with distinctive, eye-catching orange roofs.[128] By the 1930s, roadside establishments also became fertile ground for refining the relationship between building functions and the circulation and parking of automobiles, as in the evolving designs of gas stations, drive-in restaurants, and drive-in movie theaters.[129]

Legions of critics scorned the brazen commercialism and tacky aesthetics of the Great American Roadside, but for its entrepreneurs, many of whom operated on the margins of the economy, the desire to make a living by catering to the growing stream of passing motor-ists superseded all ideas about the "proper" aesthetic qualities of the countryside.[130] Many farmers subdivided roadside property into com-mercial lots and rented or sold to the highest bidders. Others erected small villages of tourist cabins, a small grocery, and a filling station and went into business themselves. The economic logic for doing so was impeccable—tourist cabins, to take just one example, were the only sector of the construction industry to expand during the worst years of the Great Depression.[131] Yet the cumulative effects of road-side commerce appalled critics who denounced the rampant com-mercialism as a cancerous blight. "Hot Dog Trail has stretched its vulgar, desecrating length over hill and valley, beach and cliff, until the most permanent memory of what the automobile associations optimistically call 'ideal tours' is the memory of a string of Eddie's Red Hot Eats, of Charlie's Camper's Cottages, of Gus's Free Air and Water, not forgetting Ye Olde Tyme Gyfte Shoppes," wrote one frus-trated observer in 1928. "Whole communities ha[ve] been thoroughly grounded in the practice of regarding 'nature' as a background for mercantile information."[132]

Although some could not see beyond what Agee described as "the scorching ugliness of badly planned and laid out concrete roads peppered with impudent billboards," others saw the Great American Roadside as a purely logical response to an increasingly mobile, motorized American consumer.[133] To collect some of these new consumers' money, entrepreneurs jettisoned long-held ideas about the location of retail establishments and experimented—successfully—with roadside operations.[134] Bypass routes and approach strips, especially, became popular retail locations since each was well sited to attract customers from among town residents *and* from highway through traffic.

Taken as a whole, the Great American Roadside represents one of the nation's earliest and most thoroughly car-dominated landscapes. Oriented entirely around the needs of motorists and easily accessible only by motor vehicle, roadside commerce expanded rapidly during the interwar years, creating an entirely new type of American landscape—the motor age's version of Main Street. Though it and other car-oriented landscapes were still new enough during the interwar years to be noteworthy—still the exception rather than the rule—they were prevalent enough to be quite familiar to millions of American motorists. "Oh yes, you know this road," Agee concluded, "and you know this roadside."[135]

CONCLUSION

The interwar changes to the American landscape may seem chaotic, but the actions of three important groups stand out for their significance. First were those charged with the herculean task of adapting the nation's roads and streets to the motor age. This included both highway builders (who had significant resources at their disposal) and city planners and traffic engineers (who did not). How they decided to adapt roads and streets to the flood of automobiles made car use significantly easier, yet even their best efforts failed to resolve the traffic crisis. Second were motorists themselves. Reliable automobiles and rapidly expanding networks of smooth roads overcame long-standing environmental constraints on transportation, creating new options for personal mobility that sharply contrasted with railroad- and streetcar-based mobility. As motorists experimented with new uses for their automobiles, they unlocked whole new realms of possibilities and began altering their everyday activities in response. Third were those who began to redesign various institutions around motorists' new mobility patterns by devising new, thoroughly car-oriented land uses. Rural institutions centralized, diversified, and expanded, while urban real estate developers and retailers experimented with decentralization strategies and car-focused site layouts that targeted large and growing numbers of motorists.

Ironically, because the caretakers of the nation's streets and highways found themselves constantly trying to catch up to the enormous demands of skyrocketing automobile ownership, they did much less to reshape the American landscape than they might have, particularly given the enormous sums at their disposal. Instead it was private entrepreneurs seeking ways to profit from growing legions of motorists who designed and introduced the most significant new car-oriented landscapes.

On the surface, the new land-use patterns that resulted were mundane: the growth of small-town businesses catering to farmers, the profusion of consolidated rural schools, the creeping growth of suburban districts of single-family homes, the smattering of new neighborhood shopping centers with small parking lots, the gas stations and restaurants that sprouted along every highway of any consequence. Taken alone, none of these qualified as revolutionary, but taken together they pointed toward the steady spread of Car Country's signature car-dependent landscapes. As car-oriented institutions proliferated, people increasingly needed cars to take advantage of what those institutions had to offer. It remained relatively easy to get around without a car in most big cities, but—aided by the spread of smooth roads, the careful calibrations of planners and traffic engineers, and a profusion of car-oriented institutions—getting places by car was often easier, faster, more convenient, and more pleasant than the available alternatives. Moreover, outside of big cities, institutions that were *not* car-centered either disappeared entirely or significantly narrowed their offerings during the interwar years. In such places, living without a car became increasingly difficult.

FIVE

FUELING THE BOOM

THE SAME SWELLING CAR USE THAT SPAWNED A NEW MOTOR-AGE geography had environmental repercussions that extended well beyond the emergence of the nation's first car-dependent landscapes. Among these, soaring car use generated surging demand for gasoline, which had particularly portentous implications for the environment. Fueled by automotive demand, oil companies entered a period of rapid, sustained growth that catapulted an industry originally designed to supply kerosene for lamps into direct competition with coal as the major supplier of the nation's energy needs. Moreover, the same sky-rocketing demand for gasoline that transformed the oil industry also offered a serendipitous solution—in the form of gasoline taxes—to the long-standing problem of how to pay for phenomenally expensive improvements to the nation's vast highway system.

Panorama of the oil fields, Los Angeles, California, 1906. E. W. Kelley, courtesy of Library of Congress Prints and Photographs Division, LC-USZ62-72117.

As a result, vast quantities of inexpensive oil became a cornerstone of the country's political economy during the interwar period, providing the fuel for swelling numbers of vehicles and financing the spread of an ever-more-expensive infrastructure of highways, particularly as states began to forge nearly unassailable legal links between gasoline-tax revenue and highway improvements. Together with new planning methods, these developments created a dynamic, politically insulated system in which growing car use and expanding road construction fed one another in a self-fueling cycle. Yet even as the pieces of this powerful new system moved into place, the combination of growing traffic problems and outspoken advocates for a national system of toll-financed "superhighways" threatened to upend the carefully crafted designs of highway administrators as the nation prepared to enter World War II.

FUELING CARS

Of the new establishments populating the interwar period's Great American Roadside, the most essential—and most completely car-oriented—was the gasoline filling station. Filling stations with dedicated pumping equipment had begun to appear in the mid-1910s to cater to motorists seeking a more convenient alternative to the assortment of grocery stores, hardware stores, drug stores, repair shops, machine shops, car dealers, and automotive garages that made the vast majority of gasoline sales during the 1910s.[1] This changed dramatically during the 1920s, however, as filling stations blossomed into an omnipresent feature of the American landscape. By 1927, roughly 265,000 curbside and drive-in filling stations accounted for better than 80 percent of all gasoline pumps in the United States.[2] Even during the Great Depression, gasoline retail outlets expanded even faster than car ownership, leaping from 317,000 in 1929 to 450,000 in 1939. Filling stations accounted for virtually all of the increase.[3]

Filling stations soon added new services, built stronger ties to big oil companies, and developed more car-friendly layouts. Beginning in Los Angeles, and becoming ubiquitous nationally by the mid-1930s, specialized filling stations began to remake themselves into "one-stop shops" for automobile service, repair, and upkeep by selling automotive accessories, performing repairs and maintenance, and eventually even adding car washes.[4] Likewise, service stations that had once been characterized by healthy numbers of independent owner-operators became increasingly affiliated with large oil companies, which were fighting to vertically integrate their operations as a way to ensure reliable outlets for growing quantities of fuel.[5] In addition, as owners of one of the first entirely car-oriented businesses, gasoline station proprietors were among the earliest to experiment with radical new ways to handle the on-site circulation and storage of automobiles, developing site arrangements that profoundly influenced the site layouts that other car-oriented retailers adopted.[6]

The proliferation of filling stations—and, eventually, the fortunes of the entire oil industry—closely paralleled the rise of the automobile. During the first American oil boom, which began in 1859 after Edwin L. Drake struck oil in Titusville, Pennsylvania, oil's market value derived from the illuminant kerosene, and it was upon kerosene that John D. Rockefeller built Standard Oil, the ruthlessly effective monopoly that dominated the industry until 1911, when the Supreme Court ordered its dissolution.[7] In these early years, many refiners simply dumped gasoline, a volatile and inexpensive by-product of kerosene production that was notoriously prone to explosions.[8] When the number of cars began multiplying in the 1910s, however, demand for gasoline surged.[9] "Then it was how to find an adequate and profitable market for [gasoline]," proclaimed the Oil and Gas Journal in 1912. "Now it is how to meet the ever-increasing demand for it."[10] Domestic gasoline distribution more than quadrupled from 89 million barrels in 1919 to 382 million barrels in 1929.[11] Even during the Great Depression, rising per-car fuel consumption offset most of the early 1930s dip in car ownership. Across the Depression, gasoline sales rose from 382 million barrels in 1929 to 668 million barrels in 1941, a reflection both of rising car ownership and of the growth of per-vehicle gas consumption from 525 gallons in 1929 to 648 gallons in 1941.[12] In one measure of gasoline's importance to the oil industry, by 1940 refineries earned 62 percent of their income from gasoline sales.[13]

To manage growing demand, the oil industry sought ways to improve its systems for finding and extracting oil, refining it into gasoline, and distributing it to filling stations. The first step was finding oil. It helped that the United States had vast oil reserves—enough to produce nearly twice as much annually as the rest of the world combined throughout the interwar period.[14] Sometimes described as "fossilized sunlight," oil is what remains of ancient organisms, such as plankton, that settled on the bottom of oceans some 10 million to 400 million years ago and became buried under layers of sediment. Geological processes then subjected it to huge pressure and heat over millions of years, ultimately transforming it into oil. Because it is liquid, much oil ultimately seeped upward to the surface and dispersed. But much also remained underground, trapped in deposits with ancient saltwater and natural gas, typically in reservoirs of porous sandstone and limestone underneath impermeable cap rock, such as chalk or shale.[15] As late as 1920, oil discoveries were still guided by studying aboveground geophysical structures—along with substantial guesswork and luck. By the mid-1920s, though, some prospectors began to adopt new gravimetric, seismic, and magnetic techniques that gave substantially more information about belowground geophysical structures.[16]

To bring oil to the surface, prospectors drilled wells through the cap rock and let the reservoir's natural pressure force its oil aboveground. This often produced that early symbol of the oil frontier, a "gusher": a spectacular, roaring jet of crude oil, gas, water, sand, and rock crashing upward through the derrick and hundreds of feet into the air before operators capped and captured the flow. Intense production in so-called flush fields created chaos and waste as producers scrambled to recover their investments before production peaked and surging production caused prices to drop.[17] Once the reservoir depressurized, pumps got to work. Eventually, as the reservoir drew down over a period of months or decades, the oil's viscosity increased enough that it was no longer economical to extract the often-sizable amounts of oil remaining underground.[18]

As late as 1899, fully 93 percent of American production came from the original Appalachian and Lima-Indiana oil fields, but a series of new discoveries, beginning with the massive Spindletop gusher in January 1901—visible four miles away in Beaumont, Texas—steadily shifted production westward. By 1919 the Appalachian and Lima-Indiana fields accounted for less than 10 percent of the national total.[19] Oil discoveries occurred all over the country, but Texas, California, Oklahoma, Louisiana, and Kansas were the biggest producers, with smaller but still significant fields in half a dozen other states.[20] The discovery of so many flush fields prompted a flurry of investment, drilling, and wealth but also caused violent oscillations between gluts and shortages that made oil a risky business. Fears of oil shortages in the early

1920s, for example, morphed into fears of overproduction by the 1930s. Profits waxed and waned accordingly.[21]

Oil's liquid character made it much easier to transport than coal, the nation's main energy source before 1950. Although similar geological processes produce both coal and oil, coal is bulkier and more difficult to handle. In addition, oil's energy density is approximately 50 percent higher than most coals. Whereas coal's bulk created dependence on rail- and water-based transportation, relatively small pumps could send oil flowing at low cost through dedicated pipelines from field to refinery.[22] As a result, an elaborate system of oil pipelines—a sort of national plumbing system dedicated to oil and its products—spread across the continent. Trunk pipeline mileage grew by 20,000 miles in the 1920s and then by another 14,000 miles in the 1930s.[23] Most pipelines linked oil fields directly to refineries, though some created indirect links via port and tanker.

Next in the chain, refineries distilled oil into a variety of commodities, the most valuable of which was gasoline. In its belowground state, crude oil is a complex mixture of hydrocarbons and organic compounds, and "refining" it initially meant separating its various components, known as "fractions." As refineries shifted from kerosene production to a wider range of products, however, they developed new processes to break the longer, complex molecules of crude's heavier, less valuable fractions into the shorter, more volatile molecules of the fuel fractions. The first such process, "thermal cracking," evolved between 1913 and 1920 and used carefully calibrated heat and pressure to wring roughly double the amount of gasoline from each barrel of crude.[24] Conflicting patent claims initially limited the technique's spread, but after their resolution the amount of cracked gasoline doubled from 34.4 million barrels in 1924 to 68.6 million in 1925, and then it nearly doubled again to 122.6 million barrels in 1928.[25] In the 1930s, automaker experiments with higher engine-compression ratios launched an "octane race," prompting a new round of experiments among refiners that led in the late 1930s to the commercialization of a second new process, "catalytic cracking." Catalytic cracking produced a better-quality fuel with higher octane ratings, and as military demand for high-quality fuels swelled after 1939, the process spread rapidly through the industry.[26]

Because demand for their most valuable products, like kerosene and gasoline, came from individuals making small-quantity purchases, refineries developed a system of "bulk stations" to receive and redistribute their output in smaller quantities to retailers. Through the late 1920s, most deliveries to bulk stations came by railroad tank cars, barges, or tankers. Then, in the 1930s, refineries began building new "product pipelines"—modeled on crude pipelines but devoted exclusively to refined products—that reduced reliance on expensive railroad tank cars. The new pipelines also undercut the advantages that refineries near large markets held over those located closer to oil fields. From bulk stations, early gasoline deliveries went out by horse-drawn tank car, supplemented in the 1920s by growing numbers of short-distance motor-truck deliveries. By the early 1930s, as automakers developed better tank trucks and as paved highways spread, refineries began delivering directly to filling stations up to 150 miles away from terminals, which significantly reduced the costs of bulk-station operations.[27]

Because of these arrangements, motorists during the interwar years could pull into any of a rapidly growing number of filling stations without any awareness of the environmental implications attached to filling their tanks. Indeed, as with much of the modern industrial economy, the oil industry's complex, geographically far-flung organization put significant distance between consumers and the processes that transformed oil into cheap, readily available gasoline. As a result, interwar motorists had little reason to feel any connection to the oil industry's environmentally destructive activities. By contrast, very little distance separated motorists from their own tailpipes: motorists bought gasoline, after all, with the explicit intention of burning it. Yet in the interwar context—with its coal-darkened skies and various accumulated sooty residues—many observers saw gasoline's relatively clean combustion as environmentally benign.[28] Indeed, scientific evidence for many of what today are recognized as the biggest environmental problems associated with large-scale car use did not accumulate until after World War II. The initial invisibility of these oil-related environmental problems—and the continuing degree to which they are difficult to see easily even today—is a significant part of their legacy.

Unlike burning gasoline, producing oil created obvious environmental damage and pollution. Beginning with the iconic gushers signaling a new oil strike, oil seeped everywhere from the production process in ways that disrupted aboveground ecosystems. Oil leaked profusely from the chaos enveloping flush fields, contaminating nearby streams and farms, seeping into the water table, and fueling frequent oil-field fires that sometimes raced out of control. "Contamination of groundwater supplies is quite common in and near oil fields," a 1935 study reported, "often because of careless drilling and casing operations or in the case of old fields because of defective and corroded well casings."[29] In the midcontinent oil-producing states, finding ways to dispose of oil-field brines without contaminating water supplies also created substantial challenges.[30]

Oil proved equally difficult to contain after it left the oil fields. Pipelines and tank cars leaked, manufacturers dumped used lubricants in waterways, and tanker captains discharged oil-contaminated ballast upon reaching port. The resulting pollution (and related harbor fires) became significant enough to prompt passage of the federal Oil Pollution Act of 1924—a toothless law, but also the only major twentieth-century federal legislation regarding water pollution before 1948.[31] Refinery wastes, too, created a range of problems. According to one investigation, these included "increased chlorine demand and tastes and odors in public water supplies, damage to bathing and other recreational areas, tainted flavor and destruction of fishes, shellfish and other aquatic life, ruination of waters for livestock and depletion of dissolved oxygen of receiving waters."[32] Refineries also posed serious safety and health hazards for their workers and nearby residents, who suffered from abnormally high cancer rates.[33] At filling stations, leaking storage tanks both above- and belowground contaminated groundwater supplies.[34] "It may be safely stated that all agencies engaged in the production, transportation, handling, or use of oil, must be considered as actual or potential sources of pollution," a 1930 study concluded. "In addition to the marine sources, consideration must be given to such land sources as wells and fields, oil terminals or loading points, refineries, railroads, and a host of industrial plants of different kinds, not excluding public service stations and garages."[35]

In addition to the pollution that extracting, transporting, refining, and distributing oil created, serious resource-management issues wracked the interwar oil industry. The nub of the industry's problem originated in American property law, which operated on a principle inherited from English common law known as the "rule of capture." This rule stated that, although all property owners had access rights to mineral resources below their property, no one owned them until they were "captured" and in the owner's direct possession. The result was a classic race to the bottom: because the land above most oil fields was extensive and divided into many parcels, because the rule of capture conferred ownership only upon oil's extraction, and because oil was liquid and thus migrated underground, those who extracted the most oil before the pumps failed profited most. Conversely, the longer anyone above a field waited to drill, the less oil—and thus profit—would remain.[36] The predictable profusion of wells that resulted caused reservoir pressures to drop quickly, so that on average 60 to 90 percent of the oil in any given reservoir remained underground as too expensive to recover.[37] "The losses thus caused [by the rule of capture]," proclaimed Henry Bates, the dean of the University of Michigan Law School, in 1935, "unquestionably mount into the billions of dollars and constitute the most reckless, extravagant waste of natural resources which even the American people have been guilty of."[38]

In a curious twist, the federal government ultimately imposed rules that reduced the industry's wasteful practices, not because those practices left too much oil underground, but because they brought too much to the surface. Fears of oil shortages during the early 1920s quickly gave way after 1926 to chronic overproduction as prospectors discovered one major oil field after another. Prices plummeted as production soared, prompting big oil companies to integrate their activities in the face of ruinous competition. When the stock market crashed in 1929, the upward trajectory of demand for oil suddenly leveled out. Then, in October 1930, when things already seemed to be at their worst, the first well blew in on East Texas's "Black Giant"—a reservoir five to ten miles wide and forty-five miles long that dwarfed other big American oil fields. Production in East Texas surged, and average per-barrel oil prices, which had already dropped from $1.85 in 1926 to $1.00 by 1930, plunged to $0.15 in May 1931. State-imposed production quotas—enforced by several thousand National Guardsmen and Texas Rangers—instilled temporary order, but an elaborate smuggling system for "hot oil" developed and by 1933 prices had fallen again.

The federal government finally intervened in 1933 to save the industry from its own excess, creating an "Oil Code" under the National Industrial Recovery Act (NIRA) that created and enforced production quotas allotted by state. With the rule of capture terminated, prices rose. When the Supreme Court ruled NIRA unconstitutional in 1935, a new federal-state system of voluntary quotas replaced the old Oil Code. Prices remained stable, and industry insiders breathed a long sigh of relief.[39]

Like production-related pollution and wasted resources, tailpipe emissions also had significant environmental implications, although two of the most important of these—smog and greenhouse gas emissions—went virtually undetected in the interwar period. The first major smog incident, for example, did not occur until July 1943, when an eye-burning, brownish-blue cloud enveloped Los Angeles. The episode prompted a concerted civic response and led to the first scientific explanation of the problem in 1950. After a decade of stalling by automakers, California created its Motor Vehicle Pollution Control Board in 1959, although the issue did not enter federal politics until the 1960s, when smog became a national problem.[40] By contrast, awareness of global warming did not emerge until much later. The 1950s saw the first research into the "greenhouse effect" hypothesis, which posits that emitting massive quantities of heat-trapping gasses into the atmosphere is changing the earth's climate. Few people had heard of the issue before the hot summer of 1988, however, when experts first began to call for public action. Even then, not until 2001 did the Intergovernmental Panel on Climate Change, a blue-ribbon panel of climate scientists, declare that "most of the observed warming over the last 50 years is likely to have been due to the increase in greenhouse gas concentrations," with "likely" defined as a "66–90% chance."[41] In both cases, interwar tailpipe emissions contributed to problems whose implications took decades to understand.[42]

By contrast, the rapid spread and large-scale use of lead as a gasoline additive, which began in the early 1920s and continued well after World War II, sparked a brief but intense national debate over public health. The product of a research effort led by Charles Kettering between 1916 and 1921, the discovery of tetraethyl lead (TEL) was hailed by the auto industry as a low-cost gasoline additive that solved the problem of engine "knock." It had the additional advantages of improving fuel efficiency in existing cars by roughly 50 percent and of enabling automakers to double their engine compression ratios, thus dramatically increasing power. The former advantage seemed particularly compelling amid early-1920s fears of gasoline shortages, and the holders of the key patents (General Motors, DuPont, and Standard Oil of New Jersey) quickly formed the Ethyl Corporation in 1924 to capitalize on the innovation. The problem—a big one—was that lead was a well-known neurotoxin that does not break down in the environment. Yet using TEL as an additive involved such small quantities that few were confident on the issue of whether or not its use posed a public health hazard. When five workers in a TEL manufacturing facility died and another thirty-five were hospitalized in late 1924, prompting national coverage of "Standard Oil's Death Factory," the Ethyl Corporation temporarily halted its operations and a serious debate about TEL's safety ensued.[43]

Although TEL's opponents included several distinguished experts, the debate's outcome was in many ways a foregone conclusion. No federal agency at the time had the power to regulate a product like leaded gasoline, and without a serious public outcry new legislation was unlikely. Moreover, industry officials argued that TEL's benefits gave it incredible importance—one executive hyperbolically called it a "gift of God."[44] The immediate safety issues involved in making and distributing leaded gasoline, they insisted, could be engineered away. Even more significantly, the burden of proof lay on TEL's opponents to demonstrate that it posed a serious public health hazard. Those who proposed, as one did, that "no possible new chemical substance should be put into retail use until proof of its harmlessness has been shown beyond doubt," were well ahead of their time in arguing for what eventually became known as the "precautionary principle."[45] In 1926 the Public Health Service quelled public fears with a reassuring— but deeply flawed—study that showed no clear negative health effects on a small sample of drivers and garage workers exposed to leaded gasoline over a two-year period.[46] The Ethyl Corporation launched a national publicity campaign, automakers began designing new high-compression engines to capitalize on the new fuel, and sales rose. By 1940, 70 percent of all U.S. gasoline sales were of leaded gasoline.[47] Studies of TEL's environmental and health effects ceased until the late

1960s, when leaded gasoline reentered public environmental debates, and the Clean Air Act of 1970 ultimately led to its phaseout between 1976 and 1986. In hindsight, the long-term negative effect predicted by TEL's opponents proved disturbingly accurate.[48]

In addition to these problems with pollution, wasted resources, and environmental toxins, the shift from oat-eating animals to gasoline-burning vehicles had several more indirect—but nonetheless significant—environmental consequences. First, in stark contrast to the earlier history of the United States, Car Country as it developed was a land without draft animals. As late as 1910, the nation had better than 27 million horses and mules, including large numbers in cities; by 1940 fewer than 14 million remained, mostly on farms, and by 1960 the number stood barely above 3 million.[49] As some contemporaries pointed out, there were clear benefits to eliminating the manure, horse carcasses, and various diseases associated with large-scale urban horse use—not to mention the benefits of removing large, sometimes unpredictable animals from crowded city streets.[50] Advocates of tractors also proclaimed their advantages, although they met significant opposition from those arguing for the superiority of horses and mules.[51]

Whatever the vices or virtues of horses versus motor vehicles, the dramatic decline of draft animal populations had far-reaching implications for the basic structure of the American landscape. By one estimate, for example, American draft animals ate roughly 27 percent of all crops harvested in the United States between 1880 and 1920. Cropland devoted to their feed peaked at 93 million acres in 1915 and declined steadily thereafter—reaching 65 million acres in 1930 and then plummeting to 5 million acres in 1960. Most of this land subsequently shifted to commodity grain production. The 80 million acres of pasturage devoted to draft animals in 1910, too, shifted to new uses, typically either crop production or pasturage for dairy cows and beef cattle.[52] Aside from the obvious presence of motor vehicles, Car Country's agricultural landscape differed markedly and in environmentally significant ways from its predecessors.

Second, a vast new American petrochemical industry emerged from the oil-refining industry in the decades after World War II. During the interwar years, the nascent industry launched a research agenda focused on understanding and finding uses for the gaseous hydrocarbon fractions that were by-products of cracking oil to produce gasoline. As research and experimentation produced greater knowledge about how heat and pressure rearranged hydrogen and carbon atoms, scientists developed new techniques to derive a wide range of chemicals from petroleum-based hydrocarbons. During World War II, for example, rubber shortages prompted extensive federal investment in an accelerated program to manufacture synthetic rubber from petroleum. The industry expanded quickly from an estimated investment in plant facilities of $350 million in 1940 to roughly $3 billion by 1953, by which time roughly a quarter of all chemicals produced in the United States were derived from petroleum. Among the industry's products were a wide range of plastics, synthetic rubber, agricultural fertilizers and pesticides (including DDT), new industrial solvents, and various synthetic detergents—all of which featured prominently in post–World War II environmental debates. To the extent that these materials originated in the quest to wring more gasoline from oil, and to find profitable markets for the by-products of gasoline production, these, too, were part of Car Country's environmental legacy.[33]

Finally, the automobile led the way in the larger shift from coal toward oil as the nation's dominant power source. Oil's relative position began expanding during the 1910s and especially during World War I, prompting Lord Curzon's famous claim that the Allies had "floated to victory upon a wave of oil."[54] By the end of World War I, petroleum had become the second most important fuel in the United States, although oil and natural gas combined accounted for just 16.4 percent of the U.S. energy supply in 1919, measured in British thermal units (Btu), versus coal's 78 percent. As car use exploded after World War I, petroleum began closing the gap. By 1941, oil and natural gas accounted for 42.3 percent of the nation's energy use, while coal slipped to just 54.1 percent of the total. From an environmental standpoint, the most remarkable thing about these changing percentages is that the growth of oil and natural gas consumption came in addition to, rather than in place of, coal consumption. In 1919, for example, coal supplied 78 percent of the American energy market with 14,602 trillion Btu; in 1941, it supplied 54.1 percent with 15,004 trillion Btu—an absolute increase over 1919. The 11,741 trillion Btu supplied by oil and natural gas in 1941 represented new energy consumption.[55]

Supplying all that energy was an enormous—and enormously profitable—enterprise. By the mid-1950s, one-third of all billion-dollar corporations in the United States were oil companies, holding combined assets of $21.1 billion dollars.[56] Yet the significant story of oil's rise as a profitable fuel for burgeoning numbers of motorists is only half of the story of oil's environmental significance in the rise of Car Country. As it turned out, the same demand for gasoline that made oil such a profitable business also held the key to financing the phenomenally expensive efforts of highway administrators to catch up to cars by remaking the American landscape.

FUELING ROADS

By the end of World War I, traditional revenue sources could no longer keep up with the escalating costs of road construction.[57] Before the war, a little over half of all rural highway funds came from state-issued bonds. Property taxes, another major source of highway revenue, funded most local government programs and projects—not just roads—and were already strained to produce sufficient revenue to meet growing highway demands. Poll taxes and labor levies, other traditional sources for rural highways, disappeared as road work shifted from being a labor-intensive enterprise to a capital-intensive one. In addition, World War I caused construction costs to skyrocket at precisely the same time that traffic demands became overwhelming. As late as 1921, road revenues still came from a mix of property taxes, general-fund allocations, bonds, federal aid, and motor-vehicle license and registration fees. Even with the substantial new income from license and registration fees (which, almost overnight, had come to account for roughly one-fifth of state highway revenues), road-related revenues lagged significantly behind demand.[58]

Gasoline taxes provided a relatively uncontroversial solution to an increasingly contentious fiscal problem. Three states, led by Oregon, adopted modest one cent per gallon gasoline taxes in 1919, which legislators justified as a highway "user tax" along the lines of license and registration fees. As such, this tax had a number of obvious advantages: it targeted the primary users of improved highways, it taxed motorists roughly in proportion to their use of roads, and it generated substantial revenue that states could use for road work or as security for bond issues. It also allowed less-populated states to collect revenue from out-of-state tourists and, most importantly, had very low administrative costs, since states assessed a small number of wholesalers rather than a large and dispersed group of gasoline retailers.[59]

As state after state became aware of its strengths—in part because the American Association of State Highway Officials (AASHO) aggressively championed the idea—the new tax spread quickly. Five years after the first appearance of the tax in 1919, thirty-six states had adopted a gas tax; by 1929 all forty-eight had followed suit. Moreover, because the tax was invisible at the pump and because new oil-field discoveries and booming production in the second half of the 1920s caused oil prices to fall more or less steadily, states were able to raise gasoline taxes to a national average of four cents per gallon by 1931 without appearing to affect the falling price of gasoline.[60] The prices that motorists paid at the pump actually fell even as gas taxes inched significantly upward (fig. 5.1).

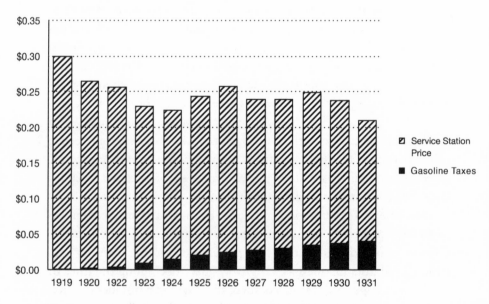

5.1 Average per gallon gasoline tax and service station prices, 1919–1931. American Petroleum Institute, *Petroleum Facts and Figures*, 156.

As a source of new revenue, the gas tax was substantial enough to underwrite mushrooming state road-building budgets, which, from 1902 to 1927, skyrocketed from 2 to 25 percent of total state expenditures. Together, gas taxes and motor-vehicle fees generated an expanding proportion of state highway funding, rising from 20.4 percent in 1921 to 59.5 percent in 1930. In addition, because politicians justified both gas taxes and vehicle fees as road-user taxes, most states devoted gas tax income exclusively to highways. The result was a de facto segregation of road-user revenues from general funds. Income from gas taxes exploded from $5.3 million in 1921 to $431.4 million in 1929, pushing gas taxes past vehicle fees as the primary source of highway revenue. By the end of the decade, twenty-one states had eliminated property taxes as a highway funding source (fig. 5.2).[61]

Motorists had good reasons to support gas taxes during the 1920s. The principle of user taxes, for example, seemed fair enough, given, in this case, the strains that escalating automotive traffic put on the nation's highways and the widespread desire among motorists for better roads. The tax was neither onerous nor obvious—paid a few

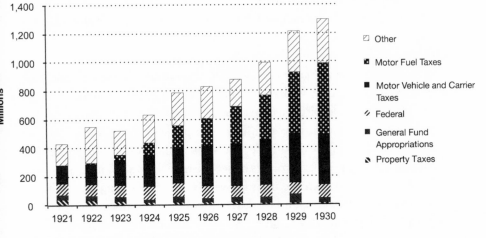

5.2 Major sources of state highway revenue, 1921–1930.
Federal Highway Administration, *Highway Statistics to 1985*, 136.

cents at a time, with the exact amount unadvertised—and it funded conspicuous, large-scale road construction. Moreover, gas taxes had strong support among state legislators and initially even garnered the support of oil-industry executives, who noted a direct link between better highways and growing gasoline sales. This widespread support for a substantial new tax took many by surprise—"Who ever heard, before, of a popular tax?" asked Tennessee's chief tax collector in 1926. Yet in the context of the general prosperity, falling oil prices, and rising automobile use of the 1920s, many regarded the gas tax as a deus ex machina that saved state treasuries from bankruptcy and state legislators from having to say no to a growing motorized constituency clamoring for more, better, and faster road improvements.[62]

When the Great Depression struck, most government receipts declined precipitously, but the gas tax proved remarkably resilient and stable as a source of revenue. Personal and corporate income tax revenues, for example, both fell in 1932 to just half of 1927 levels; property tax revenues also plummeted. By comparison, state gas tax income rose in the first years of the Depression to a record high of $537.4 million in 1931, dipped a negligible 4.3 percent in 1932 to $514.1 million, and then began to climb again, reaching $948 million in 1941. By that time, gas taxes produced half of all state highway revenues (fig. 5.3). Gas taxes proved such a reliable generator of revenue that the federal government introduced its own one cent per gallon levy as part of the Revenue Act of 1932, which for the next two decades consistently produced more revenue than Congress appropriated as federal aid for highways.[63]

The combination of gas taxes, vehicle taxes, and federal spending kept large state highway budgets intact through the worst years of the Great Depression, despite massive revenue shortfalls that caused total state and local contributions to highway expenses to plummet. Federal aid offset part of the difference, and substantial federal work-relief grants earmarked for road projects offset the rest (fig. 5.4). With a quarter of the civilian workforce unemployed in 1933, for example, roads proved an ideal place to spend work-relief money. Not only could state highway departments put large numbers of people to work immediately, but compared to so-called make-work jobs like raking leaves, road and street work produced durable, tangible—and thus politically

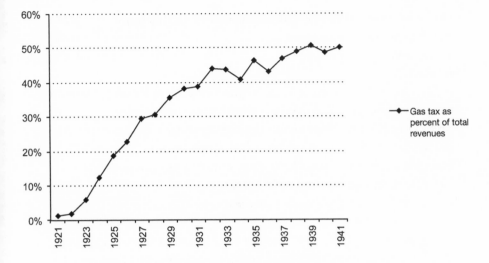

5.3 Gasoline tax as a percentage of total state highway revenues, 1921–1941.
Federal Highway Administration, *Highway Statistics to 1985*, 136.

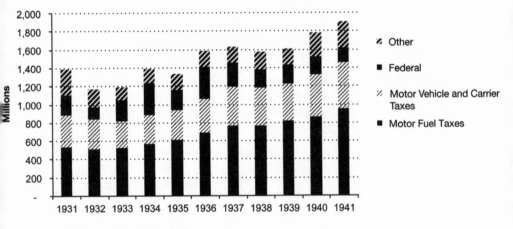

5.4 Major sources of state highway revenue, 1931–1941.
Federal Highway Administration, *Highway Statistics to 1985*, 136.

attractive—results. Between 1933, when Franklin D. Roosevelt took office, and 1942, the first full year of U.S. participation in World War II, federal work-relief agencies devoted $4 billion to roads and streets and in the process expanded the parameters of federal aid for roads beyond the traditional focus on rural highways. Buoyed by stable gas tax revenue and greatly expanded federal spending, highway budgets fell only slightly in 1932 and 1933; by 1934, and then through the rest of the decade, both expenditures and highway income exceeded 1929 levels.[64]

In that context, many state legislatures began to allocate portions of the large, steady income from gas taxes toward nonhighway expenses, provoking the first widespread backlash against the tax. Before the Depression, this practice, which came to be known as "diversion," had been insignificant, claiming between 2 and 3.3 percent of total collections between 1927 and 1931. As the Depression deepened, however, that range became even higher (between 15.9 and 18 percent from 1934 to 1937), prompting intense opposition from the automobile and road-building industries (fig. 5.5). The National Highway Users Conference (NHUC), for example, which formed in 1932, became the biggest opponent of diversion. Chaired by Alfred P. Sloan, the president of General Motors, and led by representatives from various automobile, oil, bus, truck, road, and farm organizations, the NHUC aggressively lobbied Congress to prohibit the practice. It achieved at least part of its goal with the passage of the Hayden-Cartwright Act of 1934, which reiterated NHUC arguments almost verbatim, proclaiming it "unfair and unjust to tax motor vehicle transportation unless the proceeds of such taxation are applied to the construction, improvement, or maintenance of highways." In a huge loophole, however, the law would penalize a state for diversion only if it exceeded its current rate—grandfathering in the large-scale diversion occurring in predominantly large, heavily urbanized northeastern states. In addition, the law had an ironic do-as-I-say-not-as-I-do element: Congress at the time allocated just 60 percent of federal gas tax income to highway purposes and diverted the remainder to the general fund.[65]

A more significant and longer-lasting legacy of NHUC's antidiversion campaign can be seen at the state level. Growing numbers of state legislatures enshrined the principle of "linkage"—that highway user-tax receipts should be used exclusively to fund highway spending. A more extreme form of linkage (and one nearly impossible to reverse), first seen in Minnesota in 1920 and next in Kansas in 1928, came in the form of constitutional amendments earmarking gas taxes for highway expenses. Sixteen states adopted such amendments between 1934 and

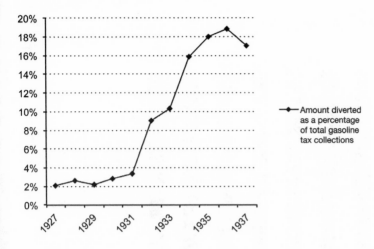

5.5 State gasoline taxes spent on nonhighway purposes as a percentage of total gasoline collections, 1927–1937. Crawford, *Motor Fuel Taxation in the United States*, 69.

1945, and another nine did so by 1956, thus making linkage a constitutional requirement in a majority of states. By 1974, forty-six of fifty states required linkage either by statute or by constitutional amendment.[66]

What began as opposition to diversion eventually became opposition to higher gas taxes, dampening further increases in the second half of the 1930s. Between 1918 and the passage of Hayden-Cartwright in 1934, for example, the gas tax rose more or less steadily from nothing to a national average of 5.21 cents per gallon. From 1934 until 1941, by contrast, the average increased less than half a cent (fig. 5.6). Gas tax income continued to grow on the strength of expanding automobile ownership and rising per-vehicle gasoline consumption, but steady increases in the tax rate effectively ceased by the mid-1930s.[67]

Most important, as state after state legally linked the large, stable income from gas taxes to highway-improvement budgets, highway administrators forged a significant new relationship between gas tax revenues and highway planning. As it had with the principle of linkage, the Hayden-Cartwright Act gave highway planning a big boost, allowing states to use up to 1.5 percent of federal-aid funds on planning activities. The Bureau of Public Roads (BPR) pushed states to spend this money on detailed, standardized highway-planning surveys, which began in 1936. The surveys compiled detailed inventories

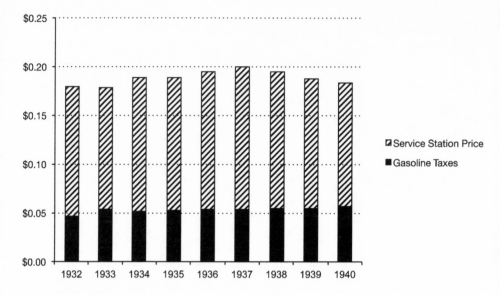

5.6 Average national gasoline tax and service station prices, 1932–1940.
American Petroleum Institute, *Petroleum Facts and Figures*, 156.

of the physical characteristics of every mile of road in state highway systems—ranging from isolated country roads to heavily traveled highways, such as the famed Route 66—and conducted extensive statewide traffic counts. Together, the surveys gave state and federal highway planners an unprecedented amount of detailed information on traffic patterns and road conditions across the nation. Just as significantly, the planning surveys included detailed financial studies designed to identify and classify every dollar of revenue collected for (and expended upon) roads and streets. These studies, in conjunction with new systems of data analysis, allowed planners for the first time to develop an accurate picture of the exact relationships among road expenses, traffic volumes, and highway user taxes. The goals, at least initially, were to account precisely for how all of the many levels of government spent user taxes and thereby to identify the extent to which user revenues actually paid to improve and maintain individual highways. How much of each highway, in other words, did gas taxes (and other user fees) really fund?[68]

The answers that the studies produced—and the method they used to produce them—marked both an environmental watershed and a significant moment in the transformation of the United States into Car Country. The method was startlingly simple: for any given stretch of road, administrators determined how much "income" it generated by multiplying its traffic volume by the average per-mile user-tax revenue that each motorist paid. By comparing the resulting figure with the improvement and maintenance costs for the same stretch of road, administrators could determine, with compelling accuracy, which highways carried enough traffic to "pay for themselves"—and which did not. This simple calculation allowed planners to create a cost-effectiveness index and classification system for different types of roads and to justify traffic-service priorities in clear-cut economic terms. "Highway builders are proceeding on the principle," explained Thomas MacDonald, chief of the BPR, in 1938, "that the utilization of the highways must produce directly the revenues with which to finance their construction." As long as states did not make "large diversions of this income to other purposes" or spread them "over an ever-increasing mileage," MacDonald reassured the nation's politicians, highway planners could provide self-liquidating highways that would not make unpredictable demands on state budgets.[69]

When that formula combined with the new state-level budgetary principle of linkage, a powerful, self-replicating system emerged: gas taxes funded more and better roads, more and better roads generated new traffic and longer trips, new traffic and longer trips consumed more gas, higher gas consumption created more tax revenue, and more tax revenue funded more and better roads. The new plans rested on a majestic vision of self-fueling growth and promised ever-improved highway facilities. And the entire system rested on the premise of the steadily growing consumption of a seemingly limitless supply of cheap, minimally taxed gasoline.

GAS TAXES OR TOLLS?

In the mid-1930s, as the BPR was creating the planning surveys that cemented its vision of a self-replicating, self-fueling system of highway expansion, the combination of staggering traffic fatalities and growing traffic congestion raised new questions about the adequacy of the highway system that gas taxes were funding. In 1935 alone, for example, roughly 827,000 reported accidents killed 37,000 people and seriously harmed 105,000 more. Although most commentators blamed this toll either on faster speeds or on careless drivers, highways themselves also increasingly came under fire. "The road never was very efficient as a channel for motor traffic, but recent jumps in the speed of the car have thrown its inadequacies into sharp relief," editorialized *Fortune* in 1936. "The cold fact is: traffic today is a combination of an eighty-mile-an-hour car in the hands of a twenty-mile-an-hour driver struggling to adjust itself to a thirty-mile-an-hour road. And it doesn't work out very well."[70]

The growing sense that two decades of enormous expenditures on highways had created an incomplete system of highways, most of which were being rendered obsolete by faster and faster automobiles, prompted a fierce debate that destroyed the broad agreement about construction priorities that had prevailed among highway builders since the early 1920s. In one camp, the BPR marshaled its forces to bolster the federal-aid system by shifting its priorities toward the strained urban sections of the system that carried the most traffic (and had the most self-liquidating highways). In another camp were those who saw the new German *autobahnen*—an integrated national system of superhighways built to the highest standards—as a cure-all for the obvious problems facing the American highway infrastructure. "Germany has the roads while we have the traffic," complained Michigan's highway commissioner in 1939 after returning from a visit. "It seems to me that if Germany can build roads of this type, the United States, the home of the world's automobile industry, can do the same."[71]

If superhighways had much to recommend them, they also had a clear Achilles' heel: they were spectacularly expensive. The vast majority of America's primary highway system constructed in the interwar years consisted of two-lane highways—one lane in each direction—with narrow shoulders on a limited right-of-way. Most of the costs associated with their improvement consisted of materials and labor. For some projects, like extensively widening a roadway or eliminating a hazardous at-grade intersection, land acquisition added significantly to the price. The land requirements for superhighways, on the other hand—with their extrawide rights-of-way, on- and off-ramps, multiple lanes in each direction, extensive medians, and wide shoulders—were lavish by comparison, particularly on expensive urban real estate where the thickest traffic clogged existing thoroughfares. Worse, motorist-oriented businesses like gas stations, restaurants, and tourist cabins had dramatically boosted land values along the most heavily traveled sections of the highway system that most needed improvement, raising the condemnation costs involved in updating the routes to superhighway standards to stratospheric levels.

The same dynamic that made superhighways so expensive increased the cost of a business-as-usual approach to highway improvement as the interwar period progressed. The premise of the BPR's "stage construction" policy, which had long guided highway improvements, was that it was both possible and desirable to match road improvements to existing traffic demands. In places with little traffic, inexpensive improvements would suffice; where thick traffic prevailed, multiple lanes of expensive concrete or asphalt were in order. This policy, however, failed to anticipate either surging traffic or changing land-use patterns. Many businesses relocated along improved highways, and each such business had patrons, suppliers, and in- and outgoing shipments that became part of the highway's baseline traffic load. Growing traffic attracted new businesses, further boosting both land values and traffic. More traffic meant greater wear and tear on the highway—necessitating more frequent maintenance—and higher speeds exposed highways with inadequate design speeds. "By the time it became evident that functional obsolescence had overtaken a large portion of the road and street system, homes and businesses had grown up along the narrow and unprotected rights of way to form continuous ribbons of roadside encroachments," the authors of one study explained. "When redesign and reconstruction became essential to accommodate the continuing rise in traffic volume and speed, the land and damage costs involved in widening and straitening these inadequate rights-of-way had risen to exorbitant levels."[72]

Undeterred by daunting costs, superhighway advocates argued that they could finance their projects by levying tolls—and thus avoid competing with the established federal-aid system for gas tax revenues. Although tolls had been a popular method of financing hard-surfaced highways in the early nineteenth century, opponents attacked them as an antidemocratic affront to "public" roads. In the face of these attacks, and more importantly in the face of competition from a growing network of railroads, toll highways had faded from existence. The first federal-aid legislation in 1916 and 1921 had cemented the earlier era's anti-toll philosophy into the nation's highway policy by barring tolls on federal-aid highways. Despite this official anti-toll policy, many politicians regarded tolls as the only revenue source left untapped for highway development, particularly given the new, well-organized opposition to higher gas taxes. Several toll bills appeared in Congress in 1936 that attracted enough interest for both congressional road committees to schedule hearings on the subject in 1937.[73]

The BPR had long discouraged both toll-road and transcontinental highway schemes, and after its experts testified in the 1937 congressional hearings, both committees ultimately ratified their negative judgment of the proposed tollway legislation. The idea behind the proposals refused to die, however, and so when Congress asked the BPR for a full report on the subject in 1938, the agency delivered a comprehensive report titled *Toll Roads and Free Roads* (1939) that coupled a scathing assessment of the viability of a transcontinental system of toll-supported superhighways and a counterproposal for a new system of "modernized" interregional highways to be funded by existing gas-tax revenues.[74]

The report unequivocally opposed a new transcontinental superhighway system, arguing that the possibilities for such a system's success boiled down to a single straightforward question: would people pay a premium for a long-distance superhighway if a parallel free road could get them to the same destination? The traffic data, the report argued, suggested that the answer was no. Marshaling an impressive array of statistics derived from the comprehensive state traffic surveys conducted as part of the highway-planning studies launched in 1936, the report concluded that of the 14,336 miles in the proposed toll-highway system, only 172 *might* be able to retire the bonds required to finance them from toll revenue, even if 1960 traffic grew 250 percent over present levels. Moreover, only 547 miles would be likely to generate even 70 percent of their costs, while the vast majority would fare even worse. The entire system, the report estimated, would generate enough revenue to recoup just 40 percent of total costs. Even combining the income from tolls with gas tax revenue in proportion to projected traffic levels, the report concluded, "would make no important change in the conclusions reached since the annual deficit for the entire system would be reduced by about only 14 percent."[75]

But the report did not stop there. Instead, it went on to argue that the real question American highway policy had to address was how to deal with growing vehicular traffic. This traffic, the bureau's data revealed, was overwhelmingly local and primarily urban in character. Trips of five miles or less accounted for an average of 25.7 percent of all automobile traffic, with that percentage ranging as high as 43.8 percent in one state. On average, the data showed, just 5.7 percent of all automobile trips were longer than thirty miles, and just 0.7 percent exceeded one hundred miles. Given the long distances between the access points on toll highways, it stood to reason that they would attract very little of this predominantly local traffic—and thus would not help solve the pressing traffic needs of the major metropolitan regions where most traffic concentrated and where the greatest costs of toll-road construction would accrue.[76]

A better alternative, the report argued in its second part, "A Master Plan for Free Highway Development," would be to create a new 26,700-mile system of interregional highways—paid for through existing user-tax revenues—to connect the country's major population centers. This system would, in essence, "modernize" the existing primary system with better alignments and sight distances, wider pavements, separation of grades, and restricted access, while continuing to provide just one lane in each direction for the majority of the system's lightly traveled rural mileage. By reorienting the attention of highway builders decidedly toward urban areas, where traffic problems were at their worst, the system would provide urban expressways to handle what the report called "the daily peak of 'in-and-out' city traffic" created by urban commuters; it would also provide belt lines and bypasses to keep through traffic away from congested areas. "Improved as a system of public roads along lines chosen to facilitate the important traffic awaiting its service," the report argued, "it will attract traffic and generate new activity, in contradistinction to the traffic-repelling tendency of the proposed toll-road system." The new system would also "effect a greater reduction in the highway accident rate than could be made by an equivalent sum spent for highways in any other way."[77]

The report's coup de grâce, however, was its argument that investing in a modernized interregional highway system would be necessary *even if* Congress proceeded with a transcontinental tollway system. The tollways, the report projected, would at best attract about one-third of anticipated traffic between cities, while the remaining two-thirds of motorists would choose slower, parallel free roads to avoid paying a toll. Those parallel free roads, the report concluded, simply could not handle even that level of traffic without the significant improvements called for in its interregional highway system proposal. The report temporarily killed discussion on Capitol Hill about toll-financed transcontinental superhighways, but it failed to reorient the discussion of future policy as decisively as the BPR's chief, Thomas MacDonald, had hoped.[78]

In part, the report's failure to recast the debate stemmed from a handful of state-level events that seemed to contradict the BPR's conclusion that few toll-charging superhighways could hope to pay for themselves. The Pennsylvania Turnpike, a 160-mile superhighway that began construction in November 1938 and opened to traffic in 1940, provided the first and most dramatic piece of evidence. Built on an abandoned railroad right-of-way through the state's mountainous terrain, the project had proceeded only with significant federal support—a $29.25 million grant from the Public Works Administration for work relief and an additional $40.8 million bond purchase by the Reconstruction Finance Corporation—and over the objections of the state highway department. The facility attracted toll-paying motorists far above the pessimistic rates projected by the BPR, suggesting that the agency's mountains of data were less authoritative than they appeared. Above all, two experts concluded, the turnpike's success demonstrated "that motorists are willing to pay more for roads if by doing so they can enjoy better service and at the same time realize savings in vehicle operating costs."[79]

The Pennsylvania Turnpike's success inspired a rash of imitators. Pennsylvania quickly authorized two extensions in 1940 and 1941, adding 167 miles that opened to traffic until 1950 and 1951, respectively. Similarly inspired, Connecticut began charging a ten-cent toll in 1938 to finance an extension of the Merritt Parkway. Despite the nearby presence of the Boston Post Road, a free but highly congested parallel route, the Merritt had attracted fifty million paying users by 1951. New York's Hutchinson Parkway added a toll in 1939 with similar results. By 1941, five states had created toll-road commissions to pursue various new toll-road projects. Over the strong opposition of federal highway planners, growing numbers of states thus began to consider toll financing as a potentially viable alternative to publicly financed highways.[80]

CONCLUSION

Although the Pennsylvania Turnpike and its followers seemed to point the way toward a new method of financing superhighways that did not depend on gas taxes, the momentum behind toll roads halted when the United States entered World War II in December 1941. For the rest of the highway system, user taxes remained the politically preferred method of financing. Moreover, a grand new vision of a self-funding, self-perpetuating system of highway finance had become well entrenched at the state level. In exchange for legally "linking" highway budgets to gas tax revenues, thereby removing highway allocations from political negotiation, highway engineers promised state legislators modern, well-maintained highway systems that would not make unpredictable demands on state budgets. Equipped with comprehensive traffic surveys, detailed road costs, and new cost-effectiveness indexes that allowed highway administrators to identify and prioritize self-liquidating projects, the highway community was becoming increasingly certain that it could finally get a handle on the nation's long-standing traffic problems.

Underneath the politics, fueling both highway budgets and the nation's growing automotive traffic, was oil itself. The oil industry possessed the interesting combination of widespread visibility (in the form of aggressive national advertising and the ubiquitous gas station itself) and invisibility, particularly where environmental problems like tetraethyl lead and greenhouse gas emissions were concerned. Inexpensive, abundant, and easily available, gasoline fueled Car Country's rise in profoundly important ways.

SIX

THE PATHS OUT OF TOWN

CONSIDER TWO PLACES. FIRST: IT IS 1928, AND YOU ARE SUSPENDED midair above Ford's River Rouge factory on the edge of Dearborn, Michigan. It spreads before you, a vast complex of buildings—more than you can easily count—and bristles with belching smokestacks. A dense network of tracks interlaces the facility, which is built tight against the curving bank of the river. A long, perfectly straight slip protrudes from the river into the facility, paralleling a series of buildings on one side and giant rectangular bins on the other. Enormous piles of materials, which range widely in color and consistency, fill the bins.

Ford's River Rouge facility, Dearborn, Michigan, 1928. From the collections of The Henry Ford, THF24040.

Civilian Conservation Corps road-building crew in the Modoc National Forest, California, 1934. National Archives, NARA 95-G-290289.

Huge scoops unload a ship's cargo, transferring it via a huge horizontal crane into one of the bins. Is that sand? Dirt? Crushed rock? From this distance it is hard to say.

Second: It is 1934, and you are in the Modoc National Forest in northeastern California, twenty or thirty miles from the Oregon and Nevada borders. Mount Shasta rises from the high plains to the west. You are with a Civilian Conservation Corps crew based in Hackamore, which pauses for a moment to take a picture. Some of the workers sweat through their shirts, others are shirtless, and everyone wears tall work boots. They are building a road. They perch atop two pieces of heavy equipment, one with caterpillar treads, the other with scrapers and rollers for finer grading work. Conifers rise behind them, but the foreground is a raw cut in the earth, as yet ungraded. Who are these men, and why are they building this particular road?

Places such as these add detail and texture to our understanding of the many ways that the physical work of building Car Country transformed the American landscape during the interwar years. The first car-oriented landscapes and the self-fueling system of rising traffic, fuel consumption, and road construction were both significant yet still account for only a subset of Car Country's environmental consequences. Manufacturing cars and building roads—especially on the scale required to make driving a standard part of American life—entailed rearranging diverse ecosystems on a massive scale. Peering into Ford's vast materials bins along the Rouge River and making sense of young men collecting government paychecks to build roads in remote forests allows us to follow what one environmental historian has called "the paths out of town"—and thereby to see the connections between what was happening in these places and the powerful forces transforming the rest of the nation.[1]

Both the auto and road-construction industries had a voracious appetite for raw materials, the demand for which remade the often-distant ecosystems where they originated. Both generated pollution and rearranged the ecosystems they inhabited, prompting ecological changes that were at once both intensely localized and widely dispersed. Both created new divisions—and forged new connections—in the American landscape. And, together, both created an unprecedented new mobility that put growing numbers of people in close contact with "nature"—or at least the beautiful, green, romanticized version of it as a place of therapeutic retreat from the modern world. Along these paths out of town, both literal and metaphorical, the United States began to refashion itself as Car Country during the interwar decades.

INDUSTRIAL FOOTPRINTS

By the early 1920s, mass-production techniques had swept through the automobile industry, launching it into the front ranks of American industry and significantly expanding its environmental footprint. In some ways, the environmental consequences of manufacturing cars resembled those of other heavy industries, particularly in their intense pollution and significant consumption of raw materials. Yet the auto industry's scale and scope stood apart from other large industries, both in its manufacturing operations and in its demands for natural resources.[2]

A sense of how thoroughly mass production transformed the auto industry's scale of operations can be glimpsed in the almost magical increases in new-car sales, which more than doubled from 895,930 in 1915 to 1.9 million in 1920—and then more than doubled again to a peak of 4.5 million in 1929.[3] By the mid-1920s, one in eight American workers owed their jobs to making, selling, or servicing cars, and by the late 1930s the number had increased to one in seven.[4] New-car sales sank to just 1.1 million in 1932 but rebounded steadily thereafter, reaching 3.9 million in 1937. Total sales for the decade reached 25.4 million passenger cars, just 18 percent fewer than the 31.1 million sold during the booming 1920s.[5] During the entire interwar period, the industry's retail sales never strayed more than a few percentage points from the national index of industrial production—with the exception of 1927–1928, which can be attributed entirely to Ford's complete shutdown during the switchover from the Model T to the Model A.[6]

In addition to the industry's sheer scale of production, its scope of production also stood apart for the complexity of the product that it manufactured. "An automobile is a city in itself," Henry Ford once told an interviewer. "It contains samples of nearly all raw materials, all arts, all crafts and trades."[7] Mass producing an automobile, in other words, meant manufacturing a broad range of parts, some simple and others sophisticated, and then assembling them into a unified product. For the industry to maintain its prodigious output, every one of those parts— upholstered seats and rubber tires, plate-glass windows and hardwood floorboards, brakes and carburetors, engines and speedometers, gearshift levers and steering wheels, plus thousands of others—had to be mass manufactured. Only then could the industry deliver completed automobiles to a mass market. As a manufacturing enterprise, then, the auto industry is best understood as a *conglomeration* of manufacturing industries, many of them very different from one another and each with its own needs, practices, and environmental effects. All of these different industries operated in unity on the same gargantuan scale, together producing enough parts to build a combined sixty-four million new automobiles between 1920 and 1941.[8]

The Ford Motor Company's operations highlight the industry's manufacturing requirements during the interwar years. Unlike most automakers, which contracted with specialty manufacturers for most of their parts, a practice that tended to obscure the full scope of activities involved in making a car, Ford famously brought nearly every step in the manufacturing process under the company's control. At the center of Ford's integrated system stood its River Rouge facility—often simply referred to as "the Rouge"—which during the 1920s supplanted its Highland Park factory as the foundation of the company's operations. The Rouge expanded quickly between 1919, when construction began in earnest, and 1926, when it began making its own steel. An inventory of the factory's major activities, which were housed in some ninety-three buildings on 1,100 riverside acres—more than quadruple Highland Park's acreage—reveals the diversity of its operations. By the early 1920s the Rouge had its own blast furnaces, coke ovens, foundry, electric furnaces, power plant, machine shops, body plant, sawmill, glass factory, paper mill, cement plant, and shop for repairing railroad locomotives. Eventually, it added an open hearth and rolling mills for steel production.

In addition to its manufacturing activities, a complex network of transportation facilities integrated the Rouge's operations and forged links to ecosystems beyond the factory. Ninety miles of railroad track crisscrossed the Rouge, for example, including five tracks along the "High Line," a concrete structure forty feet high and three-quarters of a mile long, which served as the interface between the enormous raw-materials bins on one side and the factory on the other. A mile-long turning basin adjacent to the storage bins and extensive dredging along the river transformed the factory by 1923 into a deepwater port, giving it direct access to carriers from the Great Lakes and beyond via the St.

Lawrence Seaway.[9] To augment its control over transportation, in 1920 the company acquired the Detroit, Toledo & Ironton Railroad (D.T. & I.) and in 1924 began operating a shipping fleet with what were allegedly the two largest ore carriers on the Great Lakes.[10] "The visitor can stand on the roof of the Ford power house at his River Rouge plant today and see the iron ore, limestone and coal coming in on his boats and railroad at one end of the plant," the New York Times reported in 1925, "and at the other see that crude dirt emerging as parts of the finished Ford automobile, packed away in freight cars ready to be assembled when they reach their destination."[11] Only Ford attempted all of these operations itself, but all automakers depended on the same vast range of what the trade press called "ancillary industries" to keep assembly lines moving. The environmental impact of mass producing automobiles, in other words, represents in microcosm the expanding activities of the nation's entire industrial sector during the interwar years.

One important environmental implication of the auto industry's shift toward mass production was its growing reliance on mechanization, which meant burning ever-greater quantities of fossil fuels—and especially coal, which was essential both for producing the electricity that ran factory machinery and for making steel, the major component of automobiles. Although the industry's trade organization, the Automobile Manufacturers Association, did not keep statistics on the industry's total fossil fuel usage, by the mid-1920s the Ford Motor Company's Rouge facility alone consumed 2,750 tons of coal per day, or a bit over a million tons per year.[12] Ford's own comprehensive estimate was that automakers (and the many suppliers that supported them) had to burn 6 tons of coal to complete a single automobile—a figure that translates into roughly 384 million tons between 1920 and 1941.[13] Combined with the industry's own products, which by 1939 were responsible for the annual consumption of 20.7 billion gallons of gasoline—90 percent of the total U.S. consumption that year—the auto industry was responsible for a significant portion of the nation's fossil fuel usage during the interwar years.[14]

The industry also generated prodigious air and water pollution. Automakers and their suppliers did attempt to reduce pollution during this period, especially by experimenting with new technologies like higher smokestacks that dispersed smoke more broadly and various smoke-abatement devices that removed particulates from smoke. Many also tried to cut back on wasteful operations, a practice that resulted in less pollution as companies developed more efficient processes and found ways to extract and make use of by-products that otherwise would have remained in the waste stream.[15] Although such efforts did reduce pollution, they put only a small dent in the total. When the first systematic water-quality measurements were taken for the Detroit River after World War II, for example, industrial sources contributed the bulk of phenolic compounds, cyanides, ammonium compounds, suspended solids, and oils and greases, contributing pollution equivalent to that expected from a city with a population of 916,000.[16] Writing in Sports Afield in 1948, Bill Wolf described a boat trip through the area in more visceral terms. "I have seen some foul rivers, but will stake the River Rouge from the Ford plant down to where the Rouge enters and contaminates the Detroit against any stream for absolute, concentrated filth," he wrote. "It's only a short distance from Ford to the Detroit River, but the oil sludge on the surface is so thick that a boat must push its way through it."[17]

Despite its enormity, the auto industry's pollution sparked almost no protest during the interwar years. In this, the industry differed little from other heavy industrial polluters of the time. Smoke pollution, for example, had grown in proportion to the expansion of coal-fired industry in the late nineteenth and early twentieth centuries, provoking an antismoke campaign in the 1890s that hinged on the common-law tradition empowering municipalities to regulate nuisances. A flurry of regulations into the early 1900s, however, gave way in the 1910s to engineering-oriented solutions relying on improved antismoke devices, professional inspectors, and a new conceptualization of smoke as an economic (rather than environmental) problem.[18] In addition, because most civic leaders privileged economic progress over environmental quality, they conceded nearly free reign in environmental matters to big employers. Heavy industries thus generally used local environments as sinks for the pollution that they generated with the understanding that in exchange they would provide jobs and make good-faith efforts to invest in economically beneficial antipollution technologies.[19] Somewhat ironically, most of the media coverage that the auto industry received on "environmental" subjects during the interwar years focused on the Ford Motor Company's industrial conservation activities—which included large-scale efforts to recycle materials, make use of by-products, and reduce waste in resource use—rather than on the industry's large-scale pollution.[20]

In addition to pollution, mass producing cars generated prodigious demand for a wide range of natural resources. In 1922, for example, American automakers devoured 69 percent of all leather sold in the United States, along with 67 percent of the rubber.[21] The next year they also purchased significant percentages of the annual output of iron and steel (10.2 percent), hardwood lumber (14 percent), aluminum (9.3 percent), lead (12 percent), and nickel (10 percent).[22] "If the motor car industry were suddenly removed from the field of production," reported *Literary Digest* in 1923, "there are a number of industries that would die, and a number of others that would languish and have to be entirely revised."[23] By 1929 the industry's appetite had become even more voracious for rubber (84.2 percent), iron (52 percent), steel (18 percent), hardwood lumber (17.7 percent), aluminum (37.4 percent), lead (31.2 percent), and nickel (26 percent). In addition, the industry had become a leading consumer of copper (15.7 percent) and tin (23.6 percent).[24] Even the Great Depression did little to change these overall trends. In 1938, for example, the industry continued to consume roughly the same percentages of rubber, iron, steel, lead, nickel, and copper that it had in 1929.[25]

It is easy to see the raw materials that went into automobiles as little more than abstract commodities—as pure products of the marketplace. Behind the market mechanisms that delivered the huge quantities of materials that kept assembly lines moving, however, coal and metal still originated deep within the earth, lumber in forests, and leather as the hide of an animal. Even as highly engineered a consumer good as an automobile still owed its existence not only to human labor and ingenuity but also to the host of plants, animals, and minerals that comprised its constituent parts.

Again, the Ford Motor Company's integrated activities make it possible to see both the scale and range of raw materials that automakers required. In the same years that Ford was adding one manufacturing capacity after another at the Rouge, it was acquiring its own sources of raw materials at a parallel pace. By the mid-1920s, the company owned nearly half a million acres of forest in Michigan's Upper Peninsula, five large coal properties in Kentucky and West Virginia, and an iron mine in northern Michigan.[26] Ford publicists bragged that its supplies made it "independent of strikes, price fluctuations or shortage of raw materials such as coal, iron, and timber," yet company-owned raw materials never provided more than a fraction of what the Rouge required.[27] In part this was due to the staggering daily quantity of materials that the Rouge consumed by the mid-1920s: 1,535 tons of iron ore, 570 tons of limestone, 2,750 tons of coal, 74 tons of steel, 1,020 tons of sand, 385,000 board feet of lumber, and 50,000 pounds of sulfuric acid—to cover just the key materials.[28] In the face of this demand, the company's iron mines could not keep even one of the Rouge's blast furnaces operating full-time, its vast timber holdings met just 20 percent of its wood requirements, and even the company's substantial coal operations did not satisfy all of the company's needs.[29]

In environmental terms, of course, it mattered little if automakers acquired raw materials directly or through intermediaries; more important was the growing size and variety of the industry's cumulative demands. Each ton of iron ore or coal, each pound of rubber or sulfuric acid, and each board foot of lumber arriving in Detroit originated in—and had been extracted from—some distant ecosystem. And the sheer range, quantity, and diverse sources of raw materials flowing into the industry's factories, which transformed them into a machine that a few decades before had been just a twinkle in inventors' eyes, testified to the environmental demands of mass producing automobiles.

The ways that these demands ramified backward through an elaborate supply chain to refashion distant places—ecologically, economically, and socially—is best encapsulated in the histories of places like Iron Mountain, Michigan, the seat of Ford's lumbering operations, and Fordlandia, Brazil, the company's ambitious but ill-fated attempt to hack a giant rubber plantation out of the Amazonian rain forest. Iron Mountain, a small community in Michigan's Upper Peninsula, first became enmeshed in Ford's operations in late 1919, when Henry Ford acquired some 300,000 acres and chose a 2,000-acre location on the edge of town to erect a new lumber mill, chemical plant, drying kilns, and factory for fabricating wooden parts. The area by the plant grew rapidly from a small community of forty people into what was soon incorporated as the town of Kingsford. By 1925 the company employed 8,000 workers on two shifts and had built a 240-foot dam and hydroelectric plant on the nearby Menominee River. At its peak, the sawmill handled 215,000 board feet of lumber, its fifty-two kilns boasted a capacity of 6.5 million board feet, and its facilities converted wood wastes into a variety of chemicals plus close to one hundred tons of charcoal briquettes per day. Iron Mountain's operations were supplemented by smaller operations at locations scattered across Michigan's Upper Peninsula, including Sidnaw, L'Anse, Pequaming, Alberta, Big Bay, and Munising, which together had a combined total milling capacity greater even than Iron Mountain.[30]

All of Ford's Iron Mountain activities rested on lumber purchased from outside contractors and from forestry operations in roughly half a million acres of Ford-owned forests, whose hardwood composition (roughly 60 percent birch, maple, and elm) had spared them from the late-nineteenth-century logging boom that had made northern Michigan one of the nation's leading sources of white pine.[31] In light of earlier logging operations, which in little more than a generation had transformed seemingly limitless forests into ravaged stumplands, Ford executives were anxious, as one internal company document put it, to display "the adoption of proper methods of conservation in their woods operations." This mainly translated into following, and in some cases surpassing, the best forestry practices of the day: cutting stumps as low as possible; trying to keep felled trees from damaging smaller trees; sending tops, smaller logs, and bigger branches to the chemical plant; and removing fire hazards by burning the slash that remained after sawyers finished their work. The company eventually even practiced selective logging.[32]

The cumulative ecological effects of these forestry activities, however, reflected the company's substantial demands for lumber as much as its conservation techniques—however progressive they were for their time. "Total yearly lumber requirements for the Ford Motor Company exceed 300,000,000 board feet," *Ford News* reported in 1924, "which means that 175,000 square feet of virgin timberland must be cleared each day."[33] Moreover, Ford's sizable forestry operations satisfied just one-fifth of the company's demand for lumber at its peak in the mid-1920s; the company met the rest through contractors, some of whom operated in Ford-owned forests and others of whom had operations in separate locations that are now hard to trace.

As it turned out, however, Ford's demand for lumber shrank dramatically in the second half of the decade—a decline that had very different environmental consequences. The industry's demand for wood had boomed in the first half of the 1920s, the same years that Ford built its operations in northern Michigan, primarily because of the swelling popularity of closed-body cars, which catapulted from roughly 10 percent of new-car sales in 1920 to almost 90 percent of sales by 1929.[34] Because closed bodies required substantially more lumber to construct, the industry's use of hardwood lumber doubled from an average of 160 board feet per vehicle in 1919 to 320 board feet in 1923 and 1924.[35] As lower roofs and new closed-steel bodies became popular, however, wood requirements fell to an average of 240 board feet per vehicle between 1925 and 1931.[36] This trend toward smaller amounts of wood in auto bodies accelerated in the early 1930s with the growing popularity of bright, colorful finishes, because the new paints dried fastest when baked at temperatures too hot for wooden body frames.

By the early 1930s, body suppliers had cut their wood usage considerably.[37] In 1934, for example, the year before the Budd Manufacturing Company introduced the first truly all-metal auto body, the average vehicle required just 97 board feet of wood, with floorboards and running boards accounting for most of the total.[38] Ford actually began eliminating wood before the rest of the industry, starting with its new touring and roadster bodies in 1922 and spreading to other models over the next several years, which it designed in conjunction with improved (black) baking paints.[39] The company's demands fell even further with the Model T's quick and inglorious demise in 1927, prompting a string of new designs, each with progressively smaller wood requirements, beginning with the Model A and followed in 1932 by the Ford V-8.[40] As a result, operations at Iron Mountain slowed after 1927 and then decelerated drastically during the Depression. After a brief resurgence during World War II, Ford left the community it had created to fend for itself in 1951.[41]

Ford's attempts to establish a huge Brazilian rubber plantation also originated in the early 1920s, when the owners of British and Dutch rubber plantations, who operated a virtual monopoly in the Far East, orchestrated a series of events designed to inflate global rubber prices. The cartel's actions irked Henry Ford—owner of the largest company in the industry that consumed two-thirds of the world's rubber—prompting a series of secret negotiations that led, in late 1927, to a 2.5-million-acre land concession from the Brazilian government to begin a rubber plantation. Located in the jungle along the Tapajós River, 110 miles upriver from its confluence with the Amazon, the concession lay in the heart of Brazil's rubber-producing region, which had boomed before Far Eastern plantations had superseded it in the 1910s. Whereas the British and Dutch exports came from large-scale commercial plantations growing clones that had been carefully cultivated to produce a high yield, Brazil's production had relied on the lower-yield *Hevea brasiliensis* that grew wild in the jungle. Ford's characteristically grand venture—dubbed "Fordlandia"—would in one stroke, if successful, defy the British-Dutch cartel, bring large-scale rubber production back to the Western Hemisphere, and advance the Ford Motor Company's strategy of vertical integration. "The production of such an area, on the basis of 1,200 pounds of rubber per acre annually," reported the *New York Times*, offering a sense of the venture's potential to alter the global rubber industry, "would be five times the total world production estimated by experts for this year."[42]

Upon arriving at Fordlandia, workers immediately set about transforming the jungle into something resembling a small midwestern town. In their first full year, they cleared 1,000 acres of jungle, planted 972 acres of rubber trees, erected a sawmill, and began permanent construction in the town. By 1930, three thousand employees had put nearly 2,000 acres into cultivation after clearing more than 3,000 acres of jungle; by 1934 the totals were 8,400 acres cleared and 1.39 million rubber trees planted. In town, the company had erected three schools, a modern 125-bed hospital, a 900-bed dormitory, a water tower outfitted with a factory whistle, and more than two hundred bungalow-style homes.[43] With the first trees expected to mature enough to produce rubber for export within ten to fifteen years, the endeavor seemed to be off to a successful start.

But all was not well. Along with significant labor unrest, a rift within the plantation's leadership, and a string of poor decisions, a host of environmental problems beset Fordlandia. Many of these stemmed from a poorly chosen site: hilly land necessitated expensive and time-consuming terracing to prevent erosion during heavy rains, for example, and the river's seasonal low-water point exposed a rock ledge fifty miles downstream that blocked access by deep-draft vessels during the lengthy dry season.[44] Even more significant was the wave after wave of native diseases and insects—absent in the Far East—that attacked plantation trees as they began to mature enough to form a closed canopy. Amazonian rubber trees, it turned out, had adapted to the region's numerous pests and diseases by spreading out in the jungle at the rate of only a few trees per acre. From a bug's-eye view, Ford's decision to plant them in a vast monoculture of closely spaced trees was the equivalent of inviting them to a banquet.

Even after Ford abandoned over half a million trees as unsalvageable, brought in James Weir, a plant pathologist with extensive experience on Far Eastern rubber plantations, and swapped Fordlandia's undeveloped acreage for a more suitable site upriver, the results turned out much the same. Workers cleared more jungle, built a new midwestern-style town, launched an intensive insect-control campaign involving both hand-picking insects from plants and spraying pesticides, and even developed a sophisticated new triple-grafting technique that combined high-yield clones with locally adapted, disease-resistant stock. By 1941, the new location's 3.6 million trees were approaching tappable age, inspiring high hopes in the company. But in late 1942 a massive caterpillar infestation, followed by a wave of leaf blight and the onset of dry weather, killed huge swaths of the plantation's trees.[45] In 1945, having invested better than $20 million in the endeavor, Ford turned the two plantations over to the Brazilian government for $244,200.[46]

The same pattern evident at Iron Mountain and Fordlandia—significant investment, rapid environmental change, a period of high hopes and general prosperity, and eventual bust and disinvestment—affected the very heart of Ford's industrial empire, not just its peripheral operations. When Ford switched from the Model T to the Model A in 1927, for example, operations shifted from Highland Park to the Rouge at an accelerating rate, and eventually even the final assembly lines relocated to the Rouge. As the Rouge's role grew, jobs, vitality, population growth, and booming real estate values followed—as did significant air and water pollution.[47] Meanwhile, Highland Park, the birthplace of mass production and the Five Dollar Day, the famous "Crystal Palace" that manufactured the car that changed the world, began a long, slow slide into oblivion. By 1933, the plant was a ghost of its former self, its vitality and prosperity drained, with some parts rented out and others devoted to storage. Today it stands abandoned, boarded over, and surrounded by barbed wire, a complex of brick buildings hulking up behind a small strip mall—one of many abandoned factories littering Detroit's landscape.[48]

ROAD ECOLOGY

If the environmental repercussions of manufacturing cars encapsulate the changes that assembly-line production and consumer capitalism set in motion, booming interwar road construction had effects that were in some ways much more subtle and in other ways more pervasive. One major difference is that roads touched virtually every ecosystem in the country—roughly one mile of road, on average, exists for each square mile of land in the United States.[49] Some of the ecological effects of such an extensive road network flowed from the ways that building, using, and maintaining roads during the interwar period restructured the immediate ecosystems in the vicinity of each road, introducing road cuts, erosion, and hydrological changes that restructured communities of roadside plants and animals. Other ecological changes flowed from the ways that roads *divided* landscapes, generating noise, fracturing habitat, and creating barriers to the easy and safe movement of animal populations. Still others flowed from the ways that roads *connected* landscapes, becoming vectors for various plant and animal movements (including invasive species) and forging links that facilitated commerce, natural-resource extraction, new roadside land uses, and individual travel.[50] Sustained scientific attention to the ecological effects of roads did not emerge until after World War II, but numerous interwar groups maintained an active interest in the different ways that roads interacted with the environments through which they ran.

Although the cumulative mileage of interwar construction projects gave them a remarkably wide reach, most individual projects during the 1920s, especially in rural areas, had predominantly localized ecological effects. The era's piece-by-piece approach to road improvements, in which contractors improved small sections of road one at a time, coupled with the stage-construction policy of the Bureau of Public Roads (BPR) that encouraged incremental improvements as traffic volumes grew, meant that the era's road-construction efforts rarely created sudden, dramatic changes along roads. In addition, during the 1920s most road-construction projects focused on upgrading pre-existing routes, not on creating completely new roads on new rights-of-way. Bigger projects often attracted significantly heavier traffic and prompted new roadside land uses, but for most rural projects in the 1920s, even significant upticks in traffic translated into relatively light usage in absolute terms. This changed by the late 1920s and early 1930s, however, by which time design standards had risen and the environmental manipulations of highway work had become more substantial. By the late 1920s, for example, the BPR calculated that the typical mile of federal-aid road work required 17,491 cubic yards of excavation.[51]

Because of its scope, the interwar road-construction boom generated significant demand for a variety of raw materials. By the late 1920s, for example, the BPR estimated the average per-mile quantities of highway construction materials at 3,726 square yards of pavement, 16,000 pounds of reinforcing steel, 4,325 pounds of structural steel, and 68 cubic yards of structural concrete.[52] This did not include materials such as sand, gravel, and rock, which had to be extracted, graded, and transported to road sites. Asphalt pavements required both crushed rock and bitumen, which by the interwar period came primarily from petroleum refineries rather than from the natural "asphalt lakes" that were the main source before the early twentieth century.[53] Reflecting both the material's growing popularity as a car-friendly pavement and the interwar road-construction boom, asphalt consumption skyrocketed from 2.3 million barrels in 1919 to 35.5 million barrels in 1941.[54]

Concrete pavements, whose use also soared in the interwar period, particularly for highways with heavy traffic loads, required crushed rock, sand, and Portland cement, a dry powder binder produced in a particularly energy-intensive process.[55] Especially in the West, which had long stretches of sparsely traveled roads, various oil- and tar-based sealants known as "road oil" gained popularity as a way to give dirt roads inexpensive surfaces and avoid dust problems. As a result, American refineries nearly doubled their output of road oil from 5.1 million barrels in 1931 to 9 million barrels in 1941.[56] Finally, as the period progressed, construction techniques slowly shifted from extensive use of human and animal labor toward fossil-fuel-powered earthmoving equipment, which reduced per-yard costs of large-scale cut-and-fill procedures by 40 percent between 1927 and 1940, making it much easier and cheaper to manipulate huge volumes of soil during roadbed preparation.[57]

Highway engineers displayed intense interest in gaining a scientific understanding of the relationship between roads and the natural world, although their concerns were narrowly limited to the knowledge they needed to build durable, structurally sound roads. One major research focus was developing solid and reliable subgrades for expensively paved roads. Building on the research that had begun with investigating the properties of sand and clay, exhaustive soil studies during the 1920s ultimately produced several simple tests for measuring the "soil constants" of any given location, which by 1929 were being used to place all soils into one of eight categories, each with a different set of engineering specifications for pavements.[58] A second major research focus was on durable, all-weather pavements. Engineers experimented extensively with various pavements, construction methods, reinforcing materials, and methods of mixing and laying asphalts and concrete. By the mid-1930s they had standardized and drastically reduced the number of specifications used for asphalt pavements and Portland cement aggregates, making it easier for engineers to specify—and suppliers to furnish—consistent materials for contractors. In these and similar research projects, engineers used their hard-earned knowledge to reduce the natural world's complexity into a handful of abstract categories. This in turn allowed them to build durable highways more efficiently and effectively—without continuing careful attention to the particularities of place.

In contrast to the attention that they lavished on foundations and surfaces, engineers largely ignored or treated as an afterthought the effects of road-improvement projects on roadsides and their associated communities of plants and animals. Those who did pay attention to roadsides tended to focus on their aesthetic deficiencies—particularly the "ugly" intrusion of roadside commerce (and, to a lesser extent, litter). "When people drive forth in automobiles," opined the *New York Times* in a typical critique, "they go not to see advertisements but the scenery. Ugly and barren roadsides are an eyesore."[59] Aside from a handful of states that adopted roadside tree-planting programs during the 1920s and continual railing in the press against billboards and other "blatant commercial advertising signs," aesthetic objections gained little traction.[60]

Roadside beautification efforts fared better in the 1930s. First, parkways—which typically included landscape architects on their design teams—began to gain substantial notice for their fully integrated aesthetic approach to highway design and construction. In addition, landscape architects became important members of the design teams working both on a number of prominent national park roads and on the Mount Vernon Memorial, Blue Ridge, and the Natchez Trace Parkways, all of which emphasized scenic beauty as part of their design criteria.[61] Second, the wider roads and changing design concepts of the 1930s, which made extensive use of new heavy earthmoving equipment, resulted in more obviously "scarred" roadsides that inspired growing interest in mitigating their raw appearance and tendency toward erosion. In 1932, for example, the American Association of State Highway Officials and the Highway Research Board formed the Joint Committee on Roadside Development, which issued a string of bulletins over the remainder of the decade promoting the concept of "complete highway" design. Third, the massive infusion of federal relief money into the road-building field, beginning with the National Industrial Recovery Act of 1933, set aside money that first allowed, and eventually required, a small percentage of federal aid to be used for roadside beautification and the creation of rest stops with bathroom facilities.[62]

Only a few groups paid much attention to the larger ecological implications of roads during the interwar period. Roadside soil erosion began to attract sustained attention in 1935, for example, when the Highway Research Board brought together the Soil Conservation Service, BPR, Tennessee Valley Authority, and various state highway officials to discuss the issue, prompting the formation of a Subcommittee on Erosion within the Joint Committee on Roadside Development. Members worried especially about growing use of heavy machinery for large road cuts and fills, which created modified slopes with loose fill that were particularly vulnerable to erosion. One experimental remedy, pioneered in various Tennessee Valley Authority projects, involved research into plant ecology and the use of native plants to help stabilize soil and reduce erosion.[63] In addition to erosion, the subject of automobile-related wildlife deaths—or "roadkill"—attracted some scientific attention. Most early work consisted of taking a census of dead animals, and especially birds, over given stretches of road.[64] The issue also inspired some interest for its impact on driver safety, prompting Pennsylvania's state highway department to post "deer crossing" warning signs along stretches of road with frequent collisions. Similarly, the federal Works Progress Administration produced a poster headlined "Don't Kill Our Wildlife," picturing two deer running across a road, perilously close to the looming headlights of an oncoming automobile.[65]

Despite these various efforts, the most sustained interest in roads' ecological effects came from engineers, who focused narrowly on advancing their road-building agenda and lessening potentially disruptive problems like erosion. Most other efforts focused more on aesthetic deficiencies than on ecological impact. Indeed, the desire for beautiful roads had its own important consequences, particularly as various groups embraced the task of transforming roads—too frequently overrun, in their opinion, by the "ugly" commerce of the Great American Roadside—into exemplars of a new kind of car-friendly nature.

CONSTRUCTING A CAR-FRIENDLY NATURE

During the boom years of the 1920s, as automakers and road builders restructured the nation's ecosystems around ever-growing numbers of automobiles, motorists began using their cars in ways that altered how motorists understood and interacted with the natural world. In particular, newfound mobility fostered a recurring quest for closer contact with nature. On this quest, motorists received remarkable aid and support. Automakers, for example, modified cars in ways that increased the sense of mastery over nature—and in the process made recreational driving more comfortable and pleasant. The road-building industry extended a network of smooth roads into almost every corner of the country. The National Park Service and state park departments created extensive, car-oriented facilities that welcomed motorists, fostered a sense of remoteness, and put spectacular scenery on full display. And the parkway movement inspired a profusion of picturesque highways that delivered motorists into the pastoral delights of the countryside. Together these trends set the stage for growing numbers of motorists to forge powerful emotional bonds with a carefully constructed "nature" as a green, beautiful place of therapeutic retreat from modern life. By putting such places within easy reach of motorists, these various car-friendly natures helped to create the illusion that cars and roads were agents of delivery from environmental problems—including those problems for which the rise of Car Country itself was responsible.

Having overcome the major obstacles to mechanical reliability that had dominated the pioneering era, automakers responded to the interwar road-construction boom with design changes that capitalized on the rapid spread of smooth roads. Growing numbers of automakers introduced changes that had been impractical in the era of poor roads, such as lowering vehicle suspensions and introducing more sensitive steering systems. In addition, smooth roads opened the possibility of driving at higher speeds, and automakers consequently incorporated bigger engines (and better brakes) into their designs.[66] Perhaps the most important design shift of the 1920s, however, was the dramatic swing toward closed-body designs as the proliferation of smooth roads helped eliminate the once-justified fear that enclosed cars would rattle apart during normal use on rough roads.[67] The paradigm shift toward enclosed cars, which had completed itself by the end of the 1920s, had at least two significant implications. First, closed cars banished dust, sun, rain, wind, and cold much more effectively than aftermarket accessories ever had, and as a result motorists could suddenly take for granted the ability to drive comfortably even in the foulest of weather. Second, since the cabins of closed cars did not have to withstand constant exposure to the elements, automakers began to equip them with an unprecedented degree of stylish, comfort-oriented amenities.

These changes, especially when coupled with smooth roads, transformed the ways that motorists interacted with the natural world. In stark contrast to the direct exposure to the elements that characterized early motor travel, in which mud and ruts, wind and rain, and heat and cold had dominated the motoring experience, the enclosed cars of the late-1920s and 1930s insulated drivers from weather extremes and isolated them from the elements. With car interiors becoming luxurious worlds unto themselves, the era's stylish, powerful cars fostered the illusion that drivers finally confronted a nature that was under their mechanical control. These changes had subtle but profound effects. For motor tourists, especially, the combination of smoother roads, enclosed cars, and bigger engines transformed what had once been slow, laborious treks through the elements into speedier, more comfortable jaunts across the countryside. In effect, closed cars allowed motorists to define nature as "scenery" rather than as "weather" or "mud." These changes made driving itself less of an adventure— increasingly mediated during the day by smooth highways and sleek automobiles, and at night by clever camping gadgets or inexpensive roadside accommodations. As a result, growing numbers of motorists turned toward the brand of nature that the American tourist industry packaged and promoted, which emphasized nature as a destination to visit and as scenery to view through a windshield.

Two significant trends in interwar road construction, each of which enticed motorists with a different version of car-friendly nature, responded to and built upon changes in recreational driving. The first trend originated in various federal government agencies as they searched for ways to promote motor tourism on public lands. Although a variety of agencies at the federal and state levels ultimately became involved, none went further or had a greater influence than the National Park Service, which before World War II remade the national parks into recreational wonderlands designed first and foremost to be engaged from the seats of automobiles. The second significant trend— a boom in parkway construction—originated in and around New York City in the mid-1920s and then spread to various federal projects overseen by the BPR. By combining the scenery and careful landscaping of parks with novel car-oriented engineering features that made them the most advanced highways of the time, parkways were in some ways the ultimate form of car-friendly nature. Parkway designers meticulously coordinated roadway engineering features and the parklike qualities of roadside landscaping to enhance the motoring experience. Tucked away in the cocoonlike cabins of enclosed cars, motorists connected with nature in the form of beautiful scenery and lush vegetation, transforming driving into a pleasant trip through a park.

Stephen Mather, who served as the first director of the National Park Service from 1916 until 1929, believed that the national parks needed to be broadly accessible to tourists—and especially motor tourists—to fulfill the democratic ideals that guided his agency's mission.[68] He became, for example, an early supporter of the National Park-to-Park Highway Association, which erected signs along a six-thousand-mile loop of highways in 1920 that connected the major national parks in nine western states. Mather expressed unequivocal support for a similarly car-friendly infrastructure within the parks themselves. "In the national parks there is one thing that the motorists are doing, and that is making them a great melting pot for the people of America," he told an audience of state park officials in 1924. "This will go far in developing a love and pride in our own country and a realization of what a wonderful place it is. There is no way to bring it home to them in a better way than by going from park to park, through the medium of an automobile, and camping out in the open."[69] To this end, Mather pursued congressional appropriations for new national park roads, winning a three-year, $7.5 million appropriation in 1924 and a ten-year, $51 million appropriation in 1927. Mather insisted from the beginning that the tourist infrastructure harmonize with the natural feel of the national parks. "In the construction of roads, trails, buildings, and other improvements," the Park Service proclaimed in its "Statement of Policy" in 1918, "particular attention must be devoted always to the harmonizing of these improvements with the landscape."[70]

Mather's efforts gained the BPR's full support after it completed the federal-aid system's final transmountain links in the mid-1920s, which freed the bureau to help accommodate growing motor-tourist traffic in national parks and forests.[71] Beginning in 1926, the BPR helped the Park Service plan over fifteen hundred miles of park road improvements, and by 1927 it had surveyed and constructed seventy-four miles of new roads in Crater Lake, Sequoia, Yosemite, Glacier, Mount Rainier, Grand Canyon, Lassen Volcanic, General Grant (the forerunner of King's Canyon), and Rocky Mountain National Parks. "These are merely a few of the important roads now under construction in the parks," BPR chief Thomas MacDonald wrote in 1927. "When they are completed they are likely to be rated among the most interesting tourist roads in America."[72] From the Transmountain Highway in Glacier National Park, parts of which were carved out of solid rock across the Continental Divide, to $1 million of improvements to the Valley Highway in Yosemite, the BPR—once a vociferous opponent of allocating scarce resources to recreational highways—had by the late 1920s become a crucial collaborator in the design and construction of some of the nation's most iconic motor-tourist roads.[73] It further extended this position in the early 1930s with projects in Zion Canyon, Rocky Mountain, and Yosemite National Parks, although the BPR's showpiece was the stunning Going-to-the-Sun Road in Glacier National Park, completed in 1933.[74]

Working with BPR engineers and landscape architects, Mather's National Park Service designed park roads to create what one historian has labeled "windshield wilderness"—unblemished natural landscapes easily accessible to (and viewable by) motorists via rustic roads crafted to blend into their surroundings.[75] The new park roads actively structured the experiences of visitors, guiding them from one attraction to another, focusing motorists' attention outward from the road toward each park's scenic features: mountains and valleys, meadows and forests, streams and waterfalls, geysers and glaciers, flora and fauna—all visible through the windshield in an ever-changing tapestry of awe-inspiring scenes. And along these roads were growing numbers of parking lots, easily accessible to those with cars, which provided jumping-off points for even closer contact via an elaborate infrastructure of hiking trails, canoe docks, picnic areas, and campsites. By the end of Mather's tenure, during which he oversaw the addition of 1,298 miles of new roads, 3,903 miles of trails, and extensive new campground facilities, the process of remaking the national parks into sites of car-friendly nature was well on its way.[76]

These trends accelerated in the 1930s, when New Deal work-relief programs elevated the project of making nature more accessible to motorists into a cornerstone of federal policy. In this, no government program was more important than the Civilian Conservation Corps (CCC). Originally designed to put young men to work on resource conservation projects in forestry and soil conservation, the CCC broadened in 1935 to include work on the nation's outdoor-recreation infrastructure. By 1942, CCC crews had constructed 125,000 miles of new roads, improved 600,000 miles of existing roads, and created over 8 million square yards of parking lots—in state and national parks across the country. Combined with other tourist-friendly improvements, including sanitary facilities, hiking shelters, bathhouses, running water, park administration buildings, picnic grounds, and the creation or improvement of over 128,000 miles of hiking trails and 90,000 acres of campgrounds, the CCC made motorized access to national parks easier than ever before. Americans responded enthusiastically as this car-friendly version of nature spread: national park system attendance soared roughly 600 percent in the 1930s, and record crowds of motorists poured into state parks.[77] In this sense, spreading car ownership, together with the creation of easily accessible, car-oriented landscapes in state and national parks, enabled generations of American motorists to find—and develop an interest in preserving—picturesque landscapes devoted to outdoor recreation.

Although the surging popularity of car-based outdoor recreation boosted interest in conservation, some of the movement's leaders viewed the trend with growing alarm. Aldo Leopold, for example, a forester and specialist in wildlife management who later wrote one of conservation's signature books, A Sand County Almanac (1949), worried that road construction and motor tourism seriously threatened the integrity of wild places. "Generally speaking," he wrote in 1925, "it is not timber, and certainly not agriculture which is causing the decimation of wilderness areas, but rather the desire to attract tourists."[78] Like Leopold, Robert Sterling Yard, a close friend of Stephen Mather's and an important publicity agent for the national parks during their formative first decade, became disenchanted in the late 1920s with the Park Service's emphasis on recreational access. When construction activities expanded in the 1930s, he moved into outright opposition. Arguing that motor roads were destroying what he called the "primitive" characteristics of the parks, Yard became a forceful advocate of roadlessness as a way of protecting large swaths of the primitive areas that he valued.[79]

The automobile—that quintessentially modern machine—struck both men as simply incompatible with the undeveloped, isolated characteristics of the places that they hoped to preserve. How could one have the experience, Leopold wondered, of *"facing nature alone, without any hotels, guides, motors, roads, or other flunkeys or reinforcements,"* if public agencies made everything accessible by road?[80] From these stirrings of discontent, Leopold, Yard, and six others founded the Wilderness Society in 1935. In its first meeting, its members drafted a statement of principles. "Cheerfully, we are willing that [motorists] should have opened to them the bulk of the 1,800,000,000 acres of outdoor America, including most of the superlative scenic features in the country which have already been made accessible to motorists," they declared. "All we desire to save from invasion is the extremely minor section of outdoor America which yet remains free from mechanical sights and smells."[81] Over the next three decades, the Wilderness Society became the most important advocacy organization fighting to preserve wilderness, achieving its signal success with the Wilderness Act of 1964.

During the same years that the Park Service created and then expanded its motor-tourist infrastructure, a parkway boom centered around New York City was developing a different sort of car-friendly nature. As with national park roads, parkway designers carefully managed their rights-of-way to present motorists with picturesque scenery and pleasant vistas, although designers intended for parkways to provide drivers with a bucolic, parklike retreat from the city, not to deliver them into a windshield wilderness.

The seeds of the mid-1920s parkway renaissance were planted in the second half of the nineteenth century. Frederick Law Olmsted Sr. coined the term "parkway" in 1868 for roads with two novel design elements. First, parkways were lined on either side with broad strips of city-owned park land, which gave roadways a secluded, parklike feel that contrasted markedly with the frenetic activity of commercial urban streets. These strips of parkland also ensured that no private property would abut directly on the road. As a result, the common-law tradition granting abutters free access to adjacent roads did not apply, which meant that parkways could limit the number and location of access points—a revolutionary idea that gained significance after the advent of high-speed automotive travel. Second, in another break with tradition, landscaped medians divided the roadway into multiple lanes, thus segregating commercial, pedestrian, and recreational traffic onto specified paths. Olmsted eventually advocated entire intercon-nected systems of parkways snaking through cities, which he hoped would put parklike surroundings within easy reach of all urbanites. Buffalo, Boston, Chicago, Minneapolis, and Kansas City all developed extensive parkway systems in the 1880s and 1890s to connect new city parks, although most were located in wealthy neighborhoods on the edge of town rather than in the heart of the city, as Olmsted originally envisioned. Parkways consequently developed an elitist reputation that caused them to fall out of favor after 1900.[82]

Interest in parkways revived in the mid-1920s with a spate of con-struction in and around New York City that brought Olmsted's ideas into the motor age. North of the city, for example, Westchester County began work on an extensive parkway system that, as the *New York Times* reported, was designed to make "Westchester the favorite run of great throngs of automobilists."[83] In the two decades following comple-tion of the Bronx River Parkway in 1925, the county built over seventy miles of parkways, including the Taconic, Saw Mill River, Hutchinson River, and Cross County Parkways, which together prompted a rush on county real estate by developers for car-based suburban enclaves. "Acreage Being Cut Up into Building Plots Finds Good Market," blared one headline. "Westchester Booming."[84] East of the city, New York's "master builder," Robert Moses, opened the Wantagh, North-ern State, and Southern State Parkways on Long Island in 1929, along with the Meadowbrook in 1934–1935, giving city dwellers direct access to the beaches of Long Island's southern shore, most notably at Jones Beach State Park, which Moses outfitted with enough parking to accommodate twenty-three thousand automobiles.[85]

Most of these parkways differed markedly from regular highways, partly because they barred trucks, buses, and commercial vehicles and partly because they spared no expense to make driving a pleas-ant experience. Highway engineers partnered with landscape archi-tects to endow parkways with design features that made driving on them resemble a trip through pastoral countryside even when pass-ing through well-settled areas. Their wide flanks featured thick plant-ings of picturesque native vegetation, creating the sense of being surrounded by nature. This also discreetly screened drivers from development that clashed with the desired naturalistic aesthetic. Rustic bridges, lampposts, and guardrails heightened the effect. In addition—and in stark contrast to the interwar period's strong preference for straight highway alignments—parkway layouts conformed to the topography of the surrounding area. This gave them sinuous, gently winding curves that minimized the need for cut-and-fill operations during construction. Combined with their other aesthetic features, parkways thus fostered a sense of unity with nature that attracted many admirers. In a ceremony bestowing eighteen design awards on the creators of the Bronx River Parkway in 1929, for example, New York's Arts and Sciences Society described the parkway as "a masterly living picture which could only be painted by nature itself, guided by the imaginative will of man."[86]

In addition to this carefully cultivated natural aesthetic, parkways included innovative engineering features that made driving safer and sped the flow of traffic. In combination with Olmsted's original provisions for limited access, engineers added entrance and exit ramps to minimize the disruption of cars turning on or off the roadway and used bridges to eliminate at-grade intersections with heavy cross traffic. The gentle, contour-hugging curves of the parkways also gave drivers easier grades and better sight lines than other highways of the day. Some of the earlier parkways, especially the Bronx River Parkway, had problems that drivers who exceeded intended speeds subsequently exposed—including narrow lanes, unbanked turns, and no median to separate cars going different directions—thus pointing the way toward improved designs in subsequent parkway projects. The innovative engineering of these years reached its apotheosis in the Mount Vernon Memorial Highway, which the BPR constructed between 1929 and 1932 as a showcase for cutting-edge design for the highway engineering community.[87]

Beginning in the early 1930s, New Deal work-relief money sparked a profusion of new parkway projects across the country. Some of these, such as Cleveland's Strongsville-Brecksville River Parkway and Milwaukee's Root River, Honey Creek, and Oak Creek Parkways, were small-scale projects with clear recreational purposes. Others, such as New York City's Henry Hudson, Grand Central, Cross-Island, Gowanus, and Interborough Parkways, were traffic movers that lacked the elaborate naturalistic landscaping of their predecessors, conforming to the letter but not the spirit of New Deal work-relief provisions limiting construction to "park access roads."[88]

The New Deal's signature parkways, though, were the Natchez Trace Parkway and especially the Blue Ridge Parkway, both low-speed recreational parkways with broad rights-of-way that ran more than four hundred miles through scenic countryside.[89] The Blue Ridge Parkway, which traversed spectacular mountainous terrain between the Great Smoky Mountains and Shenandoah National Parks, eventually brought together the National Park Service, BPR, and two state highway departments with several alphabet-soup organizations, including the Public Works Administration, Works Progress Administration, and Civilian Conservation Corps. To create what the Blue Ridge Parkway's major historian has described as a "super-scenic motorway," battalions of workers transformed raw road cuts into gently rounded banks, erected miles of quaint split-rail fences, and created recreational areas with hiking trails, picnic areas, shelters, and sanitary facilities.[90] In order to maintain what one designer working on the project called its careful "illusion of unspoiled countryside," the parkway's landscape architects transplanted appropriately picturesque log cabins along the road, erected new structures that evoked a pioneer past, and demolished buildings that were out of harmony with the desired aesthetic effect.[91]

In the same years that the Blue Ridge Parkway pushed the aesthetic of car-friendly nature toward the extreme end of the recreational spectrum, Connecticut's thirty-seven-mile Merritt Parkway, which opened in sections between 1938 and 1940, adapted its own version of car-friendly nature to the needs of high-speed suburban commuters. In contrast to Westchester's parkways, which originated as part of the county park system and were later embraced by commuters, the Merritt was designed from the beginning to relieve the traffic burden of the Boston Post Road, the major artery between Connecticut and New York City. Built on a three-hundred-foot right-of-way, the four-lane Merritt included numerous proto-expressway features designed to improve the speed and safety of heavy traffic: a wide, landscaped median, cloverleaf entrance and exit ramps, banked curves, and long straightaways. When combined with careful landscaping and rustic overpasses, the finished product attracted abundant praise. "It shows what the highway of the future should really look like," editorialized the *Bridgeport Post*, "a highway where the eye is filled with beauty and the mind with peace as the car purrs safely along."[92] Despite its success, the Merritt marked one of the last significant attempts to merge car-friendly nature with heavy commuter traffic. Highway engineers embraced its traffic-moving and safety features but dismissed its attention to aesthetic details as an unnecessary (and expensive) extravagance. The future of urban and suburban traffic-moving highways, they believed, lay in the direction of efficient, limited-access expressways—not in the carefully cultivated rusticity of parkways.[93]

CONCLUSION

The spread of Car Country changed American ecosystems—and American relationships with those ecosystems—in significant ways. Some changes, such as new roads and growing traffic in formerly inaccessible places, and the billowing smoke and polluted rivers near manufacturing facilities, are easy to identify. Others, like gravel pits, the changing distribution of plants and animals along roadsides, and logging operations in Michigan's Upper Peninsula, bear less obvious connections to the forces that called them into being and require some specialized knowledge to see the connections clearly. Still others, such as the various car-friendly, nonurban places that have been consciously designed and carefully crafted to celebrate close contact with nature, have a more ambiguous legacy. On one hand, they have subjected more and more places to car-based development, simplifying ecosystems and subjecting them to new pressures; on the other, they have introduced legions of Americans to a particularly attractive version of "nature," often fostering feelings of closeness, awe, and even the desire to engage, especially through outdoor recreation, or to protect, especially through conservation measures and protective legislation. Yet these aspects also implicitly cultivate the illusion that, by climbing into a car and driving out "into nature," individuals can escape, at least temporarily, the environmental consequences of modern urban-industrial society, and even of Car Country itself.

Photo Gallery Two

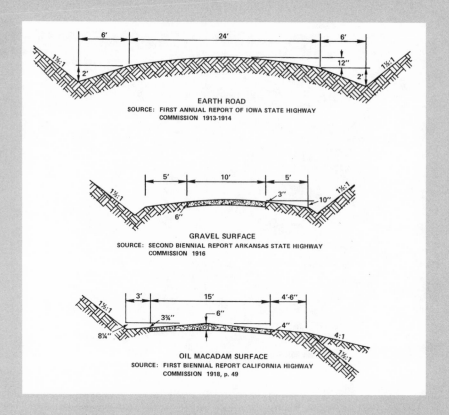

EARTH ROAD
SOURCE: FIRST ANNUAL REPORT OF IOWA STATE HIGHWAY
COMMISSION 1913-1914

GRAVEL SURFACE
SOURCE: SECOND BIENNIAL REPORT ARKANSAS STATE HIGHWAY
COMMISSION 1916

OIL MACADAM SURFACE
SOURCE: FIRST BIENNIAL REPORT CALIFORNIA HIGHWAY
COMMISSION 1918, p. 49

Evolution of typical road sections, 1900–1920. As vehicular traffic on rural roads changed in character and volume, so too did road design: pronounced crowns got flatter, and solid pavements replaced earth and gravel. From Federal Highway Administration, *America's Highways*, 383.

An annotated aerial photograph of University City, Missouri, early 1930s, highlighting development according to the city's zoning plan. As interwar city planners embraced zoning, they unintentionally wove greater transportation requirements into newly developed landscapes by segregating land uses into distinct single-purpose zones. Papin Aerial Service, St. Louis, from Bartholomew, *Urban Land Uses*, ii.

A typical traffic-flow map of the era produced by Miller McClintock's Erskine Bureau, 1930. Interwar traffic engineers responded to the crush of automotive traffic by systematically applying traffic-control techniques, ranging from stop signs to automated traffic lights, to create coordinated systems for traffic circulation across entire metropolitan regions. From Albert Russel Erskine Bureau, *A Traffic Control Plan for Kansas City* (Kansas City: Chas. E. Brown Printing Co., 1930), 56.

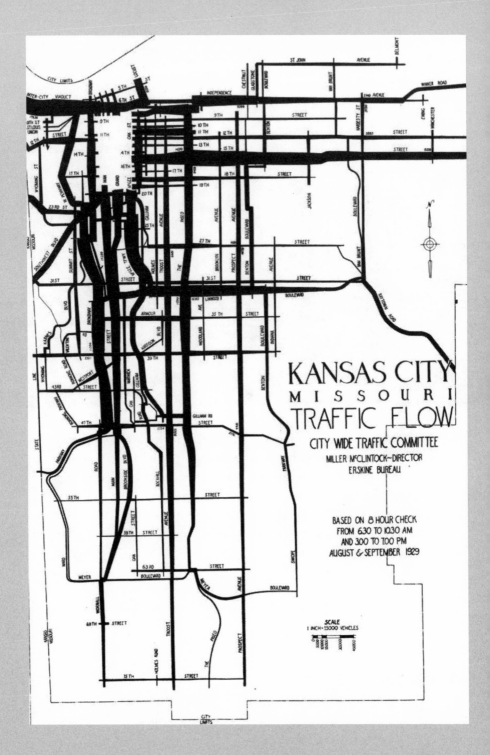

KANSAS CITY
MISSOURI
TRAFFIC FLOW

CITY WIDE TRAFFIC COMMITTEE
MILLER McCLINTOCK~DIRECTOR
ERSKINE BUREAU

BASED ON 8 HOUR CHECK
FROM 6.30 TO 10.30 AM
AND 3.00 TO 7.00 PM
AUGUST & SEPTEMBER 1929

SCALE
1 INCH = 15000 VEHICLES

231

New houses in a car-oriented suburb, Cincinnati, Ohio, 1935. As real estate speculators began marketing areas without access to the streetcar system to motorists—note the driveways providing off-street parking—residents of such areas relied on their cars to maintain easy access to important institutions and services. Carl Mydens, courtesy of Library of Congress Prints and Photographs Division, LC-USF34-000647-D.

Downtown Omaha, Nebraska, November 1938. Parking meters proliferated in the late 1930s as their dual benefit to cities became clear:
they increased the turnover of prime on-street parking spots and created a reliable new revenue stream for city governments. John Vachon,
courtesy of Library of Congress Prints and Photographs Division,
LC-DIG-ppmsca-10438.

Hi-Way Sandwich Shop, outside Waco, Texas, 1939. A legion of entrepreneurs followed swelling interwar traffic onto the nation's highways,
creating what the writer James Agee dubbed "the Great American
Roadside": a seemingly endless proliferation of gas stations, restaurants, bars, roadhouses, and overnight accommodations aimed at
attracting the business of motorists. Russell Lee, courtesy of Library
of Congress Prints and Photographs Division, LC-USF33-012503-M5.

"Sold into Slavery," 1929. The cumulative effects of roadside commerce appalled critics who denounced the rampant commercialism as a cancerous blight. "Whole communities," wrote one frustrated critic in 1928, "ha[ve] been thoroughly grounded in the practice of regarding 'nature' as a background for mercantile information." William Ferguson, from *Nature Magazine* 13 (June 1929): 1.

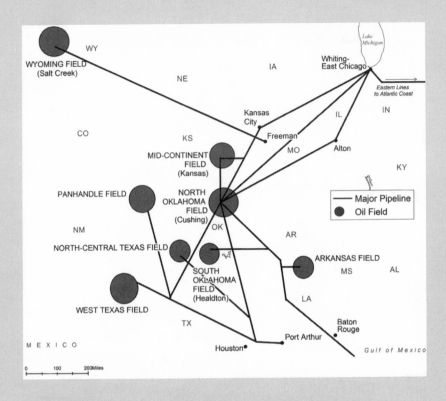

Structure of major U.S. pipelines, 1929. Whereas coal's bulk created dependence on rail- and water-based transportation, relatively small pumps could send oil, the lifeblood of the automobile, flowing at low cost through dedicated pipelines from field to refinery. A sort of national plumbing system dedicated to oil and its products evolved in response. Based on Williamson et al., *American Petroleum Industry*, vol. 2, *The Age of Energy, 1899–1959*, 342. Cartography by Sarah Horowitz, 2011.

"An Earthen Hell," 1923. Beginning with the iconic gushers signaling a new discovery, oil seeped everywhere from the production process in ways that disrupted aboveground ecosystems. Oil leaked profusely from the chaos enveloping flush fields, contaminating nearby streams and farms, seeping into the water table, and fueling frequent oil-field fires that sometimes raced out of control. Frank and Frances Carpenter Collection, courtesy of Library of Congress Prints and Photographs Division, LC-USZ62-98529.

A Santa Fe, New Mexico, gas station's tongue-in-cheek accounting of the various components determining gasoline's cost, 1938. Because government assessed a gas tax on wholesalers rather than retailers, motorists could not (and, today, still cannot) see the tax at the pump, rendering curiously invisible the backbone of the dedicated revenue stream that funded the interwar highway construction boom. Dorothea Lange, courtesy of Library of Congress Prints and Photographs Division, LC-USF34-019287-E.

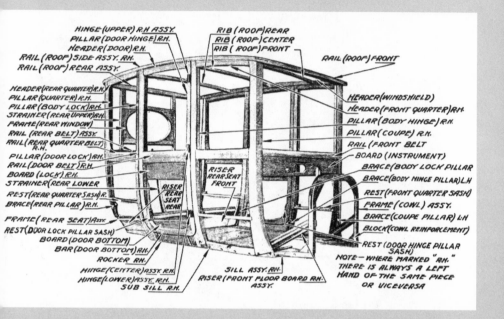

Diagram of the wooden parts in the Model T's closed-body sedan, 1923. The growing popularity of closed-body designs in the 1920s stimulated demand for lumber, putting new demands on distant forest ecosystems. As designs changed and steel replaced wood, however, lumbering operations like Ford's substantial Iron Mountain facility became increasingly obsolete, setting in motion a process of disinvestment and decline that carried a very different set of environmental consequences. From Ford Motor Company, *Ford Price List of Body Parts, Model T, Effective September 1, 1923* (Detroit: Ford Motor Company, 1923), 22.

"Don't Kill Our Wild Life," ca. 1936–1940. The interwar road construction boom had profound ecological implications, but the effects of roadside erosion and roadkill were two of the only subjects to prompt publicity or generate scientific research. Works Progress Administration, Federal Art Project, courtesy of Library of Congress Prints and Photographs Division, LC-USZC2-1001.

Motorists stop at a scenic overlook in Mount Rainer National Park, 1920s. For motor tourists, especially, the combination of smoother roads, enclosed cars, and bigger engines helped transform what had once been slow, laborious treks through the elements into speedier, more comfortable jaunts across the countryside, allowing motorists to reconceive nature as "scenery" rather than as "weather." Mount Rainier National Park Archives.

Bronx River Parkway, 1929, the iconic project that launched the interwar parkway boom. Aesthetic touches like rustic bridges, lampposts,
and guardrails; sinuous, gently winding curves; and careful naturalistic landscaping—especially when combined with innovative engineering features like limited access and the elimination of at-grade
intersections—distinguished parkways from typical rural highways
and created a distinctive new brand of car-friendly nature. From *Public
Roads* (Apr. 1929): 21.

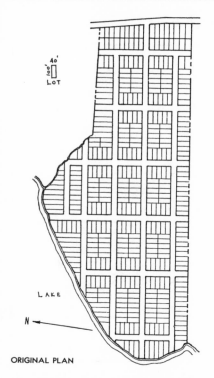

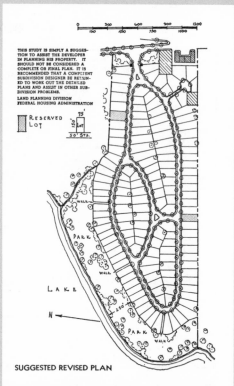

ORIGINAL PLAN

SUGGESTED REVISED PLAN

An excessive amount of street construction, the rigid and monot-onous layout of streets, the use of "butt" lots, and the subdividing of the wooded lakeshore, as shown in the original scheme, would have made this project costly to develop and difficult to market.

The revised plan has overcome these objections and every lot has been made a desirable building site. Although this plan pro-vides fewer lots, the changes permit a greater financial return and quicker sales for the developer and a better investment for the buyer.

A Federal Housing Administration publication contrasts a developer's "Original Plan" for subdividing a property with its own "Suggested Revised Plan," 1940. FHA development standards, which favored larger lots, winding streets, and especially "a greater financial return and quicker sales for the developer and a better investment for the buyer," profoundly shaped the land-use practices of postwar suburban developers. From Federal Housing Administration, *Successful Subdivisions*, 26-7.

Zoning for Off-Street Parking

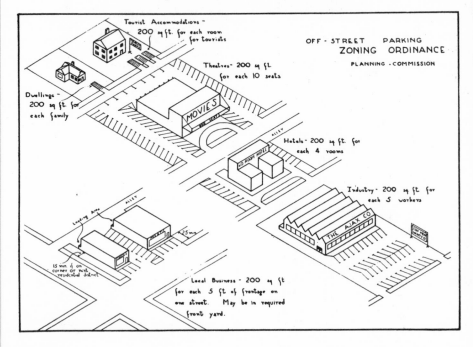

"Zoning for Off-Street Parking," illustrating parking requirements in a typical post–World War II zoning ordinance, 1947. After World War II, the integration of ample, free, convenient, on-site parking—a key component of Car Country—became a staple of new development, partly because it made good business sense and partly because municipalities began to require it through zoning ordinances like this one. From Levin, "Zoning for Parking Facilities," 13, reproduced from *The Tennessee Planner* (State Planning Commission, Dec. 1947).

Great Neck Shopping Center, Great Neck, Long Island, 1952. Viewed from the outside, shopping centers were entirely dependent on automobiles, located for the maximum convenience of motorists near heavily traveled suburban routes, with ample (and free) on-site parking. Courtesy of Library of Congress Prints and Photographs Division, LC-G613-61201.

The open-air mall of Prince George Plaza, Hyattsville, Maryland, 1959. Viewed from the inside, the well-appointed, pedestrian-only malls of regional shopping centers belied their reliance on automobiles, creating idealized (and car-free) downtown streetscapes for residents of the booming postwar suburbs. Gottscho-Schleisner Inc., courtesy of Library of Congress Prints and Photographs Division, LC-G613-74127-B.

Investigators interview motorists at a checkpoint in the Phoenix-Maricopa County Traffic Survey, 1956 or 1957. Origin-destination surveys like this one gave highway planners detailed information about travel routines, which helped them determine the "optimal" paths for new urban expressways, including the interstates, based strictly on traffic priorities. City of Phoenix, from *Better Transportation for Your City* (1958), 14.

Buses in downtown St. Louis, 1950s. For a variety of reasons—and by a variety of methods—cities across the country paved over streetcar tracks and adopted bus systems in the years after World War II. St. Louis Public Service Company, from *Better Transportation for Your City* (1958), 23.

Construction crews erect Boston's Central Artery, 1956–1959. Likening expressway construction to downtown's equivalent of essential heart surgery, urban boosters began pushing radical reconstruction as the key to solving downtown America's problems. In 1956, the momentous Federal-Aid Highway Act provided federal financing to realize these dreams. Courtesy of the Bostonian Society, vw0022/21

A sound street plan calls for proper integration of the four basic classes of streets. Note in this scene how the major arterial (vertical in photo) is linked with the expressway and also connects with collector streets. The latter provide access to the local streets.

A handbook for urban transportation planning presents this exit-ramp neighborhood as the epitome of good practice. The car-centric approach to transportation planning worked hand in glove with equally car-centric land-use planning practices, characterized by rigidly separated land uses, segregated into large single-use zones with ample off-street parking. California Division of Highways, from *Better Transportation for Your City* (1958), 46.

PART IV

New Patterns, New Standards, New Landscapes, 1940–1960

SUBURBAN NATION

WHEN WORLD WAR II ENDED, THE FIRST CAR-DEPENDENT LAND-scapes were already creeping across the United States. Especially in outlying rural locations where small neighborhood institutions had disappeared and in suburban areas that lacked public transportation, cars had become a necessary and important part of many people's lives. Such car-dependent places remained relatively few and far between, but the residents and retailers who populated them had demonstrated their profitability. Rather than withering and dying—the fate many observers had predicted—many car-dependent suburbs retained or increased their property values, enriching their developers and satisfying their residents. Moreover, outlying retailers had demonstrated that businesses catering to an automotive clientele could thrive, even during the most difficult years of the Great Depression. In contrast to the high-rent central business districts of cities, where prospects for resuming the vigorous growth of the 1920s seemed dim, undeveloped suburban areas struck postwar business leaders as a promising and expansive frontier.

Suburban Denver, Colorado, mid-1940s: large lots, no side-walks, single-use residential zoning. Stephen P. Jarchow, from Urban Land Institute, *Community Builders Handbook* (Washington, D.C.: Urban Land Institute, 1947), 67. Reprinted with permission of the Urban Land Institute.

As housing developers and retailers eyed the urban fringe in the first decade after World War II, car-dependent landscapes became central to the basic administrative, financial, and growth strategies of several powerful sectors of the American economy. Postwar leaders in the housing, retail, and transportation industries capitalized on new transportation and land-use policies to redefine "development" as "car-oriented development," which was stimulated by federal incentives, planned by experts who operated from the narrow perspective of their training and expertise, and subject to stringent land-use regulations designed to shield large real estate investments from risk. Offices and manufacturing facilities soon followed housing and retail into the sub-urbs, leaving cities reeling under the burdens of a contracting popula-tion, rapid demographic change, an aging infrastructure, expanding slums, and an eroding tax base—on top of other long-standing chal-lenges facing central business districts, such as tangled traffic, severe parking shortages, and deteriorating streetcar service.

After a decade of runaway suburbanization, just as things seemed to be at their worst for big American cities, the federal government elevated its incentives for suburbanization to an even higher level, most notably with the Federal-Aid Highway Act of 1956, which guar-anteed federal funding for 90 percent of the cost of a 41,000-mile sys-tem of superhighways. The system—designed by highway engineers almost entirely without consulting city planners or public transporta-tion officials—represented a supreme triumph over the environmental constraints that had long bedeviled efforts to maximize the potential speed and flexibility of cars. First, limited-access interstates dramati-cally changed the landscapes that they crossed, concentrating devel-opment and traffic at entrance and exit ramps while erecting otherwise impermeable boundaries between motorists and adjacent landscapes. Second, the interstates created an entirely new driving environment in which all the physical details of the roadway were designed to maxi-mize the speed, flexibility, and safety of automotive travel—whether driving in a snowstorm, across challenging mountainous terrain, or through the heart of a densely settled city. The interstates also directly challenged long-distance railroad traffic by linking all major metropol-itan areas via a transcontinental system of high-speed, multilane, toll-free, limited-access highways. Perhaps most importantly, however, the new interstates dramatically expanded the area available for profitable development in and near metropolitan areas. Additional federal subsidies for real estate development, combined with the car-oriented land-use development standards established in the first postwar decade, ensured that the explosive new growth along the new highways would be low-density, car-oriented growth. As the interstates spread, car-dependent landscapes began to dominate all others. With these basic building blocks in place, the United States completed its transformation into Car Country.

HOUSING

By the end of World War II, a serious, long-term housing shortage wracked American cities, big and small alike. By 1945, housing starts had failed to keep up with demand for new housing through sixteen straight years of depression and war. The number of urban rental apartments actually contracted from 16.3 million in 1940 to just 13 million in 1950 as rentals converted into owner-occupied homes, highlighting the acuteness of the shortage as soldiers began to return home.[1] The housing industry moved quickly to address these problems. Drawing on a host of new construction methods, including an adapted version of assembly-line techniques, housing construction boomed after World War II, adding roughly 15 million new housing units over the next decade. The overwhelming majority of these were single-family homes.[2] With the housing sector booming, national homeownership rates crept upward. Homeowners reached majority status in the United States for the first time in the late 1940s, climbing to 55 percent in 1950 and 62 percent in 1960.[3] Nearly all of the increase came in car-dependent suburbs, where homeownership nearly doubled between 1940 and 1950.[4]

Historians have noted that the explosive nature of the postwar housing boom made it look like a rapid, unplanned response to an overwhelming need, imbuing it—especially in retrospect—with a sense of inevitability. They have also noted, however, that what appeared unplanned and spontaneous was in fact the product of more than a decade of careful planning, innovation, and lobbying.[5] Two questions in particular place the postwar suburban boom—and the economic interests that engineered it—in the context necessary to understand Car Country's evolution. First, why did the housing industry respond to postwar demand with almost exclusively *suburban* construction? And second, why did suburban growth overwhelmingly take the form of *car-dependent* landscapes?

The answers to both questions lie, in large part, in the powerful role that the Federal Housing Administration (FHA) played in guiding the postwar housing boom, favoring land-use practices and solutions to transportation problems that privileged car-dependent suburban growth. Created as part of the National Housing Act of 1934, the FHA was the signature program in New Deal efforts to rescue the then-ailing housing industry. Designed with significant input from reformers, bankers, and realtors, Congress created the FHA "to encourage improvement in housing standards and conditions, to facilitate sound home financing on reasonable terms, and to exert a stabilizing influence on the mortgage market."[6]

To achieve these goals, FHA administrators targeted a variety of land-use problems and business practices plaguing the interwar housing industry, especially those facing large-scale developers. First on the agency's list was to eliminate the disorderly, corner-cutting suburban developers known as "curbstoners." In addition to cutting into big-builder profits, these speculative subdividers had gained notoriety for saddling buyers with low-quality improvements and wave after wave of special assessments as cities installed various utilities and other necessary upgrades. Second, the FHA sought to replace the typical urban practice of "promotional" zoning, in which municipalities used zoning as a tool for maximizing tax revenue, with "protective" zoning, in which they used zoning to protect neighborhoods from new, value-disrupting land uses. Finally, the FHA sought a way to overcome generally poor long-range urban planning for the development of streets, parks, and other public works, particularly beyond city boundaries where planning ranged between scant and nonexistent.[7]

The FHA addressed these problems through the mechanism of federal mortgage insurance—and, more particularly, insurance for long-term, fixed-rate, low-interest, low-down-payment, self-amortizing mortgages. Mortgage insurance gave bankers a powerful inducement to make home loans: before 1934, the typical home loan required a down payment of at least 30 percent of the home's value, and the combination of high interest rates and commissions, short terms of repayment, and daunting mortgage foreclosure rates discouraged would-be lenders.[8] Mortgages, in other words, were risky for banks— and thus hard to get. To increase loan availability, the FHA insured mortgages that met its strict underwriting standards, which were carefully crafted to insure long-term financial soundness. These standards detailed physical specifications for streets, utilities, sewers, and drainage; dictated minimum lot size and house setbacks; required zoning protection from competing, value-disrupting uses such as retail and industry; and developed minimum quality standards for house construction.[9] In the postwar years, obtaining FHA mortgage insurance often spelled the difference between proceeding with a project or not, so that even in suburban jurisdictions lacking building codes, builders used the FHA's minimum property standards as a de facto building code.[10] As a result, developers (and suburban municipalities) hoping to attract FHA insurance for new projects had a powerful incentive to adhere to the car-oriented template of large lots, comparatively low densities, and protective single-use zoning that the FHA demanded.

During the postwar construction boom, FHA mortgage standards created powerful incentives to home buyers, big builders, and lenders alike. Adding to the FHA's influence, the new Veterans Administration (VA), which was created in 1944 as part of the GI Bill, followed the FHA's standards and procedures to insure loans for sixteen million returning servicemen.[11] For home buyers, federal insurance made it much easier to find a home loan on favorable terms—the FHA and VA together secured loans for ten million new homes between 1946 and 1953 alone.[12] In many cases, borrowers paid lower monthly mortgage payments than they had paid before in rent, even after factoring in extra expenses.[13] The FHA mortgage standards also benefited big builders, particularly a provision known as Title VI, which offered "conditional commitments" for FHA-approved projects even before they had buyers.[14] These commitments allowed builders to obtain construction loans for much larger projects than banks had been willing to finance before and to get them on more favorable terms.[15] Lenders, too, benefited from the new arrangements, reaping the financial rewards of significantly expanded lending while the FHA assumed the most substantial risks. Insured against defaults, mortgages proved to be quite profitable.

The FHA standards changed the face of the entire housing industry. Before World War II, most suburban developers had been subdividers: platting land, improving it for building, and selling lots to people who arranged their own construction and financing. In the postwar period, by contrast, the industry was dominated by large-scale "merchant builders" who controlled every aspect of development, including land acquisition, the planning and construction of entire subdivisions of finished houses, and arranging financing for their buyers. The shift from the basic product of a lot in a developing neighborhood to the basic product of a finished house in a completed subdivision inherently favored big builders capable of handling the complexity and expense of construction at the neighborhood level or larger. It also worked to the disadvantage of speculative investors looking for a quick score.[16] In addition, the FHA's conditional commitments to builders explicitly favored "neighborhood unit" developments over those conducted on a smaller scale.[17] In a sign of how thoroughly things changed after the war, large builders constructed roughly two-thirds of all new housing by the late 1950s. In the interwar decades, by contrast, small construction firms that finished five houses or less per year built roughly one-third of all new homes, and owner-builders another third.[18]

The biggest developers captured generally favorable national headlines, with enormous companies like Levitt & Sons attracting significant coverage for their new technologies, advanced techniques, and efficient management. The Levitts secured their reputation with three famous "Levittown" developments between the late 1940s and early 1960s, including a 17,400-house development on Long Island, a 16,000-home project in Bucks County, Pennsylvania, built adjacent to the Pennsylvania Turnpike, and a similarly large development in Willingboro, New Jersey, just off the New Jersey Turnpike. The largest, on Long Island, took advantage of several of Robert Moses's signature park and parkway projects of the 1920s, nestling adjacent to the Wantagh Parkway by its western border, which provided easy access to Jones Beach, fifteen miles away; the Southern State Parkway, which led to New York City, was located by its southern border. It housed eighty-two thousand residents, the largest ever for a single

American developer, and included seven small "village greens," plus a variety of small recreational areas, including baseball fields, swimming pools, and playgrounds.[19] Since the Levitts proceeded without a master plan, however, and since they expanded Levittown's size as their land purchases accumulated, this handful of amenities, together with seven small shopping strips and a "town hall"—strictly a concession to appearances, given that the unincorporated community had no government for it to house—constituted the majority of the "city planning" that went into this city-sized development.[20]

Smaller merchant builders, who operated at the "merely big" neighborhood level of one or two hundred houses, had even less incentive than the Levitts to provide—or even reserve space for—the institutions and amenities that city planners championed. The FHA encouraged, but did not require, builders to reserve sites for schools and churches "if a subdivision is large enough to warrant," to include neighborhood shopping centers "where needed," and to create small parks to "render the entire tract more marketable," but the agency focused on the profitability and long-term stability of developments, not on securing conveniently located schools, churches, shopping, and parks for residents.[21] Most developers believed their projects were not big enough, by themselves, to justify the expense of reserving sites for community spaces and institutions, and so few provided them. Instead, most focused on what FHA regulations *did* require by hiring engineers to lay out streets, design utilities, and determine lot details, house placement, and setback lines. Because the FHA operated primarily outside the context of regional planning, nearly all of the era's suburban developments reflected that fact.[22] As subdivisions proliferated, the resulting agglomerations of housing earned the sobriquet "sprawl" for their infrequent and primarily unplanned public open spaces and community institutions.[23]

The same incentives that enriched buyers, banks, and big builders channeled investment away from urban neighborhoods. The FHA secured only first mortgages for homes, for example, so loans for rehabilitating or remodeling older structures did not qualify. In addition, its underwriting standards drew on appraisal techniques created by the Home Owners Loan Corporation (HOLC), which branded both older neighborhoods and racially and economically heterogeneous neighborhoods as "declining"—or too risky for investment. Known as "redlining" after the color used on HOLC maps to designate noncreditworthy areas, the standards automatically excluded neighborhoods with nonwhite residents from qualifying for mortgage insurance, creating an insidious federal endorsement of racially segregated housing—justified in the name of ensuring the long-term soundness of investments. By the same standards, the FHA did not insure even new, custom-built homes on vacant lots in established urban neighborhoods if those neighborhoods themselves contained too many old houses, multifamily dwellings, or diverse residents. Since all three were characteristics of cities, the resulting system starved cities of new residential investment and hurt the urban tax base by subsidizing the move of affluent citizens into the suburbs.[24]

If the resulting growth patterns hurt cities, they were a bonanza for suburban areas—prompting most local metropolitan-area governments to collaborate with big developers. Most localities, for example, quickly created the necessary planning mechanisms and zoning laws required for FHA approval if they did not already exist.[25] Local authorities also tended to approve projects and to file maps quickly, important practices for undercapitalized builders for whom time was money. Zoning determinations almost always favored builders, reflecting a negotiated balance between the builder's desire to keep costs down and public officials' desire to secure long-lasting, high-value construction.[26] Even when local officials differed on other issues, they could often agree on the desirability of growth—effectively agreeing to operate local government as a "growth machine."[27]

Fueled by federal incentives, postwar growth machines churned out subdivisions outside nearly every American city, the residents of which experienced near-complete segregation by race, income, and, to a lesser extent, age. Because FHA underwriting standards privileged homes in racially homogenous neighborhoods as the only truly safe investment risks, cities lost a whole generation of predominantly young, moderately affluent white citizens to the suburbs. In addition to establishing the homogeneity of the suburbs, this out-migration accelerated changes in urban demography that helped redefine cities as places occupied by the poor and people of color.[28]

Postwar growth machines also produced car-dependent landscapes on a theretofore unprecedented scale. Between 1950 and 1960, for example, the U.S. metropolitan population grew by roughly 45 percent while the square mileage that urban populations occupied doubled.[29] Again, FHA standards and the norms for suburban development that they fostered help explain the shift. First, they favored single-family homes on large lots—low-density development that reduced the number of buildings within walking distance of any given residence. Second, they mandated single-use residential zoning coupled with deed restrictions designed to protect large new subdivisions from potentially value-disrupting land uses, such as the construction of unplanned multifamily dwellings, retail establishments, offices, or factories.[30]

Such zoning and deed restrictions usually served their value-protecting purposes but did so at a cost to the walkability of suburban landscapes: they insured that the nearest possible location for retail, community institutions, and places of employment was at the edge of a subdivision.[31] Sometimes this produced retail clusters within walking distance of homes, but more often the distances were too long to cover conveniently by foot. Equally important, and in contrast to older streetcar suburbs, where only building lots within easy walking distance of at least one streetcar line were marketable, the builders of postwar subdivisions often made no provision for public transportation. Although FHA standards did take "accessibility" into account, they focused prominently on access by road.[32] Most suburban public transportation consisted of buses that stopped relatively infrequently along main collectors or arterials at the edge of subdivisions and thus required a long walk for residents to access.

By the mid-1950s, residents of many sprawling new metropolitan developments had only tangential everyday connections to downtown, which until very recently had been the universal focus of city life. "This is the kind of district where a housewife's remark that she is just going to step out to take the children over to the neighbor's house means that she is going to drive them five miles down a country road," explained *Harper's Magazine* in 1958. "Or if she says she's just running down to the store, she may drive fifteen miles to a shopping center, or a supermarket, or an upholsterer."[33]

RETAIL

That the *Harper's* proverbial housewife in 1958 would drive fifteen miles to a shopping center—rather than a much shorter distance downtown—reflected a significant change in the postwar American landscape. In the decade after World War II, American retailers followed the housing boom into the green fields of the suburbs, accelerating the shift toward car-dependent locations that began before the war. As in earlier decades, retailers chose locations outside the central business district for a variety of reasons, including the attempt to escape problems of downtown congestion and the desire to be closer to affluent suburban consumers. Even among big downtown retailers with no intention of abandoning their central city locations, establishing suburban branch stores—as opposed to expanding downtown facilities—represented the clear avenue for growth during the postwar years. In a fiercely competitive climate, big retailers moved swiftly to identify and colonize the best suburban locations ahead of their competitors.[34]

Car-oriented retailers continued to congregate in locations selected for maximum convenience to motorists. Major urban thoroughfares and arteries that connected new outlying subdivisions to the city, which were almost always zoned for retail, continued their transformation into long, traffic-choked ribbons of restaurants, Laundromats, auto dealers, motels, gas stations, auto-parts stores, and other similar enterprises, most featuring off-street parking and large signs designed to attract passing motorists. Secondary business districts established during the interwar years expanded by attracting new tenants, as did many smaller neighborhood business streets. An occasional small retail cluster here and a scattered individual store there continued to crop up where zoning permitted.

In addition to these string-street and cluster developments, developers began to expand in scale and scope the design of the neighborhood shopping center, which had emerged in the 1930s, producing large new "community" shopping centers and even enormous new "regional" shopping centers that competed with downtown in both the range and diversity of their offerings.[35] In contrast to the chaotic growth of the automotive strips, the developers of planned shopping centers often launched elaborate location studies to guide their siting decisions, analyzing local population characteristics and income, the traffic load and overall capacity of major roads, the expected driving time from targeted neighborhoods, the anticipated overall trade area, and estimated necessary parking.[36]

Both the planned and unplanned retail developments of the postwar years embraced car-oriented site features to a much greater degree than had decentralized interwar retailers. One crucial difference was the degree to which postwar retailers integrated ample, free, convenient, on-site parking into their sites.[37] "The basic need of the suburban shopper is for [a] conveniently accessible, amply stocked shopping area with plentiful and free parking," wrote Victor Gruen, a prominent postwar shopping center designer. "This is the purely practical need for which the shopping center was originally conceived and which many centers most adequately fulfill."[38] Other car-friendly features, including easy on-site circulation and quick access to and from the road, reached their apotheosis in an explosion of new "drive-in" service windows, which appeared not only at increasingly popular drive-in "fast-food" restaurants but also at banks, dry cleaners, liquor stores, and even some less likely institutions, including funeral homes and churches.[39]

Providing ample free parking made good business sense, but its widespread appearance among postwar restaurants and retailers, including those that had found curbside parking sufficient in the interwar years, also reflected a profusion of zoning codes that *required* businesses to furnish it, most often in a fixed ratio to floor space. Virtually unheard of before the war, zoning requirements for parking proliferated in the late 1940s, making off-street parking requirements the most prevalent form of zoning-code revision during that period.[40] In 1950, a comprehensive national survey of the subject found 155 municipalities that had created zoning provisions requiring off-street parking; in 1954, a follow-up survey identified 311.[41]

The most iconic postwar use of off-street parking lots came with the rising popularity of planned suburban shopping centers. Here, again, FHA underwriting standards played a role, particularly in the diffusion of neighborhood shopping centers, the smallest and most abundant type. As early as 1936, the FHA began to encourage neighborhood shopping center construction among developers who were planning projects in areas that lacked an adequate number of stores in the vicinity—even going so far as to supply them with generic shopping center plans. Designed to be anchored by a supermarket or variety store, plus a drug store, all arranged around a shared parking lot, such developments were envisioned by the FHA as serving the everyday shopping needs of somewhere between three and fifteen thousand nearby residents—or at least 750 families. By the postwar period, larger developments routinely included shopping centers with large, on-site parking lots, not least because they continued to generate revenue long after the final house sold and the builder had moved on. The FHA's apparently secondary goal of discouraging unplanned, agglomerating strip developments along suburban arteries, on the other hand, proved significantly less successful.[42]

Retailers embraced planned shopping centers of all sizes for many reasons. First, tenants benefited generally from the work of management companies, which owned and operated each shopping center as a unit. This allowed a management company to control the tenant mix, preventing unwanted competition from moving in next door. Second, tenants benefited from the management company's planning work, which often included location studies and other legwork that ensured the viability of the entire enterprise, such as working with local governments to resolve conflicts over development issues.[43] Third, tenants divided the expenses of upkeep, parking, lighting, signs, and shared public spaces. Fourth, and perhaps most importantly, shopping centers benefited from the same phenomenon that downtown boosters had always thought of as a product of "central location," but which postwar shopping center developers called "synergy"—the tendency of stores to generate more business when carefully grouped together than when located in isolation. Shoppers already visiting a shopping center to pick up groceries, for example, could more easily grab additional convenience goods they needed from another store in the same complex rather than driving to a competitor.

The resulting pattern of retail development took overwhelmingly car-dependent forms. Even neighborhood shopping centers serving a relatively concentrated population tended to locate on the edge of new subdivisions rather than at their center, which would have put them in easier walking distance of residents. They did so in part because FHA guidelines strongly discouraged locating retail within neighborhoods and in part because locating on a more trafficked collector or artery increased accessibility to motorists from beyond the neighborhood. For the same reasons, community shopping centers (designed to serve 15,000 to 100,000 people, typically featuring at least one junior department store as an anchor tenant) and regional shopping centers (designed to serve from 100,000 to 1 million people, featuring one or two major branch department stores, plus goods and services in a depth and breadth nearly matching the central business district) located themselves near the intersections of heavily traveled suburban routes. Because these shopping centers were designed to serve considerable numbers of people, most of their customers would have to come from unwalkable distances. Their vast parking lots and carefully selected locations maximized the convenience of access by automobile, leaving no doubt as to how developers expected most patrons to arrive.[44]

Regional shopping centers, which replicated something akin to downtown's offerings in one fell swoop, were phenomenally expensive endeavors, and early postwar developers took significant business risks to create them. Such massive undertakings took a long time— one prominent planner estimated an "incubation time" of between one and one-half and six years—and developers typically had to carry planning costs for most of that before they could secure financing. This involved selecting a site; planning for growth, traffic, and merchandising; designing and engineering the shopping center; finding tenants and securing leases; and securing all of the necessary public approvals and zoning changes.[45] In part because of the risks, and in part because there were faster profits in developing suburban houses, the first planned regional shopping center did not open until 1949, on the edge of Raleigh, North Carolina. Similar developments followed outside Seattle, Los Angeles, Boston, and Milwaukee—all featuring open-air pedestrian malls. Between 1949 and 1953, regional shopping centers opened at the slow but steady rate of between one and three per year, followed by record years in 1954 (seven) and 1955 (five). The first fully enclosed regional mall, Southdale—a two-level mall with seventy-two stores and five thousand parking spots—opened outside Minneapolis in 1956.[46]

If shopping centers were entirely car-centered on the outside, sitting in the midst of great seas of parking, their key interior feature—because of which they became known colloquially known as "malls"—was their use of a large, central, pedestrian corridor that completely excluded automobiles. Designed as idealized downtown streetscapes for residents of the booming postwar suburbs, the earliest regional malls featured unified "modern" design, elaborate landscaping, comfortable open spaces, and a diverse mix of retail establishments, including full-scale department stores. Enclosed malls went a step further, offering a completely climate-controlled shopping experience. In addition to excluding traffic and the weather, enclosed malls conspicuously tackled downtown's worst problems as defined by most of the malls' white, middle-class patrons: parking shortages, congested traffic, the presence of "undesirable" social elements, unruly establishments like bars and pool halls, and the general noise, dirt, and dynamism associated with shopping downtown. As one of the foremost historians of shopping centers has noted, in eliminating these elements malls also commercialized public space, subordinated traditional rights to free speech to management's desire for public order and decorum, and fostered an identity among women as consumers but not producers.[47]

Meanwhile, downtown retailers suffered. In Philadelphia, for example, the number of customers at flagship department stores declined in 1953 and then again in 1954—the beginning of a long, slow decline that lasted more than two decades.[48] In Los Angeles, which had taken decentralization further than any other American city, downtown's share of the metropolitan region's retail business fell from 30 percent in 1930 to 11 percent in 1948, prompting *Business Week* to declare in 1951 that downtown Los Angeles's doom had been sealed. The changes were not just a matter of poor public transportation: even in cities with well-developed rapid-transit systems, including New York, Chicago, Boston, and Philadelphia, outlying business districts gained position relative to downtown.[49]

As cities struggled, downtown leaders girded for a fight. Big-city chambers of commerce adopted a tried-and-true mixture of statistical quibbling, praise for the plucky entrepreneurship of downtown business owners, faith in the everlasting importance of central location, and elaborate plans for improving downtown's infrastructure. "The proportion of sales downtown may decline, but an aggressive selling program can counteract this trend to increase the physical volume," proclaimed one typical booster in 1954. "Smart merchandising, neat stores, an attractive central business district, better access highways, an improved free-moving traffic pattern, convenient public transit, and more adequate parking guarantees the prime position occupied by the central district."[50]

Postwar boosters agreed with near unanimity on all of these proposals, but plentiful parking topped most wish lists. The profusion of zoning codes requiring new businesses to provide off-street parking applied only to new construction, and retroactively applying parking requirements to existing downtown merchants was of dubious legality. As a result, zoning for parking increased the accessibility of outlying businesses without improving conditions downtown.[51] By the late 1940s and early 1950s, some cities began to go into the parking business for themselves, using steady parking-meter revenue to secure financing for municipally owned parking facilities. Large new parking garages in more than a dozen cities, both public and private, appeared by the mid-1950s, but parking shortages remained a problem, especially in the biggest cities.[52] In 1950, for example, American cities with half a million residents or more averaged just twelve downtown parking spots per thousand residents, and 30 percent of downtown parkers walked at least 800 feet to reach their destination.[53]

Second on most wish lists was constructing the high-speed, limited-access freeways that traffic engineering studies had been championing since the 1930s. "We are suffering from hypertension in our central business district, much as humans suffer from hypertension when too much blood is fed to the heart," declared the director of New Orleans's planning and zoning commission. "Only, in this case, the arteries are our streets and the cars are our blood. When a human has such troubles, he goes to a doctor for relief, often for surgery. Our surgery is to build better streets and to construct expressways."[54] Leaders in other cities agreed. The astronomical costs of condemning land downtown to make room for freeways had kept most freeway plans on the drawing boards through the Depression and war, but in the early postwar period, as federal aid for urban extensions became more generous, some cities actually began to build. By the mid-1950s, New York, Boston, Detroit, Cleveland, Chicago, Pittsburgh, Los Angeles, San Francisco, and a handful of other cities had all begun or completed short sections of freeway. Many other cities had active planning under way, but the expense—and, in the late 1940s, the politics of razing houses during a housing crisis—proved formidable.[55]

As leaders struggled to make downtown more accessible by car, the 1954 Congress revised the tax code in a way that inadvertently created a massive new subsidy for suburban commercial real estate development. Responding to a mild economic downturn in 1953, Congress designed the subsidy to stimulate new capital investment in industry by dramatically reducing the period—from forty years to just seven—over which taxpayers could "write off" losses from the depreciation of capital equipment, including buildings. Although the legislation included investments in commercial real estate almost as an afterthought, it had its most profound impact in this area, transforming commercial real estate investment into a giant tax shelter. Investors could now significantly reduce their taxes by writing off the paper "losses" incurred by claiming the rapid depreciation of new buildings.[56]

Investors took immediate advantage of the new rules by pouring money into new projects, prompting a speculative boom in suburban commercial development—nearly all of which followed the car-dependent standards for location and site layout developed in the first postwar decade. In a sign of the significance of "accelerated depreciation" to commercial developers, one early study showed that by 1959, 97.9 percent of all real estate partnerships took advantage of the new incentive—as opposed to a rate among overall eligible businesses of about 17 percent.[57] For the largest and most expensive real estate projects, such as regional shopping centers, accelerated depreciation dramatically reduced the risks and increased the rewards of investment. In 1956 alone, just long enough after the tax code revision to rush a major project through its "incubation period," developers completed twenty-five new regional shopping centers totaling 15.6 million square feet. This was an astonishing number of projects, especially considering that in the entire period from 1949 to 1955 developers had completed just twenty-one such shopping centers totaling 16.4 million square feet. New regional malls added roughly 10 million square feet of new suburban retail space in car-dependent locations every year from 1957 to 1959 and 20 million square feet per year from 1960 to 1962.[58] By October 1960, fifty-eight regional suburban shopping centers boasted at least half a million square feet of floor area.[59] Similar tax benefits accrued to speculative investors and big businesses—particularly the many franchises and chains that spread like wildfire over the next two decades—who rushed to expand the Great American Roadside.[60]

TRANSPORTATION

As new land-use regulations and incentives channeled the growth of the housing and retail industries in car-dependent directions, a series of fitful changes in transportation policy and infrastructure development made it easier than ever before to get around by car. Highway budgets soared after World War II, but state highway departments continued to play the familiar game of catch-up, particularly in expanding metropolitan regions with the heaviest traffic.[61] By 1946, total state highway disbursements reached $1.8 billion, just below their prewar peak; thereafter they expanded rapidly, more than tripling to $6.9 billion by 1956 after Congress informally began "linking" highway allocations to federal gas tax income.[62] In some ways, state highway departments were well prepared for postwar construction, having spent the war planning ambitious new projects, including urban expressways. Yet the postwar housing boom created steel and lumber scarcities, which slowed construction, and postwar inflation offset some increased spending.

The continuing growth of traffic presented by far the most important challenge for highway planners. During the postwar years, motorists added tens of billions of vehicle miles traveled annually, setting new records every year from 1946 until 1952. The lion's share of the increase came in metropolitan areas, and though state highway departments focused growing resources on urban roads, total freeway mileage remained relatively small. Other urban projects, especially arterial street widenings, did little to improve traffic conditions along routes into the booming suburbs, particularly as new businesses lined even the widest highways with near-solid walls of traffic-generating commerce.[63] Then, in the early 1950s, just as engineers began to finish plans in 116 cities for new federally funded arterials, materials shortages due to the Korean War slowed construction once again.[64]

The blueprint for postwar highway construction efforts, which had been established during World War II, extended the traffic-service vision that had dominated the interwar period. In April 1941, in response to the Pennsylvania Turnpike's success, President Roosevelt appointed a National Interregional Highway Committee comprised of a mix of highway engineers, urban planners, and politicians but dominated by Thomas MacDonald, the chief of the newly renamed Public Roads Administration (PRA), to study once again "the need for a limited system of national highways" for interregional transportation.[65] The resulting report, *Interregional Highways* (1944), recapitulated the main points of *Toll Roads and Free Roads* (1939), including its emphasis on traffic-service priorities, its commitment to urban express highways, its opposition to toll financing, and its vision of a new interregional highway system. New in the report was the proposed size of the interregional system (whose mileage rose from 26,000 to 39,000 miles), the recommendation that the entire system have restricted access (despite the fact that just seventeen states had laws enabling limited-access roads), and a proposal to build parking facilities near traffic interchanges on the edge of big-city downtowns. The report paid lip service to the power of urban expressways as "a powerful force tending to shape the future development of the city," but it nevertheless privileged engineering techniques and traffic-service priorities in its guidelines for locating expressways, which ignored the social and aesthetic criteria that animated many urban planners.[66]

In contrast to earlier years, when near unanimity among state highway officials had resulted in the passage of bills virtually identical to the recommended legislation put forth by the American Association of State Highway Officials, their professional organization, disagreement within the prohighway community gave politicians a good excuse to wrangle over the Federal-Aid Highway Act of 1944. The resulting legislation produced the largest-ever federal highway bill to that point, approving $500 million of federal aid per year for three years, of which $225 million went to the federal-aid system, $125 million to urban extensions, and $150 million to rural secondary and feeder highways. In a break from tradition that promised to help cities laboring to fund new expressways, the legislation authorized use of federal-aid money for up to one-third of the costs of acquiring rights-of-way. And, of enormous significance, it authorized—but did not dedicate any specific funding to—a new forty-thousand-mile system based on the proposals in Interregional Highways, which it named the National System of Interstate Highways.[67]

At the PRA's request, state highway departments immediately began designating the routes of the new interstate system, and in August 1947 the Federal Works Administrator approved locations for all but 2,319 miles—all urban bypasses and connectors set aside for further study.[68] All urban portions of the system were designed to penetrate deep into cities to facilitate access to downtown. Reflecting the general lack of collaboration at the time between land-use planners and transportation officials, nothing in the enabling legislation stipulated a role for city-planning officials in mapping out these routes, nor did it establish any review mechanism to ensure that the new interstates would conform to existing comprehensive urban plans. The legislation left it up to state highway departments and city councils to determine the exact process for selecting the new highway routes, but in most cases highway officials did the planning and route selection on their own and then asked cities to approve their recommendations.[69]

Not surprisingly, the techniques that highway officials used to map out the new routes grew from their training as engineers and from their traffic-service priorities. Their main tool was the "origin-destination survey," in which investigators interviewed motorists at checkpoints and urban residents in their homes to establish detailed information about travel routines. Between 1944 and 1945, officials conducted such surveys in 135 cities with populations of fifty thousand or less and in 30 large metropolitan areas, with the goal of generating a more sophisticated understanding of travel patterns than traffic counts and traffic-flow maps could reveal. In order to differentiate between the routes people actually took and those that they would take if a more direct option existed, officials created "desire-line" maps comprised of straight lines connecting the origin and destination of each trip recorded in their surveys. The routes where lines overlapped the most, in theory, should reveal the best routes to serve traffic needs. Planners used this information to identify "control points" along the desired route and then mapped the interstates through the nation's cities by connecting these control points together.[70] Bigger social, economic, and environmental questions about the new expressways, their relationship with future urban growth, and their impact on other modes and patterns of urban transportation all took a backseat to this traffic-service approach to location.[71]

Meanwhile, urban public transportation underwent its own sea change as buses replaced streetcars and total ridership fell precipitously. The switchover from streetcars to buses, which began in the late 1930s and was largely complete by 1955, provides one of the more colorful stories in American transportation history. The major characters and events included a nationwide, General Motors–led conspiracy involving various tire, oil, and truck companies; a family of brothers who parlayed a small business busing miners and schoolchildren around Minnesota's Mesabi Iron Range into National City Lines, the nation's largest transit company; thousands of miles of scrapped streetcar lines and tens of thousands of scrapped streetcars; a criminal conviction in 1949 for federal antitrust and restraint-of-trade violations, coupled with penalties of just $5,000 on each company and $1 each on a handful of executives; and a sensationalistic presentation and report on the conspiracy to the U.S. Senate, just after the oil shock of 1973.[72]

Historians continue to debate the conspiracy's significance, but amid the various points of contention several points remain clear. First, although National City Lines ultimately controlled streetcar systems in some forty-five American cities, virtually all cities with streetcar systems confronted a long-term decline in streetcar ridership, which fell from 12 billion rides in 1928 to 7.2 billion rides in 1937. World War II briefly pushed ridership to 8.1 billion rides in 1947, but then it crashed to 1.2 billion rides in 1955.[73] Second, the switchover took place within a particular political context. For many politicians, replacing streetcars with buses provided an opportunity to restructure the politics of urban public transportation along more advantageous lines.[74] Finally, combined public transportation ridership declined sharply after World War II. Bus, trolley, and streetcar ridership combined hit a postwar peak of 19.6 billion rides in 1947 but then plunged to just 9.7 billion rides in 1955.[75] Together these trends caused revenues to plummet, prompting further cuts in the frequency of service, the elimination and consolidation of routes, and deferred maintenance, creating a vicious feedback loop of deteriorating service and declining revenues.

While public transportation struggled, the toll-road movement thrived. The creation of the interstate system in 1944 had briefly renewed faith in the possibility of financing a modern, nationwide system of free roads, but with traffic growing, Congress's failure to fund the interstates, and new financial-needs studies projecting highway requirements of roughly $60 billion over the next fifteen years, the jangling coins in the Pennsylvania Turnpike Authority's coffers enticed many states to reconsider.[76] In 1945, Maine began work on a forty-seven-mile toll road and New York instituted tolls on two major parkways into the city. Interest in these profitable ventures snowballed, and by 1954 twenty-two states had established toll road authorities that together had completed 1,239 miles of toll highways and had begun work on another 1,382 miles. Plans in various stages of approval were in the works for another 3,314 miles.[77] Despite what appeared to be irresistible momentum, however, toll-road construction crested in 1953. In part this was due to the Bureau of Public Roads (BPR), which continued to argue that tolls should be a last-ditch measure and to point to the 5,620 miles of interstates already completed with federal-aid financing by the end of 1953 (albeit to lower standards than the system later required) as evidence that existing funding was enough to build most interstates.[78]

When the Korean War ended in mid-1953, attention in Washington, D.C., returned to domestic issues, with highway needs high on the list of priorities. Over the next three years, two developments elevated the interstate system from an underfunded, largely unexecuted plan into the most wide-ranging, landscape-altering public works project in U.S. history. The first was the Federal-Aid Highway Act of 1954, which earmarked the first money specifically for the interstate system ($175 million) while raising total federal aid to highways by roughly 50 percent for 1956 and 1957 so that expenditures matched gas tax income. The second development came when President Eisenhower became actively involved in highway politics, declaring his intention to create a new transcontinental system that would solve the nation's increasingly well-publicized highway woes. The resulting maneuvers, countermaneuvers, plans, and counterplans, which are among the best-studied in American highway history, ultimately ended with passage of the momentous Federal-Aid Highway Act of 1956 and the Highway Revenue Act of 1956.[79]

In addition to expanding funding for the existing federal-aid program, these two pieces of legislation upgraded, slightly expanded, and fully funded the interstate system that Congress had originally approved in 1944, officially renaming it—in a sop to cold war politics—the National System of Interstate and Defense Highways. The legislation differed notably from previous federal-aid acts in three areas. First, with the exception of adding one thousand miles to the system and formally reviewing the urban routes designated in 1947, the "new" interstate system was the same transcontinental highway network established in 1944.[80] By stipulating that the entire system be built to uniformly high, multilane superhighway standards, however—even in locations where traffic volume did not justify them—Congress greatly expanded the system's scope and took a step beyond the long-standing engineering principle that traffic demands alone should shape the nation's highways. The entire interstate system was to reflect the highest possible engineering standards, however small the traffic volume of its more remote stretches.

Second, the 1956 legislation funded the construction of the entire interstate system, treating it as a single project to be finished in a designated period. This broke with the basic understanding that had guided both federal aid and the various formally designated federal-aid highway systems since at least 1921. Federal aid had always reflected an ongoing process of dividing available money among states, not a program designed to build a fixed, predetermined highway system. In contrast to the 1956 legislation, earlier federal-aid systems had existed primarily to ensure that limited expenditures would not be dispersed in an uncoordinated way.[81]

Third, and crucial to its political success in Congress, the legislation formally enshrined "linkage" as federal policy. To meet the 90 percent federal share of the interstate system's cost, Congress raised the federal gasoline tax by one cent and created new excise taxes on tires and vehicles. The resulting revenue, along with other existing highway-user income, flowed into a new Highway Trust Fund, whose sole purpose was to pay interstate construction bills. The Trust Fund effectively insulated this revenue from political debates over appropriations, even after the cost estimates for completing the system began to balloon—rising from $27 billion to $39.5 billion between 1954 and 1958 alone. Meanwhile, rising gasoline consumption, coupled with another one-cent hike in the federal gas tax in late 1959, kept Trust Fund coffers full. Because its moneys were "linked" to interstate construction, they guaranteed the system's completion even after the political winds of antihighway sentiment began to blow with growing force in future decades.[82]

Like federal incentives for housing and commercial real estate development, federal funding for the interstate system had profound implications for the American landscape. First, because the interstates sliced through cities with the explicit intention of making downtown more accessible to motorists, they profoundly reshaped cities. Huge swaths of built-up real estate had to be cleared for the new expressways, often in conjunction with long-standing "slum clearance" priorities that disproportionately displaced poor and minority populations. Moreover, the new freeways, and especially elevated freeways, often had a blighting effect, prompting deterioration and decay in previously healthy adjacent neighborhoods. The interstates did create easier access to downtown for motorists, although greater access did not revitalize downtown in the ways that city leaders had hoped. Instead, freeways seemed to accelerate the trends of declining public transit usage and the residential shift to the suburbs; worse, in nearly all big cities, the average number of trips that metropolitan-area residents took downtown continued to decline.[83]

Second, the interstates acted as a vector for spreading new development and economic activity across a broad metropolitan region that extended ever-farther away from downtown. Nearly all such development followed the low-density, car-dependent patterns that had come to dominate housing and commerce in the first postwar decade. One result was a new sort of Great American Roadside, with motels, gas stations, fast-food restaurants, and truck stops congregating at interstate exchanges, even in remote areas, to serve travelers. New ribbon developments also emerged along suburban arterials where they crossed the interstates, often attracting new community and regional shopping centers. The interstate system's various urban bypasses and ring roads also acted as magnets for new development, including a variety of new offices and industries, eventually leading to the kind of doughnut-shaped development that one writer has described as "edge city."[84]

Third, the interstates—and the swelling number of big rigs that traveled them—became a powerful tool for postwar agribusinesses to remake the economic geography of rural regions that had once been beholden to railroad rates and timetables into "trucking country." Exploiting a truck-sized loophole in the Motor Carrier Act of 1935 that was intended to exempt small farmers from the freight-hauling regulations administered by the Interstate Commerce Commission, agribusinesses and their "free-market" allies in the Department of Agriculture embraced the transportation flexibility that unregulated long-haul truckers provided. Free from the regulated pricing structure and fixed routes of railroads, resistant to the organizing efforts of the powerful Teamsters Union, and subject to hypercompetitive conditions, "independent" truckers were linchpins in the successful efforts of food processors to deploy a variety of seemingly mundane technologies to remake food distribution and marketing. Chicago's big four meatpackers, for example, saw their empire crumble as upstart companies such as Iowa Beef Packers used new breeds of cattle, industrial feedlots, decentralized "cinderblock" meatpacking facilities, and mechanically refrigerated tractor trailers to deliver low-priced beef to supermarket display cases across the nation. Significantly, the new monopolistic systems that postwar agribusinesses created generated little political concern in Washington, D.C., since they kept farm incomes high and consumer food prices low—in large part because of the low-cost, flexible transportation that unregulated truckers provided.[85]

Finally, and in some ways most importantly, the linkage of federal gas tax revenues to interstate construction cemented an even grander version of the self-fueling system that highway planners had first conceived during the Great Depression, which coupled the nation's steadily expanding automotive infrastructure to steadily expanding gasoline consumption. In comparison to the interwar system of primary highways, the interstates generated new traffic, new dedicated income, new traffic-generating roads, and new car-dependent landscapes on a much larger scale. As a result, the principle of dedicating ever-growing gasoline tax revenue to highways became solidified as a cornerstone of the American political economy for the next half century.[86]

OFFICES AND INDUSTRY

As suburban residential and commercial districts boomed, other sectors of the urban economy followed, including white-collar offices and blue-collar manufacturing industries, prompting accelerating car-oriented land-use practices that might best be described as the "urbanization of the suburbs."[87] A variety of factors fueled the trend. Major changes in communication technology, for example, reduced the importance of concentrating the office functions of large businesses, making it unnecessary to maintain enormous facilities on expensive downtown real estate. Branch and regional offices became increasingly common, sometimes in stand-alone facilities and sometimes in new suburban office parks. Some corporate headquarters also relocated to suburban areas, often to new "campuses" with elaborately landscaped grounds, large parking lots, and multiple buildings.[88]

Among manufacturers, the postwar years brought yet another round of decentralization. Both light and heavy industry had a long track record of locating beyond the limited space and high rents of central business districts, dating back to late-nineteenth-century enterprises in places such as Pullman, Illinois, and Homestead, Pennsylvania. In Detroit, automakers had begun in the 1910s to concentrate along a rail corridor six miles outside of downtown, and in the 1920s some relocated to even larger outlying facilities in order to capitalize on new, horizontally oriented mass-production techniques. (To put things in perspective, Ford's River Rouge facility occupied twice the acreage taken by Detroit's entire central business district.)[89] In the interwar years, bigger trucks and improved highways freed some light industry from dependence on railroad transportation, further stimulating movement toward the periphery.[90] By the end of World War II, aging plants, new materials-handling methods, spreading assembly-line techniques, parking shortages, the desire to reserve room for future growth, and a shift toward transportation by truck and highway all sped industry's move into the suburbs.[91]

The industrialization of the suburbs affected some cities more than others, having the most profound effect on the old "industrial heartland." Between 1947 and 1958, for example—even before new interstates, bypasses, and ring roads accelerated the suburban shift—Chicago's central city lost 18.5 percent of its manufacturing jobs, while its suburban industry grew by 49.4 percent. In other industrial cities, the numbers were equally dramatic: Pittsburgh, manufacturing jobs down 25.3 percent and suburban industry up 18.1 percent; Cleveland, down 22.4 percent and up 98.4 percent; Detroit, down 42.9 percent and up 41.5 percent.[92] Even in smaller manufacturing cities, the suburbanization of industry had profound effects. In Wilmington, Delaware, for example, two-thirds of all jobs were inside Wilmington in 1940; twenty years later, that percentage had plummeted to just under one-third.[93] By 1963, for the first time, the bulk of American manufacturing occurred in suburbs rather than cities.[94]

As the proportion of jobs in suburbs rose in relation to downtown, car-dependent landscapes became even more prevalent. When offices and factories traded urban locations for suburban ones, for example, they usually traded wide accessibility by public transportation for easier access by private car. For some employees, and especially those who already drove to work, the relocation sometimes meant an easier, more convenient commute. For those who formerly walked or took public transportation, on the other hand, commuting suddenly required access to a car, creating dependence that had not existed before. Swapping urban locations for suburban ones could also leave holes in the formerly dense urban landscape, particularly in the form of abandoned brownfield sites like Ford's Highland Park factory. As city landscapes became less dense, and as the economic vitality that big manufacturers generated in their vicinity disappeared, cities themselves became less walkable: places that had once been destinations became large expanses of empty space to get around, repelling traffic rather than attracting it.

AUTOMOBILES

As sector after sector of the urban economy spread its operations into the suburbs, creating vast, new car-dependent landscapes, automobile ownership exploded. World War II had taken a bigger bite out of American automobile ownership than even the worst years of the Great Depression, and at war's end pent-up demand for replacement cars unleashed itself in a furious rush: new-car sales jumped to 2.1 million in 1946 and then climbed steadily to 5.1 million in 1949, breaking the previous single-year record, set in 1929, of 4.5 million. Booming sales, however, soon outstripped replacement demand for old and worn-out cars: by 1952, automakers had sold more new cars since the end of the war (31.1 million) than the total number of cars in the United States in 1941 (29.6 million). Yet still the boom continued. Between 1950 and 1960, annual new-car sales *averaged* 5.9 million—1.4 million more than the old 1929 record—and set a new single-year record of 7.9 million in 1955.[95] Despite scrappage rates of over 3 million vehicles annually through the 1950s, car ownership more than doubled in the fifteen years after World War II, skyrocketing from 28.2 million in 1946 to 61.7 million in 1960.[96] Meanwhile, the percentage of American families owning automobiles rose from 51 percent in 1941 to 77 percent in 1960.[97] Even more impressive, the volume of traffic swelled faster than the number of new cars, causing the near tripling of vehicle miles traveled from 200 billion in 1945 to 588 billion in 1960.[98]

What explains this boom? Part of the answer clearly lies in the numerous, overlapping policies at all levels of government that pumped huge amounts of money into car-friendly infrastructure projects, which had the effect of making it easier and dramatically less expensive to drive even relatively long distances.[99] Part of the answer also clearly lies in the ways that automobiles opened new mobility options, resonated with powerful American values, and enticed growing numbers of increasingly affluent consumers.[100]

Yet perhaps the most important part of the answer lies in the ways that the changing structure of the postwar American landscape affected people's relationships with—and reliance upon—automobiles. In the early 1960s, researchers at the Institute for Social Research at the University of Michigan began a series of investigations into commuting patterns—known within the transportation community as "the journey to work"—with a particular focus on how residential location within expanding metropolitan areas affected decisions about commuting.[101] As part of these broader investigations, researchers isolated the most important variables accounting for differences in two important categories: car ownership and car use. Basing their work on a series of interviews with families representing a cross-section of residences in over thirty cities, the researchers conducted roughly half of their interviews in 1963 and the other half in 1965. Because the overall investigation focused on the role of residential location in urban mobility patterns, these interviews generated detailed data on the relationships among car ownership, car use, and residential location that is unavailable in most statistical sources for this period.[102] Their data, which is summarized and analyzed in the report *Automobile Ownership and Residential Density* (1967), demonstrates a strong correlation between the spread of low-density landscapes during the postwar years and growing car ownership and use. The postwar boom in car-dependent suburban development, in other words, should be understood as one of the *causes* of exploding automotive ownership rather than the other way around.

In its analysis of car ownership, the report confirmed what other studies had already demonstrated: that the three most important variables explaining car ownership levels for any given group were income, demographic composition, and degree of urbanization. Of the three, income was the strongest predictor of car ownership. In 1963, for example, 51 percent of households with income under $3,000 owned cars, as compared to 65 percent of those with an income between $3,000 and $4,000, 76 percent with an income between $4,000 and $5,000, and 87 percent with an income between $5,000 and $6,000.[103] Not surprisingly, car ownership in the United States expanded during the postwar period in proportion to both rising real wages and the falling costs of driving associated with car-oriented infrastructure improvements.

Demographic factors also affected who drove. In general, older segments of the population were much less likely to drive than younger segments, and women were somewhat less likely to drive than men—although younger women drove at much higher rates than older women. Among drivers between the ages of twenty-five and forty-four, for example, 42 percent of drivers were women, whereas they were just

24 percent of drivers seventy or older.[104] Growing numbers of women drivers helped explain another trend: the rising number of families owning more than one car. The researchers found a strong correlation between families with more than one wage earner and those with more than one car. When women took jobs outside the home, in other words, their families tended to acquire second cars.[105]

Where people lived—and especially the density of their neighborhoods—also had a measurable effect on automobile ownership. Automakers had long observed that Americans owned fewer cars per capita, both per person and per family, in the nation's largest cities. The authors of *Automobile Ownership and Residential Density* pushed this observation a step further, assessing the degree to which different neighborhood densities affected car-ownership rates for families in different income ranges (fig. 7.1a–c).

The researchers used four categories to compare residential density: "old" central cities, "new" central cities, smaller central cities, and suburban areas. The old central cities—Baltimore, Boston, Chicago, St. Louis, and Philadelphia—all had populations of at least 500,000 by 1900, which meant that the central portion of each had grown to substantial size before the advent of the motor age. The new central cities—Cleveland, Detroit, Los Angeles, Pittsburgh, San Francisco, and Washington, D.C.—all surpassed 500,000 residents during the motor age and had comparatively lower residential densities.

Using these four categories, the authors concluded "that the character of the urban environment does have a substantial influence on automobile ownership." First, residential density markedly affected ownership in households with an income of $4,000 or less. In old cities, just 15 percent of families in this lower income bracket owned cars, compared to a whopping 84 percent for families with the same income living in suburban areas. Second, high residential density suppressed multiple-car ownership in affluent households with incomes of $7,500 or more. In old cities, just 19 percent of families in this higher income bracket owned two or more cars, compared to 61 percent of similar families in the suburbs. Whatever a family's income, the correlation was clear: the lower the density of settlement—a good if imperfect indicator of areas with many opportunities per square mile—the higher the rate of car ownership.[106]

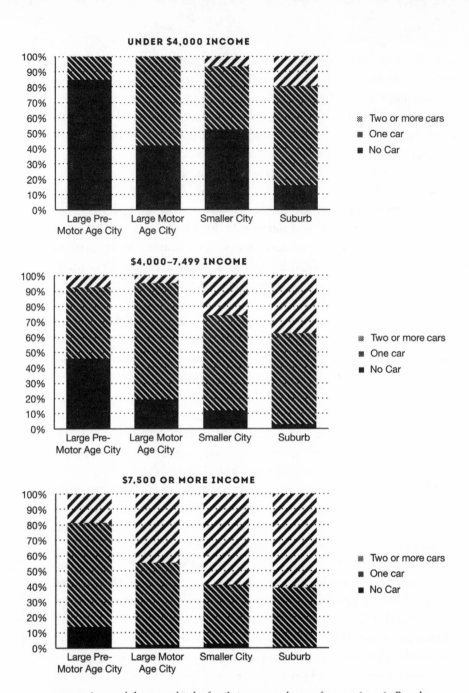

7.1A–C Automobile ownership by family income and type of area, 1963–1965. Based on Lansing and Hendricks, *Automobile Ownership and Residential Density*, 16 (table 5).

In addition to examining rates of car *ownership*, the researchers also examined the variables governing car *use*. Because most data on car usage in the postwar decades was gathered as "vehicle miles traveled"—at the unit of all vehicles combined rather than the unit of the household—the statistical opportunities for analyzing the role of automobiles at the household level were limited.[107] Because the authors of *Automobile Ownership and Residential Density* collected and analyzed their data per household (rather than per vehicle), and because they were able to correlate interview responses with income, demographic factors, and residential location, their results provide a rare and suggestive glimpse into how the proliferation of suburbs in the first two postwar decades affected the size and scale of burgeoning urban traffic during the same years.[108]

As with car ownership, the researchers found that income, age, and gender all affected car use, prompting the conclusion that family income correlated closely enough to predict annual miles traveled.[109] Even more significantly, the researchers found large differences in total car use according to residential density (fig. 7.2a–b). For the sample counting all respondents, including families without a car, households in old cities drove an average of just 3,900 miles—well less than half that of families in new cities (9,700 miles) and well less than one-third the amount of driving among families living in suburban areas (14,600 miles). Significant differences in the total amount of driving also occurred among car-owning families according to the density of their neighborhoods. Car-owning families in old cities averaged 6,700 miles per year of driving—much less than the residents of new cities (11,000 miles), smaller central cities (12,800 miles), and suburban areas (15,200 miles).[110]

There are both negative and positive explanations for why residents of high-density neighborhoods—both then and now—drive less than residents of low-density neighborhoods. On the negative side of the ledger, owning and operating a car in a high-density neighborhood can be expensive and inconvenient. Finding on-street parking may be difficult, vehicle security may be an issue, and leaving the vehicle exposed to the weather—particularly during the winter in the snowbelt—may be a hassle. Off-street parking, on the other hand, may be unavailable, inconveniently located, or prohibitively expensive. In addition, any

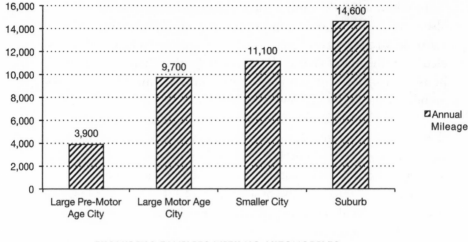

INCLUDING FAMILIES WITH NO AUTOMOBILES

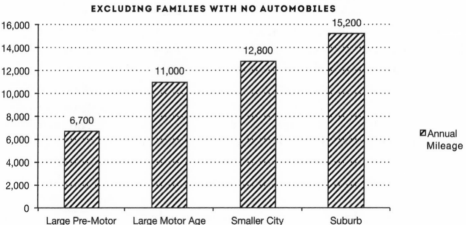

EXCLUDING FAMILIES WITH NO AUTOMOBILES

7.2A–B Mean annual mileage on all automobiles for families living in different types of areas, 1963–1965. Based on Lansing and Hendricks, *Automobile Ownership and Residential Density*, 28 (graph 5).

parking scarcities affecting the immediate area near a car owner's residence are likely to affect nearby businesses as well, reducing the attractiveness of using a car to visit them. Densely settled urban areas also generally have thicker, slower-moving traffic than low-density areas, which might also discourage car use, especially for short, quick trips.

On the positive side, densely settled areas with mixed land uses have a wider range of "opportunities per square mile" than low-density areas, ensuring the location of most everyday goods and services within a small radius. Public transportation also tends to be better in high-density locations, running more frequently and getting riders to their destinations with greater speed and convenience. In low-density neighborhoods, on the other hand, where homes are spread out and where goods and services are located beyond the boundaries of the neighborhood, the everyday need for mobility over unwalkable distances is strong, and driving provides the fastest and most convenient way to satisfy that need.

In short, *Automobile Ownership and Residential Density* reported a compelling link between how much postwar Americans drove and the physical structure of the landscapes they inhabited. In high-density areas where mixed land uses prevailed, a lower percentage of households owned cars—and those that did drove them much less than average. In low-density areas, on the other hand, and especially in low-density suburban areas divided into large, single-use tracts that were well serviced by an expensive car-oriented infrastructure, much larger percentages of households owned automobiles, were considerably more likely to own multiple vehicles, and accumulated significantly more miles of travel each year than those in higher-density areas.

Not surprisingly, during the same postwar decades that Americans moved in large numbers to low-density, single-use residential suburbs, where they needed to drive more often and over greater distances to accomplish their various daily activities, both car ownership and national vehicle miles traveled soared. As older suburban "bedroom communities" became newly "urbanized suburbs," in other words, trips became less focused on downtown destinations and more dispersed across large metropolitan regions. The distances that all city residents—and especially suburban residents—had to drive to conduct their daily affairs increased accordingly.

All of this suggests that the conventional historical explanation of the relationship between skyrocketing car sales and booming suburbanization during the postwar decades—that cars "enabled" suburban development—requires revision.[111] Although this point is not wrong, since automobiles were, and remain, a prerequisite for car-dependent landscapes, it nevertheless sidesteps the question of causality.

A suburban residence may, in practice, require a car to be practical, but the reverse does not hold true: owning a car does not require a suburban residence. A better explanation is that cars made suburban development possible, but mushrooming suburban developments made cars essential. As car-dependent landscapes multiplied along new high-speed highways across vast metropolitan regions, beginning with suburban homes for affluent urbanites and then spreading to other important sectors of the economy, car use exploded. Why? Because when people live in Car Country, they *drive*.

CONCLUSION

Car Country did not emerge overnight, and nothing about its spread was foreordained. Indeed, its overwhelming successes in the United States since World War II have hinged on four variables, all of which were in place by 1956: car-oriented transportation policies motivated by a traffic-service vision and laid out to maximize convenience from a motorist's-eye view; large government subsidies for low-density, car-oriented development; legal and institutional sanction of car-oriented development as the only acceptable form of new development; and reliable profitability for developers. Large government subsidies fueled Car Country's spread in a variety of ways, including, among others, FHA insurance for home mortgages and construction loans; federal tax incentives for commercial suburban developments (accelerated depreciation) and home ownership (mortgage interest deductions); and legally mandated "linkage" between highway budgets and automobile user-fee revenues, especially gasoline taxes. Similarly, Car Country became the legally and institutionally sanctioned form of development in the United States. The postwar housing industry focused overwhelmingly on large, low-density subdivisions, located on greenfield sites on the urban fringe. Local governments zoned large acreages for single-family homes on large lots, banishing commercial and industrial enterprises from residential areas and requiring businesses to provide expansive on-site parking. As other sectors of the urban economy followed housing outward into the suburbs and along the new interstates, each sector evolved its own car-oriented standards for development that zoning and construction codes increasingly reinforced as requirements. Together, government subsidies, car-oriented development standards, and car-based transportation policies shielded investors from risk, insured the profitability of car-oriented development, and kept the costs of driving relatively low for individual motorists.

Taken together, these four variables produced an almost irresistible momentum for Car Country's spread. More residentially zoned suburbs, more heavily segregated land uses, and more and faster highways have translated directly into more people living in car-dependent surroundings. The result has been an American landscape and environment so thoroughly remade around car-based mobility that older ways of moving around have become difficult, if not impossible, for most Americans.

As the standards for the endless replication of Car Country into new areas got locked in, so too did significant environmental problems. Making cars, building roads, burning gasoline, and developing low-density sprawl carry significant interlocking—and mutually amplifying—environmental costs. These costs have not gone unnoticed. Indeed, anti-automobile and antiroad protests have had a significant presence in the United States, particularly since the 1960s.[112] For better or worse, however, protests against the social and environmental costs of car dependence did not gain national prominence until *after* the nation's political economy had already elevated into a position of prominence the transportation priorities and development standards that perpetuate low-density sprawl. *Growth* in the interstate era has meant *car-dependent growth*. Car Country has been the result.

EPILOGUE
Reaching for the Car Keys

In real life . . . the implications of accommodating a few more cars and a few more cars and a few more cars are a little harder to see. But swiftly or slowly, the positive feedback is at work. Swiftly or slowly, greater accessibility by car is inexorably accompanied both by less convenience and efficiency of public transportation, and by thinning-down and smearing-out of [land] uses, and hence by more need for cars.
　　—Jane Jacobs (1961)[1]

AFTER 1956, CAR COUNTRY QUICKLY BECAME THE NATION'S SIGNA-ture landscape: sprawling, single-use, low-density, and bound together by an overwhelmingly car-oriented transportation system. Remaking the nation as Car Country has had its benefits. It has made it dramatically easier to drive, for example, helping expand homeownership to previously unfathomable levels and making real estate investments more profitable and secure. Yet it has also had drawbacks, most notably, that Car Country's one-size-fits-all landscape does not, in fact, fit all: it only fits cars. To take an agricultural metaphor, Car Country is a monoculture, a landscape designed to maximize the benefits of car-based mobility. Yet it succeeds by imposing a brittle simplicity on the landscape that sacrifices environmental resiliency and complexity. As a result, ever more complicated and expensive technological and managerial interventions are necessary to keep it functioning smoothly. In the case of Car Country, we might add that the lost complexity is not just ecological, but social, technological, and economic as well.

　　Among the postwar critics who decried the complex mix of incentives, regulations, and planning practices that gave rise to Car Country, perhaps the most perceptive and outspoken was Jane Jacobs. Jacobs, a writer, community activist, and resident of Greenwich Village in New York City, first became interested in the negative effects of urban renewal on cities while working as an associate editor for *Architectural Forum*

Advertisement for Jane Jacobs, *The Death and Life of Great American Cities* (1961). Courtesy of Random House.

in the mid-1950s, a period when federal slum-clearance programs were remaking American cities in significant ways. In the spring of 1956, she "stepped into prominence at a planners' conference at Harvard," as Lewis Mumford, the urban planner and historian, later described it. "Into the foggy atmosphere of professional jargon that usually envelops such meetings, she blew like a fresh offshore breeze to present a picture, dramatic but not distorted, of the results of displacing large neighborhood populations to facilitate large-scale rebuilding."[2] She expanded her critique for a national audience in a provocative essay in *Fortune* titled "Downtown Is for People" (1958) and then again in a bombshell of a book, *The Death and Life of Great American Cities* (1961), which combined a fierce and eloquent defense of urbanism with a trenchant critique of prevailing city-planning orthodoxies. "This book," it began with characteristic forthrightness, "is an attack on current city planning and rebuilding."[3]

Jacobs devoted little attention to new car-dependent development on the urban periphery, the era's most visible part of Car Country. But she generated significant insight into such places by focusing on what she saw as Car Country's antithesis: the nation's "great" cities, which she considered the nation's historical hubs of economic, political, and social innovation. In contrast to the bird's-eye view of most planners, she took a street-level view of city life, celebrating the "intricate ballet" of city people's comings and goings in an effort to understand what made cities vibrant, vital, and safe. Jacobs disparaged city planners for trying to transform even very dense cities into car-friendly places, but she was surprisingly ambivalent about cars themselves. "Automobiles are often conveniently tagged as the villains responsible for the ills of cities and the disappointments and futilities of city planning," she wrote. "But the destructive effects of automobiles are much less a cause than a symptom of our incompetence at city building."[4] Jacobs, in other words, was one of the first prominent critics to understand that land-use decisions—and not just a car-friendly transportation infrastructure—profoundly shaped the context in which cars operated.

Wherever one found car-friendly transportation and land-use policies in city planning, Jacobs argued, one could find cars having a destructive impact. This was true, she argued, mainly because cars "compete with other [land] uses for space and convenience." In vibrant, walkable cities, she believed, even the smallest efforts to accommodate motorists sacrificed, in zero-sum fashion, exactly those needs of pedestrians and local land uses that created vibrancy and walkability in the first place. "Erosion of cities by automobiles entails so familiar a series of events that these hardly need describing," she wrote. "Because of vehicular congestion, a street is widened here, another is straightened there, a wide avenue is converted to one-way flow, staggered-signal systems are installed for faster movement, a bridge is double-decked as its capacity is reached, an expressway is cut through yonder, and finally whole webs of expressways. More and more land goes into parking, to accommodate the ever increasing number of vehicles while they are idle." These "piecemeal corrosive changes," she argued, "cumulatively eat away a city," making it less vibrant, resilient, and walkable. "Swiftly or slowly," she concluded, "greater accessibility by car is inexorably accompanied both by less convenience and efficiency of public transportation, and by thinning-down and smearing-out of [land] uses, and hence by more need for cars."[5]

Yet if cars were central to these changes, she insisted that the real problem was less cars themselves than the misguided effort to increase urban mobility by catering to motorists. The changes that fostered urban car dependence were not "all thought out in advance, in some Olympian scheme or master plan," she argued, rejecting the conspiracy theory for the automobile's success in the United States. "If they were, they would not be nearly as effective as they are. In the main, they occur as direct, practical responses to direct, practical problems as those problems appear. Every move thus counts; few are gestures and boondoggles."[6]

The same forces that Jacobs described in "great" cities were also at work in other walkable places, from small rural towns to streetcar suburbs. That new suburbs designed around cars create car dependence is certainly no surprise. But Jacobs showed by analogy how other places that once functioned well without cars could sink into car dependence. Even minor, seemingly benign changes designed to improve the mobility of motorists, she argued, could create car-oriented land-use patterns that reduced the number of opportunities per square mile and decreased the convenience and efficiency of other forms of transportation. In the case of St. Paul's Macalester-Groveland neighborhood, for example, by the mid-1950s, when buses replaced streetcars, average wait times for public transportation had already doubled or even quadrupled compared to the late 1920s, depending on the route and the time of day, making it harder for nonmotorists to access goods, services, and jobs outside the neighborhood. In addition, as the new economic geography of the motor age prompted a shuffling of local stores and institutions—a grocery store closing here, a hardware store closing there—everyday goods and services once located within an easy walk often relocated farther away. As a result, and despite the fact that the relative density and mixed land-use patterns of Macalester-Groveland give it much lower built-in mobility needs today than an exit-ramp suburb like Eagan, most residents nevertheless depend on personal vehicles to conduct their daily affairs. Macalester-Groveland is Car Country, too—just a much less extreme version than Eagan.

Much to Jacobs's consternation, by the time she published *Death and Life* in 1961, the system of self-fueling, car-oriented land-use and transportation priorities that have been the focus of this book, as well as the "piecemeal corrosive changes" eating away at walkable places large and small, had already established deep roots in professional transportation and city-planning practice. A dense thicket of car-friendly regulations, incentives, and procedures regarding land-use practices had also grown up in all levels of government. Although Jacobs attracted a wide audience and inspired a host of other critics, she experienced personally the rigors of fighting even a single project when she led a successful battle against the proposed Lower Manhattan Expressway—a project pushed by New York City's famous "master builder," Robert Moses—a victory that inspired antifreeway coalitions across the country.[7] "It is not easy for uncredentialed people to stand up to the credentialed, even when the so-called expertise is grounded in ignorance and folly," she wrote in a new preface for *Death and Life* in 1992. "This book turned out to be helpful ammunition against such experts. But . . . the book neither collaborated with car people nor had an influence on them."[8]

In the end, Jacobs argued, the city-planning profession's "arrogant gatekeepers" discredited her ideas among younger planning professionals, who were "being rigorously trained as anticity and antistreet designers and planners."[9] As a result, she concluded,

"Anticity planning remains amazingly sturdy in American cities. It is still embodied in thousands of regulations, bylaws, and codes, also in bureaucratic timidities owing to accepted practices, and in unexamined public attitudes hardened by time."[10]

With the weight of existing rules and regulations working against those trying to "knit up holes and tatters in a city neighborhood," the efforts against the solidifying status quo became "a daunting ordeal at best, and often enough heartbreaking."[11] Even in the early 1960s, the forces behind Car Country's expansion were already too institutionalized, too powerful, for even small-scale efforts to preserve vital, walkable landscapes to proceed without being forced into one energy-sapping battle after another, without clear prospects for success.[12]

To the gatekeepers, regulations, bylaws, codes, bureaucratic timidities, and unexamined public attitudes that Jacobs identified—as if this list were not already long enough!—we must also add heavy government subsidies and the influence of those with powerful interests in maintaining car-friendly transportation policies and land-use regulations. Even before Jacobs burst onto the scene, taxpayer dollars and entrenched economic interests had already tilted the playing field in favor of car-oriented landscapes. As a result, both the transportation and land-use aspects of Car Country have come to appear as uncomplicated and natural products of "free-market" choices: depending on cars is, for most Americans, the natural state of being. If most car-owning Americans "choose" to live in Car Country, that choice means little, given that Car Country is more often than not the *only* option available.[13]

The lack of meaningful choice has had consequences. From an environmental perspective, Car Country's most significant costs have been "externalized," that is, they have taken the form of environmental degradation not reflected in the market price of owning and operating a car. In just the narrow category of air quality, for example, better than a century of burning gasoline to fuel American cars has generated significant environmental problems—in forms as varied and scientifically complex as smog, lead contamination, and the buildup of atmospheric greenhouse gasses—the costs of which are borne not by motorists as a group but by society at large, motorists and nonmotorists alike. Yet trying to account for these externalized costs is a monumental task. Simply taking an inventory of problems, for example, poses a daunting list-making challenge, with items piling up on top of one another, devoid of rhyme, reason, or hierarchy. "So widespread is [the automobile] that it seems impossible to break down and calculate all its bells and whistles: the oil filters, mufflers, and catalytic converters, the hoses and belts, not to forget the oils in road building or the coolants from air conditioners," writes Jane Holtz Kay in her anticar tirade, *Asphalt Nation*. "The automobile's abuse overruns our capacity to record it."[14] Even focusing on calculating the full costs of something seemingly more manageable, such as Car Country's ubiquitous free on-site parking, can quickly devolve into something like Ahab's quest to capture the white whale, as Donald C. Shoup's doorstop of a book, *The High Cost of Free Parking*, vividly demonstrates.[15]

Given the daunting challenges of identifying and analyzing Car Country's externalities, most critics have focused on its most obvious liability: the problems that come with a national transportation system that now burns upwards of 130 billion gallons of gasoline annually.[16] The first problem is cost. In many ways, Car Country rests on the premise that personal vehicles are relatively inexpensive to own and operate. Because Car Country's rise to dominance coincided with the golden age of cheap and abundant oil, the price of gasoline has seldom challenged this premise. Yet, as numerous critics have argued, oil is both a finite natural resource and subject to the laws of supply and demand. Should oil supplies tighten and prices rise significantly over a long enough period—whether due to dwindling supplies, rising extraction costs, increased global demand, or instability in oil-producing regions does not really matter—the costs of driving could skyrocket. Barring a rapid conversion from oil to another, less expensive fuel, Car Country's future economic health depends on the continuing reliable flow, and low price, of a limited (and geopolitically contentious) natural resource.

Yet even replacing oil-chugging engines with clean electric motors—itself a monumental undertaking—would address only Car Country's oil-related environmental externalities. Swapping polluting personal vehicles for nonpolluting equivalents would not address, for example, the environmental problems related to acquiring the raw materials for new cars and roads, mass manufacturing cars, building and maintaining roads, or rolling out sprawling new suburbs. Nor would it do anything to change the large mobility requirements and car-dependent characteristics that are part of the American landscape. Making the transition to vehicles fueled by something other than oil would also present a political problem that few advocates of electric vehicles ever discuss: what sorts of new taxes would be necessary to offset the loss of the enormous revenues dedicated to car-based transportation that gas taxes currently provide?

Perhaps Car Country's most important historical legacy, then, is that in surmounting one set of environmental constraints it has made itself increasingly subject to others—while limiting its flexibility to respond to them. Drawing on a complex mix of transportation and land-use policies, the nation has rebuilt the American landscape in ways that allow drivers to overcome long-standing natural limits on personal transportation. In doing so, the United States has delivered unprecedented freedom, mobility, and flexibility to the vast majority of its inhabitants. Yet the same changes that broke down old barriers to easy transportation also wove a growing dependence on cars into the very fabric of the landscape. When it is time to go to work, most of us reach for the car keys. When we need a gallon of milk or a loaf of bread, most of us reach for the car keys. When we want to go out to eat, to visit a friend, or to drop a package by the post office, most of us reach for the car keys. That reaching for the car keys has become the default national gesture to initiate most travel testifies to the incredible advantages of Car Country. For those who own cars, driving is cheap. It is easy. It is fast. It is weatherproof. Cars—and the elaborate transportation system and land-use practices that cater to them—have, for car-owning Americans, reduced once-formidable environmental constraints on easy travel to a distant memory. But one of the cruel ironies of Car Country is that other, very different environmental limits— including a destabilized climate and the depletion of a crucial natural resource, oil—now pose the greatest threats to its future. The arena of Car Country's greatest successes has become its chief liability.

NOTES

PROLOGUE: A CAR OF ONE'S OWN

1 Lewis Mumford, *The Highway and the City* (New York: Mentor Books, 1964), 246.

2 This last obligation was remarkably affordable, though it felt onerous at the time. In the second half of 1989, when I first got the truck, the national average price for a gallon of regular unleaded actually *fell* from $1.09 to $0.98, and with the exception of a short spike in late 1990, when prices briefly soared to $1.37, prices seldom exceeded $1.10 per gallon. See Energy Information Administration, "May 2008 Monthly Energy Review," Table 9.4: Motor Gasoline Retail Prices, U.S. City Average, http://tonto.eia.doe.gov/merquery/mer_data. asp?table=T09.04 (accessed June 16, 2008).

3 On Atlanta's development policies after 1975, which heavily favored low-density, automobile-oriented growth over an extensive area, see Carlton Basmajian, "Projecting Sprawl? The Atlanta Regional Commission and the 1975 Regional Development Plan of Metropolitan Atlanta," *Journal of Planning History* 9, 2 (2010): 95–121.

4 Frank Coffey and Joseph Layden, *America on Wheels: The First 100 Years, 1896–1996* (Los Angeles: General Publishing Group, 1996), 9.

5 Peter Norton has traced the origins of the love-affair thesis, which has been popular in both popular and scholarly histories of the automobile in the United States, to the *DuPont Show of the Week* episode called "Merrily We Roll Along," first broadcast on NBC on 22 October 1961. See Norton, "Americans' Affair of Hate with the Automobile: What the 'Love Affair' Fiction Concealed," in *Automobile: Les cartes du désamour*, ed. Mathieu Flonneau (Paris: Descartes and Cie, 2009), 93–104. Among the popular works that explicitly invoke the love affair, including those that believe that the romance has faded and the relationship should be dissolved, see Frank Donovan, *Wheels for a Nation: How America Fell in Love with the Automobile and Lived Happily Ever After . . . Well, Almost* (New York: Thomas Y. Crowell, 1965) ; Leon Mandel, *Driven: The American Four-Wheeled Love Affair* (New York: Stein and Day, 1977); David K. Wright, *America's 100 Year Love Affair with the Automobile: And the Snap-On Tools That Keep Them Running* (Osceola, Wisc.: Motorbooks International, 1995); Jane Holtz Kay, *Asphalt Nation: How the Automobile Took Over America and How We Can Take It Back* (New York: Crown Publishers, 1997); Katie Alvord, *Divorce Your Car! Ending the Love Affair with the Automobile* (Gabriola Island, B.C.: New Society Publishers, 2000); and Tim Falconer, *Drive: A Road Trip through Our Complicated Affair with the Automobile* (Toronto: Viking Canada, 2008). Although scholars have attacked the love-affair thesis directly—see especially Norton,

"Americans' Affair of Hate with the Automobile," and Norton, *Fighting Traffic: The Dawn of the Motor Age in the American City* (Cambridge, Mass.: MIT Press, 2008)—serious scholars continue to invoke it in their work. For recent examples, see David Blanke, *Hell on Wheels: The Promise and Peril of America's Car Culture, 1900–1940* (Lawrence: University Press of Kansas, 2007); Tom McCarthy, *Auto Mania: Cars, Consumers, and the Environment* (New Haven, Conn.: Yale University Press, 2007); John A. Jakle and Keith A. Sculle, *Motoring: The Highway Experience in America* (Athens: University of Georgia Press, 2008); and John Heitmann, *The Automobile and American Life* (Jefferson, N.C.: McFarland & Co., 2009).

6   A. Q. Mowbray, *Road to Ruin: A Critical View of the Federal Highway Program* (Philadelphia: J. B. Lippincott, 1968); Helen Leavitt, *Superhighway—Superhoax* (Garden City, N.Y.: Doubleday, 1970); Albert Kelley, *The Pavers and the Paved* (New York: D. W. Brown, 1971); Bradford Snell, *American Ground Transport: A Proposal for Restructuring the Automobile, Truck, Bus, and Rail Industries* (Washington, D.C.: Government Printing Office, 1974); David Saint Clair, *The Motorization of American Cities* (New York: Praeger, 1986); James Howard Kunstler, *The Geography of Nowhere: The Rise and Decline of America's Man-Made Landscape* (New York: Simon and Schuster, 1993); Jack Doyle, *Taken for a Ride: Detroit's Big Three and the Politics of Pollution* (New York: Four Walls Eight Windows, 2000). A number of historians have eschewed the conspiracy thesis in favor of systematically tracing the political processes and events that produced a wide range of policies heavily favoring automobiles and highways over other forms of transportation. For notable examples, see Paul Barrett, *The Automobile and Urban Transit: The Formation of Public Policy in Chicago, 1900–1930* (Philadelphia: Temple University Press, 1983); Bruce E. Seely, *Building the American Highway System: Engineers as Policy Makers* (Philadelphia: Temple University Press, 1987); Mark Rose, *Interstate: Express Highway Politics, 1939–1989*, rev. ed. (Knoxville: University of Tennessee Press, 1990); Tom Lewis, *Divided Highways: Building the Interstate Highways, Transforming American Life* (New York: Penguin Books, 1997); and Owen Gutfreund, *Twentieth-Century Sprawl: How Highways Transformed America* (New York: Oxford University Press, 2004).

7   For an excellent overview and assessment of the extensive research on the relationship between travel behavior and land-use patterns, including a trenchant critique of various faulty assumptions at the core of much of the research, see Jonathan Levine, *Zoned Out: Regulation, Markets, and Choices in Transportation and Metropolitan Land-Use* (Washington, D.C.: Resources for the Future, 2006), esp. 21–49. Although the research is at times inconclusive or contradictory, a recent comprehensive study of the subject concludes that large-scale adoption of more compact, mixed-use development is highly likely to reduce total vehicle miles traveled, to reduce energy consumption, and to lower associated greenhouse gas emissions. See Transportation Research Board, *Driving and the Built Environment: The Effects of Compact Development on Motorized Travel, Energy Use,*

and CO2 Emissions (Washington, D.C.: Transportation Research Board, 2009). For the case that this study actually *understates* the effects of more compact development, see Calthorpe Associates, "The Role of Land Use in Reducing VMT and GHG Emissions: A Critique of TRB Special Report 298," Aug. 2010, www.calthorpe.com/news/link-between-better-land-use-transportation-and-greenhouse-gas-emissions-calthorpe-associates-r (accessed 8 Oct. 2010).

8   It is worth noting that my everyday needs fell within a relatively narrow spectrum that, both as a student and as a graduate student, a "college town" admirably satisfied. It was enough to be surrounded by restaurants and dining halls, bookstores and libraries, coffee shops and bars, cheap apartments and classroom buildings—because these things satisfied most (if not all) of my everyday needs and desires. Not everyone needs and wants the same things, of course. A less demographically narrow population would require a much more diverse landscape than either college town supplied in order to be broadly walkable for its residents.

9   It also ignores the genuine advantages that automobiles offer and the transportation problems that they solve for individuals who live in car-dependent landscapes. For a sustained critique of the tendency among critics of the automobile to overlook its positive attributes, see James A. Dunn Jr., *Driving Forces: The Automobile, Its Enemies, and the Politics of Mobility* (Washington, D.C.: Brookings Institution Press, 1998). For an introduction to the emerging field of "envirotech," comprised of historians attempting to blend the major insights of environmental history with those of the history of technology, see especially Jeffrey K. Stine and Joel A. Tarr, "At the Intersection of Histories: Technology and the Environment," *Technology and Culture* 39 (Oct. 1998): 601–40; Martin Reuss and Stephen H. Cutliffe, eds., *The Illusory Boundary: Environment and Technology in History* (Charlottesville: University of Virginia Press, 2010); and Edmund Russell et al, "The Nature of Power: Synthesizing the History of Technology and Environmental History," *Technology and Culture 52* (Apr. 2011): 246–59.

10   Notably, the system's managers have begun to take steps to change this pattern by redeveloping some of the system's stops. See Sharon Feigon, David Hoyt, and Gloria Ohland, "The Atlanta Case Study: Lindbergh City Center," in *The New Transit Town: Best Practices in Transit-Oriented Development*, ed. Hank Dittmar and Gloria Ohland (Washington, D.C.: Island Press, 2004), 176–92.

11   Planners typically refer to this as "transit-oriented development" (TOD)—the template that Atlanta's system is using in projects like the Lindbergh City Center cited above. On TOD, see especially Peter Calthorpe, *The Next American Metropolis: Ecology, Community, and the American Dream* (New York: Princeton Architectural Press, 1993); Michael Bernick and Robert Cervero, *Transit Villages in the 21st Century* (New York: McGraw-Hill, 1997); and Hank Dittmar and Gloria Ohland, eds., *The New Transit Town: Best Practices in Transit-Oriented Development* (Washington, D.C.: Island Press, 2004).

12 Sperling's Best Cities, Compare Saint Paul, MN, and Eagan, MN, Housing, www.bestplaces.net/city/default.aspx?cat=HOUSING&city=St._Paul_MN &ccity=Eagan_MN&p=2758000&op=2717288 (accessed June 23, 2008).

13 The location of the commercial nodes shown on the figure 2 map is derived from detailed maps created in 1927 by the Sanborn Fire Insurance Company. See Sanborn Map Company, *Digital Sanborn Maps, 1867–1970* (Ann Arbor, Mich.: ProQuest UMI, 2001).

14 Distances shown on figure 3 are actual distances based on a "representative" residential address in each neighborhood—a relative's house and a friend's house.

15 Others have adopted the term "automobility," coined by John C. Burnham in 1961, to describe the complex technological and cultural systems in which automobiles operate, including, as James J. Flink has put it, "the combined impact of the motor vehicle, the automobile industry and the highway plus the emotional connotations of this impact for Americans." Burnham, "The Gasoline Tax and the Automobile Revolution," *Mississippi Valley Historical Review* 48 (Dec. 1961): 435–59; Flink, "Three Stages of American Automobile Consciousness," *American Quarterly* 24 (Oct. 1972): 451 (quotation), 451–73. In part because scholarly definitions range widely and vary greatly in the particular features included in the "system" of automobility, and in part because the term obscures rather than illuminates the degree to which the "system" evolved over time, I have chosen not to use it here.

16 For a brilliant account of the long history of the automobile's critics, see Brian Ladd, *Autophobia: Love and Hate in the Automotive Age* (Chicago: University of Chicago Press, 2008).

17 Pete Seeger, "Little Boxes," lyrics by Malvina Reynolds, recorded on Columbia, 1963, 45 rpm single.

18 In general, the key exceptions have been critics focusing on "sprawl"—a term popularized by William Whyte, cited below. Especially important have been urban and regional planners, "New Urbanist" architects, and urban historians. For some of the more influential examples, see Benton MacKaye, "The Townless Highway," *New Republic* 62 (12 Mar., 1930): 93–95; Benton MacKaye and Lewis Mumford, "Townless Highways for the Motorist: A Proposal for the Automobile Age," *Harper's Magazine* 163 (Aug. 1931): 347–56; William Whyte, ed., *The Exploding Metropolis* (New York: Doubleday, 1958); Mumford, *Highway and the City*; Real Estate Research Corporation of Chicago, *The Costs of Sprawl: Environmental and Economic Costs of Alternative Residential Development Patterns at the Urban Fringe*, 3 vols. (Washington, D.C.: Government Printing Office, 1974); Calthorpe, *Next American Metropolis*; Kunstler, *Geography of Nowhere*; Robert W. Burchell, Naveed A. Shad et al., *Costs of Sprawl Revisited* (Washington, D.C.: Transportation Research Board, 1998); Peter Newman and Jeffrey Kenworthy, *Sustainability and Cities: Overcoming Automobile Dependence* (Washington, D.C.: Island Press, 1999); Andres Duany, Elizabeth Plater-Zyberk, and Jeff Speck, *Suburban Nation: The Rise of Sprawl and the Decline of the American Dream* (New

York: North Point Press, 2001); Richard Register, *Ecocities: Building Cities in Balance with Nature* (Berkeley: Berkeley Hills Books, 2002); Robert W. Burchell, George Lowenstein et al., *Costs of Sprawl: 2000* (Washington, D.C.: Transportation Research Board, 2002); Barrett, *Automobile and Urban Transit*; Kenneth T. Jackson, *Crabgrass Frontier: The Suburbanization of the United States* (New York: Oxford University Press, 1987); and Gutfreund, *Twentieth-Century Sprawl.*

1. ROADS AND REFORMERS

1   Isaac B. Potter, *The Gospel of Good Roads: A Letter to the American Farmer* (New York: Evening Post Job Printing House, 1891), 5. *Good Roads* also reproduced "Gospel of Good Roads" in its first two issues.

2   "Filthy Streets Up Town," *New York Times*, 14 Feb. 1882, p. 8.

3   "Filthy Thoroughfares," *New York Times*, 13 Feb. 1882, p. 8.

4   George E. Waring Jr., *Street-Cleaning: And the Disposal of a City's Wastes; Methods and Results and the Effect Upon Public Health, Public Morals, and Municipal Prosperity* (New York: Doubleday and McClure, 1898), 9 (quotation), 1–42.

5   The clearest statement of this thesis remains Robert H. Wiebe, *The Search for Order, 1877–1920* (New York: Hill and Wang, 1967). The literature on Progressive reform is voluminous and rife with disagreement, but for key works that both extend and revise Wiebe's arguments in ways that have influenced my interpretations here, see Alfred D. Chandler, *The Visible Hand: The Managerial Revolution in American Business* (Cambridge, Mass.: Harvard University Press, 1977); Olivier Zunz, *Making America Corporate, 1870–1920* (Chicago: University of Chicago Press, 1990); William Cronon, *Nature's Metropolis: Chicago and the Great West* (New York: W. W. Norton, 1991); Peter C. Baldwin, *Domesticating the Street: The Reform of Public Space in Hartford, 1850–1930* (Columbus: Ohio State University Press, 1999); Daniel T. Rodgers, "In Search of Progressivism," *Reviews in American History* 10 (Dec. 1982): 113–32; Hal S. Barron, *Mixed Harvest: The Second Great Transformation in the Rural North, 1870–1930* (Chapel Hill: University of North Carolina Press, 1997); Howard Lawrence Preston, *Dirt Roads to Dixie: Accessibility and Modernization in the South, 1885–1935* (Knoxville: University of Tennessee Press, 1991); Bruce E. Seely, *Building the American Highway System: Engineers as Policy Makers* (Philadelphia: Temple University Press, 1987); and Peter J. Ling, *America and the Automobile: Technology, Reform and Social Change* (New York: Saint Martin's Press, 1990).

6   For one discussion of the spatial arrangement of these "walking cities," see Kenneth T. Jackson, *Crabgrass Frontier: The Suburbanization of the United States* (New York: Oxford University Press, 1985), 14–16.

7   On the shift from the craft apprentice system to the factory system, see especially W. J. Rorabaugh, *The Craft Apprentice: From Franklin to the Machine Age in America* (New York: Oxford University Press, 1986). For a vivid description of the spatial transformation of a neighborhood in Rochester, New York, see Paul

E. Johnson, *A Shopkeeper's Millennium: Society and Revivals in Rochester, New York, 1815–1837* (New York: Hill and Wang, 1978), 48–55. For an overview of urban spatial transformations in the nineteenth century, see Gunther Barth, *City People: The Rise of the Modern City Culture in Nineteenth-Century America* (New York: Oxford University Press, 1980), 28–57.

8   Jackson, *Crabgrass Frontier*, 20 (quotation). See also Zane L. Miller and Patricia M. Melvin, *The Urbanization of Modern America: A Brief History*, 2nd ed. (New York: Harcourt Brace Jovanovich, 1987), 86–87.

9   Ted Steinberg, *Down to Earth: Nature's Role in American History* (New York: Oxford University Press, 2002), 157; American Public Works Association (hereafter APWA), *History of Public Works in the United States, 1776–1976* (Chicago: APWA, 1976), 66.

10 Clay McShane, *Down the Asphalt Path: The Automobile and the American City* (New York: Columbia University Press, 1994), 21; APWA, *History of Public Works*, 66.

11 Miller and Melvin, *Urbanization of Modern America*, 72; APWA, *History of Public Works*, 66.

12 McShane, *Down the Asphalt Path*, 28. In practice, hills, lakes, mountains, and other geographical obstacles all affected the actual area that electric trolleys made available, as did the number and routes of streetcars available in each city.

13 Miller and Melvin, *Urbanization of Modern America*, 132. On the rise and fall of the municipal annexation movement, see Jackson, *Crabgrass Frontier*, 138–56.

14 Delos F. Wilcox, *The American City: A Problem in Democracy* (New York: Macmillan Co., 1904), 123 (quotation). On the significance of balloon-frame construction for rapid urban growth, see Jackson, *Crabgrass Frontier*, 124–28. On the urban pollution crisis generally, see Martin V. Melosi, *Effluent America: Cities, Industry, Energy, and the Environment* (Pittsburgh: University of Pittsburgh Press, 2001), 23–48; and David Stradling, *Smokestacks and Progressives: Environmentalists, Engineers, and Air Quality in America, 1881–1951* (Baltimore: Johns Hopkins University Press, 1999).

15 Allan G. Bogue, "An Agricultural Empire," in *The Oxford History of the American West*, ed. Clyde A. Milner, Carol A. O'Connor, and Martha A. Sandweiss (New York: Oxford University Press, 1994), 294–96, 299, 303; Richard White, *"It's Your Misfortune and None of My Own": A History of the American West* (Norman: University of Oklahoma Press, 1991), 229, 271–72; Robert V. Hine and John Mack Faragher, *The American West: A New Interpretive History* (New Haven, Conn.: Yale University Press, 2000), 341–42; Paul K. Conkin, *A Revolution Down on the Farm: The Transformation of American Agriculture since 1929* (Lexington: University of Kentucky Press, 2008), 5–15. For a case study of how these processes changed a single place, see John Mack Faragher, *Sugar Creek: Life on the Illinois Prairie* (New Haven, Conn.: Yale University Press, 1986).

16 John C. Hudson, "Settlement of the American Grassland," in *The Making of the American Landscape*, ed. Michael Conzen (Boston: Unwin Hyman, 1990), 169–85.

17   Cronon, *Nature's Metropolis*, esp. 55–93, 104–19.

18   Ibid., 315–18.

19   Ibid., 324–27.

20   Ibid., 333–40. See also David Blanke, *Sowing the American Dream: How Consumer Culture Took Root in the Rural Midwest* (Athens: Ohio University Press, 2000); Ronald R. Kline, *Consumers in the Country: Technology and Social Change in Rural America* (Baltimore: Johns Hopkins University Press, 2000); Barron, *Mixed Harvest*; and Gordon L. Weil, *Sears, Roebuck, U.S.A.: The Great American Catalog Store and How It Grew* (New York: Stein and Day, 1977).

21   On the Grange, see Thomas A. Woods, *Knights of the Plow: Oliver H. Kelley and the Origins of the Grange in Republican Ideology* (Ames: Iowa State University Press, 1991).

22   Andrew Wood and James A. Baer, "Strength in Numbers: Urban Rent Strikes and Political Transformation in the Americas, 1904–1925," *Journal of Urban History* 32 (Sept. 2006): 865. See also Barth, *City People*, 41–53. On hotels and boardinghouses, which were somewhat more hospitable, see A. K. Sandoval-Strausz, "Homes for a World of Strangers: Hospitality and the Origins of Multiple Dwellings in Urban America," *Journal of Urban History* 33 (Sept. 2007): 933–64.

23   McShane, *Down the Asphalt Path*, 29–30, 58, 62, 64–65; "Report of the Board of Experts on Street Paving in Philadelphia, Pa.," *Engineering News and American Contract Journal* 12 (9 Aug. 1884): 61; Stanley K. Schultz, *Constructing Urban Culture: American Cities and City Planning, 1800–1920* (Philadelphia: Temple University Press, 1989), 177; APWA, *History of Public Works*, 66; Baldwin, *Domesticating the Street*, 52–53.

24   "Growth of City Travel," *Engineering News and American Contract Journal* 14 (7 Nov. 1885): 303.

25   David E. Nye, *Electrifying America: Social Meanings of a New Technology* (Cambridge, Mass.: MIT Press, 1990), 88–89; Jon C. Teaford, *The Unheralded Triumph: City Government in America, 1870–1900* (Baltimore: Johns Hopkins University Press, 1984), 237; Jackson, *Crabgrass Frontier*, 107–9; McShane, *Down the Asphalt Path*; Martin V. Melosi, *Garbage in the Cities: Refuse, Reform, and the Environment, 1880–1980* (College Station: Texas A&M University Press, 1981), 25; Jackson, *Crabgrass Frontier*, 111.

26   Clay McShane, "Transforming the Use of Urban Space: A Look at the Revolution in Street Pavements, 1880–1924," *Journal of Urban History* 5 (May 1979): 279–307; McShane, *Down the Asphalt Path*, 57. See also Eric Schatzberg, "Culture and Technology in the City: Opposition to Mechanized Street Transportation in Late-Nineteenth-Century America," in *Technologies of Power: Essays in Honor of Thomas Parke Hughes and Agatha Chipley Hughes*, ed. Michael Thad Allen and Gabrielle Hecht (Cambridge, Mass.: MIT Press, 2001), 84–85; and Melosi, *Garbage in the Cities*, 137.

27   On overhead wires, see Schatzberg, "Culture and Technology," 65–82. On anti-streetcar sentiment, see Scott L. Bottles, *Los Angeles and the Automobile:*

The Making of the Modern City (Berkeley: University of California Press, 1987), 4, 11–12, 22–51; and Nye, *Electrifying America*, 97–104. On protective legislation, see McShane, *Down the Asphalt Path*, 73–75. On the perceived "moral influence" of streetcars themselves—whatever the shortcomings of the businessmen who operated them—see Joel A. Tarr, "From City to Suburb: The Moral Influence of Transportation Technology," in *The Search for the Ultimate Sink: Urban Pollution in Historical Perspective*, ed. Joel A. Tarr (Akron, Ohio: University of Akron Press, 1996); and Sam Bass Warner Jr., *Streetcar Suburbs: The Process of Growth in Boston, 1870–1900* (Cambridge, Mass.: Harvard University Press, 1962), 26–27.

28   "The Convention of the American Society of Municipal Improvements," *Engineering Record* 38 (5 Nov. 1898): 498.

29   Robert M. Fogelson, *Downtown: Its Rise and Fall, 1880–1950* (New Haven, Conn.: Yale University Press, 2001), 45.

30   Jackson, *Crabgrass Frontier*, 113–14; Fogelson, *Downtown*, 45; Nye, *Electrifying America*, 112–14.

31   Schatzberg, "Culture and Technology," 83; Nye, *Electrifying America*, 97–104; Bottles, *Los Angeles and the Automobile*, 4, 11–12, 22–51.

32   Melosi, *Garbage in the Cities*, 24. See also McShane, *Down the Asphalt Path*, 42–44.

33   "The Break-Down of Municipal Administration in New York," *New York Times*, 11 Feb. 1873, p. 4 (quotation); McShane, *Down the Asphalt Path*, 51 (statistics).

34   "Our Filthy Thoroughfares," *New York Times*, 14 Feb. 1874, p. 3.

35   "Brooklyn's Mud Burden: Commissioner Adams Will Not Lift It," *New York Times*, 12 March 1890, p. 3.

36   Martin V. Melosi, *The Sanitary City: Urban Infrastructure in America from Colonial Times to the Present* (Baltimore: Johns Hopkins University Press, 2000), 91; Suellen Hoy, *Chasing Dirt: The American Pursuit of Cleanliness* (New York: Oxford University Press, 1995), 68; Schultz, *Constructing Urban Culture*, 166. See also Joel A. Tarr and Francis Clay McMichael, "Decisions about Wastewater Technology: 1850–1932," *Journal of the Water Resources Planning and Management Division* (May 1977): 48–51; and Tarr and McMichael, "Historic Turning Points in Municipal Water Supply and Wastewater Disposal, 1850–1932," *Civil Engineering-ASCE* 47 (Oct. 1977): 82–83. A number of cities—including Brooklyn, Chicago, Providence, New Haven, Boston, Cincinnati, and Indianapolis—had installed smaller sewer systems for the removal of stormwater between 1850 and 1870, but none integrated them with their water systems. See Melosi, *Sanitary City*, 93.

37   "Filthy Thoroughfares," 8.

38   Martin V. Melosi, "Environmental Crisis in the City: The Relationship between Industrialization and Urban Pollution," in *Pollution and Reform in American Cities, 1870–1930*, ed. Martin V. Melosi (Austin: University of Texas Press, 1980), 17–18; Nancy Tomes, *The Gospel of Germs: Men, Women, and the Microbe in American Life* (Cambridge, Mass.: Harvard University Press, 1999). See also Hoy, *Chasing Dirt*, 60–65.

39   "Our Tenement Houses," *New York Times*, 9 June 1891, p. 4.

40   "What Patronage Does in This City," *New York Times*, 23 Feb. 1873, p. 4.

41   At the national level, the fight against patronage ultimately produced the Pendleton Act in 1883, creating the Civil Service Commission. The commission administered a civil service exam to judge the qualifications of applicants for a steadily expanding number of federal jobs. Although most federal jobs were part of the system by the end of the nineteenth century, state and especially municipal government jobs were another story. In New York City, for example—despite complaints like those from the *New York Times* quoted above and waves of reform efforts in the late nineteenth and early twentieth century—the city's civil service was not fully reformed until the 1930s. See Bruce M. Stave, *Urban Bosses, Machines, and Progressive Reformers* (Malabar, Fla.: Robert E. Krieger Publishing Co., 1984); James L. Merriner, *Grafters and Goo Goos: Corruption and Reform in Chicago, 1833–2003* (Carbondale: Southern Illinois University Press, 2004); John M. Dobson, *Politics in the Gilded Age: A New Perspective on Reform* (New York: Praeger, 1972); Ari Arthur Hoogenboom, *Outlawing the Spoils: A History of the Civil Service Reform Movement, 1865–1883* (Urbana: University of Illinois Press, 1961); and Kenneth Ackerman, *Boss Tweed: The Rise and Fall of the Corrupt Pol Who Conceived the Soul of Modern New York* (New York: Carroll and Graf, 2005).

42   George Rogers Taylor, *The Transportation Revolution, 1815–1860* (New York: Rinehart and Co., 1951), 156; Federal Highway Administration (hereafter FHWA), *America's Highways, 1776–1976: A History of the Federal-Aid Program* (Washington, D.C.: Government Printing Office, 1976), 29; John B. Rae, *The Road and the Car in American Life* (Cambridge, Mass.: MIT Press, 1971), 25–26; Seely, *Building the American Highway System*, 9.

43   Casper Tabott, "The Personal Labor System of Road Tax," *Good Roads* 1 (Jan. 1892): 38. The contrast between American and European roads emerged as a popular theme among late-nineteenth-century road reformers. See, for example, Potter, *Gospel of Good Roads*; and Charles Kendall Adams, "A Word of Contrast," *Good Roads* 1 (June 1892): 298.

44   For an overview of American road laws through the early 1890s, see Office of Road Inquiry (hereafter ORI), *Bulletin No. 1: State Laws Relating to the Management of Roads* (Washington, D.C.: Government Printing Office, 1893); and Office of Public Road Inquiry (hereafter OPRI), *Bulletin No. 32: Public-Road Mileage, Revenues, and Expenditures in the United States in 1904* (Washington, D.C.: Government Printing Office, 1907): 10, 16. On controversies over the statute-labor system, see Philip P. Mason, "The League of American Wheelmen and the Good-Roads Movement, 1880–1905" (Ph.D. diss., University of Michigan, 1957), 224–25; and Barron, *Mixed Harvest*, 25–27.

45   For the argument that road builders' apolitical technological expertise played a central role in the growth and development of the American highway system, see Seely, *Building the American Highway System*.

46 On this point, see especially John Stilgoe, "Roads, Highways, Ecosystems," from National Humanities Center, "Nature Transformed," http://nationalhumanitiescenter.org/tserve/nattrans/ntuseland/essays/roads.htm (accessed 12 Oct. 2010).

47 Wilcox, American City, 29.

48 For an approach that does not emphasize the centrality of streets for many of these subjects, see Joel A. Tarr and Gabriel Dupuy, eds., Technology and the Rise of the Networked City in Europe and America (Philadelphia: Temple University Press, 1988).

49 On the debates over "combined" versus "separate" sewer systems, see Stanley K. Schultz and Clay McShane, "To Engineer the Metropolis: Sewers, Sanitation, and City Planning in Late Nineteenth-Century America," Journal of American History 65 (Sept. 1978): 389–411. For statistics on the growth of sewer systems, see Joel A. Tarr, James McCurley, and Terry F. Yosie, "The Development and Impact of Urban Wastewater Technology: Changing Concepts of Water Quality Control, 1850–1930," in Pollution and Reform in American Cities, ed. Melosi, 68; and Teaford, Unheralded Triumph, 219–20. On the growth of the separate system of sewerage, see Hoy, Chasing Dirt, 68. On the divergent development of sewers in large and small cities, see Stanley K. Schultz and Clay McShane, "Pollution and Political Reform in Urban America: The Role of Municipal Engineers, 1840–1920," in Pollution and Reform in American Cities, ed. Melosi, 162.

50 In Boston, for example, abutters footed the entire bill for sewers. They could choose, however, either to wait for the city to install them and to assess their cost against the owners of adjacent property or to contract with a private firm to construct the sewers "under the superintendence of city officials." See "Recent Municipal Work in Boston, Mass.," Engineering Record 28 (8 July 1893): 91. On early municipally owned sewer systems, see Schultz and McShane, "Pollution and Political Reform," 162.

51 See Melosi, Sanitary City, 95–97.

52 Melosi, Garbage in the Cities, 30; Melosi, Sanitary City, 187. For a short account of New York City's involvement in street cleaning from the 1840s through 1881, see "Clean Streets Demanded," New York Times, 19 Mar. 1881, p. 5.

53 See, for example, "How Boston Keeps Clean," New York Times, 25 July 1880, p. 7; "Boston's Street-Cleaning Work," The Engineering Record 25 (27 Feb. 1892): 214; and "Recent Municipal Work," 91–92.

54 Judith Walzer Leavitt, The Healthiest City: Milwaukee and the Politics of Health Reform (Madison: University of Wisconsin Press, 1982), 70–71, 122–23, 243–44.

55 On unequal treatment of poor and wealthy areas, see "Our Streets," New York Times, 6 Jan. 1870, p. 8; and Melosi, Sanitary City, 188–89.

56 For two of Waring's own accounts of his activities, see George E. Waring Jr., "The Cleaning of the Streets of New York," Harper's Weekly 39 (26 Oct. 1895): 1022, 1024; and Waring, Street-Cleaning. For a contemporary summation of his efforts, see "Street Cleaning in New York," Engineering Record 37 (8 Jan. 1898):

121–22. For historical accounts of his activities, see Melosi, *Garbage in the Cities*, 58–65; Melosi, *Sanitary City*, 191; Hoy, *Chasing Dirt*, 79; McShane, *Down the Asphalt Path*, 52–53; and Teaford, *Unheralded Triumph*, 232. For a good account of the street-cleaning crusade in Hartford, Connecticut, see Baldwin, *Domesticating the Street*, 50–55.

57 For some representative contemporary accounts of the relationship between asphalt and street-cleaning efforts, see "The Economy of Asphalt over Stone Pavements," *Engineering News* 34 (29 Aug. 1895): 136; "Improved Macadam," *Engineering Record* 47 (16 May 1903): 510; and "The Cost of Sweeping and Cleaning Asphalt," *Engineering Record* 47 (18 Apr. 1903): 406. See also Melosi, *Garbage in the Cities*, 141–45.

58 U.S. Bureau of the Census, *Statistics of Cities Having a Population of 8,000 to 25,000: 1903* (Washington, D.C.: Government Printing Office, 1906); ORI, *Bulletin No. 45: Data for Use in Designing Culverts and Short-Span Bridges* (Washington, D.C.: U.S. Department of Agriculture, 1913), 92–97, and "Street Cleaning Methods," *Municipal Journal and Engineer* 26 (24 Mar. 1909): 485–89, both cited in Melosi, *Garbage in the Cities*, 141–43.

59 "The Use of the Public Street as a Catch-All," *Engineering Record* 47 (14 Mar. 1903): 275.

60 Warner, *Streetcar Suburbs*, 31. For an excellent discussion of electric and gas utilities based on case studies of Kansas City and Denver, see Mark H. Rose, *Cities of Light and Heat: Domesticating Gas and Electricity in Urban America* (University Park: Pennsylvania State University Press, 1995), 13–38.

61 "The Pole and Wire Question," *New York Times*, 6 Dec. 1883, p. 4. See also Schatzberg, "Culture and Technology," 64–65; and Teaford, *Unheralded Triumph*, 231.

62 Schatzberg, "Culture and Technology," 64–65.

63 For a particularly good overview of reform arguments along these lines, see Peter Derrick, *Tunneling to the Future: The Story of the Great Subway Expansion That Saved New York* (New York: New York University Press, 2001), esp. 90–122.

64 Fogelson, *Downtown*, 46; Edwin G. Burrows and Mike Wallace, *Gotham: A History of New York City to 1898* (New York: Oxford University Press, 1999), 1053–55; McShane, *Down the Asphalt Path*, 26; Charles N. Glaab and A. Theodore Brown, *A History of Urban America* (New York: Macmillan, 1967), 149.

65 Crane as quoted in Burrows and Wallace, *Gotham*, 1055. On court challenges and protests against the elevated trains, see ibid., 1056; McShane, *Down the Asphalt Path*, 74–75; and Fogelson, *Downtown*, 46–47.

66 Burrows and Wallace, *Gotham*, 1058.

67 Wilcox, *American City*, 38–39.

68 Fogelson, *Downtown*, 55–68; Jane Holtz Kay, *Lost Boston*, expanded and updated ed. (Boston: Houghton Mifflin, 1999), 249–51.

69 The pioneering work on street pavements is McShane, "Use of Urban Space," 279–307. See also McShane, *Down the Asphalt Path*, 9, 58–61. On asphalt, see I. B. Holley Jr., "Blacktop: How Asphalt Paving Came to the Urban United States,"

Technology and Culture 44 (Oct. 2003): 703–33. For an engineering textbook that discusses how to lay these pavements and evaluates their individual strengths and weaknesses, see William Pierson Judson, *City Roads and Pavements Suited to Cities of Moderate Size*, 2nd revised and enlarged ed. (New York: Engineering News Publishing Co., 1902).

70   APWA, *History of Public Works*, 67.

71   "Street Paving in Philadelphia," 62.

72   "The Streets of New York City," *Engineering News* 24 (5 July 1890): 20; "Recent Municipal Work," 91.

73   See, for example, "Street Paving in Philadelphia," 61; and "Recent Municipal Work," 91. In Boston, legislators had the new rule written into the city charter. See "Street Cleaning in New York," 409.

74   "A City's Control of Its Highways," *Engineering Record* 25 (30 Jan. 1892): 140.

75   This section draws on research and ideas first presented in Christopher W. Wells, "The Changing Nature of Country Roads: Farmers, Reformers, and the Shifting Uses of Rural Space, 1880–1905," *Agricultural History* 80 (Spring 2006): 143–66.

76   For more on this point, see ibid., 148–51.

77   John M. Stahl, "Will Good Roads Bankrupt the Farmer?" *Good Roads* 7 (Feb. 1895): 67.

78   Mason, "League of American Wheelmen," esp. ch. 2; Gary Allan Tobin, "The Bicycle Boom of the 1890s: The Development of Private Transportation and the Birth of the Modern Tourist," *Journal of Popular Culture* 7, 4 (1974): 838–49; Wiebe E. Bijker, *Of Bicycles, Bakelites, and Bulbs: Toward a Theory of Sociotechnical Change* (Cambridge, Mass.: MIT Press, 1995), 19–100; Stephen B. Goddard, *Colonel Albert Pope and His American Dream Machines: The Life and Times of a Bicycle Tycoon Turned Automotive Pioneer* (Jefferson, NC: McFarland & Co., 2000); Robert A. Smith, *A Social History of the Bicycle: Its Early Life and Times in America* (New York: American Heritage Press, 1972); David V. Herlihy, *Bicycle: The History* (New Haven, Conn.: Yale University Press, 2004).

79   For a typical statement of this position, see ORI, *Bulletin No. 23: Road Conventions in the Southern States and Object-Lesson Roads Constructed under the Supervision of the Office of Public Road Inquiries, with the Cooperation of the Southern Railway* (Washington, D.C.: Government Printing Office, 1902), 7.

80   On ORI and OPRI activities during this period, see FHWA, *America's Highways*, 44–52; W. Stull Holt, *The Bureau of Public Roads: Its History, Activities and Organization* (Baltimore: Johns Hopkins University Press, 1923), 7; Mason, "League of American Wheelmen," 83–206; and Seely, *Building the American Highway System*, 11–23.

81   For more on this point, see Wells, "Changing Nature of Country Roads," esp. 147–48.

82   Speech delivered before the Iowa Bankers' Association annual meeting, Council Bluffs, Iowa, 24 May 1893, quoted in ORI, *Circular No. 26: Going into Debt for*

Good Roads (Washington, D.C.: Government Printing Office, 1897), 1.

83   *Southern Pines, N.C., Tourist*, 31 May 1907, quoted in Preston, *Dirt Roads to Dixie*, 24.

84   Barron, *Mixed Harvest*, 19–42.

85   David W. Lewis, "Country Roads: Who Should Be Responsible for Them?" *Good Roads* 5 (May 1894): 179.

86   Quoted in Barron, *Mixed Harvest*, 30.

87   Potter, *Gospel of Good Roads*, 10.

88   For example, see ibid., 8–9.

89   Ibid., 24.

90   ORI, *Circular No. 16: Highway Taxation: Comparative Results of Labor and Money Systems* (Washington, D.C.: Government Printing Office, 1894), 1 (first and second quotations), 2 (third quotation). See also ORI, *Circular No. 24: Highway Repairing* (Washington, D.C.: Government Printing Office, 1896).

91   For two examples of this exercise, see ORI, *Circular No. 19: Traffic of the Country Roads* (Washington, D.C.: Government Printing Office, 1896), 2; and Potter, *Gospel of Good Roads*, 10–11.

92   "Address Delivered at the Southern Immigration and Industrial Congress, Augusta, Ga., June 1, 1894," in ORI, *Circular No. 14: Addresses on Road Improvement* (Washington, D.C.: Government Printing Office, 1894), 3. The urban historian Owen Gutfreund has skewered the use of statewide taxes to fund rural roads, which became a cornerstone of rural road financing in future years, as "a system of transfer payments from urbanized regions to rural regions, and from all taxpayers generally to those who drove automobiles." Gutfreund, *Twentieth-Century Sprawl: How Highways Transformed America* (New York: Oxford University Press, 2004), 27.

93   See, for example, Potter, *Gospel of Good Roads*, 11.

94   Martin Dodge, *Report of the Office of Public Road Inquiries* (Washington, D.C.: Government Printing Office, 1903), 332. The best sources for charting the course and expansion of the object-lesson roads program are the annual director's reports, beginning in 1897. Other descriptions of the program include FHWA, *America's Highways*, 45–47; and Seely, *Building the American Highway System*, 14–16.

95   "Good Roads Train and Road Improvement Exhibits" flier, File 530, Box 95, Entry 2, RG 30, National Archives and Record Administration, College Park, Maryland (hereafter NARA). The OPRI correspondence files contain a variety of information about the agency's participation in the Good Roads Train endeavors. See "Good Roads Train, 1902–1903," File 68, Box 29; M. O. Eldridge to Martin Dodge, 7 Sept. 1904, "Frisco Good Roads Train," File 56, Box 20; M. V. Richards, Land and Industrial Agent, Southern Railway, to M. O. Eldridge, "Benefits of Road Improvement, 1898–1907," 24 Sept. 1906, File 17, Box 7, all in Entry 2, RG 30, NARA; and Dodge, *Report* (1902 and 1903). See also Seely, *Building the American Highway System*, 17–18; and FHWA, *America's Highways*, 48–50.

96   ORI, *Bulletin No. 9: State Aid to Road-Building in New Jersey* (Washington, D.C.: Government Printing Office, 1894); Dodge, *Report* (1903), 342–43; Austin F. MacDonald, *Federal Aid: A Study of the American Subsidy System* (New York: Thomas Y. Crowell Company, 1928), 86; FHWA, *America's Highways*, 43. The ORI/OPRI published a variety of pamphlets and circulars during the 1890s and early 1900s with detailed descriptions of state aid acts (and proposed laws), and the office's annual director's reports in this period routinely address changes in state road laws. For an overview of early state aid programs, see Mason, "League of American Wheelmen," 234–36, 240.

97   On the links between RFD and the good-roads movement, see Wayne E. Fuller, *RFD: The Changing Face of Rural America* (Bloomington: Indiana University Press, 1964), esp. 177–98; Fuller, "Good Roads and the Rural Free Delivery of Mail," *Mississippi Valley Historical Review* 42 (June 1955): 67–83; and Wells, "Changing Nature of Country Roads," 157–58.

98   Ibid., 158–59.

99   OPRI, *Bulletin No. 32*, 8–9.

100   On the importance of engineering ideas in some of these transformations, see especially Schultz and McShane, "To Engineer the Metropolis"; and Melosi, *Sanitary City*.

101   Steinberg, *Down to Earth*, 171.

2. AUTOMOTIVE PIONEERS

1   Parts of this chapter were originally published in slightly different form as Christopher W. Wells, "The Road to the Model T: Culture, Road Conditions, and Innovation at the Dawn of the American Motor Age," *Technology and Culture* 48 (July 2007): 497–523. Reprinted by permission of the author and publisher.

2   On the *Chicago Times-Herald* race, see Allan Nevins, *Ford*, vol. 1, *The Times, the Man, the Company, 1915–1933* (New York: Charles Scribner's Sons, 1954), 139–41; and Stephen W. Sears, *The American Heritage History of the Automobile in America* (New York: American Heritage Publishing Co., 1977), 20–26. On the industry's early growth, see James M. Laux et al., *The Automobile Revolution: The Impact of an Industry*, ed. and trans. James M. Laux (Chapel Hill: University of North Carolina Press, 1982), 15; National Automobile Chamber of Commerce (hereafter NACC), *Facts and Figures of the Automobile Industry* (New York: NACC, 1928), 6; and Federal Highway Administration (hereafter FHWA), *Highway Statistics: Summary to 1985* (Washington, D.C.: Government Printing Office, 1987), 25.

3   Ibid., 25.

4   Ibid., 39.

5   Henry Ford, with the collaboration of Samuel Crowther, *My Life and Work* (Garden City, N.Y.: Doubleday, Page and Co., 1922), 73; Charles Merz, *And Then Came Ford* (Garden City, N.Y., Doubleday, Doran & Co., 1929), 304.

6   Clay McShane, *Down the Asphalt Path: The Automobile and the American City*

(New York: Columbia University Press, 1994), 82–83. Most histories of the automobile or the automobile industry sketch the development of motor-vehicle
technology in the eighteenth and nineteenth centuries. For more in-depth discussions of the topic, see T. P. Newcomb and R. T. Spurr, *A Technical History of
the Motor Car* (Bristol: Adam Hilger, 1989), 3–22; Sears, *Automobile in America*,
9–16; John B. Rae, *The American Automobile: A Brief History* (Chicago: University of Chicago Press, 1965), 1–15; James J. Flink, *America Adopts the Automobile,
1895–1910* (Cambridge, Mass.: MIT Press, 1970), 12–25; and Flink, *The Automobile
Age* (Cambridge, Mass.: MIT Press, 1988), 1–14.

7   NACC, *Facts and Figures* (1928), 6 (statistics). Most of these had electric or steam
     engines.

8   This list includes, among others, the Duryea brothers, Albert Pope, George E.
     Whitney, Elwood P. Haynes, Ransom E. Olds, Alexander Winton, Henry Ford,
     and the brothers Francis and Freelan Stanley.

9   Albert Pope, "Automobiles and Good Roads," *Munsey's* 29 (May 1903): 168. On
     the good-roads movement during this period, see Christopher W. Wells, "The
     Changing Nature of Country Roads: Farmers, Reformers, and the Shifting
     Uses of Rural Space, 1880–1905," *Agricultural History* 80 (Spring 2006): 143–66.

10   Hiram Percy Maxim, *Horseless Carriage Days* (New York: Harper & Brothers,
     1936), 79, 80.

11   McShane, *Down the Asphalt Path*, 130–31, 220–21; "W. K. Vanderbilt Dies in
     Home Here," *New York Times*, 8 Jan. 1944. On the connections between Ameri-
     can elites and road-improvement efforts in New York, see Peter J. Hugill, *The
     Elite, the Automobile, and the Good Roads Movement in New York: The Develop-
     ment and Transformation of a Technological Complex, 1904–1913*, Discussion Paper
     Series (Syracuse: Department of Geography, Syracuse University, 1981).

12   "The Road Improvement Fallacy: Cry for Improved Roads as Necessary Condi-
     tion for the Progress of the Motor Vehicle Industry Ill Founded and Likely to
     Lead Construction and Design into Unprofitable Channels," *Motor Age* 1 (1899):
     83.

13   Newcomb and Spurr, *Technical History of the Motor Car*, 23–24, 35–36; Laux et al.,
     Automobile Revolution, 34–35; Flink, *Automobile Age*, 33–35; Peter J. Hugill, "Tech-
     nology and Geography in the Emergence of the American Automobile Industry,
     1895–1915," in *Roadside America: The Automobile in Design and Culture*, ed. Jan
     Jennings (Ames: Iowa State University Press for the Society for Commercial
     Archeology, 1990), 29–39, esp. 31–34; Peter J. Hugill, "Technology Diffusion in
     the World Automobile Industry, 1885–1985," in *The Transfer and Transformation
     of Ideas and Material Culture*, ed. Peter J. Hugill and D. Bruce Dickson (College
     Station: Texas A&M University Press, 1988), 110–42; Guy Jellinek-Mercédès,
     My Father Mr. Mercédès, trans. Ruth Hassell (Philadelphia: Chilton Books, 1961),
     esp. 87–100. Before 1903, American manufacturers who used gasoline engines
     utilized the horseless-carriage design, mounting the engine under or behind the
     vehicle's seat.

14 M. C. Krarup, "The Automobile," *Outing* 37 (Feb. 1901): 620; "Growth of the Automobile Industry," *Nation* 88 (7 Jan. 1909): 8.

15 Hrolf Wisby, "Camping Out in an Automobile," *Outing* (Mar. 1905): 740 (first quotation); H. P. Burchell, "America Sets the Automobile Pace," *Outing* 45 (Mar. 1905): 747.

16 In recent years, scholars have generated a host of fresh insights into the shifting contours of the early auto industry, both before and after the advent of the Model T. Much of this work has been inspired by the observation that *social context* actively shapes definitions of technological merit—and thus the success and failure of different technologies. For one notable example of this approach, see Ronald Kline, *Consumers in the Country: Technology and Social Change in Rural America* (Baltimore: Johns Hopkins University Press, 2000). I am here making the case that *environmental context* played a significant role as well in shaping the evolution of automotive technology in the United States.

17 "Automobile Not a Plaything," *Outing* 43 (Oct. 1903): 354.

18 Eustace Clavering, "The Twentieth Century Runabout," *Munsey's* 28 (Dec. 1902): 388 (quotation); Flink, *America Adopts the Automobile*, 280–84; Newcomb and Spurr, *Technical History of the Motor Car*, 47. Most European manufacturers also faced horsepower taxes, which made them hesitant to adopt big, powerful engines.

19 Frederick Dwight, "Automobiles: The Other Side of the Shield," *Independent* 65 (3 Dec. 1908): 1300 (quotation); Ralph C. Epstein, *The Automobile Industry: Its Economic and Commercial Development* (Chicago: A. W. Shaw Co., 1928), 76, 91; Nevins, *Ford*, vol. 1, 275.

20 "The Automobile of 1904," *Outing* 43 (Mar. 1904): 734; Flink, *Automobile Age*, 31–39. As James J. Flink and others have demonstrated, the widely held notion that Henry Ford was the first to think of building low-priced motor vehicles in large quantities is mistaken. Ford did stand alone, however, in applying the idea on a much grander scale than others ever envisioned was possible.

21 On high-wheeler production, see Flink, *Automobile Age*, 34–35 and Hugill, "Technology and Geography," 34–36. By 1909 nearly fifty firms, concentrated almost entirely in the Midwest, produced high-wheelers. The indispensable compendium of information on American motor vehicles during this period is Beverly Rae Kimes and Henry Austin Clark Jr., *Standard Catalog of American Cars, 1805–1942*, 3rd ed. (Iola, Wisc.: Krause Publications, 1996).

22 "Automobile of 1904," 734.

23 For three discussions of this problem, see Hugill, "Technology and Geography," 34, 36, 38; Flink, *America Adopts the Automobile*, 281–88; and Newcomb and Spurr, *Technical History of the Motor Car*, 36, 85–86. The ratios cited here are calculated based on information in Association of Licensed Automobile Manufacturers, *Handbook of Gasoline Automobiles, 1904–1906* (New York: Dover Publications, 1969), 268–69. On Henry Ford's understanding of the role that steel played in this equation, see Henry Ford, "Special Automobile Steel," *Harper's*

Weekly 51 (16 Mar. 1907): 336G. On Ford's early recognition of this problem, see Nevins, *Ford*, vol. 1, 276–77.

24 Nevins, *Ford*, vol. 1, 338; Kimes and Clark, *Standard Catalog*, 571.

25 Henry Ford, "Arranging to Build 20,000 Runabouts" (letter to the editor), *The Automobile*, 11 Jan. 1906, 107.

26 Accounts of Ford's first encounter with vanadium steel vary. Ford himself claimed he came across it "almost by accident" when he salvaged a valve stem from a wrecked French racing car in Palm Beach, Florida. Ford, *My Life and Work*, 65–66. As Allan Nevins points out, however, accounts of vanadium steel and its properties had been published in scientific journals that Ford executives read and had been exhibited at an engineering convention in 1905 that a chief Ford executive had attended. Nevins, *Ford*, vol. 1, 348–49. Douglas Brinkley concludes that C. Harold Wills, Ford's most influential designer at the time, discovered the alloy for the company. Brinkley, *Wheels for the World: Henry Ford, His Company, and a Century of Progress* (New York: Penguin Books, 2003), 101–2. Thomas J. Misa, on the other hand, claims that Wills came across the alloy only when he hired J. Kent Smith, a British metallurgical engineer, as a consultant. Misa, *A Nation of Steel: The Making of Modern America, 1865–1925* (Baltimore: Johns Hopkins University Press 1995), 223–25. As the company's metallurgical sophistication grew, its goal of a strong, lightweight design remained, but its use of vanadium steel declined. The company's chief metallurgist, John Wandersee, came to realize that heat treatments were of equal or greater importance than an alloy's component parts for producing steels with the particular characteristics that engineers desired for different parts. Vanadium steel proved impractical for crankshafts, for example, whereas properly heat-treated manganese carbon steel worked admirably in that capacity. See John Wandersee, "The Reminiscences of Mr. John Wandersee" (bound), 20–27, Acc. 65, The Henry Ford, Benson Ford Research Center, Dearborn, Michigan (hereafter BFRC). "With the proper kind of heat treat you could improve any kind of steel," Wandersee said. "Any steel that had enough alloy or carbon content to permit hardening could be tempered to the requirements" (24–25). Other considerations included price, ease of machining, and availability. See also Ford, *My Life and Work*, 66–69. Ford's belief in vanadium steel was thus crucial to the development of the Model T, but at the same time he put unfounded faith in the "revolutionary" nature of the alloy.

27 For two detailed accounts of the Model T's development, see Nevins, *Ford*, vol. 1, 388–93; and Brinkley, *Wheels for the World*, 99–106. See also Galamb, "Reminiscences" (draft), Acc. 65, Box 21, Folder "Oral Histories—Galamb"; and C. J. Smith, "The Reminiscences of C. J. Smith" (bound), Acc. 65, both in BFRC.

28 Galamb, "Reminiscences," 18. Henry Ford and C. Harold Wills were the other influential members of the design team.

29 Ford, "20,000 Runabouts," 119.

30 Quoted in Flink, *America Adopts the Automobile*, 278.

31   Most histories of the automobile in the United States devote space to describing the Model T and its design. See especially Nevins, *Ford*, vol. 1, 387–93; Bruce W. McCalley, *Model T Ford: The Car That Changed the World* (Iola, Wisc.: Krause Publications, 1994); Wells, "Road to the Model T"; and Robert Casey, *The Model T: A Centennial History* (Baltimore: Johns Hopkins University Press, 2008), 13–31.

32   Because the Model T's initial low price has often been misunderstood and exaggerated, it is important to qualify this statement. When the Model T debuted at $850 in 1908, its cost put it near the top of the "low-cost" category, well above most high-wheelers and runabouts—including Ford's own Model N at $600. Not until 1 October 1910 did Ford institute its famous policy of annual price cuts by lowering the price of the Model T touring car from $950 to $780. It cut the price to $690 in 1911 and to $600 in 1912. Nevins, *Ford*, vol. 1, 646–47. The 1912 price marked the first time the Model T's price dropped below the average annual wage in the United States, indicating the extent to which motor-vehicle ownership remained a privilege of the wealthy and the well-off, even in the early Model T era. Flink, *Automobile Age*, 38. In 1910, for example, there were fully 130.9 Americans aged fifteen years or older for every motor vehicle in the country—underlining the extent to which "low cost" remained a relative term. FHWA, *Highway Statistics: Summary to 1965* (Washington, D.C.: Government Printing Office, 1967), 37. Only after the introduction of assembly line techniques in 1914 did the Model T begin to become more widely affordable.

33   "Halt Here on Run to Pacific," *New York Post-Standard*, 3 June 1909 (first quotation), in Acc. 717, Box 5, Folder "1909 Race—General," BFRC; Ford Motor Company, "The Story of the Race" (second quotation); Acc. 717, Box 5, Folder "1909 Race—General," BFRC. On cross-country automobile trips during this period, see Curt McConnell, *Coast to Coast by Automobile: The Pioneering Trips, 1899–1908* (Stanford, Calif.: Stanford University Press, 2000).

34   "Driver Chapin Tells of Shawmut's Trip," *Seattle Daily Times*, 23 June 1909, Acc. 717, Box 5, Folder "1909 Race—General," BFRC.

35   Smith, "Reminiscences," 9–10.

36   "Fast Time Made in Seattle Race," *New York Times*, 27 June 1909. Judges disqualified the winning Model T five months later for having used unauthorized parts for a section of the race, but Ford continued to describe its "win" in its advertisements, and fifty years later the company even staged a reenactment of the Model T's "victory" as part of a celebration of the construction of the fifty-millionth Ford automobile. See "50 Million Fords Ago . . . ," Acc. 717, Box 1, BFRC.

37   "The New York–Seattle Race" (advertisement), *Ford Times*, 15 July 1909.

38   F. Eugene Melder, "The 'Tin Lizzie's' Golden Anniversary," *American Quarterly* 12 (Winter 1960): 468. It should be noted that a utilitarian focus was common in automobile advertising of this period. See Pamela Walker Laird, "'The Car without a Single Weakness': Early Automobile Advertising," *Technology and Culture* 37 (Oct. 1996): 796–812.

39   Ford manufactured its replacement parts on a large scale and sold them at very

low prices, one of many attractive selling points of the Model T. In contrast, most auto manufacturers charged significantly more for replacement parts, partly because they manufactured them on a more limited scale, which raised production costs, and partly because they had a monopoly on available replacements. The widespread availability of Ford dealerships proved yet another selling point. During the 1909 race from New York to Seattle, for example, one of the drivers of the Shawmut car told a reporter that the extensive Ford dealer network had given it a big advantage during the race. "At another point we were laid up another sixteen hours to make repairs," he explained, "although the Ford car lost but little time in repairing through the fact that there is a Ford agency in almost every city and large town while there are few Shawmut cars in operation west of New York State." See "Shawmut's Trip." By the end of 1912, the Ford Motor Company had over seven thousand dealers in the United States, with at least one dealership for every town with two thousand or more residents. See "Petitioners' Statement of Facts," 18 Apr. 1927, Dodge et al. vs. Commissioner of Internal Revenue, vol. 1, p. 79, Acc. 84, Box 1, BFRC. Joseph Anthony Interrante has estimated that by the onset of World War I few rural residents lived more than fifteen miles from a Ford dealership. See Interrante, "A Moveable Feast: The Automobile and the Spatial Transformation of American Culture, 1890–1940" (Ph.D. diss., Harvard University, 1983), 90.

40 Ronald Kline and Trevor Pinch, "Users as Agents of Technological Change: The Social Construction of the Automobile in the Rural United States," *Technology and Culture* 37 (1996): 763–95, esp. 773–77; Kline, *Consumers in the Country*, 55–86.

41 David Beecroft, "Farmers Are Converting Wheat into Motor Cars," *Motor Age* 28 (11 Feb. 1915): 18–19.

42 Ford, *My Life and Work*, 67, 68. The decision to build only one model—using an identical chassis for the Model T runabout, touring car, town car, and delivery car—came in 1909. See Nevins, *Ford*, vol. 1, 452.

43 NACC, *Facts and Figures* (1924), 4.

44 Although models and types of tops varied, most of the smaller tops that covered just one seat, such as those for cars with runabout bodies, had the option of folding down behind the seat when not in use, much like the roof of a modern-day convertible. Others, and especially those designed to cover both the front and back seats of longer touring-car bodies, had to be disassembled and removed.

45 Hugo Alois Taussig, *Retracing the Pioneers: From West to East in an Automobile* (San Francisco: Philopolis Press, 1910), 67. For descriptions of many early transcontinental trips by automobile, see McConnell, *Coast to Coast*.

46 The travel accounts of early motorists are often a litany of encounters with weather-induced road problems. For just one of many examples of motorists hiring a farmer to haul a stuck vehicle from the mud, see Effie Price Gladding, *Across the Continent by the Lincoln Highway* (New York: Brentano's, 1915), 53, 134–36.

47 E. B. White, "Farewell, My Lovely!" in *The Second Tree from the Corner* (New

York: Harper and Row, 1984), 34, originally published as Lee Strout White, *Farewell to Model T* (New York: G. P. Putnam's Sons, 1936).

48   The Model T accessories industry grew along with the Ford factory's output, ensuring that Model T accessories became as ubiquitous as the automobile for which they were designed. For two accessible collections of advertisements for Model T accessories, see Floyd Clymer, *Henry's Wonderful Model T, 1908–1927* (New York: McGraw-Hill, 1955), 191–218; and James L. Kenealy, *Model "T" Ford: Authentic Accessories, 1909–1927*, 3 vols. (Seattle: James L. Kenealy, 1976). A good primary source is the national magazine *Scientific American*, which published an annual review of automobile accessories in the years 1915–1920. Sears catalogs after 1915 are also an excellent source for charting the increasing availability of Model T accessories. "Only one page in the current catalogue is devoted to parts and accessories for the Model T," E. B. White wrote in 1936, "yet everyone remembers springtimes when the Ford gadget section was larger than men's clothing, almost as large as household furnishings." White, "Farewell, My Lovely!" 32.

49   O. O. McIntyre, "How Many Gadgets on Your Car?" *Motor* (Nov. 1924): 54, quoted in Kathleen Franz, "Narrating Automobility: Travelers, Tinkerers, and Technological Authority in the Twentieth Century" (Ph.D. diss., Brown University, 1999), 171.

50   Bruce W. McCalley has meticulously documented when the Ford factory first offered various equipment options and when they became standard. See McCalley, *Model T Ford*.

51   Quoted in Sears, *Automobile in America*, 88.

52   Fred J. Wagner, "Useful Talks and News about Automobiles," *American Suburbs* 3 (Jan. 1912): 152.

53   McCalley, *Model T Ford*, 277. The starter came as standard equipment on the coupe and sedan styles, as an option for the touring and runabout styles, and was altogether unavailable for the truck.

54   Epstein, *Automobile Industry*, 106.

55   H. L. Maher, "Reminiscences" (draft), 28, Acc. 65, BFRC.

56   Ford, *My Life and Work*, 71.

57   *Motor World* 17 (17 Oct. 1907): 106, quoted in Nevins, *Ford*, vol. 1, 352–53. Ford expanded on this idea two years later in Henry Ford, "System the Secret of Ford's Success," *New York Times*, 3 Jan. 1909, p. S7.

58   From a letter published in the *Ford Times*, 15 Apr. 1908, pp. 14–15, quoted in Nevins, *Ford*, vol. 1, 387.

59   The Ford production year ran from 1 October of one year through 30 September of the next.

60   It is a widely held—but incorrect—assumption that the Model T's design never changed. In fact, it changed all the time, although the company worked hard to ensure compatibility as new parts and components replaced old ones. "It is next to impossible to describe every variation in the car," writes Bruce McCalley, the

former editor of *Vintage Ford* and author of the definitive study of the Model T's mechanical evolution. "There were almost constant changes in detail, many being no more than the result of a different supplier of some component. Furthermore, Ford did not stop using one part and begin using another on any given date. New pieces were added and at the same time the old supply was being used up. There seems to have been considerable overlap in new versus old when a new style was introduced." See McCalley, *Model T Ford*, iii. The company replaced a number of its forged parts, for example, with less expensive stamped-metal equivalents after acquiring the John R. Keim Mills in Buffalo, New York, which it entirely relocated to Highland Park in 1912. In addition to making changes based on production considerations, the company also responded to consumer complaints. "The changes in the car usually came through the Complaints Department," explained Joseph Galamb. "The complaints always came to me. They would ask the Service Department how they were going to fix it. I was the go-between between Mr. Ford and the Service Department. When Service would have too many complaints on one thing, I would design it differently so it would hold up, but without any change." See Galamb, "Reminiscences," 101.

61 David A. Hounshell, *From the American System to Mass Production, 1800–1932* (Baltimore: Johns Hopkins University Press, 1984), 221 (quotation), 228–34. Advances in the machine-tool industry proved crucial to Ford's ability to manufacture automobiles on such a large scale. Just as vanadium steel had enabled the strong and lightweight design of the Model T, harder steels made it possible for machine-tool manufacturers to build stronger, faster-running, more precise tools for auto manufacturers like Ford.

62 The Model T production figures are for the calendar year named, as compiled in McCalley, *Model T Ford*, 502–36. McCalley's numbers differ slightly from those in Hounshell, *American System to Mass Production*, 224, which are 20,727 in 1910, 53,488 in 1911, and 82,388 in 1912. Only the 1912 numbers differ significantly. The price changes of Model T touring cars, all of which were made on 1 October of the year mentioned, appear in Nevins, *Ford*, vol. 1, 646–47, as compiled from the files of the *Ford Times*. Each Model T body type—runabout, roadster, town car, coupe, landaulet, and touring car—had its own price. I cite the touring-car price as the most popular of the available options.

63 Flink, *Automobile Age*, 38. For comparison purposes, the Bureau of Economic Analysis in the U.S. Department of Commerce calculated the average annual wage (per job) in the United States in 2008 as $50,259, while the National Automobile Dealers Association reported the average price of a new car at $28,400. See Bureau of Business and Economic Research, University of New Mexico, http://bber.unm.edu/econ/us-wage.htm (accessed 31 Jan. 2010); and Federal Trade Commission, www.ftc.gov/bcp/edu/pubs/consumer/autos/aut11.shtm (accessed 31 Jan. 2010). Although it cost much more as a percentage of average salary than most cars today, the Model T continued to be priced very low compared to the industry's overall average, which did not fall below $2,000 until

1915. See Carlos Arnaldo Schwantes, *Going Places: Transportation Redefines the Twentieth-Century West* (Bloomington: Indiana University Press, 2003), 52.

64 FHWA, *Highway Statistics to 1965*, 37.

65 J. J. Seaton, "Small Car and its Uses," *Harper's Weekly* 54 (8 Jan. 1910): 26.

66 "Building an Automobile Every 40 Seconds," 759 (quotation), one of a series of sixteen articles in *American Machinist* published between 8 May and 27 Nov. 1913 (vols. 38 and 39).

67 The classic primary source on early mass production is Horace Lucien Arnold and Fay Leone Faurote, *Ford Methods and the Ford Shops* (1915; New York: Arno Press, 1972). The book is a compilation of articles originally published in *Engineering Magazine* that were based on a detailed study of the Highland Park plant conducted in 1914, shortly after it had been developed. Also important are various reminiscences conducted during the preparation of the company's official history in the 1950s, available in Acc. 65 of the BFRC; see, for example, the reminiscences of William Klann, Charles Sorensen, Richard Kroll, William Pioch, and A. M. Wibel. Charles Sorensen, *My Forty Years with Ford* (New York: W. W. Norton, 1956), 115–32, also provides an account of the development of assembly-line techniques by one of the major developers of the process. Hounshell, *American System to Mass Production*, 217–61, remains the definitive history of the subject. See also Nevins, *Ford*, vol. 1, 447–80.

68 Hounshell, *American System to Mass Production*, 248, 249, 253–55.

69 On the importance of "system" as a component of Fordism, see Thomas P. Hughes, *American Genesis: A Century of Invention and Technological Enthusiasm, 1870–1970* (Chicago: University of Chicago Press, 1989), 203–20.

70 McCalley, *Model T Ford*, 506–13. Hounshell, *American System to Mass Production*, 224, places the production figures at 189,088 in 1913 and 585,388 in 1916. The price of the Model T touring car is from Nevins, *Ford*, vol. 1, 647.

71 McCalley, *Model T Ford*, 502–36. The industry's total output is as compiled in NACC, *Facts and Figures* (1928), 6.

72 Stephen Meyer, *The Five Dollar Day: Labor Management and Social Control in the Ford Motor Company, 1908–1921* (Albany: State University of New York Press, 1981).

73 Merz, *Then Came Ford*, 116, 117. By 1926, the term "mass production" referred to the entire range of Ford's innovations, including "mechanization, high wages, low prices, and large-volume output"—not just large-scale production. See Hounshell, *American System to Mass Production*, 305. On Ford and the press, see David L. Lewis, *The Public Image of Henry Ford: An American Folk Hero and His Company* (Detroit: Wayne State University Press, 1976); and Reynold M. Wik, *Henry Ford and Grass-Roots America* (Ann Arbor: University of Michigan Press, 1972).

74 It is worth noting that corporations, including the Ford Motor Company itself, never relinquished the search for ways to benefit from dramatic productivity increases without raising salaries.

75   The environmental historian J. R. McNeill has gone so far as to argue that the advent of Fordism marked "the historic compromise of the twentieth century between industrial workers and employers," amounting to "a renegotiation of the social contract of industrial society." McNeill, *Something New Under the Sun: An Environmental History of the Twentieth-Century World* (New York: W. W. Norton, 2000), 316–17.

76   NACC, *Facts and Figures* (1921), 7.

77   As calculated from Ford production statistics in McCalley, *Model T Ford*, 502–36, and industry production statistics in NACC, *Facts and Figures* (1928), 6.

78   Darwin S. Harch, "Out of the Chrysalis of Past Effort," *Motor Age* 31 (4 Jan. 1917): 6. This number is slightly less accurate than it appears, for it excludes manufacturers and models that were not already on the market in early January but that came into existence during the year.

79   NACC, *Facts and Figures* (1928), 6 (production figures); Alfred D. Chandler, *Giant Enterprise: Ford, General Motors, and the Automobile Industry* (New York: Harcourt, Brace, and World, 1964), 33 (Model T prices). See also Flink, *Automobile Age*, 80–83.

3. BUILDING FOR TRAFFIC

1   Quoted in John B. Rae, *The Road and the Car in American Life* (Cambridge, Mass.: MIT Press, 1971), 5.

2   Some states—particularly the larger, wealthier states of the Northeast and East Coast, such as New York and Massachusetts—developed significant road-building programs and expertise without much federal influence, although scholars are just beginning to focus on these state-level initiatives. For an insightful case-study of New York's "subfederal road-building regime" in the years before 1920, see Michael R. Fein, *Paving the Way: New York Road Building and the American State, 1880–1956* (Lawrence: University Press of Kansas, 2008), esp. 18–76.

3   Bruce E. Seely, *Building the American Highway System: Engineers as Policy Makers* (Philadelphia: Temple University Press, 1987), 24. On Page's background and training, see ibid., 21–22; and Federal Highway Administration (hereafter FHWA), *America's Highways, 1776–1976: A History of the Federal-Aid Program* (Washington, D.C.: Government Printing Office, 1976), 64.

4   Office of Public Roads (hereafter OPR), *Circular No. 91: Sand-Clay and Earth Roads in the Middle West* (Washington, D.C.: Government Printing Office, 1910), 29.

5   This is not to suggest that Page did not believe in the social justification for good roads that preachers of the good-roads gospel advanced. He believed, quite strongly, in a clear link between road improvements and rural uplift. Neither did Page abandon the promotional techniques pioneered by those before him, as the OPR's participation in various expositions and a series of road-improvement train excursions beginning in 1911 indicated. Page's sermon, however, was one

of scientific competence and bureaucratic efficiency, and his activities differed qualitatively in content and emphases from preachers of the good-roads gospel like Stone and Dodge. "Whatever the technical subject of the engineers' talks," Bruce Seely has argued, "the foundation was the good roads gospel, for that social message generated excitement essential to this 'educational' program. Thus Page the disinterested reformer built a promotional program identical in all but tone to that of his predecessor." My argument here is that Page's emphasis on local knowledge, technical competence, and bureaucratic efficiency differed in substantive ways—not merely in tone—from his predecessors' policies, even though some of his techniques (such as the use of object-lesson roads, promotional displays, speeches, and road-improvement trains) remained the same. Page's goal remained one of rural uplift, but he was not a preacher of the "good-roads gospel," a set of beliefs that evolved in an earlier era and that embodied a substantially different set of reform ideas. See Seely, *Building the American Highway System*, 36 (quotation), 35–36.

6 Logan Waller Page, "Object-Lesson Roads," *Yearbook of the United States Department of Agriculture, 1906* (Washington, D.C.: Government Printing Office, 1907), 137–50.

7 Logan Waller Page, *Report of the Director of the Office of Public Roads* (Washington, D.C.: Government Printing Office, 1905), 432.

8 Page, *Report of the Director* (1907), 19.

9 Page, *Report of the Director* (1908), 5. Earth roads accounted for 39 percent of all object-lesson-road yardage in 1908, outstripping macadam roads at 33 percent and sand-clay roads at 19 percent. In 1909 the percentage of earth roads rose to 46 percent, and by 1910 approached 65 percent. Sand-clay mileage peaked at 30 percent in 1909 before falling to 18 percent in 1910, but sand-clay roads retained a sizable margin over macadamized roads (at 14 percent and 5 percent, respectively) in both years. See Page, *Report of the Director* (1909), 4; and *Report of the Director* (1910), 769.

10 Page, *Report of the Director* (1907), 18.

11 OPR, *Circular No. 91*, 7.

12 Ibid., 9.

13 John Scott-Montagu, "Automobile Legislation: A Criticism and Review," *North American Review* 179 (Aug. 1904): 170.

14 John Farson, "The Rights of the Automobilist," *The World To-Day* 10 (Mar. 1906): 307.

15 The intense yet brief anti-automobile sentiment in the United States has fascinated historians and lay observers alike. Among the latter, it stands as a symbol of the "backward" rural civilization that the automobile helped to erase. See, for example, M. M. Musselman, *Get a Horse! The Story of the Automobile in America* (Philadelphia: J. B. Lippincott, 1950), the title of which refers to a popular derisive phrase that passersby yelled at broken-down motorists early in the century. Among academic historians, interest has been even more intense. For the more

important explanations of the phenomenon, most of which attribute its decline to the increasing affordability of automobiles to prospective rural owners, see Michael Berger, *The Devil Wagon in God's Country: The Automobile and Social Change in Rural America, 1893–1929* (Hamden, Conn.: Archon Books, 1979), 13–52; James J. Flink, *America Adopts the Automobile, 1895–1910* (Cambridge, Mass.: MIT Press, 1970), 64–70; Reynold M. Wik, *Henry Ford and Grass-Roots America* (Ann Arbor: University of Michigan Press, 1972), 17; Joseph Anthony Interrante, "You Can't Go to Town in a Bathtub: Automobile Movement and the Reorganization of Rural American Space, 1900–1930," *Radical History Review* 21 (Fall 1979): 152–56; Ronald Kline and Trevor Pinch, "Users as Agents of Technological Change: The Social Construction of the Automobile in the Rural United States," *Technology and Culture* 37 (Oct. 1996): 763–95, esp. 768–73; and Ronald Kline, *Consumers in the Country: Technology and Social Change in Rural America* (Baltimore: Johns Hopkins University Press, 2000), 55–86, esp. 57–62. One of the more significant treatments of the subject is Clay McShane, *Down the Asphalt Path: The Automobile and the American City* (New York: Columbia University Press, 1994), 173–202, which describes the dynamics of anticar sentiment in urban and suburban areas. One of the most interesting and creative accounts is Thomas Martin McCarthy, "The Road to Respect: Americans, Automobiles, and the Environment" (Ph.D. diss., Yale University, 2001), 92–144, which attributes both the intensity and the rapid disappearance of anticar sentiment to rural envy of wealthy urban motorists.

16 "Motorists Don't Make Socialists, They Say," *New York Times*, 4 Mar. 1906, p. 12. For a discussion of Wilson's remarks and its place in the automotive historiography, see McCarthy, "Road to Respect," 132n91.

17 For two typical statements of this position, see "The Bicycle and the Automobile," *Scientific American* 93 (23 Sept. 1905): 234; and Augustus Post, "Automobile Opportunities," *Outing* 53 (Feb. 1909): 651–52. For similar arguments in France, see Catherine Bertho Lavenir, "How the Motor Car Conquered the Road," in *Cultures of Control*, ed. Miriam R. Levin (Amsterdam: Harwood Academic Publishers, 2000), 113–34, esp. 114 and 125–26.

18 "Unjust Automobile Laws," *Outing* 46 (1905): 639.

19 FHWA, *Highway Statistics: Summary to 1965* (Washington, D.C.: Government Printing Office, 1967), 23.

20 Most explanations for the clash between farmers and motorists focus on how people felt about *cars* rather than on how they felt about *roads*. This is true even of those who make sophisticated and interesting arguments about the significance of roads in American life and about the period's clashes over rural space. In his excellent study of the origins of the modern wilderness movement, for example, Paul S. Sutter describes the conflict between farmers and motorists, at its base, as one "between mechanical and biological forms of transportation," stressing the tensions between urban recreation and rural work. See Sutter, *Driven Wild: How the Fight against Automobiles Launched the Modern Wilderness*

Movement (Seattle: University of Washington Press, 2002), 30–31. Thomas McCarthy, on the other hand, attributes the clash over automobiles in rural areas to class antagonisms and rural envy. See McCarthy, "Road to Respect," 130–39. For an excellent study of the conflicts between rural Americans and motor tourists—and the slow process by which they mutually accommodated one another in increasingly sophisticated ways, see Warren James Belasco, *Americans on the Road: From Autocamp to Motel* (Cambridge, Mass.: MIT Press, 1979).

21   Roy Stone to H. I. Budd, 21 Dec. 1897, Entry 2, Series 28, Box 67: Rural Free Delivery, 1897–1906, National Archives and Record Administration, College Park, Maryland (hereafter NARA).

22   Frederick Dwight, "Automobiles: The Other Side of the Shield," *Independent* 65 (Dec. 1908): 1302. On the issue of the "dust problem," see also Joseph Anthony Interrante, "A Moveable Feast: The Automobile and the Spatial Transformation of American Culture, 1890–1940" (Ph.D. diss., Harvard University, 1983), 80.

23   "Modern Road Problems," *New York Press*, 2 Mar. 1911, Entry 2, Series 6, Box 9: Clippings 1908–1912, NARA.

24   The effects of automobiles on improved roads became an increasingly important topic of conversation in the years after 1907. For a good summary of the level of technical understanding of the subject by 1913, see OPR, *Bulletin No. 48: Repair and Maintenance of Highways* (Washington, D.C.: Government Printing Office, 1913), 20.

25   Page, *Report of the Director* (1907), 20.

26   OPR, *Circular No. 47: Tar and Oil for Road Improvement; Report of Progress of Experiments at Jackson, Tenn.* (Washington, D.C.: Government Printing Office, 1906). These experiments were performed in conjunction with the city engineer of Jackson, Tennessee. Neither motorists nor farmers were entirely happy with the results. "The oily and tarry preparations that have been used from time to time in some places, do lay the dust but they ruin roads by keeping them soft and by encouraging skidding," wrote one motorist. "When this dampening material is freshly applied, the spattering substance that is thrown up by wheels is ruinous to clothing and, when it dries out, the fine dust the wind carries away contains oily particles, and where they rest on houses and porches they leave an ineradicable stain." See John Harrison, "Troubles of the Automobile Owner," *American Suburbs* 2 (Feb. 1911): 164.

27   OPR, *Circular No. 89: Progress Reports of Experiments with Dust Preventatives* (Washington, D.C.: Government Printing Office, 1908); OPR, *Circular No. 90: Progress Reports of Experiments in Dust Prevention, Road Preservation, and Road Construction* (Washington, D.C.: U.S. Department of Agriculture, 1909). These tests were performed in conjunction with the Massachusetts Highway Commission on a stretch of the main highway to New York City about sixteen miles outside of Boston. See also OPR, *Bulletin No. 34: Dust Preventatives* (Washington, D.C.: Government Printing Office, 1908).

28 The best sources for tracing the evolution of the OPR's dust-prevention experiments before World War I are the OPR's annual director's reports and *Bulletin No. 48*; *Circular No. 47*; *Circular No. 89*; *Circular No. 90*; and *Circular No. 93: Bitumens and Their Essential Constituents for Road Construction and Maintenance* (Washington, D.C.: Government Printing Office, 1911). See also FHWA, *America's Highways*, 67–69; Seely, *Building the American Highway System*, 28; and A. E. Johnson, *American Association of State Highway Officials: A Story of the Beginning, Purposes, Growth, Activities and Achievements of AASHO* (Washington, D.C.: American Association of State Highway Officials, 1965), 34–37.

29 McShane, *Down the Asphalt Path*, 219.

30 Office of Public Roads and Rural Engineering, *Bulletin No. 390: Public Road Mileage and Revenues in the United States, 1914-; A Summary* (Washington, D.C.: Government Printing Office, 1917). For the 1909 figures, see also Office of Road Inquiry (hereafter ORI), *Bulletin No. 32: Public-Road Mileage, Revenues, and Expenditures in the United States in 1904* (Washington, D.C.: Government Printing Office, 1907), 40–41.

31 Emily Post, *By Motor to the Golden Gate* (New York: D. Appleton and Co., 1916), 245.

32 The notable exception was the lobbying effort of the Automobile Club of America (later the AAA) in 1903–1904 in support of the Brownlow bill, the first of the major proposals in the campaign for federal aid. See Seely, *Building the American Highway System*, 19; and FHWA, *America's Highways*, 215–16.

33 Allan Nevins, *Ford*, vol. 1, *The Times, the Man, the Company, 1915–1933* (New York: Charles Scribner's Sons, 1954), 259.

34 "Address of Dr. F. L. Bartlett, President Colorado Automobile Club," in *Proceedings of the Good Roads Conference, Held at Denver December 4, 5, 6, 1906* (Denver: Denver Chamber of Commerce, 1906), 10.

35 American Automobile Association, *Highways Green Book: Third Annual Edition* (Washington, D.C.: American Automobile Association, 1922), vi.

36 See, for example, "The A.A.A. Good Roads Convention," *Good Roads Magazine* 10 (Sept. 1909): 322–23.

37 Fisher was by no means the first person to envision a long-distance tourist road, but the Lincoln Highway was the first such scheme to propose a coast-to-coast rock-surfaced highway of permanent all-weather construction. (Following the success of Wayne County, Michigan's experiments with concrete roads, the organization, and especially its president, Henry B. Joy, became enthusiastic advocates of making the Lincoln Highway of concrete "wherever practicable.") Along with the significant degree of national enthusiasm that the memorial highway engendered and its role in starting a fierce debate over road-construction priorities, this makes the Lincoln Highway notable as the first of its kind despite many earlier but less successful schemes.

38 The Roy Dikeman Chapin Papers in the archives of the Bentley Historical Library at the University of Michigan (hereafter BHL) contain a wealth of primary

sources that document the activities and difficulties of the Lincoln Highway Association—which in many ways recapitulated the difficulties of the OPR in slightly different form. On the Lincoln Highway generally, see Lincoln Highway Association, *The Lincoln Highway: The Story of a Crusade That Made Transportation History* (New York: Dodd, Mead & Co., 1935); Drake Hokanson, *The Lincoln Highway: Main Street across America* (Iowa City: University of Iowa Press, 1988); Phil Patton, *Open Road: A Celebration of the American Highway* (New York: Simon and Schuster, 1986), 39–44; and Marguerite Shaffer, *See America First: Tourism and National Identity, 1880–1940* (Washington, D.C.: Smithsonian Institution Press, 2001), 149–53. On the Dixie Highway, see Tammy Leigh Ingram, "Dixie Highway: Private Enterprise and State Building in the South" (Ph.D. diss., Yale University, 2007); Howard Lawrence Preston, *Dirt Roads to Dixie: Accessibility and Modernization in the South, 1885–1935* (Knoxville: University of Tennessee Press, 1991), 52–60; Seely, *Building the American Highway System*, 38; and FHWA, *America's Highways*, 83, 109. On the National Highways Association, see Charles Henry Davis, *National Highways to Bring About Good Roads Everywhere* (Washington, D.C.: National Highways Association, 1913); and Shaffer, *See America First*, 154–60.

39   The bicycle industry suffered a startling collapse in the late 1890s and ceased to be much of a presence in the good-roads movement as the twentieth century wore on.

40   For a case study of the tension between the farm-to-market and motor-tourist blocs within the good-roads movement in the South, see Preston, *Dirt Roads to Dixie*. For a case study of these tensions in a small town in Illinois, including a discussion of the dynamics of small-town boosters and their relationship with various systems of transportation, including railroads, electric interurban railways, and motor roads, see Norman C. Moline, *Mobility and the Small Town, 1900–1930: Transportation Change in Oregon Illinois*, Research Paper No. 132, (Chicago: Department of Geography, University of Chicago, 1971). See also FHWA, *America's Highways*, 109–10.

41   "The View Point of the Automobile Manufacturer Towards the Improvement of Country Roads in Michigan," 5 (italics added), enclosure in A. F. Bement to R. D. Chapin, 20 Jan. 1917, Box 3: 1917 January 16–25, Roy Dikeman Chapin Papers, BHL.

42   For a list of top priorities, see American Association for Highway Improvement, *Papers, Addresses, and Resolutions Before the American Road Congress in Richmond, Va., Nov. 1911* (Baltimore: Waverly Press, 1912), 187–90, cited in FHWA, *America's Highways*, 78.

43   L. W. Page to A. G. Spalding, 2 May 1912, Entry 2, Series 50, Box 141: Trans-Continental Highways, 1897–1911, NARA.

44   Quoted in Roy Chapin, "The Automobile Manufacturer in Relation to the Good Road," speech to the National Association of Automobile Manufacturers, 1914, Box 2: Miscellaneous 1914, Roy Dikeman Chapin Papers, BHL.

45   See Federal Aid Good Roads Convention, *Proceedings of the Federal Aid Good*

Roads Convention: Held at Washington, D.C., Jan. 16 and 17, 1912, Called by the American Automobile Association (Washington, D.C.: American Automobile Association, 1912).

46   W. Stull Holt, The Bureau of Public Roads: Its History, Activities and Organization (Baltimore: Johns Hopkins University Press, 1923), 14; FHWA, America's Highways, 81; Wayne E. Fuller, RFD: The Changing Face of Rural America (Bloomington: Indiana University Press, 1964), 193.

47   "Federal Aid to Good Roads," House Doc. 1510, 63rd Cong., 3rd Sess. (1916).

48   Dorsey Shackleford, "Federal Road Legislation," in Proceedings, Third American Road Congress (Washington, D.C.: American Highway Association, 1914), 57, cited in FHWA, America's Highways, 86.

49   "I have your courteous favor of the 10th and it seems to me that your analysis of the Shackleford Bill coincides exactly with my own views," wrote Senator Charles E. Townsend, a Republican from Michigan, to Roy D. Chapin, president of the Hudson Motor Car Company. "To me it means absolutely nothing as a contribution to good roads. It is constructed for political purposes only." C. E. Townsend to R. D. Chapin, 13 Mar. 1914, Box 1: 1914 March, Roy Dikeman Chapin Papers, BHL.

50   "View Point of the Automobile Manufacturer," 4. For a succinct summary of the debate—from the perspective of an advocate of national highways—see Charles Henry Davis, Arguments for and Against National Highways versus Federal Aid (Washington, D.C.: National Highways Association, 1914). For arguments more clearly advanced from the position of motorists, see also Davis, How National Highways are Necessary to the Automobile (Washington, D.C.: National Highways Association, 1914).

51   For a detailed analysis of the role of Page and the OPR in crafting the Federal Aid Road Act of 1916, see Seely, Building the American Highway System, 36–45.

52   The act capped the maximum federal contribution at $10,000 per mile, which limited the ability of states to build with the most expensive road surfaces.

53   For the most thorough discussion of the implications of excluding cities from the federal-aid system, see Owen D. Gutfreund, Twentieth-Century Sprawl: Highways and the Reshaping of the American Landscape (New York: Oxford University Press, 2004). Most histories of the American highway system discuss the Federal Aid Road Act of 1916 in some detail. See, for example, Rae, Road and the Car, 36–39; Seely, Building the American Highway System, 41–45; and FHWA, America's Highways, 84–87. Information on the formation of new state highway departments in 1916 and 1917 comes from Public Roads Administration, Highway Statistics, Summary to 1945 (Washington, D.C.: Government Printing Office, 1947), 54. In addition to the seven new state highway departments, eighteen states reorganized existing departments and another nine benefited from new state laws expanding their power. See Seely, Building the American Highway System, 47. The act also appropriated $10 million at $1 million per year for use on roads on national forest lands.

54　FHWA, *America's Highways*, 87. The regulations were issued in September as U.S. Department of Agriculture, *Circular No. 65: Rules and Regulations of the Secretary of Agriculture for Carrying out the Federal Aid Road Act* (Washington, D.C.: Government Printing Office, 1916).

55　J. Pennybacker and L. Boykin, "Federal Aid to Highways," in *Yearbook of the United States Department of Agriculture, 1917* (Washington, D.C.: Government Printing Office, 1918), 135 (quotation), 127–38.

56　A. G. Gutheim, "Highway Department and Railroad Cooperation for Transportation of Materials," *Public Roads* 2 (Dec. 1919): 33–36; FHWA, *America's Highways*, 95; Seely, *Building the American Highway System*, 50.

57　Chapin's papers are the best source of information on this endeavor. For a good summary, see Roy D. Chapin, speech to the Highway Industries Association, December 1918, Box 6: Miscellaneous 1918, Roy Dikeman Chapin Papers, BHL. See also FHWA, *America's Highways*, 93–96.

58　"The Highways of the Country and Burden They Must Carry," *Public Roads* 1 (June 1918): 4.

59　Quoted in Fuller, *RFD*, 197.

60　See Seely, *Building the American Highway System*, 51–52; and FHWA, *America's Highways*, 101.

61　FHWA, *America's Highways*, 102.

62　A. G. Batchelder to R. D. Chapin, 3 Jan. 1919, Box 6: 1919 January 1–5, Roy Dikeman Chapin Papers, BHL.

63　ORI, *Bulletin No. 32*, 8–9.

64　U.S. Bureau of the Census, *Historical Statistics of the United States: Colonial Times to 1970*, vol. 2 (Washington, D.C.: Government Printing Office, 1975), 710; "Authorized Road Bond Issues Total Nearly $500,000,000," *Engineering News-Record* 84 (22 Jan. 1920): 202; Thomas H. MacDonald, *Report of the Chief of the Bureau of Public Roads* (Washington, D.C.: Government Printing Office, 1920), 13.

65　Leonard D. White, "Public Administration," in *Recent Social Trends in the United States*, ed. President's Research Committee on Social Trends (New York: McGraw-Hill, 1933), 1421.

66　Clay McShane and Joel Tarr have done the pioneering work on this subject. See McShane and Tarr, *The Horse in the City: Living Machines in the Nineteenth Century* (Baltimore: Johns Hopkins University Press, 2007). See also McShane, *Down the Asphalt Path*, 41–56, esp. 43–44; and Ann Norton Greene, *Horses at Work: Harnessing Power in Industrial America* (Cambridge, Mass.: Harvard University Press, 2008).

67　Mark S. Foster, *From Streetcar to Superhighway: American City Planners and Urban Transportation, 1900–1940* (Philadelphia: Temple University Press, 1982), 14.

68　Arthur Woods, "Keeping City Traffic Moving," *World's Work* 31 (Apr. 1916): 628. At Park Row near the Brooklyn Bridge, the ratio was 296,500 pedestrians to 6,700 vehicles. Other counts revealed similar pedestrian dominance elsewhere: Fifth Avenue and Thirty-Fourth Street, 142,230 to 25,580; Fifth Avenue and

Twenty-Third Street, 158,260 to 9,645. Ibid., 628–29.

69 Boston Chamber of Commerce, *Street Traffic in the City of Boston* (Boston: Boston Chamber of Commerce, 1914), 28 (quotation), 26–28.

70 Robert M. Fogelson, *Downtown: Its Rise and Fall, 1880–1950* (New Haven, Conn.: Yale University Press, 2001), 117–19.

71 See, for example, Sidney Ososski, "Clearing Our Crowded Streets," *World To-Day* 19 (Aug. 1910): 874. Motor-vehicle traffic was not among Ososski's seven "principal causes of traffic congestion in the big cities of the world." On the arguments of proponents of building-height limits as a solution to traffic woes, see Fogelson, *Downtown*, 126–28. For a more politically charged explanation of the causes of congestion, see Benjamin Clark Marsh, *An Introduction to City Planning: Democracy's Challenge to the American City* (1909; New York: Arno Press, 1974), 21–26.

72 FHWA, *Highway Statistics: Summary to 1975* (Washington, D.C.: Government Printing Office, 1975), 45.

73 No exact statistics for early commuters exist during this period. For a more detailed discussion of the evidence showing a rise of commuting in big American cities before 1920, see McShane, *Down the Asphalt Path*, 190–91. On traffic exceeding automobile registrations, see Robert H. Whitten, "Unchoking Our Congested Streets," *American City Magazine* 23 (Oct. 1920): 353.

74 David Beecroft, "The Conquering Motor Car," *World To-Day* 12 (Feb. 1907): 159. See also "Automobiles May Solve the Traffic Problem," *The Automobile* 20 (28 Jan. 1909): 196.

75 Paul Barrett, *The Automobile and Urban Transit: The Formation of Public Policy in Chicago, 1900–1930* (Philadelphia: Temple University Press, 1983), 57; Edward H. Bennett and William E. Parsons, *Plan of St. Paul* (St. Paul: City Planning Board, 1922), 30–34, cited in McShane, *Down the Asphalt Path*, 190.

76 Woods, "Keeping City Traffic Moving," 625. See also "Regulation of Street Traffic," *American City* 13 (Sept. 1915): 174; and Alfred A. Benesch, "Regulating Street Traffic in Cleveland," *American City* 13 (Sept. 1915): 182–84.

77 For a strong monographic treatment of this subject that analyzes the social construction of streets as a technology, see Peter D. Norton, *Fighting Traffic: The Dawn of the Motor Age in the American City* (Cambridge, Mass.: MIT Press, 2008).

78 "Traffic Congestion and the Citizen's Pocketbook," *American City* 17 (Aug. 1917): 165.

79 McShane, *Down the Asphalt Path*, 174–75. For a case study of the "deadly competition for public space" in Chicago, see Barrett, *Automobile and Urban Transit*, 47–81.

80 William B. Bailey, "Street Accidents in New York City," *Independent and Weekly Review* 76 (Dec. 1913): 552. By comparison, in Los Angeles, which was less centralized and had more open space where children could play, only 9 percent of all traffic deaths between 1910 and 1913 were children. See McShane, *Down the Asphalt Path*, 176.

81 Woods, "Keeping City Traffic Moving," 631.

82 National Automobile Chamber of Commerce, *Facts and Figures of the Automobile Industry, 1921* (New York: National Automobile Chamber of Commerce, 1922), 22.

83 Woods, "Keeping City Traffic Moving," 621.

84 Charles S. Adams, "Relation of Speed to Automobile Dangers," *Scientific American* 95 (13 Oct. 1906): 263. On this point, see also Barrett, *Automobile and Urban Transit*, 137–38.

85 McShane, *Down the Asphalt Path*, 176.

86 Barrett, *Automobile and Urban Transit*, 58.

87 Dwight, "Automobiles: The Other Side of the Shield," 1303.

88 Farson, "Rights of the Automobilist," 307.

89 "Recklessness as a Cause of Accidents," *Literary Digest* 45 (10 Aug. 1912): 231. This was a frequently repeated claim. See, for example, "Accidents Due to the Foreign Chauffeur—The American Coachman Is Said to Be More Cautious," *Scientific American* 94 (24 Feb. 1906): 174; and "Blame for Speeding Put on Chauffeurs: The Only Way to Check Reckless Driving, Says the Highways Protective Society," *New York Times*, 3 Feb. 1910, p. 7.

90 "How to Avoid Automobile Accidents," *Outing* 47 (Jan. 1906): 503–4.

91 Automobile Club of Hartford, "Diary of a Hartford Motorist," *Bulletin* 1, 2 (1911): 13–14, quoted in Peter C. Baldwin, *Domesticating the Street: The Reform of Public Space in Hartford, 1850–1930* (Columbus: Ohio State University Press, 1999), 219.

92 For an influential statement of this position by a historian, see McShane, *Down the Asphalt Path*, 176–77.

93 For the typical range of infractions that landed boys in juvenile court in Chicago, see the list compiled in Jane Addams, *The Spirit of Youth and the City Streets* (New York: Macmillan Co., 1909), 55–56.

94 For the most influential statement of this thesis, see Clay McShane, "Transforming the Use of Urban Space: A Look at the Revolution in Street Pavements, 1880–1924," *Journal of Urban History* 5 (May 1979): 279–307; and McShane, *Down the Asphalt Path*. For the most compelling qualifications to McShane's arguments, see Baldwin, *Domesticating the Street*.

95 Miller McClintock, *Street Traffic Control* (New York: McGraw-Hill, 1925), 187; McShane, *Down the Asphalt Path*, 184. Philadelphia formed its traffic squad in 1904, New York in 1907.

96 Even though streetcars technically had right-of-way, their smooth rails enticed slow-moving teamsters hauling heavy loads, and track-bound streetcars carrying scores of passengers had no choice but to slow down behind them—and to halt entirely behind vehicles attempting left-hand turns across thick oncoming traffic, or behind wagons unloading freight on narrow streets. For a case study of the confrontation between streetcars and teamsters in Chicago, see Barrett, *Automobile and Urban Transit*, 48–56.

97 William Phelps Eno, *Street Traffic Regulation* (New York: Rider and Driver Publishing Co., 1909), 50.

98 Boston Chamber of Commerce, *Street Traffic*, 30. For a substantial overview of police traffic regulation in the 1910s and the early 1920s, see Norton, *Fighting Traffic*, 47–64.

99 *Rules for Driving* (New York: Police Department of the City of New York, 1903), 4, reproduced in William Phelps Eno, *The Story of Highway Traffic Control, 1899–1939* (Saugatuck, Conn.: Eno Foundation for Highway Traffic Control, 1939), 13. On Eno, see also McShane, *Down the Asphalt Path*, 185–86; and Norton, *Fighting Traffic*, 50–54.

100 Eno, *Street Traffic Regulation*, ii–iii.

101 William Phelps Eno, *Science of Highway Traffic Regulation, 1899–1920* (Washington, D.C.: Brentano's, 1920), title page.

102 Joseph Sabath, "What a Traffic Court Can Do," *American City* 17 (Aug. 1917): 126–27. On the creation of New York City's first traffic court, see Woods, "Keeping City Traffic Moving," 630–31. On the relationship between courts and motorists in the first decade of the century, see also Flink, *America Adopts the Automobile*, 195–99. On the significance of "safety first" and the work of safety councils, especially during the 1920s, see Norton, *Fighting Traffic*, 21–46.

103 On the question of pedestrians' rights to the streets as they evolved in the motor age, see especially Norton, *Fighting Traffic*, 65–101, esp. 66–70.

104 *Oxford English Dictionary* dates the word "jaywalker" from 1917, labeling it "originally U.S." It cross-references "jay," which colloquially referred after 1900 to "a stupid or dull person, a simpleton. Also (as adjective) dull, unsophisticated; inferior, poor." Thus pedestrians who stupidly ignored traffic while crossing the street inspired this appellation. Peter Norton has uncovered seven uses of the term in American cities dating as early as 1909, and he traces its evolving rhetorical role in the conflict between pedestrians and motorists, focusing primarily on the 1920s. See Norton, "Street Rivals: Jaywalking and the Invention of the Motor Age Street," *Technology and Culture* 48 (Apr. 2007): 331–59, esp. 341–44; and Norton, *Fighting Traffic*, 71–79.

105 For a range of perspectives on the subject from New York, see "Rights Afoot at Crossing," *New York Times*, 13 Jan. 1912, p. 12; Richard Welling, "The Pedestrian's Right to Go Safely," *New York Times*, 22 June 1915, p. 14; "Middle-Block Crossing Is Defended," *New York Times*, 2 Dec. 1915, p. 10; and Richard Welling, "Pedestrians' Rights: Total Misconception of Speeders Needs to Be Corrected by Law Like Seattle's," *New York Times*, 31 Oct. 1920, p. XII. Filmstrips showing downtown street traffic from the early twentieth century are perhaps the most vivid source for understanding the street-crossing habits of pedestrians during this period; for photographs illustrating the same point, see Norton, *Fighting Traffic*, 67–68.

106 "Making the Streets Safe," *American City* 7 (Dec. 1912): 535.

107 Baldwin, *Domesticating the Street*, 174. See also Norton, *Fighting Traffic*, 21–46.

108 Scott-Montagu, "Automobile Legislation," 168.

109 Woods, "Keeping City Traffic Moving," 630. On the efforts of auto clubs to combat speed limits, see McShane, *Down the Asphalt Path*, 178–82; and Flink, *America Adopts the Automobile*, 179–86.

110 Baldwin, *Domesticating the Street*, esp. 189–92.

111 On the effects of excluding cities from the federal-aid system, see Gutfreund, *Twentieth-Century Sprawl*.

112 Daniel H. Burnham and Edward H. Bennett, *Plan of Chicago*, ed. Charles Moore (1908; New York: Princeton Architectural Press, 1993), 80.

113 Ibid., 82.

114 Ibid., 88 (on residential streets versus traffic streets), 97 (on circumferential distributors). For Burnham's complete vision of proposed modifications to Chicago's street system, see the map following p. 100. On the *Plan of Chicago* and its context, see T. S. Hines, *Burnham of Chicago: Architect and Planner* (New York: Oxford University Press, 1974); McShane, *Down the Asphalt Path*, 209–13; Barrett, *Automobile and Urban Transit*, 45, 73–81; Foster, *Streetcar to Superhighway*, 42–44; Peter Hall, *Cities of Tomorrow: An Intellectual History of Urban Planning and Design in the Twentieth Century*, updated ed. (Malden, Mass.: Blackwell Publishers, 1996), 179–83; and Paul Boyer, *Urban Masses and Moral Order in America, 1820–1920* (Cambridge, Mass.: Harvard University Press, 1978), 266–76. For a typical contemporary summary of the plan, see George E. Hooker, "A Plan for Chicago," *The Survey* 22 (4 Sept. 1909): 778–90.

115 Burnham and Bennett, *Plan of Chicago*, 39. For an overview of Burnham and the city beautiful planners, see Mel Scott, *American City Planning since 1890: A History Commemorating the 50th Anniversary of the American Institute of Planners* (Berkeley: University of California Press, 1969), 31–109.

116 For an overview, see Barrett, *Automobile and Urban Transit*, 73–81.

117 Harold Jacobs Howland, "The City Practical," *Outlook* 97 (Feb. 1911): 394, 395. For an overview of the "city efficient" planning tradition, also sometimes called "city functional," see Scott, *American City Planning*, 110–82.

118 As Frederick Law Olmsted Jr. became famous in his own right, he dropped the abbreviation "Jr." in his name. Frederick Law Olmsted Sr. died on 28 August 1903.

119 Frederick Law Olmsted, "How to Organize a City Planning Campaign," *American City* 9 (Oct. 1913): 305.

120 These various engineering studies are enshrined in the many city plans that individual cities released during the 1910s. Several cities, like Boston, published traffic studies independently. See Boston Chamber of Commerce, *Street Traffic*. They were also much discussed and frequently summarized in the engineering press, most notably *American City* and *Municipal Journal and Engineer*. See also Eno, *Street Traffic Regulation*, which includes suggestions for both minor and major changes to city streets to improve the flow of traffic. James C. Scott has labeled this process of reducing social and physical reality to quantifiable

categories for easy review by centralized administrators "administrative legibility." See Scott, *Seeing Like a State: How Certain Schemes to Improve the Human Condition Have Failed* (New Haven, Conn.: Yale University Press, 1998).

121 "Efficiency in City Planning," *American City* 8 (Feb. 1913): 142–43.

122 McShane, "Use of Urban Space," 280. The cities are New York, Chicago, St. Louis, Cleveland, Cincinnati, Buffalo, San Francisco, New Orleans, Detroit, Milwaukee, and Washington, D.C., the eleven largest for which McShane could find reliable data sets. The high percentage of unpaved streets in 1902 should be understood in geographically relative terms: in the downtown areas of large cities, few streets other than alleys were completely unpaved. Moreover, the annexations of the 1880s and 1890s brought large peripheral territories with unpaved streets under the control of city governments. The closer one got to the center of any big city at the turn of the century, the more paved streets one could expect to find. For a compilation of paving statistics for the twenty largest cities in the United States between 1900 and 1930, see Clay McShane, "American Cities and the Coming of the Automobile" (Ph.D. diss., University of Wisconsin–Madison, 1975), 301–8. The reasons behind the spread of asphalt pavements are complex, but it is clear that the desire to smooth a path for motorists was only one of many factors operating in asphalt's favor. See McShane, *Down the Asphalt Path*, 57–80; McShane, "Use of Urban Space," 279–307; and I. B. Holley Jr., "Blacktop: How Asphalt Paving Came to the Urban United States," *Technology and Culture* 44 (Oct. 2003): 703–33.

123 Barrett, *Automobile and Urban Transit*, 74–76. For a report on the status of urban street pavements around the nation in 1907, see "Municipal Paving: A Symposium," *Annals of the American Academy of Political and Social Science* 29 (May 1907): 559–600. See also McShane, "Use of Urban Space"; McShane, "Urban Pathways: The Street and Highway, 1900–1940," in *Technology and the Rise of the Networked City in Europe and America*, ed. Joel A. Tarr and Gabriel Dupuy (Philadelphia: Temple University Press, 1988), 67–87; and Holley, "Blacktop," 703–33. For two typical contemporary handbooks on road and street engineering, see Harwood Frost, *The Art of Roadmaking: Treating of the Various Problems and Operations in the Construction and Maintenance of Roads, Streets, and Pavements* (New York: Engineering News Publishing Co., 1910), esp. 29–445; and Charles Mulford Robinson, *The Width and Arrangement of Streets: A Study in Town Planning* (New York: Engineering News Publishing Co., 1911), esp. 1–83.

124 Frost, *Art of Roadmaking*, 310.

125 In Chicago, for example, most street-widening projects required condemning expensive commercial real estate, pushing the average cost of such improvements to over $1 million per mile for each of the 112 miles the city widened between 1915 and 1930. See Barrett, *Automobile and Urban Transit*, 145.

126 "Street Widening in New York City," *Good Roads* 2 (7 Oct. 1911): 162. Although it shared the same name, this periodical should not be confused with the League of American Wheelman's publication of the 1890s.

127 Felix Hunt, "A Practical Detail of City Planning: Street Widening in Old New York," *American City* 7 (Nov. 1912): 412. For McAneny's own account of these street-widening projects, see Edward Marshall, "How the City Can Save Millions, Told by McAneny," *New York Times*, 15 June 1913, p. SM8. McAneny was also a key player in the extension of New York's subway system in 1913 and in the passage of the city's pathbreaking zoning ordinance in 1916. See Peter Derrick, *Tunneling to the Future: The Story of the Great Subway Expansion That Saved New York* (New York: New York University Press, 2001); Seymour I. Toll, *Zoned American* (New York: Grossman Publishers, 1969); and Fogelson, *Downtown*, 160–66.

128 William Phelps Eno, "Standardized Street Traffic Regulation," *American City* 9 (Sept. 1913): 225. See also Eno, *Science of Highway Traffic Regulation*, 39. See also Harold M. Lewis, "The New York City Motor Traffic Problem," in *The Automobile: Its Province and Its Problems*, ed. Clyde L. King (Philadelphia: American Academy of Political and Social Science, 1924), 221; and McClintock, *Street Traffic Control*, 101–3.

129 Arno Dosch, "The Science of Street Traffic," *World's Work* 27 (Feb. 1914): 403.

130 "One-Way Vehicle Traffic," *New York Times*, 18 Oct. 1908, p. 10. The article further reported that the "substantial unanimity" in Boston for the one-way proposals stood in stark contrast to the disagreement that other proposed traffic rules generated.

131 E. P. Goodrich, "The Crowded Streets: Situation, Now Serious, Requires Special Measures," *New York Times*, 19 Apr. 1914, p. C6. See also "New Rules of the Road," *New York Times*, 28 Jan. 1914, p. 7.

132 "One-Way Rule Aids in Clearing Traffic: Eight Additional Streets Under New Regulation Relieve Congestion," *New York Times*, 1 Feb. 1916, p. 9.

133 "5th Av. Soon to Be A 'One-Way' Street: Merchants and Police Hope to Prevent Repetitions of Recent Auto Jams," *New York Times*, 31 Jan. 1920, p. 1.

134 See, for example, "Fight One-Way Plan for Fifth Avenue: C. P. Foute Says Merchants and Their Customers Oppose New Traffic Rules," *New York Times*, 13 Feb. 1920, p. 22. See also McShane, *Down the Asphalt Path*, 198–99.

135 "Traffic Ills Remedied," *New York Times*, 25 Mar. 1920, p. 10. The police commissioner in charge of traffic was careful to make it known that "the one-way scheme has not been withdrawn officially" and would be implemented if necessary. The American Public Works Association credits William Potts, a Detroit police officer, with installing the first red-yellow-green traffic light at the corner of Woodward Avenue and Fort Street in early 1920. See American Public Works Association (hereafter APWA), *History of Public Works in the United States, 1776–1976* (Chicago: American Public Works Association, 1976), 123–24. Fifth Avenue was finally converted to one-way traffic between 135th Street and Washington Square Park in 1966. See Peter Kihss, "5th and Madison Avenues Become One-Way Friday," *New York Times*, 12 Jan. 1966, p. 1.

136 "Guide Lines to Regulate Street Traffic," *Good Roads* 2 (5 Aug. 1911): 67; John P. Fox, "Traffic Regulation in Detroit and Toronto," *American City* 13 (Sept. 1915):

176–78; Woods, "Keeping City Traffic Moving," 630; "Street Traffic Recommendations," *American City* 13 (Sept. 1915): 184; Eno, *Science of Highway Traffic Regulation*, 10, 68; McClintock, *Street Traffic Control*, 1925; McShane, *Down the Asphalt Path*, 198.

137 Fox, "Traffic Regulation," 178; "Safety-First Traffic Signals in Portland, Ore.," *American City* 13 (Sept. 1915): 180–81; Eno, "Standardized Street Traffic Regulation," 226; Woods, "Keeping City Traffic Moving," 623–27 (illus.); Eno, *Science of Highway Traffic Regulation*, 10.

138 These included Baltimore, Washington, St. Louis, Boston, New Orleans, and New York. See Fox, "Traffic Regulation," 175; Frederick H. Elliott, "New Uniform Rules for Street Traffic," *American City* 14 (Feb. 1916): 124; Harold W. Newman, "The Umbrella Semaphore," *American City* 14 (June 1916): 628; and W. L. Bradley, "A Practical Traffic Signal and Shelter," *American City* 17 (Aug. 1917): 155–56. Toledo, Ohio, may have begun using semaphores in 1908; see APWA, *History of Public Works*, 123. For an overview of the diffusion of the technology of street traffic regulation, see Clay McShane, "The Origins and Globalization of Traffic Control Signals," *Journal of Urban History* 25 (Mar. 1999): 379–404.

139 Benesch, "Regulating Street Traffic in Cleveland," 184 (quotation), 182–84.

140 Eno, *Science of Highway Traffic Regulation*, 68; APWA, *History of Public Works*, 123–24. See also McShane, *Down the Asphalt Path*, 199; and Barrett, *Automobile and Urban Transit*, 55–62.

141 Oliver B. Harden, "Hazard of Street Crossing," *New York Times*, 5 June 1905, p. 8.

142 On the "fantasy plans" of amateur city planners, see Stanley K. Schultz, *Constructing Urban Culture: American Cities and City Planning, 1800–1920* (Baltimore: Johns Hopkins University Press, 1989), 22–32; and McShane, *Down the Asphalt Path*, 203–15.

143 "The chief drawbacks to most of the proposed plans for overhead crossings of streets, for double-deck streets, and the like," reported *American City* in 1915, "are the excessive cost, the opposition of local business interests, and the doubt if any really substantial increase in street capacity would result, or any increase at all commensurate with the price paid." See "Regulation of Street Traffic," 174.

144 Fogelson, *Downtown*, 44–111.

145 FHWA, *Highway Statistics: Summary to 1985* (Washington, D.C.: Government Printing Office, 1987), 39.

4. MOTOR-AGE GEOGRAPHY

1 Federal Highway Administration (hereafter FHWA), *Highway Statistics: Summary to 1985* (Washington, D.C.: Government Printing Office, 1987), 25.

2 Ibid., 39.

3 David Blanke, *Hell on Wheels: The Promise and Peril of America's Car Culture, 1900–1940* (Lawrence: University Press of Kansas, 2007), 56. Numbers are based on U.S. Bureau of the Census, *Statistical Abstract of the United States: 2003*, No.

HS-41, Transportation Indicators for Motor Vehicles and Airlines, 1900 to 2001 (Washington, D.C.: Government Printing Office, 2003), 77–78; and U.S. Bureau of the Census, *Historical Statistics of the United States: Colonial Times to 1957* (Washington, D.C.: Government Printing Office, 1960), 462.

4 Bruce E. Seely, *Building the American Highway System: Engineers as Policy Makers* (Philadelphia: Temple University Press, 1987), 67.

5 Quoted in "Unfit for Modern Motor Traffic," *Fortune* 14 (Aug. 1936): 90.

6 Quoted in W. Stull Holt, *The Bureau of Public Roads: Its History, Activities and Organization* (Baltimore: Johns Hopkins University Press, 1923), 31.

7 FHWA, *America's Highways, 1776–1976: A History of the Federal-Aid Program* (Washington, D.C.: Government Printing Office, 1976), 109.

8 J. L. Harrison, "Where the Highway Dollar Goes," *Public Roads* 13 (Apr. 1932): 21; FHWA, *America's Highways*, 124.

9 FHWA, *Highway Statistics to 1985*, 77–82; Mark H. Rose, *Interstate: Express Highway Politics, 1939–1989*, rev. ed. (Knoxville: University of Tennessee Press, 1990), 4.

10 FHWA, *America's Highways*, 381–95. For two contemporary descriptions of highway design and location trends, see A. G. Bruce and R. D. Brown, "The Trend of Highway Design," *Public Roads* 8 (1927): 7–14, 20; and Harry Byron Jay, "The Evolution of Road Location," *Highway Magazine* 20 (Sept. 1929): 227–29.

11 A. G. Bruce, "The Effects of Increased Speed of Vehicles on the Design of Highways," *Public Roads* 10 (Mar. 1929): 11.

12 U.S. Census Bureau, *Statistical Abstract*, Mini-Historical Statistics, 77–78, reproduced in Blanke, *Hell on Wheels*, 60.

13 For one statement of the problem and the problem-specific approach to solving it, see E. W. James, "Traffic Control and Safety," *Public Roads* 5 (Aug. 1924): 4.

14 Seely, *Building the American Highway System*, 118–35.

15 Joseph Barnett, "Safe Side Friction Factors and Superelevation Design," *Proceedings of the Highway Research Board, 16th Annual Meeting* 16 (1936): 75; FHWA, *America's Highways*, 132.

16 On the specifics of this committee's work, see FHWA, *America's Highways*, 390–95.

17 "Unfit for Modern Motor Traffic," 91.

18 Secretary of Agriculture, "Report to Congress on Study and Research of Traffic Conditions and Measures for Their Improvement" (Washington, D.C.: Government Printing Office, 1937).

19 Blaine A. Brownell, "The Commercial-Civic Elite and City Planning in Atlanta, Memphis, and New Orleans in the 1920s," *Journal of Southern History* 41 (Aug. 1975): 340, 343, 353–54; Mel Scott, *American City Planning Since 1890: A History Commemorating the 50th Anniversary of the American Institute of Planners* (Berkeley: University of California Press, 1969), esp. 110–269; Marc Weiss, *The Rise of the Community Builders: The American Real Estate Industry and Urban Land Planning* (New York: Columbia University Press, 1987), 4–5; Theodora Kimball

Hubbard and Henry Vincent Hubbard, *Our Cities To-Day and To-Morrow: A Survey of Planning and Zoning Progress in the United States* (Cambridge, Mass.: Harvard University Press, 1929). During the 1920s, Herbert Hoover's Department of Commerce oversaw two model zoning statutes designed to provide a legal basis for communities hoping to govern the planning, zoning, and subdivision of land and issued a string of publications designed to promote this sort of city planning. See, for example, U.S. Department of Commerce, *A Zoning Primer: By the Advisory Committee on Zoning* (Washington, D.C.: Government Printing Office, 1922); U.S. Department of Commerce, *A Standard State Zoning Act: Under Which Municipalities May Adopt Zoning Regulations; By the Advisory Committee on Zoning* (Washington, D.C.: Government Printing Office, 1924); and U.S. Department of Commerce, *A City Planning Primer: By the Advisory Committee on City Planning and Zoning* (Washington, D.C.: Government Printing Office, 1928).

20   For a careful case study of Bartholomew's work in St. Louis, see Eric Sandweiss, *St. Louis: The Evolution of an American Urban Landscape* (Philadelphia: Temple University Press, 2001), 212–29.

21   Brownell, "Commercial-Civic Elite and City Planning," 353–54; Norman J. Johnston, "Harland Bartholomew: Precedent for the Profession," in *The American Planner: Biographies and Recollections*, ed. Donald A. Krueckeberg (New York: Methuen, 1983), 279–300.

22   Memphis City Planning Commission, *First Annual Report* (Memphis, 1921), 11, 19–28, quoted in Brownell, "Commercial-Civic Elite and City Planning," 355.

23   Harland Bartholomew, "Reduction of Street Traffic Congestion by Proper Street Design: How St. Louis Is Meeting Its Problem," in *The Automobile: Its Province and Its Problems*, ed. Clyde L. King (Philadelphia: American Academy of Political and Social Science, 1924), 245 (quotation), 244–45; Alvan Macauley, *City Planning and Automobile Traffic Problems* (Detroit: Packard Motor Car Company, 1925). On the rise and fall of the central business district as the defining characteristic of American cities, see Robert M. Fogelson, *Downtown: Its Rise and Fall, 1880–1950* (New Haven, Conn.: Yale University Press, 2001).

24   On the history of zoning in the United States, see Seymour I. Toll, *Zoned American* (New York: Grossman Publishers, 1969); S. J. Makielski Jr., *The Politics of Zoning: The New York Experience* (New York: Columbia University Press, 1966); and Charles M. Haar and Jerold S. Kayden, eds., *Zoning and the American Dream: Promises Still to Keep* (Washington, D.C.: American Planning Association Press, 1989).

25   Ernest P. Goodrich, "Zoning and Its Relation to Traffic Congestion," in *Planning for City Traffic*, ed. Austin F. MacDonald (Philadelphia: American Academy of Political and Social Science, 1927), 222–33. The role of parking in this equation did not begin to receive systematic attention until after World War II. See Eno Foundation for Highway Traffic Control, *Zoning Applied to Parking* (Saugatuck, Conn.: Eno Foundation for Highway Traffic Control, 1947).

26   J. Rowland Bibbins, "Traffic Transportation Planning and Metropolitan

Development—The Need of an Adequate Program," in *Automobile*, ed. King, 210. See also Macauley, *City Planning and Automobile Traffic*; Hubbard and Hubbard, *Our Cities To-Day and To-Morrow*; Advisory Committee on Planning and Zoning, *The Preparation of Zoning Ordinances: A Guide for Municipal Officials and Others in the Arrangement of Provisions in Zoning Regulations* (Washington, D.C.: Government Printing Office, 1931); W. L. Pollard, ed., *The Annals of the American Academy of Political and Social Science* 155, part 2, Zoning in the United States (May 1931): 1–227; and Harland Bartholomew, *Urban Land Uses: Amounts of Land Used and Needed for Various Purposes by Typical American Cities; An Aid to Scientific Zoning Practice* (Cambridge, Mass.: Harvard University Press, 1932).

27   Paul Barrett, *The Automobile and Urban Transit: The Formation of Public Policy in Chicago, 1900–1930* (Philadelphia: Temple University Press, 1983), 148–49.

28   Howard L. Preston, *Automobile Age Atlanta: The Making of a Southern Metropolis, 1900–1935* (Athens: University of Georgia Press, 1979), 118–25.

29   Miller McClintock, *Report and Recommendations of the Metropolitan Street Traffic Survey* (Chicago: Chicago Association of Commerce, 1926), 58. See also "Unfit for Modern Motor Traffic," 85.

30   Scott L. Bottles, *Los Angeles and the Automobile: The Making of the Modern City* (Berkeley: University of California Press, 1991), 117, 275–76. On McClintock's evolving career and growing alliance with automotive interests, see Peter D. Norton, *Fighting Traffic: The Dawn of the Motor Age in the American City* (Cambridge, Mass.: MIT Press, 2008), 163–69, 202–5, 234–35.

31   McClintock, *Metropolitan Street Traffic Survey*; Miller McClintock, *A Report on the Street Traffic Control Problem of San Francisco* (San Francisco: San Francisco Traffic Survey Committee, 1927); Miller McClintock, *The Street Traffic Control Problem of the City of New Orleans* (New Orleans: New Orleans City Planning and Zoning Commission, 1928); Albert Russel Erskine Bureau, *A Report on the Street Traffic Control Problem of the City of Boston* (Boston: City of Boston Printing Department, 1928); Albert Russel Erskine Bureau, *Traffic Survey by Public Service Engineer under Direction of Joint Committee on Ordinances with Report and Recommendations* (Providence, R.I.: Oxford Press, 1928); Albert Russel Erskine Bureau, *A Traffic Control Plan for Kansas City* (Kansas City, Mo.: Chas. E Brown Printing Co., 1930); Miller McClintock, *The Greater Chicago Traffic Area: A Preliminary Report on the Major Traffic Facts of the City of Chicago and Surrounding Region* (Chicago: Committee on Traffic and Public Safety, 1932); Miller McClintock, "The Traffic Survey," in *Planning for City Traffic*, ed. MacDonald, 10. Perhaps the most notable achievement—the influence of which was as broad as McClintock's—came in New York City, which mounted a massive undertaking that combined city planning and traffic engineering as two parts of a greater whole even as it expanded the scope of city planning from the citywide to the regional. See *Regional Plan of New York and Its Environs*, 2 vols. (New York: Regional Plan of New York and Its Environs, 1929–1931).

32   Miller McClintock, *Street Traffic Control* (New York: McGraw-Hill, 1925), 11.

33   McClintock, "Traffic Survey," 8 (quotation), 8–18. See also McClintock, *Street Traffic Control*, 11–24; and Irving C. Moller, "Guiding the Traffic Flow," in *Planning for City Traffic*, ed. MacDonald, 114–17.

34   In this, traffic engineers simply acknowledged trends that had developed in the pre-automotive era. Indeed, most major cities had major radials along which streetcars connected peripheral residential neighborhoods with central business and factory districts. The regular traffic that these arteries carried made them magnets for business development, which in turn attracted greater volumes of vehicular traffic, heightening the conflict between automobiles and streetcars. Public policy reinforced the use of such radial streets as traffic carriers by giving them top priority for widening, straightening, paving, street sweeping, and snow removal, all of which tended to make them more attractive to traffic than other streets. Thus as the number of automobiles rose in the first two decades of the century, most motorists quite naturally followed these direct routes rather than negotiating a maze of backstreets that were less direct and less well maintained than the major arteries. They also flooded the few long, radial routes that lacked streetcar lines, typically prompting their quick transformation from residential streets—frequently traversing wealthy neighborhoods—into business streets that resembled the major streetcar routes. For a good discussion of these trends in Hartford, see Peter C. Baldwin, *Domesticating the Street: The Reform of Public Space in Hartford, 1850–1930* (Columbus: Ohio State University Press, 1999), 207–14.

35   As secretary of commerce, Herbert Hoover called for a National Conference on Street and Highway Safety in 1924, popularly known as the Hoover Conference, which led the field in developing nationally recognized standards. For a collection of the committee reports, including that by the Committee on Traffic Control, see National Conference on Street and Highway Safety, *First National Conference on Street and Highway Safety* (Washington, D.C.: U.S. Department of Commerce, 1924). For the report of the Committee on Uniformity of Laws and Regulations, including a suggested Uniform Vehicle Code, see National Conference on Street and Highway Safety, *National Conference on Street and Highway Safety* (Washington, D.C.: U.S. Department of Commerce, 1926). For two shorter, technical discussions of particular problems, see M. G. Lloyd, "Uniform Traffic Signs, Signals, and Markings," in *Planning for City Traffic*, ed. MacDonald, 121–27; and A. B. Barber, "Making Our Traffic Laws Uniform," in *Planning for City Traffic*, ed. MacDonald, 128–33. See also "Unmuddling our Motor Regulations," *Literary Digest* 75 (18 Nov. 1922): 73–76; Alvin Barton Barber, "How the States are Working towards a Uniform Motor Vehicle Code," *American City* 35 (Dec. 1926): 851–54; and "Automobile Fatalities Indicate Importance of Uniform Vehicle Code," *American City* 38 (Feb. 1928): 169. For an overview of efforts during the 1920s to address city street traffic, including the role of automotive interests in shaping the Hoover Conference's recommendations, see Norton, *Fighting Traffic*, esp. 175–93.

36 Burton W. Marsh, "Traffic Control," in *Planning for City Traffic*, ed. MacDonald, 94, 98. For an overview of the history of traffic-control signals, see Clay McShane, "The Origins and Globalization of Traffic Control Signals," *Journal of Urban History* 25 (Mar. 1999): 379–404.

37 B. W. Marsh, "Traffic Control," 99–107, 113. On traffic-signal installation and use in Chicago, see McClintock, *Metropolitan Street Traffic Survey*, 180–86; Barrett, *Automobile and Urban Transit*, 156–58; and Norton, *Fighting Traffic*, 134–38.

38 Barrett, *Automobile and Urban Transit*, 144, 147–49. Chicago's innovation was to use the signs to create new "boulevards" along preexisting streets not formerly regarded as boulevards; as early as 1914, the Motor Club of Michigan had paid to install octagonal red stop signs on cross streets along an existing, specially built boulevard leading to a Detroit suburb, thus reinforcing right-of-way rules already in place. See McShane, "Globalization of Traffic Control Signals," 383.

39 McClintock, *Street Traffic Control*, 126–28; T. Glenn Phillips, "The Traffic Problems in Detroit and How They Are Met," in *Automobile*, ed. King, 241–43.

40 Frederick Law Olmsted, Harland Bartholomew, and Henry Charles Cheney, *A Major Traffic Street Plan for Los Angeles* (Los Angeles: Major Highways Committee, 1924), 18, quoted in Fogelson, *Downtown*, 260.

41 For an excellent summary of growing awareness of this phenomenon (known as "induced traffic") and its role in transportation debates, see Brian Ladd, *Autophobia: Love and Hate in the Automotive Age* (Chicago: University of Chicago Press, 2008), 121–27. For a comprehensive citation of current research on its dynamics, see ibid., 123n45.

42 Few contemporaries noted the parallels between this idea and earlier elevated trains, which had used different means to achieve the same ends: providing high-speed traffic with a dedicated right-of-way in an effort to reduce the effects of congestion. On the evolving ideas behind high-speed, multilane, limited-access highways, see Charles W. Eliot, "The Influence of the Automobile on the Design of Park Roads," *Landscape Architecture* 13 (Oct. 1922): 27–37; Sidney D. Waldon, "Superhighways and Regional Planning," *Planning Problems of Town, City, and Region* (1927): 150–66; Robert Kingery, "Highways of the Future," *Transactions of the National Safety Council, 18th Annual Safety Conference* (Sept.–Oct. 1929): 72–75; W. W. Arnheim, "Express Routes Suggested to End Congestion," *Nation's Traffic* 3 (Apr. 1929): 38–40; Jay Downer, "Parkways and Super-Highways: Their Comparative Advantages in Inter-Urban Planning," *Official Proceedings of the Annual Convention of the American Society of Municipal Engineers* 36 (1930): 49–52; George D. Hall, "The 'Freeway': A New Thought for Subdividers," *Landscape Architecture* 21 (Jan. 1931): 115–18; Herbert S. Swan, "The Parkway as a Traffic Artery," *American City* 45–46 (Oct.–Nov. 1931): 73–76, 84–86; Fred Lavis, "Highways as Elements of Transportation and Discussion," *Transactions of the American Society of Civil Engineers* 95 (1931): 1021–59; Latham C. Squire and Howard M. Bassett, "A New Type of Thoroughfare: The 'Freeway,'" *American City* 47 (Nov. 1932): 64–66; W. Russell Tylor, "Social Factors in Development

of Regional Highways," *Roads and Streets* 76 (June 1933): 219–23; and Edward M. Bassett, "Zoning and Freeways," *City Planning* 9 (July 1933): 138–39.

43 On McClintock's late-1930s collaborations with Norman Bel Geddes, whose book *Magic Motorways* (New York: Random House, 1940) and General Motors-sponsored Futurama exhibit at the 1939–1940 New York World's Fair helped dramatize the idea of urban freeways for a mass audience, see Norton, *Fighting Traffic*, 248–50; and M. Scott, *American City Planning*, 361–62. For an insightful analysis of McClintock's broader role as "a safety expert for the motor age," in which he downplayed the benefits of education and enforcement while promoting the safety benefits of carefully designed, high-speed "limited ways," see Norton, *Fighting Traffic*, 234–54. On the significance of McClintock's plans relative to others, see Fogelson, *Downtown*, 271–76.

44 John A. Massen and Miller McClintock, *Limited Ways: A Plan for the Greater Chicago Traffic Area; A Report to the City Council of the City of Chicago*, vol. 2 (Chicago: Committee on Traffic and Public Safety, 1933), 26.

45 On advocates of urban freeway construction, see Fogelson, *Downtown*, esp. 270–82; and Norton, *Fighting Traffic*, 202–4, 238–41.

46 The major federal road agency, for example, was named the Bureau of Public Roads, and it gave its major research journal the name *Public Roads*.

47 William Phelps Eno, *How Traffic Regulation May Be Improved in Town and Country: A Supplement to Simplification of Highway Traffic* (Fairfield, Conn.: Eno Foundation for Highway Traffic Regulation, 1936), 21.

48 For a contemporary overview of the legal principles involved, see "Freeways and the Rights of Abutting Owners," *Stanford Law Review* 3 (Feb. 1951): 298–311.

49 See, for example, Jay, "Evolution of Road Location," 229.

50 Although automobile ownership was quite large by the end of the interwar period, with the ratio of driving-age Americans to automobiles reaching 3:1 in 1940, differences of race, class, and gender still circumscribed the access that some people had to the automobile-based mobility that I describe here. A large literature exists on the subject; some of the more notable works include Cotten Seiler, *Republic of Drivers: A Cultural History of Automobility in America* (Chicago: University of Chicago Press, 2008), 36–68, 105–28; Tom Lewis, *Divided Highways: Building the Interstate Highways, Transforming American Life* (New York: Penguin Books, 1997); Mark Foster, "In the Face of 'Jim Crow': Prosperous Blacks and Vacations, Travel and Outdoor Leisure, 1890–1945," *Journal of Negro History* 84 (Spring 1999): 130–49; Virginia Scharff, *Taking the Wheel: Women and the Coming of the Motor Age* (New York: Free Press, 1991); Georgine Clarsen, *Eat My Dust: Early Women Motorists* (Baltimore: Johns Hopkins University Press, 2008); Michael Brian Schiffer, with Tamara C. Butts and Kimberly K. Grimm, *Taking Charge: The Electric Automobile in America* (Washington, D.C.: Smithsonian Institution Press, 1994); Margaret Walsh, "Gendering Transport History: Retrospect and Prospect," *Journal of Transport History* 23 (Mar. 2002): 1–8; David Gartman, *Auto Opium: A Social History of American Automobile Design* (New York:

Routledge, 1994); and Joseph Anthony Interrante, "A Moveable Feast: The Automobile and the Spatial Transformation of American Culture, 1890–1940" (Ph.D. diss., Harvard University, 1983).

51   For an excellent monographic treatment of this subject for rural areas, see Norman T. Moline, *Mobility and the Small Town, 1900–1930: Transportation Change in Oregon, Illinois*, Research Paper No. 132 (Chicago: Department of Geography, University of Chicago, 1971). On transportation changes in the West, see Carlos Arnoldo Schwantes, *Going Places: Transportation Redefines the Twentieth-Century West* (Bloomington: Indiana University Press, 2003), esp. 58–188. On cities and streetcars, see Joel A. Tarr, *Transportation Innovation and Changing Spatial Patterns in Pittsburgh* (Chicago: Public Works Historical Society, 1978).

52   Quoted in William Cronon, *Nature's Metropolis: Chicago and the Great West* (New York: W. W. Norton, 1991), 92.

53   For one explanation of how railroads structured relationships between cities in the nineteenth century, with a focus on Chicago's role as a "gateway" city between the heavily settled East and the sparsely settled—but rapidly developing—West, see ibid., esp. 55–93.

54   Cars also had a dramatic impact on intercity transportation, although that is not the focus here. In 1910, for example, 95 percent of all intercity transportation was by railroad; within 25 years, automobiles claimed 90 percent of such trips. Between 1920 and 1933, total railroad passenger revenues fell an alarming 75 percent. See Schwantes, *Going Places*, 172–73.

55   The base map for figure 4.3 is *Railroad Commissioners' Map of Minnesota* (Chicago: Rand, McNally & Co., 1900), which mapped the routes of all operating railroads in the state of Minnesota in 1900. Travel time by rail is based on information in American Association of General Passenger and Ticket Agents, *Travelers' Official Railway Guide for the United States, Canada, and Mexico* 32 (Mar. 1900). The map is designed to approximate maximum possible travel under optimal conditions. As such, it assumes travelers took the shortest possible trip by rail (measured in time), that trains ran on time, and that travelers could switch immediately to horse-drawn transportation—and travel an average of six miles per hour in any direction—upon arriving at a stop. Poor roads, inclement weather, slow transfers, tired horses, delayed trains, missed connections, or choosing to travel on anything other than the fastest possible train all would have shrunk the size of the timesheds shown. Even very favorable conditions, on the other hand, would have been unlikely to expand the timesheds depicted here significantly.

56   The base map for figure 4.4 is *The Twin Cities in 1914* (Minneapolis: A. W. Warnock, 1914), which mapped the streetcar system of the Twin Cities in 1914. (Only those routes operating in 1900 are shown.) The frequency of streetcar runs for the city's various lines is based on information in *Free St. Paul Shopping Guide and Street Railway Directory* (St. Paul: Ramaley Publishing Co., 1906), 44–68. The map is designed to approximate maximum possible travel under optimal conditions. As such, it assumes that all streetcars traveled an average of twelve miles

per hour over their routes, including all stops, and that travelers could switch immediately to walking—and travel an average of three miles per hour in any direction—upon arriving at a stop. Inclement weather, slow transfers, and especially traffic delays all would have shrunk the size of the timesheds shown.

57   Robert Fishman, *Bourgeois Utopias: The Rise and Fall of Suburbia* (New York: Basic Books, 1987); Kenneth T. Jackson, *Crabgrass Frontier: The Suburbanization of the United States* (New York: Oxford University Press, 1985).

58   The base map for figure 4.5 is *Railroad Commissioners' Map of Minnesota* (Chicago: Rand, McNally & Co., 1900), which mapped the routes of all operating railroads in the state of Minnesota in 1900. Timetable information for the Chicago, Burlington & Northern Railroad's suburban line that ran from downtown St. Paul through St. Paul Park was generously furnished by Aaron Isaacs. The map is designed to approximate maximum possible travel under optimal conditions. As such, it assumes that travelers took the shortest possible trip by rail (measured in time), that trains ran on time, and that travelers could switch immediately to walking—and travel an average of three miles per hour in any direction—upon arriving at a stop. Poor roads, inclement weather, delayed trains, or choosing to travel on anything other than the fastest possible train all would have shrunk the size of the timeshed shown.

59   Herbert Ladd Towle, "The Automobile and Its Mission," *Scribner's* 53 (Feb. 1913): 151.

60   Malcolm M. Willey and Stuart A. Rice, *Communication Agencies and Social Life* (New York: McGraw-Hill, 1933), 47.

61   The theorist Jean Baudrillard made much of this point, arguing that although automobiles provided the sense of exercising free will, they also required motorists to sacrifice their individualism in order to share the road with other drivers as an atomized unit of the collective "traffic." See Baudrillard, *America*, trans. Chris Turner (New York: Verso, 1988), 52–3; and Karl Raitz, "American Roads, Roadside America," *Geographical Review* 88 (July 1998): 376.

62   The base map for figure 4.6 is Minnesota Department of Highways, *1930 Condition Map of Minnesota Trunk Highways* (St. Paul: Minnesota Department of Highways, 1930), which mapped the surface conditions of all trunk highways in the state of Minnesota in 1930. In contrast to figures 4.3–4.5, which approximate maximum travel under optimal conditions, figures 4.6–4.8 represent *average* daytime travel times. As such, figures 4.6–4.8 assume travel speeds of 35 miles per hour on paved roads, 25 miles per hour on surfaced roads and city streets, and 15 miles per hour on all other roads. Traffic congestion, road conditions (especially on unpaved surfaces), road construction, inclement weather, and driver behavior all would have affected actual speeds. In contrast to the fixed routes and timetables of rail-based transportation, travel by automobile reflected a much wider range of possible travel times.

63   Amos Hawley, *Human Ecology: A Theory of Community Structure* (New York: Ronald Press, 1950), 410, quoted in Moline, *Mobility and the Small Town*, 5.

64   See note 62, above, for the speed assumptions in figure 4.7.

65   Fogelson, *Downtown*, 189.

66   George H. Herrold, "The Parking Problem in St. Paul," *Nation's Traffic* 1 (July 1927): 30, 47.

67   John W. Diers and Aaron Isaacs, *Twin Cities by Trolley: The Streetcar Era in Minneapolis and St. Paul* (Minneapolis: University of Minnesota Press, 2007), 298–99.

68   See note 62, above, for the speed assumptions in figure 4.8.

69   Willey and Rice, *Communication Agencies and Social Life*, 47–48.

70   Although the focus here is on the role of private automobile ownership in rural areas, trucks played an increasingly significant role in the changing political economy of agriculture beginning in the 1930s. For a thorough and insightful analysis of trucking's growing role and impact on rural areas before World War II, see Shane Hamilton, *Trucking Country: The Road to America's Wal-Mart Economy* (Princeton: Princeton University Press, 2008), esp. 13–68.

71   John Kolb and Edmund de S. Brunner, *A Study of Rural Society* (Boston: Houghton Mifflin Co., 1946), 225–52; Edmund de S. Brunner and Irving Lorge, *Rural Trends in Depression Years: A Survey of Village-Centered Agricultural Communities, 1930–1936* (New York: Columbia University Press, 1937), 83–125.

72   Brunner and Lorge, *Rural Trends in Depression Years*, 105.

73   Harold Ickes, *Back to Work: The Story of PWA* (New York: Macmillan Co., 1935), 90.

74   Kolb and Brunner, *Study of Rural Society*, 465.

75   E. B. White, *One Man's Meat* (New York: Harper and Row, 1938), 136.

76   Kolb and Brunner, *Study of Rural Society*, 331, 336, 351–52.

77   Brunner and Lorge, *Rural Trends in Depression Years*, 83.

78   Willey and Rice, *Communication Agencies and Social Life*, 57 (italics in original).

79   Edmund de S. Brunner and J. H. Kolb, *Rural Social Trends* (New York: McGraw-Hill, 1933), 63.

80   W. M. Curtiss, *Use and Value of Highways in Rural New York*, Agricultural Experiment Station Bulletin No. 656 (Ithaca, N.Y.: Cornell University Agricultural Experiment Station, 1936), 19.

81   White, *One Man's Meat*, 136. The degree to which rural Americans depended on automobiles during the 1930s is perhaps best illustrated by the large number of poor migrant farm families, such as those described in John Steinbeck's Pulitzer prize–winning novel, *The Grapes of Wrath* (New York: Viking Press, 1939), who depended on access to automobiles, despite their poverty, to survive. The differences between poor migrants who depended on mobility for their work and homeless "transients" is explored in John N. Webb, *The Transient Unemployed: A Description and Analysis of the Transient Relief Population* (Washington, D.C.: Government Printing Office, 1935); and John N. Webb and Malcolm Brown, *Migrant Families* (Washington, D.C.: Government Printing Office, 1938). Webb found that the vast majority of migrant family groups traveled by car, either in their own (approximately 65,000) or by hitchhiking (approximately 45,000), as

opposed to the 35,000 families who used trains, either paying their fares (30,000) or "riding the rails" (5,000). "Unattached transients," on the other hand, overwhelmingly "road the rails" rather than hitchhiking—120,000 versus 35,000. Webb, *Transient Unemployed*, 68.

82 Harlan Paul Douglass, *The Suburban Trend* (New York: The Century Co., 1925), 136–37.

83 Mark S. Foster, *From Streetcar to Superhighway: American City Planners and Urban Transportation, 1900–1940* (Philadelphia: Temple University Press, 1982), 14.

84 In fact, transit engineers used the theory that ridership would increase as a square of population growth in their planning. See Fogelson, *Downtown*, 60–61.

85 C. P. Taylor, *A Traffic Officer's Training Manual* (Chicago: National Safety Council, 1930), 7.

86 Quoted in Stephen W. Sears, *The American Heritage History of the Automobile in America* (New York: American Heritage Publishing Company, 1977), 142. More serious individuals said much the same thing, such as George E. Roberts of the National Bank, who declared that "the American public is thinking more about where to park its cars than about the League of Nations." See "Wanted—More Hitching-Posts for Cars," *Literary Digest* 80 (2 Feb. 1924): 57.

87 Herbert S. Swan, "Our City Thoroughfares: Shall They Be Highways or Garages?" *American City* 27 (Dec. 1922): 497; "Banishing the All-Day Parker," *Literary Digest* 82 (20 Sept. 1924): 76–79. The first parking meters did not appear until 1935.

88 For a succinct summary of the traffic engineering profession's position situated in its broader context, see Norton, *Fighting Traffic*, 138–45.

89 When the Los Angeles parking ban went into effect, traffic thinned remarkably. The city's police chief estimated that traffic moved about 50 percent faster than before; streetcars ran on time for the first time in years; and the Public Utilities Commission reported that accidents were down even as rush-hour automobile trips had been cut by an average of ten to fifteen minutes. The ban infuriated motorists who wanted to use their cars to shop downtown, however, prompting heated letters to the editor and a case challenging the new regulations in court. In a more important form of protest, motorists also began to do their shopping elsewhere. By the end of the first week of the parking ban, alarmed downtown store owners reported sharp declines in sales, prompting the Business Men's Co-Operative Association, a former advocate of the ban, to launch a campaign against the new ordinance. Before a month passed, the restrictions had been modified, replacing the complete daytime ban with a forty-five-minute parking limit from 10:00 a.m. to 4:00 p.m. and a complete ban from 4:00 until 6:15 p.m. See Bottles, *Los Angeles and the Automobile*, 63–87; and Norton, *Fighting Traffic*, 159–62.

90 Chicago's successful parking ban in 1927, which was implemented following a survey by McClintock showing that just 1.5 percent of nearly seventy thousand department-store customers polled had parked at the curb, provides an

interesting counterpoint to events in Los Angeles. See McClintock, *Metropolitan Street Traffic Survey*, 159; Barrett, *Automobile and Urban Transit*, 135, 158–60; and Norton, *Fighting Traffic*, 145–46. McClintock conducted similar surveys in other cities but found much higher percentages of customers in those cities arrived by automobile and parked at the curb, prompting him to recommend against the outright ban that had worked in Chicago. See McClintock, *Street Traffic Control Problem of San Francisco*, 159; and McClintock, *A Report on the Parking and Garage Problem of Washington, D.C.* (Washington, D.C.: Automobile Parking Committee of Washington, 1930), 48. On parking garages, see Richard Longstreth, *City Center to Regional Mall: Architecture, the Automobile, and Retailing in Los Angeles, 1920–1950* (Cambridge, Mass.: MIT Press, 1997), 45–46; and John A. Jakle and Keith A. Sculle, *Lots of Parking: Land Use in a Car Culture* (Charlottesville: University of Virginia Press, 2004).

91 Henry Ford, *Ford Ideals: Being a Selection from "Mr. Ford's Page" in the Dearborn Independent* (Dearborn, Mich.: Dearborn Publishing Company, 1922), 157.

92 On the role of the real estate industry in shaping urban development, and particularly in the rise of the modern residential subdivision, see Weiss, *Rise of the Community Builders*.

93 For the standard account of automotive suburbanization during the interwar period, see Jackson, *Crabgrass Frontier*, 181–86.

94 On self-built suburbs, see Dolores Hayden, *Building Suburbia: Green Fields and Urban Growth, 1820–2000* (New York: Vintage Books, 2004), 97–127.

95 George A. Lundberg, Mirra Komarovsky, and Mary Alice McInerny, *Leisure: A Suburban Study* (New York: Columbia University Press, 1934), 37.

96 Roderick D. McKenzie, *The Metropolitan Community* (New York: McGraw-Hill, 1933), 174–78; Clay McShane, *Down the Asphalt Path: The Automobile and the American City* (New York: Columbia University Press, 1994), 14–19; Jackson, *Crabgrass Frontier*, 174–77; Mark S. Foster, "The Automobile and the City," *Michigan Historical Quarterly* 19 (Fall 1980): 460–62.

97 McKenzie, *Metropolitan Community*, 175.

98 Interrante, "A Moveable Feast," 171; Jackson, *Crabgrass Frontier*, 171; McShane, *Down the Asphalt Path*, 192. For a detailed analysis of the "centrifugal drift" during the 1920s, see McKenzie, *Metropolitan Community*, 173–79.

99 Jackson, *Crabgrass Frontier*, 185.

100 William S. Worley, *J. C. Nichols and the Shaping of Kansas City: Innovation in Planned Residential Communities* (Columbia: University of Missouri Press, 1990), 124–55, esp. 127–31.

101 Patricia Burgess Stach, "Real Estate Development and Urban Form: Roadblocks in the Path to Residential Exclusivity," *Business History Review* 63 (Summer 1989): 369; Jackson, *Crabgrass Frontier*, 177–78.

102 See also Jackson, *Crabgrass Frontier*, 177–78, 258–59.

103 An extensive literature exists on Los Angeles and the automobile. See, among others, Bottles, *Los Angeles and the Automobile*; Ashleigh Brilliant, *The Great Car*

Craze: How Southern California Collided with the Automobile in the 1920s (Santa Barbara: Woodbridge Press, 1989); Christopher Finch, *Highways to Heaven: The AUTO Biography of America* (New York: HarperCollins, 1992); Jackson, *Crabgrass Frontier*, 178–81; and Reyner Banham, *Los Angeles: Four Architectural Ecologies* (Harmondsworth, UK: Penguin Books, 1973). Similar trends can be seen in other cities as well. For a case study of Philadelphia with a slightly different focus, for example, see Stephanie Dyer, "Markets in the Meadows: Department Stores and Shopping Centers in the Decentralization of Philadelphia, 1920–1980" (Ph.D. diss., University of Pennsylvania, 2000); on Hartford, see Baldwin, *Domesticating the Street*; on St. Louis, see Sandweiss, *St. Louis*; on Atlanta, see Preston, *Automobile Age Atlanta*.

104 Banham, *Los Angeles*, 82. Planning for the city's famous freeway system, which began in the late 1930s, did not finish until 1947; as late as the 1980s, five of Los Angeles's seven major freeways followed former street railway routes. Eric H. Monkkonen, *America Becomes Urban: The Development of U.S. Cities and Towns, 1780–1980* (Berkeley: University of California Press, 1988), 177; Finch, *Highways to Heaven*, 50.

105 Longstreth, *City Center to Regional Mall*, 40–41.

106 Ibid., 58–63.

107 Ibid., 67–79.

108 Ibid., 104–12.

109 Ibid., 112–27.

110 Ibid., 127–41.

111 Chester Liebs, *Main Street to Miracle Mile: American Roadside Architecture* (Boston: Little, Brown, 1985), 117–35; Susan Strasser, *Satisfaction Guaranteed: The Making of the American Mass Market* (Washington, D.C.: Smithsonian Institution Press, 1989), 203–51; Richard Longstreth, *The Drive-In, the Supermarket, and the Transformation of Commercial Space in Los Angeles, 1914–1941* (Cambridge, Mass.: MIT Press, 2000).

112 Liebs, *Main Street to Miracle Mile*, 124–29; Longstreth, *Transformation of Commercial Space*. For a nuanced and insightful analysis of the politics—both governmental and social—underlying supermarkets' successes, see Tracey Deutsch, *Building a Housewife's Paradise: Gender, Politics, and American Grocery Stores in the Twentieth Century* (Chapel Hill: University of North Carolina Press, 2010).

113 Richard Longstreth, "The Neighborhood Shopping Center in Washington, D.C., 1930–1941," *Journal of the Society of Architectural Historians* 51 (Mar. 1992): 5–34, esp. 5–6, 17–21; Longstreth, *Transformation of Commercial Space*; and Longstreth, "The Diffusion of the Community Shopping Center Concept during the Interwar Decades," *Journal of the Society of Architectural Historians* 56 (Sept. 1997): 268–93.

114 Douglas Haskell, "Architecture on Routes U.S. 40 and 66," *Architectural Record* 81 (May 1937): 19, quoted in Liebs, *Main Street to Miracle Mile*, 15.

115 Fogelson, *Downtown*, 250; David Saint Clair, *The Motorization of American Cities* (New York: Praeger, 1986), 8.

116 Barrett, *Automobile and Urban Transit*; Bottles, *Los Angeles and the Automobile*; Saint Clair, *Motorization of American Cities*.

117 Fogelson, *Downtown*, 296–97.

118 Ibid., 299–302. See also Norton, *Fighting Traffic*, 200–1.

119 Fogelson, *Downtown*, esp. 381–94.

120 "The Great American Roadside," *Fortune* 10 (Sept. 1934): 53. The article ran without a byline but was later credited to Agee in a 1980 reprint. James Agee, "The Great American Roadside," *Fortune* 101 (11 Feb. 1980): 72–75. For an insightful analysis of the essay as it relates to Agee's more famous collaboration with Walker Evans, *Now Let Us Now Praise Famous Men* (Boston: Houghton Mifflin, 1941), see Jeff Allred, *American Modernism and Depression Documentary* (New York: Oxford University Press, 2010), esp. 117–21.

121 Liebs, *Main Street to Miracle Mile*.

122 Ibid., 193–224.

123 Harold F. Williamson et al., *The American Petroleum Industry*, vol. 2, *The Age of Energy, 1899–1959* (Evanston, Ill.: Northwestern University Press, 1963), 681.

124 Warren James Belasco, *Americans on the Road: From Autocamp to Motel* (Cambridge, Mass.: MIT Press, 1979); Liebs, *Main Street to Miracle Mile*, 169–91.

125 Jesse Merl Bennett, *Roadsides: The Front Yard of a Nation* (Boston: Stratford, 1936), 162; Daniel M. Bluestone, "Roadside Blight and the Reform of Commercial Architecture," in *Roadside America: The Automobile in Design and Culture*, ed. Jan Jennings (Ames: Iowa State University Press, 1990), 175; Bureau of Public Roads, *Toll Roads and Free Roads* (Washington, D.C.: Government Printing Office, 1939), 107.

126 On the broader context of how advertisers used billboards and outdoor advertising to tap into the "mobile markets" that growing numbers of motorists created—and the ways that their actions reshaped the automobile-age American landscape—see Catherine Gudis, *Buyways: Billboards, Automobiles, and the American Landscape* (New York: Routledge, 2004).

127 Jim Heimann, *California Crazy and Beyond: Roadside Vernacular Architecture* (San Francisco: Chronicle Books, 2001); "Great American Roadside," 63.

128 Liebs, *Main Street to Miracle Mile*, 199–204.

129 See John A. Jakle and Keith A. Sculle, *The Gas Station in America* (Baltimore: Johns Hopkins University Press, 1994); Jakle and Sculle, *Fast Food: Roadside Restaurants in the Automobile Age* (Baltimore: Johns Hopkins University Press, 1999); Liebs, *Main Street to Miracle Mile*, 95–115, 153–67, 193–224.

130 For more on this point, see Raitz, "American Roads," 363–87; and Gudis, *Buyways*, 163–230.

131 John J. McCarthy and Robert Littell, "Three Hundred Thousand Shacks," *Harper's* 167 (July 1933): 180–88.

132 Anne O'Hagan, "The Hot Dog Trail," *Woman's Journal* 13 (May 1928): 12–13, quoted in Bluestone, "Roadside Blight," 173.

133 "Great American Roadside," 172. On this point, see especially Gudis, *Buyways*, 37–160.

134　For a description of the four primary "types" of new roadside operations during this period, see Liebs, *Main Street to Miracle Mile*, 22–27.

135　"Great American Roadside," 53.

5. FUELING THE BOOM

1　Harold F. Williamson et al., *The American Petroleum Industry*, vol. 2, *The Age of Energy, 1899–1959* (Evanston, Ill.: Northwestern University Press, 1963), 217–28; John A. Jakle and Keith A. Sculle, *The Gas Station in America* (Baltimore: Johns Hopkins University Press, 1994), 48–50.

2　Williamson et al., *American Petroleum Industry*, vol. 2, 470.

3　Ibid., 680.

4　Richard Longstreth, *The Drive-In, the Supermarket, and the Transformation of Commercial Space in Los Angeles, 1914–1941* (Cambridge, Mass.: MIT Press, 2000), esp. 9–31.

5　Jakle and Sculle, *Gas Station in America*, esp. 50–67.

6　Longstreth, *Transformation of Commercial Space*, esp. 9–31; Chester Liebs, *Main Street to Miracle Mile: American Roadside Architecture* (Boston: Little, Brown, 1985), 95–117; Jakle and Sculle, *Gas Station in America*, esp. 130–200.

7　On Drake and the early oil industry, see Brian Black, *Petrolia: The Landscape of America's First Oil Boom* (Baltimore: Johns Hopkins University Press, 2000), 13–36. A vast literature exists on Rockefeller and Standard Oil. See, for example, Ida Tarbell, *The History of the Standard Oil Company*, 2 vols. (New York: S. S. McClure, 1904); Harold F. Williamson and Arnold R. Daum, *The American Petroleum Industry*, vol. 1, *The Age of Illumination, 1859–1899* (Evanston, Ill.: Northwestern University Press, 1959); Ralph W. Hidy, George Sweet Gibb, and Henrietta M. Larson, *History of Standard Oil Company*, 3 vols. (New York: Harper, 1955–1971); Allan Nevins, *John D. Rockefeller: The Heroic Age of American Enterprise* (New York: Charles Scribner's Sons, 1941); and Ron Chernow, *Titan: The Life of John D. Rockefeller, Sr.* (New York: Random House, 1998).

8　Harvey O'Connor, *The Empire of Oil* (New York: Monthly Review Press, 1955), 14–15; Alfred Crosby, *Children of the Sun: A History of Humanity's Unappeasable Appetite for Energy* (New York: W. W. Norton, 2006), 95; Williamson et al., *American Petroleum Industry*, vol. 2, 214; Daniel Yergin, *The Prize: The Epic Quest for Oil, Money, and Power* (New York: Simon and Schuster, 1991), 14; Tom McCarthy, "The Coming Wonder? Foresight and Early Concerns about the Automobile," *Environmental History* 6 (Jan. 2001): 49.

9　It was not inevitable that gasoline would be the most preferable fuel for internal-combustion engines. On this point, see especially T. McCarthy, "Coming Wonder?," 46–74.

10　Quoted in Williamson et al., *American Petroleum Industry*, vol. 2, 195.

11　Ibid., 443.

12　Ibid., 653–56.

13 American Petroleum Institute (hereafter API), *Petroleum Facts and Figures* (New York: API, 1941), 145. For comparison, gasoline was the third most valuable refinery product in 1909, behind illuminating oils and lubricating oils, and accounted for 16.7 percent of total refinery sales. By 1914 gasoline had taken over as the most valuable product, comprising 30.7 percent of total sales. By 1919, gasoline accounted for 46.9 percent of total sales. See Williamson et al., *American Petroleum Industry*, vol. 2, 111.

14 API, *Petroleum Facts and Figures*, 8, 16. See also D. W. Meinig, *The Shaping of America*, vol. 4, *Global America, 1915–2000* (New Haven, Conn.: Yale University Press, 2004), 41–42.

15 O'Connor, *Empire of Oil*, 46–49; Paul Roberts, *The End of Oil: On the Edge of a Perilous New World* (Boston: Houghton Mifflin, 2004), 33–34; Sonia Shah, *Crude: The Story of Oil* (New York: Seven Stories Press, 2004), xi–xxiii.

16 Yergin, *The Prize*, 218–19; Williamson et al., *American Petroleum Industry*, vol. 2, 313–16; James A. Veasey, "The Law of Oil and Gas," *Michigan Law Review* 18 (Apr. 1920): 449.

17 Williamson et al., *American Petroleum Industry*, vol. 2, 5, 22.

18 O'Connor, *Empire of Oil*, 48.

19 Williamson et al., *American Petroleum Industry*, vol. 2, 17; Roberts, *End of Oil*, 32.

20 API, *Petroleum Facts and Figures*, 64.

21 "Some Explanations for the Increased Cost of Gasoline," *Literary Digest* 65 (22 May 1920): 115–16; "Getting Ready for the Gasoline Famine," *Literary Digest* 66 (17 July 1920): 110–14; "Vision of Dollar Gasoline," *Literary Digest* 76 (17 Mar. 1923): 13–14; "Is the Price of Gasoline Getting Ready to Soar?" *Literary Digest* 83 (13 Dec. 1924): 62–64; Williamson et al., *American Petroleum Industry*, vol. 2, 332–36.

22 Crosby, *Children of the Sun*, 86.

23 Williamson et al., *American Petroleum Industry*, vol. 2, 339, 568. See also George S. Wolbert Jr., *U.S. Oil Pipelines: An Examination of How Oil Pipe Lines Operate and the Current Public Policy Issues Concerning Their Ownership* (Washington, D.C.: API, 1979), 11–19.

24 On the evolution of refineries and refining technology from 1899 to 1919, see Williamson et al., *American Petroleum Industry*, vol. 2, 110–66. For contemporary accounts, see "Manufacture of Gasoline by Cracking Heavy Oils," *Scientific American Supplement* 79 (1 May 1915): 283; C. H. Claudy, "Rittman Process of Cracking," *Scientific American* 112 (20 Mar. 1915): 267; and Claudy, "Burton Process of Cracking to Make Gasoline" *Scientific American* 112 (2 Jan. 1915): 5.

25 Williamson et al., *American Petroleum Industry*, vol. 2, 395. On refining technology and the spread of thermal cracking in the 1920s, see ibid., 373–441; and Huston Thompson, "Distribution of Gasoline and Methods of Price Control," *Annals of the American Academy of Political and Social Science* 116 (Nov. 1924): 89–90.

26 Williamson et al., *American Petroleum Industry*, vol. 2, 607; M. W. Gibney, "Battle of the Octanes," *Popular Mechanics* 58 (Nov. 1932): 698–702; "Super-Shell:

New Gas from New Cracking Process Wins Quick Popularity," *Business Week* (17 May 1933): 10; M. Bunn, "How Modern Gas Adds Power to Your Motor," *Popular Science* 124 (Feb. 1934): 56, 99; "Monsieur Houdry's Invention: Oil Refining's Great Mystery, Houdry Process, which May Change the Economic Structure of Oil," *Fortune* 19 (Feb. 1939): 56–59; "Standard Oil's Better Gasoline: Rival to the Houdry Catalytic Refining Process," *Business Week* (13 May 1939): 38–39; "Refinery Rejuvenation: Mid-Continent Petroleum Will Install Catalytic Cracking," *Business Week* (24 June 1939): 20; "Revolution in Gasoline: Refiners' Race for High Octane Ratings," *Business Week* (30 Dec. 1939): 23–24.

27   Williamson et al., *American Petroleum Industry*, vol. 2, 206–16, 466–68, 675–79.

28   Not everyone took such a position. On the early history of how automobile exhausts factored into contemporary debates about the era's "smoke nuisance," see T. McCarthy, "Coming Wonder?," 54–61.

29   "Oil Pollution and Refinery Wastes," *Sewage Works Journal* 7 (Jan. 1935): 105. See also William T. Chambers, "Kilgore, Texas: An Oil Boom Town," *Economic Geography* 9 (Jan. 1933): 76; Williamson et al., *American Petroleum Industry*, vol. 2, 319; and J. R. McNeill, *Something New Under the Sun: An Environmental History of the Twentieth-Century World* (New York: W. W. Norton, 2000), 300–301.

30   Earnest Boyce, "A Study of Oil-Well Brine Disposal," *Transactions of the Kansas Academy of Science* 38 (28–30 Mar. 1935): 131–37.

31   Douglas C. Drake, "Herbert Hoover, Ecologist: The Politics of Oil Pollution Control, 1921–1926," *Mid America: An Historical Review* 55 (July 1973): 207–28; "Federal Oil Pollution Act," *Public Health Reports* 39 (19 Dec. 1924): 3206–8; Joseph A. Pratt, "Letting the Grandchildren Do It: Environmental Planning during the Ascent of Oil as a Major Energy Source," *Public Historian* 2 (Summer 1980): 31–41; Martin V. Melosi, *Coping with Abundance: Energy and Environment in Industrial America* (Philadelphia: Temple University Press, 1984), 151–52. On pipelines, see Terry Tamminen, *Lives per Gallon: The True Cost of Our Oil Addiction* (Washington, D.C.: Island Press, 2006), 33–35.

32   "Oil Pollution and Refinery Wastes," 112.

33   Pratt, "Letting the Grandchildren Do It," 52–58.

34   Tamminen, *Lives per Gallon*, 39–40.

35   Frederick C. Lincoln, "The Menace of Oil Pollution," *The Auk* 47 (Oct. 1930): 548.

36   O'Connor, *Empire of Oil*, 45–56; Veasey, "Law of Oil and Gas," 445–69; American Bar Association, *Legal History of Conservation of Oil and Gas* (Chicago: American Bar Association, Section of Mineral Law, 1938). The key exception was when oil was discovered under large tracts of publicly owned land. Although this scenario had the potential to "solve" the problem of chaotic competition, it also produced some of the era's most spectacular political scandals, including the one involving Teapot Dome that ripped apart the Harding administration. See, for example, Yergin, *The Prize*, 211–16. On this broad theme about resources held in common in environmental history, see especially Garrett Hardin, "The

Tragedy of the Commons," *Science* 162 (13 Dec. 1968): 1243–48; Arthur F. McEvoy, *The Fisherman's Problem: Ecology and Law in the California Fisheries* (New York: Cambridge University Press, 1986); and David Feeny, Susan Hanna, and Arthur F. McEvoy, "Questioning the Assumptions of the 'Tragedy of the Commons' Model of Fisheries," *Land Economics* 72 (May 1996): 187–205.

37 O'Connor, *Empire of Oil*, 52–53. So-called secondary recovery methods, such as mining, squeezing, sucking, and especially pushing (displacement), could bring some of the remaining oil aboveground at much greater expense. These were often utilized in later decades, when the price of oil was significantly higher, to recover some of the oil that remained in what the industry euphemistically described as "dry wells." See, for example, "'Dry' Wells Yield Vast New Oil Supplies," *Science News-Letter* 88 (17 July 1965): 43.

38 Quoted in O'Connor, *Empire of Oil*, 53.

39 Yergin, *The Prize*, 223–27, 244–59; O'Connor, *Empire of Oil*, 62–77; Williamson et al., *American Petroleum Industry*, vol. 2, 535–66; Gerald D. Nash, *United States Oil Policy: Business and Government in Twentieth Century America* (Pittsburgh: University of Pittsburgh Press, 1968), 112–56; Melosi, *Coping with Abundance*, 152–55, 157–58.

40 For an excellent analysis of smog's emergence as an issue, see Tom McCarthy, *Auto Mania: Cars, Consumers, and the Environment* (New Haven, Conn.: Yale University Press, 2007), 115–28, 164–71. See also Jack Doyle, *Taken for a Ride: Detroit's Big Three and the Politics of Pollution* (New York: Four Walls Eight Windows, 2000), esp. 17–49, 64–79; James E. Krier and Edmund Ursin, *Pollution and Policy: A Case Essay on California and Federal Experience with Motor Vehicle Air Pollution, 1940–1975* (Berkeley: University of California Press, 1977); and Rudi Volti, "Reducing Automobile Emissions in Southern California: The Dance of Public Policies and Technological Fixes," in *Inventing for the Environment*, ed. Arthur Molella and Joyce Bedi (Cambridge, Mass.: MIT Press, 2003), 277–88.

41 IPCC, "Summary for Policymakers," 2001, www.grida.no/publications/other/ipcc_tar (accessed 28 Dec. 2009) (quotation). See also Spencer R. Weart, *The Discovery of Global Warming* (Cambridge, Mass.: Harvard University Press, 2003).

42 Both smog and climate change illustrate a persistent theme in environmental politics: problems that seem negligible or unimportant on an individual scale can, once aggregated, have national or even global environmental implications. Because the problems do not become clear until after large numbers of people are involved, the damaging behaviors have often accrued both widespread social acceptance and economic importance. Moreover, the causal linkage between seemingly harmless behaviors on one side and environmental problems on the other frequently requires elaborate scientific explanation. This creates opportunities for entrenched interests to challenge the science by proposing plausible alternative theories for the environmental problems, which often take time and study to disprove. As a result, "attack, delay, and ask for more research" has proven a fruitful strategy for those hoping to avoid new environmental

regulations. Moreover, because such problems frequently necessitate sweeping changes in established behaviors, effective regulations are frequently intrusive and perceived as onerous.

43 "Standard Oil's Death Factory," *Nation* 119 (26 Nov. 1924): 561–62. The literature on tetraethyl lead is extensive. See Pratt, "Letting the Grandchildren Do It"; Jamie Lincoln Kitman, "The Secret History of Lead: How Did Lead Get into Gasoline in the First Place? And Why Is Leaded Gas Still Being Sold in the Third World, Eastern Europe and Elsewhere?" *Nation* 270 (20 Mar. 2000): 11–44; William Kovarik, "Henry Ford, Charles Kettering and the 'Fuel of the Future,'" *Automotive History Review* 32 (Spring 1998): 7–27; Kovarik, "Ethyl: The 1920s Environmental Conflict over Leaded Gasoline and Alternative Fuels," paper presented at the American Society for Environmental History Annual Conference, 26–30 Mar. 2003, Providence, R.I., available at www.runet.edu/~wkovarik/papers/ethylconflict.html (accessed 30 Dec. 2009); Alan P. Loeb, "Birth of the Kettering Doctrine: Fordism, Sloanism and the Discovery of Tetraethyl Lead," *Business and Economic History* 24, 1 (1995): 72–87; David Rosner and Gerald Markowitz, "A 'Gift of God?': The Public Health Controversy over Leaded Gasoline in the 1920s," *American Journal of Public Health* 75 (Apr. 1985): 344–52; T. McCarthy, *Auto Mania*, 48–53; and Williamson et al., *American Petroleum Industry*, vol. 2, 409–14.

44 Rosner and Markowitz, "'Gift of God?,'" 344–52.

45 U.S. Public Health Service, *Proceedings of a Conference to Determine Whether or Not There Is a Public Health Question in the Manufacture, Distribution or Use of Tetraethyl Lead in Gasoline*, Public Health Bulletin No. 158 (Washington, D.C.: Government Printing Office, 1925), quoted in Pratt, "Letting the Grandchildren Do It," 47. The precautionary principle received its first major international endorsement in 1982 when the United Nations adopted the World Charter for Nature. See David Kriebel et al., "The Precautionary Principle in Environmental Science," *Environmental Health Perspectives* 109 (Sept. 2001): 871–76; Brian Mayer, Phil Brown, and Meadow Linder, "Moving Further Upstream: From Toxics Reduction to the Precautionary Principle," *Public Health Reports* 117 (Nov.–Dec. 2002): 574–86; and Gary E. Marchant, "From General Policy to Legal Rule: Aspirations and Limitations of the Precautionary Principle," *Environmental Health Perspectives* 111 (Nov. 2003): 1799–1803.

46 On the serious weaknesses of this study, which issued annual updates through 1931, see Pratt, "Letting the Grandchildren Do It," 49–50; and Rosner and Markowitz, "'Gift of God?,'" 350.

47 T. McCarthy, *Auto Mania*, 51.

48 Most damningly, one study suggests a clear link between childhood lead exposure and violent criminal behavior, arguing that the sharp fall in violent crime in the United States during the 1990s is a direct product of the dramatic reduction in childhood lead exposure during the 1970s and 1980s. See Jessica Wolpaw Reyes, *Environmental Policy as Social Policy? The Impact of Childhood Lead Exposure*

on *Crime*, National Bureau of Economic Research Working Paper No. 13097 (Cambridge, Mass.: National Bureau of Economic Research, 2007). The eventual phaseout of leaded gasoline abounded in ironies. First, the issue reemerged not because of health concerns but because lead damaged catalytic converters, a technology designed to reduce problems with smog. Second, the then-powerful argument that TEL was necessary because it improved vehicle gas mileage was becoming moot at precisely the same time that TEL was finally introduced, just as one major new oil discovery in the United States after another was made. Third, Eugene Houdry, the chemist who introduced catalytic cracking to the oil industry in the late 1930s—a process that allowed refineries to produce gasoline with a high enough octane rating to overcome engine knock without the addition of TEL—was also the inventor, in 1949, of an early catalytic converter to remove unburned hydrocarbons from motor-vehicle exhaust. Using the catalytic converter with leaded gasoline dramatically reduced its effectiveness, however, and since automakers had decided to add TEL to Houdry's higher-octane gasoline to get even more power out of their engines, leaded gasoline blocked early adoption of catalytic converters—spawning, in combination with catalytic cracking, a horsepower race in the auto industry in the 1950s.

49 "Horses, Mules and Motor Vehicles," in *USDA Statistical Bulletin No. 5* (Washington, D.C.: Government Printing Office, 1925), 2–7; U.S. Bureau of the Census, *Historical Statistics of the United States: Colonial Times to 1970*, vol. 2. (Washington, D.C.: Government Printing Office, 1975), Series K184–186, K570, K572, quoted in Alan L. Olmstead and Paul W. Rhode, "The Agricultural Mechanization Controversy of the Interwar Years," *Agricultural History* 68 (Summer 1994): 36.

50 Clay McShane and Joel Tarr, *The Horse in the City: Living Machines in the Nineteenth Century* (Baltimore: Johns Hopkins University Press, 2007), 165–77; Anne Norton Greene, *Horses at Work: Harnessing Power in Industrial America* (Cambridge, Mass.: Harvard University Press, 2008), 244–74.

51 See, for example, Olmstead and Rhode, "Agricultural Mechanization Controversy," 35–53; George B. Ellenberg, "Debating Farm Power: Draft Animals, Tractors, and the United States Department of Agriculture," *Agricultural History* 74 (Spring 2000): 545–68; and Greene, *Horses at Work*, 244–74.

52 Alan L. Olmstead and Paul W. Rhode, "Reshaping the Landscape: The Impact and Diffusion of the Tractor in American Agriculture, 1910–1960," *Journal of Economic History* 61 (Sept. 2001): 664–65. In the early 1930s, the Horse Association of America even went so far as to claim that the agricultural depression of the 1920s had its roots in the steep decline of draft animals, arguing that shifting cultivation from oats and hay to commodity grains had glutted the latter's markets, suppressing farm profits. See McShane and Tarr, *Horse in the City*, 128–29.

53 Gordon H. Turrentine, "Petrochemicals Come of Age," *Analysts Journal* 9 (Nov. 1953): 45–50. See also Shah, *Crude*, 11–13. On federal funding during World War II for alternative biological sources of rubber that could be produced

domestically, see Mark R. Finlay, *Growing American Rubber: Strategic Plants and the Politics of National Security* (New Brunswick, N.J.: Rutgers University Press, 2009), 140–225.

54 Quoted in Yergin, *The Prize*, 183.

55 Williamson et al., *American Petroleum Industry*, vol. 2, 444, 671. See also Joseph Pratt, "The Ascent of Oil: The Transition from Coal to Oil in Early Twentieth Century America," in *Energy Transitions: Long-Term Perspectives*, ed. Lewis Perelman, Gus Giebelhaus, and Michael Yokell (Boulder, Colo.: Westview Press, 1981).

56 Leo Huberman and Paul M. Sweezy, "Publisher's Foreword," in O'Connor, *Empire of Oil*, vii.

57 This section was originally published in slightly different form as Christopher W. Wells, "Fueling the Boom: Gasoline Taxes, Invisibility, and the Growth of the American Highway Infrastructure, 1919–1956," *Journal of American History* 99 (June 2012): 72–81. Reprinted by permission of the author and publisher.

58 Philip H. Burch Jr., *Highway Revenue and Expenditure Policy in the United States* (New Brunswick, N.J.: Rutgers University Press, 1962), 36; R. Rudy Higgens-Evenson, *The Price of Progress: Public Services, Taxation, and the American Corporate State, 1877 to 1929* (Baltimore: Johns Hopkins University Press, 2003), 77–91; John C. Burnham, "The Gasoline Tax and the Automobile Revolution," *Mississippi Valley Historical Review* 48 (Dec. 1961): 436–37.

59 Finla Goff Crawford, *Motor Fuel Taxation in the United States* (Syracuse, N.Y.: F. G. Crawford, 1939), 1–2; Higgens-Evenson, *Price of Progress*, 78, 89–90; James A. Dunn Jr., "The Importance of Being Earmarked: Transport Policy and Highway Finance in Great Britain and the United States," *Comparative Studies in Society and History* 20 (Jan. 1978): 42, 48; Burch, *Highway Revenue and Expenditure Policy*, 37.

60 Wilfred Owen, *A Study in Highway Economics* (Cambridge, Mass.: Phi Beta Kappa Society, 1934), 84–85; James W. Martin, "The Administration of Gasoline Taxes in the United States," *National Municipal Review* 13 (Oct. 1924): 587–600, reproduced in Richard E. Gift, ed., *State Tax Systems under Changing Technology: The Problem of the Roadways* (Lexington: College of Business and Economics of the University of Kentucky, 1980), 39; API, *Petroleum Facts and Figures*, 156; Burnham, "Gasoline Tax," 445–46.

61 Higgens-Evenson, *Price of Progress*, 61–63; Owen, *Study in Highway Economics*, 73; Charles L. Dearing, *American Highway Policy* (Washington, D.C.: Brookings Institution, 1941), 100, 102–3; Martin, "Administration of Gasoline Taxes," 39; Federal Highway Administration (hereafter FHWA), *Highway Statistics: Summary to 1985* (Washington, D.C.: Government Printing Office, 1987), 136; Burnham, "Gasoline Tax," 447. This stood in contrast to revenues for city streets, which still relied heavily on property taxes and special assessments. For an analysis of the resulting rural-urban imbalance, see especially Owen Gutfreund, *Twentieth-Century Sprawl: Highways and the Reshaping of the American Landscape* (New York: Oxford University Press, 2005).

62 Burch, *Highway Revenue and Expenditure Policy*, 37; Burnham, "Gasoline Tax," 446 (quotation), 449–52. In contrast to motorists, road builders, and politicians who lined up to support the tax during its widespread adoption in the 1920s, the petroleum industry soon began to denounce it (after early support from oil company executives). See Peter D. Norton, *Fighting Traffic: The Dawn of the Motor Age in the American City* (Cambridge, Mass.: MIT Press, 2008), 198.

63 Crawford, *Motor Fuel Taxation*, 9–11, 13; U.S. Bureau of the Census, *Historical Statistics of the United States: Colonial Times to 1957* (Washington, D.C.: Government Printing Office, 1960), Series Y384–400, p. 722; FHWA, *Highway Statistics to 1985*, 136; Burnham, "Gasoline Tax," 456–57.

64 FHWA, *Highway Statistics to 1985*, 136; Mark H. Rose, *Interstate: Express Highway Politics, 1939–1989*, rev. ed. (Knoxville: University of Tennessee Press, 1990), 10; John Bell Rae, *The Road and the Car in American Life* (Cambridge, Mass.: MIT Press, 1971), 74; Bruce E. Seely, *Building the American Highway System: Engineers as Policy Makers* (Philadelphia: Temple University Press, 1987), 88, 90–91.

65 Frederic E. Everett, "Diversion Dangers and Gasoline Tax Evasions," *American Highways* 11 (Jan. 1932): 1–2; Crawford, *Motor Fuel Taxation*, 76 (quotation), 68–71, 76–78; Rose, *Interstate*, 9–10; Gutfreund, *Twentieth-Century Sprawl*, 31–37; Dunn, "Importance of Being Earmarked," 42–43; Burch, *Highway Revenue and Expenditure Policy*, 73–74.

66 Burch, *Highway Revenue and Expenditure Policy*, 64, 66, 79; Dunn, "Importance of Being Earmarked," 42–43; Gutfreund, *Twentieth-Century Sprawl*, 33–34; Seely, *Building the American Highway System*, 210; Rose, *Interstate*, 32–33.

67 API, *Petroleum Facts and Figures*, 156; Burnham, "Gasoline Tax," 449–50; Gutfreund, *Twentieth-Century Sprawl*, 34–37.

68 On the highway planning surveys, see H. S. Fairbank, "State-Wide Highway Planning Surveys," *Civil Engineering* 7 (Mar. 1937): 178–81; Fairbank, "Newly Discovered Facts About Our Highway System," typescript [1938], Ohio Department of Transportation Library, Columbus; FHWA, *America's Highways, 1776–1976: A History of the Federal-Aid Program* (Washington, D.C.: Government Printing Office, 1976), 268–71; and Seely, *Building the American Highway System*, 166–69.

69 Thomas MacDonald, "The Trend of Modern Highways," *Motor Transportation* 64 (June 1938): 1138 (first quotation), 1135 (second and third quotations). See also Seely, *Building the American Highway System*, 161, 167; and Burnham, "Gasoline Tax," 456.

70 "Unfit for Modern Motor Traffic," *Fortune* 14 (Aug. 1936): 85 (statistics), 87 (quotation). The number of deaths for 1935 reported in U.S. Bureau of the Census, *Statistical Abstract of the United States: 2003*, is 34,494, roughly 2,500 less than reported in *Fortune*. On the framing of this public debate, see Paul G. Hoffman, "The White Line Isn't Enough," *Saturday Evening Post* 210 (26 Mar. 1938): 12ff.; J. C. Furnas, "—And Sudden Death," *Reader's Digest* 47 (Aug. 1935): 21–26; David Blanke, *Hell on Wheels: The Promise and Peril of America's Car Culture, 1900–1940* (Lawrence: University Press of Kansas, 2007); and Norton, *Fighting Traffic*.

71 Seely, *Building the American Highway System*, 147–48 (quotation); Meinig, *Shaping of America*, vol. 4, 18.

72 Wilfred Owen and Charles L. Dearing, *Toll Roads and the Problem of Highway Modernization* (Washington, D.C.: Brookings Institution, 1951), 33. On the limits of stage construction, see Bureau of Public Roads (hereafter BPR), *Toll Roads and Free Roads* (Washington, D.C.: Government Printing Office, 1939), 105–6; for a detailed discussion of problems associated with rights-of-way, see ibid., 114–21. Thomas MacDonald was particularly distressed that this pattern of development seemed to follow the bypass roads constructed during the 1930s, so that *"within a surprisingly short time we have only another city street with congested traffic."* Thomas H. MacDonald, "Tomorrow's Roads," *Engineering News-Record* 117 (17 Dec. 1936): 868 (italics in original). MacDonald argued that the only viable solution to this problem was to couple limited-access bypasses with adequate local service roads to keep local traffic and businesses from clogging the bypass.

73 Seely, *Building the American Highway System*, 147–49, 162–63; George Rogers Taylor, *The Transportation Revolution, 1815–1860* (New York: Rinehart, 1951).

74 BPR, *Toll Roads and Free Roads*; Seely, *Building the American Highway System*, 162–63, 169; FHWA, *America's Highways*, 271–73.

75 BPR, *Toll Roads and Free Roads*, 2–3, 15, 19–33 (traffic counts and estimates), 81–86 (ability to self-liquidate), 86 (quotation), 89 (influence of parallel free roads). See also Seely, *Building the American Highway System*, 169–70.

76 BPR, *Toll Roads and Free Roads*, 7–11, 20–21, 89.

77 BPR, *Toll Roads and Free Roads*, 93 (first quotation), 110 (second and third quotations), 89–98, 102–11. See also Seely, *Building the American Highway System*, 170.

78 BPR, *Toll Roads and Free Roads*, 22, 110; Seely, *Building the American Highway System*, 170–77.

79 Owen and Dearing, *Problem of Highway Modernization*, 10 (quotation), 6–10; Seely, *Building the American Highway System*, 163, 175–76; Meinig, *Shaping of America*, vol. 4, 18–19. See also Mitchell E. Dakelman and Neal A. Schorr, *The Pennsylvania Turnpike* (Portsmouth, N.H.: Arcadia Publishing, 2004); and FHWA, *America's Highways*, 136–37.

80 Owen and Dearing, *Problem of Highway Modernization*, 4–6, 14–18; Seely, *Building the American Highway System*, 175–76; FHWA, *America's Highways*, 136–37.

6. THE PATHS OUT OF TOWN

1 William Cronon, "Kennecott Journey," in *Under an Open Sky: Rethinking America's Western Past*, ed. William Cronon, George A. Miles, and Jay Gitlin (New York: W. W. Norton, 1992), 33.

2 For a detailed analysis of the automobile's environmental impact across its entire life cycle, beginning with raw-materials extraction and running all the way through use and disposal, see Tom McCarthy, *Auto Mania: Cars, Consumers, and the Environment* (New Haven, Conn.: Yale University Press, 2007).

3   Automobile Manufacturers Association (hereafter AMA), *Automobile Facts and Figures* (Detroit: AMA, 1971), 3.

4   David E. Kyvig, *Daily Life in the United States, 1920–1939: Decades of Promise and Pain* (Westport, Conn.: Greenwood Press, 2002), 22; AMA, *Automobile Facts and Figures* (1938), 51.

5   AMA, *Automobile Facts and Figures* (1971), 3.

6   AMA, *Automobile Facts and Figures* (1940), 26.

7   Quoted in Anne O'Hare McCormick, "Ford Seeks New Balance for Industry," *New York Times Magazine*, 29 May 1932, 4–5.

8   AMA, *Automobile Facts and Figures* (1971), 3.

9   For the company's own version of the Rouge and its practices, see Ford Motor Company, *The Ford Industries: Facts about the Ford Motor Company and Its Subsidiaries* (Detroit: Ford Motor Company, 1924), esp. 36–62. The most complete contemporary analysis of the Rouge and its workings appeared in *Industrial Management* in a series of thirteen articles by John H. Van Deventer between 1922 and 1923, beginning with Van Deventer, "Ford Principles and Practice at River Rouge: Links in a Complete Industrial Chain," *Industrial Management* 64 (Sept. 1922): 131–37. The best historical descriptions of the plant are Allan Nevins and Frank Ernest Hill, *Ford*, vol. 2, *Expansion and Challenge, 1915–1933* (New York: Charles Scribner's Sons, 1957), esp. 200–16; and Lindy Biggs, *The Rational Factory: Architecture, Technology, and Work in America's Age of Mass Production* (Baltimore: Johns Hopkins University Press, 1996). Before dredging operations reached their conclusion, only smaller vessels could make it up the shallow Rouge to the factory, which raised costs and forced the company to rely more extensively on rail-based deliveries. See Nevins and Hill, *Ford*, vol. 2, 212–16.

10   On the relative size of the Ford ore carriers, the *Henry Ford II* and the *Benson Ford*, see Hartley W. Barclay, *Ford Production Methods* (New York: Harper and Brothers, 1936), 92.

11   Evans Clark, "The Super-Trust Arrives in America: The Far-Spreading Vertical Combination Begins a New Economic Order—It Starts with Raw Material and Knits Processes of Manufacture and Distribution through Railroads, Mills and Sales Agencies," *New York Times*, 13 Dec. 1925, p. XX1. See also Clark, "How Super-Trust Alters Industry: Vertical and Horizontal Business Combines Illustrate Tendency to Control Output from Raw Material to Consumer," *New York Times*, 14 Feb. 1926, p. XX10. The trope of raw materials flowing in one end of the factory and finished automobiles flowing out the other was often repeated in the press's coverage of Ford's River Rouge operations. See, for example, Van Deventer, "Principles and Practice at River Rouge," 131.

12   "Rouge Plant Facts," 28 Mar. 1924, Acc. 572, Box 23, Folder 11.25, The Henry Ford, Benson Ford Research Center, Dearborn, Michigan (hereafter BFRC).

13   Ford News Bureau, press release, 29 July 1949, cited in Thomas Martin McCarthy, "The Road to Respect: Americans, Automobiles, and the Environment" (Ph.D. diss., Yale University, 2001), 332. This would have made the automobile

industry responsible for roughly 3.4 percent of all coal consumption in the United States during this period, a considerable figure based on coal's pervasive use in the industrial, residential, commercial, transportation, and steel-producing sectors at the time. The calculation is based on historical coal production figures in Richard Bonskowski, William Watson, and Fred Freme, "Coal Production in the United States: An Historical Overview," Energy Information Administration, www.eia.doe.gov/cneaf/coal/page/coal_production_review.pdf (accessed 5 Nov. 2009).

14 AMA, *Automobile Facts and Figures* (1940), 73.

15 Tom McCarthy, "Henry Ford, Industrial Ecologist or Industrial Conservationist? Waste Reduction and Recycling at the Rouge," *Michigan Historical Review* 27 (Fall 2001): 53–88. On industrial ecology, see also Christine Meisner Rosen, "Industrial Ecology and the Transformation of Corporate Environmental Management: A Business Historian's Perspective," in *Inventing for the Environment*, ed. Arthur Molella and Joyce Bedi (Cambridge, Mass.: MIT Press, 2003), 319–38; and Braden Allenby, "Industrial Ecology," in *Inventing for the Environment*, ed. Molella and Bedi, 339–72.

16 International Joint Commission of United States and Canada, *Report on the Pollution of Boundary Waters* (Washington, D.C., and Ottawa: International Joint Commission, 1951), 63–64.

17 Bill Wolf, "Running Sores on Our Land," *Sports Afield* (Nov. 1948): 91, quoted in T. McCarthy, *Auto Mania*, 110. Thomas McCarthy is the major historian of pollution at the Rouge; see his "Road to Respect," esp. 272–341.

18 David Stradling, *Smokestacks and Progressives: Environmentalists, Engineers and Air Quality in America, 1881–1951* (Baltimore: Johns Hopkins University Press, 1999), 6–152.

19 Andrew Hurley, *Environmental Inequalities: Class, Race, and Industrial Pollution in Gary, Indiana, 1945–1980* (Chapel Hill: University of North Carolina Press, 1995), 1–45; T. McCarthy, "Road to Respect," 272–341; Joel Tarr, *The Search for the Ultimate Sink: Urban Pollution in Historical Perspective* (Akron, Ohio: University of Akron Press, 1996).

20 T. McCarthy, "Industrial Conservationist?"

21 "Motor Cars as Consumers," *Literary Digest* 76 (6 Jan. 1923): 62. See also National Automobile Chamber of Commerce (hereafter NACC), *Facts and Figures of the Automobile Industry* (New York: NACC, 1923), 14–15.

22 NACC, *Facts and Figures* (1924), 15.

23 "Motor Cars as Consumers," 62.

24 NACC, *Facts and Figures* (1930), 82–83.

25 AMA, *Automobile Facts and Figures* (1939), 39.

26 Scholars have devoted significant attention to the ancillary industries that the Ford Motor Company owned and operated. The standard, basic account remains Nevins and Hill, *Ford*, vol. 2, 217–48. For more recent treatments, see especially Ford R. Bryan, *Beyond the Model T: The Other Ventures of Henry Ford*,

rev. ed. (Detroit: Wayne State University Press, 1997); David L. Lewis, "The Rise and Fall of Old Henry's Northern Empire, Part I," *Cars and Parts* 17 (Dec. 1973): 90–97; and D. Lewis, "The Rise and Fall of Old Henry's Northern Empire, Part II," *Cars and Parts* 17 (Jan.–Feb. 1974): 100–5.

27 Ford Motor Company, *The Ford Industries*, 5.

28 "Rouge Plant Facts." In addition, by the mid-1930s the Rouge required 538 million gallons of water daily to cool its turbo generators, more than required by the cities of Detroit, Cincinnati, and Washington, D.C., combined. See Barclay, *Ford Production Methods*, 133. For a discussion of raw-materials use at the Rouge through 1980, see T. McCarthy, "Road to Respect," 214–71, esp. 227–52.

29 Ford Motor Company Advertising Department to Albert E. Dunford, 18 Feb. 1924, Acc. 572, Box 11, Folder 24, BFRC; A. M. Wibel, "The Reminiscences of A. M. Wibel" (draft), 187, Acc. 79, Box 65, Oral Histories—Wibel (Folder 1), BFRC; "Rouge Plant Facts"; "Ford Developing His Iron Mines," *Literary Digest* 74 (26 Aug. 1922): 56; and Nevins and Hill, *Ford*, vol. 2, 220. Between 1920 and 1928, Ford's Imperial Mine produced less than a third of the iron ore consumed at the Rouge. See "Henry's Furnace" and "Benson's Furnace," 25 July 1928, Acc. 572, Box 23, Folder 11.25.2.4—Steel Operations, BFRC. For a detailed study of Ford's iron-mining operations from 1920 to 1980, see T. McCarthy, "Road to Respect," 230–52.

30 Beatrice Blomquist, "Ford Comes to Iron Mountain: The Birth of Kingsford," 1–20, n.d., Acc. Vertical File, Folder "FMC—Plants—North America—Michigan—Iron Mountain," BFRC; Bryan, *Beyond the Model T*, 54–55, 118–21; "Iron Mountain Is Busy Scene," *Ford News* 1 (1 Nov. 1920): 1; "100 Additional Ford Homes Under Construction at Iron Mountain," *Ford News* (1 Nov. 1924), Acc. Vertical File, Folder "FMC—Plants—North America—Michigan—Iron Mountain," BFRC; Lewis, "Northern Empire, Part I," 91–92. On the profitability of these operations, see W. E. Carnegie to Edsel Ford, P. E. Martin, E. C. Kanzler, and B. J. Craig, 11 Nov. 1925, and W. E. Carnegie to P. E. Martin, C. E. Sorensen, and W. B. Mayo, 9 Dec. 1925, both in Acc. 572, Box 14, Folder 11.12.5, BFRC; and Bryan, *Beyond the Model T*, 118–29. Kingsford brand charcoal is still manufactured today in California.

31 For a succinct treatment of the earlier boom, see Philip P. Mason, *The Lumbering Era in Michigan History, 1860–1900* (Ann Arbor, Mich.: Braun-Brumfield, 1956).

32 Hubert A. Breunair, "Reforestation of Ford Motor Company Timber Lands and Present Method of Logging Its Forest Acreage in the Upper Peninsula of Michigan: Report Prepared for C. W. Avery, Superintendent's Office, Jan 28, 1926," Acc. 60, Box 12, Folder "Lumber," BFRC; "Reminiscences of Mr. Robert Edwards," 9, Acc. 65, BFRC; "The Reminiscences of Mr. Eric Stromquist," 6, Acc. 65, BFRC. On the larger role of "conservation" ideas in Ford's operations, see especially T. McCarthy, "Industrial Conservationist?"

33 *Ford News* 4 (1 Mar. 1924): 5.

34 NACC, *Facts and Figures* (1924), 4; NACC, *Facts and Figures* (1930), 8.

35 The 1919 statistic is from Kingston Forbes, *The Principles of Automobile Body Design: Covering the Fundamentals of Open and Closed Passenger Body Design* (Philadelphia: Ware Bros., 1922), 303. By contrast, Ford Bryan places the average Model T's board-feet requirements in 1919 at 250. Bryan, *Beyond the Model T*, 118. The industry's average per-vehicle lumber usage here is calculated based on the numbers reported in the NACC's *Facts and Figures of the Automobile Industry* for each year. On wood used in automobile construction in the early 1920s, see "Lumber Used in the Motor Vehicle Industry," *Scientific American Monthly* 3 (Mar. 1921): 274–75; "Substitutes for Ash in Automobile Bodies," *Scientific American Monthly* 4 (Oct. 1921): 377; and Forbes, *Principles of Automobile Body Design*, esp. 82–87, 302–6.

36 Some call the closed-steel body an "all-steel body," but this is a misnomer since bodies of the period actually had wooden frames clad in sheet steel. On the evolution of closed-body technology, see William J. Abernathy, *The Productivity Dilemma: Roadblock to Innovation in the Automobile Industry* (Baltimore: Johns Hopkins University Press, 1978), 18–19, 183–85. On closed-body designs as a generator of increased demand for wood, see Roger White, "Body by Fisher: The Closed Car Revolution," *Automobile Quarterly* 29, 4 (1991): 56; and James J. Flink, *The Automobile Age* (Cambridge, Mass.: MIT Press, 1988), 213–14.

37 Abernathy, *Productivity Dilemma*, 25; and Flink, *Automobile Age*, 213. On the growing popularity of colorful finishes, see "Cars Now Shine in Bright Colors," *New York Times*, 9 Jan. 1927, p. A1.

38 As calculated by dividing the industry's total consumption of hardwood lumber by its total passenger-car production, using the numbers reported in NACC, *Facts and Figures* (1935), 4, 50. On the "turret top," see Abernathy, *Productivity Dilemma*, 184. For comparison, the auto industry consumed 17.7 percent of all hardwood lumber in the United States in 1929 but only 3.2 percent in 1938. NACC, *Facts and Figures* (1930), 82–83; NACC, *Facts and Figures* (1939), 39.

39 Trent E. Boggess, "The Customer Can Have Any Color He Wants—So Long As It's Black: A Study of the Materials and Methods Used to Paint Model T Fords during the Black Era," *Vintage Ford* 32, 6 (1997): 38–39. For some of the changes, see Bruce W. McCalley, *Model T Ford: The Car That Changed the World* (Iola, Wisc.: Krause Publications, 1994), 306–12, 330–36, 369–71, 375–76.

40 For a technical discussion of how the new steel bodies disrupted Ford's backward vertical integration, see Abernathy, *Productivity Dilemma*, 114–46. In contrast, General Motors (GM) and its Fisher Body Works stuck with wood into the early 1930s, leading at least one historian to conclude that the decision to avoid mass producing all-steel bodies gave GM a "chameleon-like ability to change stampings, styles, and colors" that enabled it to move toward its policy of the annual model change. See Roger White, "Body by Fisher," 57. Similarly, David Hounshell has concluded that the high costs of Ford's changeover to all-metal construction in 1925, which eliminated the last of the Model T's wooden framing, probably inspired Henry Ford to resist the necessity of abandoning the

Model T for a new design. "Ford's investment in new tooling for the T in 1925," Hounshell concludes, "should have been for the A." Hounshell, *From American System to Mass Production, 1800–1932* (Baltimore: Johns Hopkins University Press, 1984), 274–75. On the demise of the Model T more generally, and the role of changing American landscapes in particular, see Christopher W. Wells, "La morte del Modello T: Strade pavimentate, auto coperte e tecnologica desueta" [The death of the Model T: Smooth roads, closed cars, and technological maladaptation], *I Frutti di Demetra* 21 (2009): 63–75.

41 Blomquist, "Ford Comes to Iron Mountain," 1–20; D. Lewis, "Northern Empire, Part I," 95–97; T. A. Rogge, "The Reminiscences of Mr. T. A. Rogge," Accession 65, BFRC, 12, 16–17. As a sign of its untenable situation, the plant had to purchase spruce from outside suppliers for the gliders it produced, and it similarly had to purchase wood from outside sources to keep its chemical by-products plant operating.

42 "Ford Rubber Plantation Ship Leaves Detroit," *New York Times*, 27 July 1928, p. 1. On the history of rubber in Brazil and Fordlandia more generally, see Warren Dean, *Brazil and the Struggle for Rubber: A Study in Environmental History* (New York: Cambridge University Press, 1987); Barbara Weinstein, *The Amazon Rubber Boom, 1850–1920* (Stanford, Calif.: Stanford University Press, 1983); Joe Jackson, *The Thief at the End of the World: Rubber, Power, and the Seeds of Empire* (New York: Viking, 2008); and Greg Grandin, *Fordlandia: The Rise and Fall of Henry Ford's Forgotten Jungle City* (New York: Metropolitan Books, 2009).

43 W. C. Deckard, "The Ford Rubber Plantations" (undated typescript), c. 1940, Acc. 1756, Box 1, Folder 1, BFRC.

44 Grandin, *Fordlandia*, 125.

45 Ibid., 341–42.

46 Ibid., 350.

47 For a case study of Rouge-generated air and water pollution, see T. McCarthy, "Road to Respect," 272–341.

48 The plant revived during World War II, but by the 1960s it was being used for storage. Allan Nevins and Frank Ernest Hill, *Ford*, vol. 3, *Decline and Rebirth, 1933–1962* (New York: Charles Scribner's Sons, 1962), 8; Douglas Brinkley, *Wheels for the World: Henry Ford, His Company, and a Century of Progress, 1903–2003* (New York: Penguin Books, 2003), 647, 761.

49 Richard T. T. Forman et al., *Road Ecology: Science and Solutions* (Washington, D.C.: Island Press, 2003), 40. Forman has also estimated that roughly 20 percent of the land area in the United States is directly affected ecologically by public roads; see Forman, "Estimate of the Area Affected Ecologically by the Road System in the United States," *Conservation Biology* 14 (Feb. 2000): 31–35. Only in the 1990s did ecologists begin to pay sustained attention to these subjects. The first lengthy treatments of road ecology are Forman, *Land Mosaics: The Ecology of Landscapes and Regions* (New York: Cambridge University Press, 1995), 145–76; Ian F. Spellerberg, *Ecological Effects of Roads* (Enfield, N.H.: Science Publishers,

2002); and Forman et al., *Road Ecology.* For reviews of the literature, see Spell-
erberg, "Ecological Effects of Roads and Traffic: A Literature Review," *Global
Ecology and Biogeography Letters* 7 (Sept. 1998): 317–33; and Forman et al., *Road
Ecology*, 16–23.

50   The connect/divide framework is introduced in Forman et al., *Road Ecology.*
     See also David G. Havlick, *No Place Distant: Roads and Motorized Recreation on
     America's Public Lands* (Washington, D.C.: Island Press, 2002), 36–58.

51   Bureau of Public Roads (hereafter BPR), *Highway Statistics: Summary to 1945*
     (Washington, D.C.: Government Printing Office, 1947), 56.

52   Ibid., 56.

53   On the history of asphalt paving, see I. B. Holley Jr., "Blacktop: How Asphalt
     Paving Came to the Urban United States," *Technology and Culture* 44 (Oct. 2003):
     703–33.

54   Harold F. Williamson et al., *The American Petroleum Industry*, vol. 2, *The Age of
     Energy, 1899–1959* (Evanston, Ill.: Northwestern University Press, 1963), 459, 670.

55   In the mid-1920s, a single mile of concrete pavement required roughly 2,000
     cubic yards of concrete mixture, 17 railroad carloads of cement, 32 carloads of
     sand, 40 carloads of crushed stone, and 38 tank cars of water. In addition, cement
     kilns consumed an additional 390 tons of coal to produce enough cement for
     one paved mile of highway. See "A Mile of Concrete Road," *Good Roads* 68 (Aug.
     1925): 191; and "A Mile of Concrete Pavement," *Highway Engineer and Contrac-
     tor* 10 (Jan. 1924): 60, cited in I. B. Holley Jr., *The Highway Revolution, 1895–1925:
     How the United States Got Out of the Mud* (Durham, N.C.: Carolina Academic
     Press, 2008), 152. In 2009, Portland cement production accounted for approxi-
     mately 5 percent of anthropogenic sources of carbon dioxide worldwide, partly
     from burning fossil fuels to generate high temperatures in kilns and partly from
     a chemical reaction in the cement itself. See Henry Fountain, "Concrete Is
     Remixed with Environment in Mind," *New York Times*, 30 Mar. 2009.

56   Federal Highway Administration (hereafter FHWA), *America's Highways,
     1776–1976: A History of the Federal-Aid Program* (Washington, D.C.: Government
     Printing Office, 1976), 329; Williamson et al., *American Petroleum Industry*, vol. 2,
     670.

57   BPR, *Highway Statistics to 1945*, 56; FHWA, *America's Highways*, 394.

58   FHWA, *America's Highways*, 121, 325.

59   "Roadside Monstrosities," *New York Times*, 22 Sept. 1929, p. E4.

60   Quoted in FHWA, *America's Highways*, 367. See also E. L. Yordan, "Road Signs
     Under Fire," *New York Times*, 17 Nov. 1935, p. XX1.

61   Timothy Davis, "The Rise and Decline of the American Parkway," in *The World
     beyond the Windshield*, ed. Christof Mauch and Thomas Zeller (Athens: Ohio
     University Press, 2008), esp. 41–49; Timothy Davis, "Inventing Nature in Wash-
     ington, D.C.," in *Inventing for the Environment*, ed. Molella and Bedi, 31–81; Ethan
     Carr, *Wilderness by Design: Landscape Architecture and the National Park Service*
     (Lincoln: University of Nebraska Press, 1998); Richard West Sellars, *Preserving*

Nature in the National Parks: A History (New Haven, Conn.: Yale University Press, 1997), 104–5; Paul S. Sutter, Driven Wild: How the Fight against Automobiles Launched the Modern Wilderness Movement (Seattle: University of Washington Press, 2004), 100; David Louter, Windshield Wilderness: Cars, Roads, and Nature in Washington's National Parks (Seattle: University of Washington Press, 2006), esp. 59–67; FHWA, America's Highways, 134.

62 FHWA, America's Highways, 351, 368, 395.

63 Joint Committee on Roadside Development, Roadside Development Part II: Final Report, Subcommittee on Erosion (Washington, D.C.: Highway Research Board, Apr. 1940), 65–66.

64 W. P. Flint, "The Automobile and Wild Life," Science 63 (23 Apr. 1926): 426–27; William H. Davis, "The Automobile as a Destroyer of Wild Life," Science 79 (1 June 1934): 504–5; W. A. Dreyer, "The Question of Wildlife Destruction by the Automobile," Science 82 (8 Nov. 1935): 439–40; Edward R. Warren, "Casualties among Animals on Mountain Roads," Science 83 (3 Jan. 1936): 14; L. M. Dickerson, "The Problem of Wildlife Destruction by Automobile Traffic," Journal of Wildlife Management 2 (Apr. 1939): 104–16.

65 James Simmons, Feathers and Fur on the Turnpike (Boston: Christopher Publishing House, 1938), 52, 84.

66 On the major design changes of the 1920s, and the role of style as a factor in those changes, see David Gartman, Auto Opium: A Social History of American Automobile Design (New York: Routledge, 1994), 68–99; Flink, Automobile Age, 212–15; Nevins and Hill, Ford, vol. 2, 394–401; and T. McCarthy, "Road to Respect," 187–211.

67 On this point, see also Roger White, "Body by Fisher," 46–63, esp. 53–54.

68 On the broader context of rising automobile use in the national parks, see also Alfred Runte, National Parks: The American Experience, 2nd ed. (Lincoln: University of Nebraska Press, 1987), 155–79; Marguerite Shaffer, See America First: Tourism and National Identity, 1880–1940 (Washington, D.C.: Smithsonian Institution Press, 2001), esp. 130–68; Louter, Windshield Wilderness; Sutter, Driven Wild; Sellars, Preserving Nature; and Linda Flint McClelland, Presenting Nature: The Historic Landscape Design of the National Park Service (Washington, D.C.: National Park Service, 1993).

69 Quoted in Shaffer, See America First, 119.

70 Quoted in McClelland, Presenting Nature, 73.

71 The importance of outdoor recreation—and attention to developing a car-friendly infrastructure—also increased in national forests, where the percentage of visitors arriving in automobiles hovered at or near 90 percent throughout the 1920s, during which time the BPR oversaw the improvement or construction of some fifteen thousand miles of national forest roads. See L. I. Hewes, "Federal Road Building in the National Forests of the West," Public Roads 3 (June 1920): 15–28; Thomas H. MacDonald, Report of the Chief of the Bureau of Public Roads (annually through the 1920s); L. F. Kneipp, "Camping Sites in Public Parks

and Forests," in *The Automobile: Its Province and Its Problems*, ed. Clyde L. King (Philadelphia: American Academy of Political and Social Science, 1924), 64; and NACC, *Facts and Figures* (1930), 63.

72 T. MacDonald, *Report of the Chief* (1927), 33.

73 The best place to track the nature and progress of the BPR's activities in the national parks is in the annual *Report of the Chief of the Bureau of Public Roads* beginning in 1927. See also FHWA, *America's Highways*, 138–39. The links between park development and the federal government's increased attention to motor tourism and motor-tourist roads was not by any means limited to the national parks and forests of the West. For an excellent, fine-grained case study of the origins and construction of the Blue Ridge Parkway, beginning with the slow movement toward linking motor tourism and national parks in the late 1920s, see Anne Virginia Mitchell, "Parkway Politics: Class, Culture, and Tourism in the Blue Ridge" (Ph.D. diss., University of North Carolina at Chapel Hill, 1997), esp. 24–38.

74 Carr, *Wilderness by Design*, 180–86.

75 Louter, *Windshield Wilderness*. See also Gabrielle Barnett, "Drive-By Viewing: Visual Consciousness and Forest Preservation in the Automobile Age," *Technology and Culture* 45 (Jan. 2004): 30–54.

76 Sellars, *Preserving Nature*, 59 (statistics).

77 Neil M. Maher, *Nature's New Deal: The Civilian Conservation Corps and the Roots of the American Environmental Movement* (New York: Oxford University Press, 2008), esp. 70–74.

78 Quoted in Sutter, *Driven Wild*, 81.

79 This and the next paragraph summarize Sutter, *Driven Wild*, esp. 54–141.

80 Quoted in ibid., 83 (italics in original).

81 Quoted in ibid., 242.

82 See especially Frederick Law Olmsted to J. C. Olmsted, "The Projected Park and Parkways on the South Side of Buffalo," City of Buffalo, Park Commission, 1888, in *Civilizing American Cities: A Selection of Frederick Law Olmsted's Writings on City Landscapes*, ed. S. B. Sutton (Cambridge, Mass.: MIT Press, 1971), 131; Olmsted, "Report to the Brooklyn Park Commission," in *Civilizing American Cities*, ed. Sutton, 138–40; Witold Rybczynski, *A Clearing in the Distance: Frederick Law Olmsted and America in the Nineteenth Century* (New York: Scribner, 1999), 281–83; Clay McShane, *Down the Asphalt Path: The Automobile and the American City* (New York: Columbia University Press, 1994), 34–40; McShane, "Urban Pathways: The Street and Highway, 1900–1940," in *Technology and the Rise of the Networked City in Europe and America*, ed. Joel Tarr and Gabriel Dupuy (Philadelphia: Temple University Press, 1988), 71–75; Peter Hall, *Cities of Tomorrow: An Intellectual History of Urban Planning and Design in the Twentieth Century*, updated ed. (Malden, Mass.: Blackwell Publishers, 1996), 110; M. Christine Boyer, *Dreaming the Rational City: The Myth of American City Planning* (Cambridge, Mass.: MIT Press, 1983), 35; and Nelson M. Wells, "Landscaping," in *Highway Engineering*

Handbook, ed. Kenneth B. Woods (New York: McGraw-Hill, 1960), 28–26.

83 Chauncey B. Griffen, "Westchester County's New Park System Will Be One of the Finest in the Country," New York Times, 6 Apr. 1924, p. RE2.

84 "Demand for Homes in the Suburbs," New York Times, 24 Apr. 1925, p. 33.

85 Bruce Radde, The Merritt Parkway (New Haven, Conn.: Yale University Press, 1993), 7. On Robert Moses, see especially Robert Caro, The Power Broker: Robert Moses and the Fall of New York (New York: Vintage Books, 1974).

86 "Honors 18 Builders of Bronx Parkway," New York Times, 25 Jan. 1929, p. 20.

87 Timothy Davis, "Mount Vernon Memorial Highway and the Evolution of the American Parkway" (Ph.D. diss., University of Texas at Austin, 1997); T. Davis, "Rise and Decline of the American Parkway," esp. 41–42.

88 Phoebe Cutler, The Public Landscape of the New Deal (New Haven, Conn.: Yale University Press, 1985), 52–55.

89 On the Natchez Trace Parkway, see Sara Amy Leach, "The Daughters of the American Revolution, Roane F. Byrnes, and the Birth of the Natchez Trace Parkway," in Looking Beyond the Highway: Dixie Roads and Culture, ed. Claudette Stager and Martha Carver (Knoxville: University of Tennessee Press, 2006), 99–114.

90 Anne Mitchell Whisnant, Super-Scenic Motorway: A Blue Ridge Parkway History (Chapel Hill: University of North Carolina Press, 2006), esp. 266 (construction details).

91 T. Davis, "Rise and Decline of the American Parkway," 48–49; Whisnant, Super-Scenic Motorway; and Timothy Davis, "'A Pleasant Illusion of Unspoiled Countryside': The American Parkway and the Problematics of an Institutionalized Vernacular," Perspectives in Vernacular Architecture 9 (2003): 239 (quotation).

92 Quoted in Radde, Merritt Parkway, 82.

93 T. Davis, "Rise and Decline of the American Parkway," 52–56.

7. SUBURBAN NATION

1 Dolores Hayden, Building Suburbia: Green Fields and Urban Growth, 1820–2000 (New York: Vintage Books, 2004), 131; Rosalyn Baxandall and Elizabeth Ewen, Picture Windows: How the Suburbs Happened (New York: Basic Books, 2000), 109–10; "Home Ownership Doubles in Decade," American City 65 (Dec. 1950): 141.

2 James Patterson, Grand Expectations: The United States, 1945–1974 (New York: Oxford University Press, 1996), 71–73; Tom Bernard, "New Homes for $60 a Month," American City 145 (Apr. 1948): 46–47.

3 Ned Eichler, The Merchant Builders (Cambridge, Mass.: MIT Press, 1982), vii–viii.

4 "Home Ownership Doubles in Decade," 141.

5 Barry Checkoway, "Large Builders, Federal Housing Programs, and Postwar Suburbanization," International Journal of Urban and Regional Research 4 (Mar. 1980): 21–22; Hayden, Building Suburbia, 128.

6 National Housing Act of 1934, quoted in Kenneth Jackson, Crabgrass Frontier:

The Suburbanization of the United States (New York: Oxford University Press, 1985), 203. On the broader context in which the National Housing Act of 1934 originated, see especially Adam Rome, The Bulldozer in the Countryside: Suburban Sprawl and the Rise of American Environmentalism (New York: Cambridge University Press, 2001), 19–30.

7   Marc Weiss, The Rise of the Community Builders: The American Real Estate Industry and Urban Land Planning (New York: Columbia University Press, 1987), 11, 142–43; Hayden, Building Suburbia, 122–25.

8   Jackson, Crabgrass Frontier, 204–5.

9   Federal Housing Administration (hereafter FHA), Underwriting Manual: Underwriting and Valuation Procedure under Title II of the National Housing Act (Washington, D.C.: Government Printing Office, 1938); Jackson, Crabgrass Frontier, 207–9; Weiss, Rise of the Community Builders, 142–52.

10   Eichler, Merchant Builders, 54.

11   Jackson, Crabgrass Frontier, 204.

12   Hayden, Building Suburbia, 132. Buyers also benefited from another federal incentive: the ability to deduct interest on home mortgages from federal income tax. In addition, real estate taxes can also be deducted. See, for example, Marion Clawson, Suburban Land Conversion in the United States: An Economic and Governmental Process (Baltimore: Johns Hopkins Press, 1971), 42.

13   Bernard, "New Homes for $60 a Month," 46–47; Jackson, Crabgrass Frontier, 205.

14   Baxandall and Ewen, Picture Windows; Weiss, Rise of the Community Builders, 147–48.

15   Eichler, Merchant Builders, 47.

16   It should be noted that the FHA's preference for neighborhood-level construction grew from its preoccupation with the long-term soundness of the properties it insured, not from a design to privilege big businesses over small ones. As the Underwriting Manual pointed out, "A most important group of factors which affect mortgage risk is the one which embraces the relationship between the physical property and the neighborhood in which it is located. This relationship directly affects the marketability of the property." FHA, Underwriting Manual, 605. For new developments, FHA leaders determined that the level of the planned neighborhood was the smallest level that made good economic sense to insure, since that was the size for which the design of the whole was big enough to protect the value of all of its constituent parts.

17   Weiss, Rise of the Community Builders, 147–48.

18   Hayden, Building Suburbia, 132. On interwar suburban construction, see especially Hayden, Building Suburbia, 97–127; Jackson, Crabgrass Frontier, 172–89; and Weiss, Rise of the Community Builders, 17–140.

19   For a concise treatment of Levittown, see Jackson, Crabgrass Frontier, 234–38. For a sample of the contemporary press's fascination with Levitt & Sons and their construction methods, see Eric Larrabee, "Six Thousand Houses that Levitt Built," Harper's Magazine 197 (Sept. 1948): 79–88; "Up from the Potato Fields,"

Time 56 (3 July 1950): 67–72; "Levittown, Pa," Time 58 (3 Sept. 1951): 98; "Levitts to Build a New 16,000-Home Community in Bucks County," American City 66 (Nov. 1951): 109; John Normile, "Three Bedrooms, 1,000 Square Feet! House in Levittown," Better Homes and Gardens 30 (June 1952): 72–74ff.; Don Weldon, "Ready-Made City Will House 70,000," Popular Science 161 (Nov. 1952): 114–17ff.; Lawrence Lader, "Birth of a City," Reader's Digest 61 (Dec. 1952): 73–76; "Levittown on the Assembly Line," Business Week (16 Feb. 1952): 26–27; "For 60,000 People," Time 60 (22 Dec. 1952): 17–18; "Levittown Builds for 70,000 Population," American City 68 (Sept. 1953): 179; and "Family Moves In," Newsweek 50 (26 Aug. 1957): 27.

20   Hayden, Building Suburbia, 136.

21   FHA, Successful Subdivisions: Principles of Planning for Economy and Protection against Neighborhood Blight (Washington, D.C.: FHA, 1940), 13–14.

22   Mel Scott, American City Planning since 1890: A History Commemorating the 50th Anniversary of the American Institute of Planners (Berkeley: University of California Press, 1969), 457–58; Hayden, Building Suburbia, 136.

23   For a typical complaint from a contemporary planner (coupled with a typical planner's solution to the problem), see John Brewer Moore, "Wanted: More Open Space in Growing Areas," American City 71 (Jan. 1956): 94–95. On the relationship between suburbanization and the rise of environmental politics, see Rome, Bulldozer in the Countryside; and Samuel P. Hays and Barbara D. Hays, Beauty, Health, and Permanence: Environmental Politics in the United States, 1955–1985 (New York: Cambridge University Press, 1987).

24   Jackson, Crabgrass Frontier, 190–245, esp. 195–203, 241–43; Norval D. Glenn, "Suburbanization in the United States Since World War II," in The Urbanization of the Suburbs, ed. Louis Masotti and Jeffrey K. Hadden (Beverly Hills: Sage Publications, 1973), 65. The degree to which the standards became self-fulfilling prophecies for new development is striking. Consider, for example, the FHA's definition of "neighborhood": "Neighborhood is defined as a single area composed of locations separated only by publicly used land, the residential portions of which exhibit a degree of homogeneity. In general, a neighborhood is available for, or improved with, dwelling of more or less similar character, age, and quality." FHA, Underwriting Manual, 903.

25   Thomas W. Hanchett, "Federal Incentives and the Growth of Local Planning, 1941–1948," Journal of the American Planning Association 60 (Spring 1994): 200–202.

26   Eichler, Merchant Builders, 31–35.

27   Harvey Molotch, "The City as a Growth Machine: Toward a Political Economy of Place," American Journal of Sociology 82 (Sept. 1976): 309–32; Margaret Weir, "Planning, Environmentalism, and Urban Poverty: The Political Failure of National Land-Use Planning Legislation, 1970–1975," in The American Planning Tradition: Culture and Policy, ed. Robert Fishman (Washington, D.C.: Woodrow Wilson Center Press, 2000), esp. 193–96.

28   Arnold R. Hirsch, *Making the Second Ghetto: Race and Housing in Chicago, 1940–1960* (New York: Cambridge University Press, 1983); Thomas J. Sugrue, *The Origins of the Urban Crisis: Race and Inequality in Postwar Detroit* (Princeton, N.J.: Princeton University Press, 1996); Raymond A. Mohl, "Making the Second Ghetto in Metropolitan Miami, 1940–1960," *Journal of Urban History* 21 (Mar. 1995): 395–427; Raymond A. Mohl, "The Second Ghetto Thesis and the Power of History," *Journal of Urban History* 29 (Mar. 2003): 243–56; Jackson, *Crabgrass Frontier*, 241–43; Glenn, "Suburbanization," 64–74. Heavy African American migration from rural to urban areas during the same years augmented the trend. In 1940, just over half of all African Americans resided in "rural" areas according to the U.S. census; by 1966, two-thirds of all African Americans lived in cities, and the majority in the biggest cities. Clawson, *Suburban Land Conversion*, 37. Historians of postwar American suburbs have recently begun to move beyond the earlier bias toward focusing on the white, middle-class suburban majority to emphasize the diversity of suburbs in both class and racial terms. See especially Becky Nicolaides, *My Blue Heaven: Life and Politics in the Working-Class Suburbs of Los Angeles, 1920–1965* (Chicago: University of Chicago Press, 2002); Robert D. Lewis, ed., *Manufacturing Suburbs: Building Work and Home on the Metropolitan Fringe* (Philadelphia: Temple University Press, 2004); Andrew Wiese, *Places of Their Own: African American Suburbanization in the Twentieth Century* (Chicago: University of Chicago Press, 2004); and Kevin M. Kruse and Thomas J. Sugrue, eds., *The New Suburban History* (Chicago: University of Chicago Press, 2006).

29   John Rae, *The Road and the Car in American Life* (Cambridge, Mass.: MIT Press, 1971), 226.

30   The FHA's "Suggested Minimum Deed Restrictions" in 1936 recommended provisions stating that "no retail or wholesale shop or store shall be erected or any business or industry or any noxious or offensive trade shall be carried on upon the said premises nor shall anything be done there on which may be or become an annoyance or nuisance to the neighborhood." A note stating that modifying this provision "to permit the erection of retail shops on specified blocks or lots" left some room to develop planned retail areas, although these were almost always located on the periphery of developments, near a major road. See FHA, *Planning Neighborhoods for Small Houses* (Washington, D.C.: FHA, 1936), 32. On the links between suburban zoning ordinances and restrictive deed covenants in the post–World War II era, see also Patricia Burgess, "Of Swimming Pools and 'Slums': Zoning and Residential Development in Post–World War II Columbus, Ohio," in *Inventing for the Environment*, ed. Arthur Molella and Joyce Bedi (Cambridge, Mass.: MIT Press, 2003), 213–39.

31   Zoning laws also effectively erected barriers against future "densification" of areas zoned exclusively for residential use, barring developers from bidding to acquire land for other purposes as it became more valuable. As a result, zoning the majority of metropolitan land for residential-only purposes has had the effect of exacerbating urban decentralization by pushing new intensive land

uses ever farther from already developed areas. For an extended analysis of these dynamics, see Jonathan Levine, *Zoned Out: Regulation, Markets, and Choices in Transportation and Metropolitan Land Use* (Washington, D.C.: Resources for the Future Press, 2006).

32 Especially during the 1930s, the FHA paid lip service to accessibility by public transportation. "The subdivision should be easily accessible by means of public transportation and adequate highways to schools, employment, and commercial centers," it explained in one of its publications, but then the agency offered a rationale for a more road-and-car-based form of accessibility: the income levels of expected inhabitants. "The convenience of public transportation and the accessibility to employment centers and schools becomes increasingly important as the income range of the prospective purchasers decreases," it explained. "Not only should the transportation facilities such as are afforded by streetcars and buses be adequate but there should be convenient access by motor car through arterial highways which provide easy approach to industrial, recreational, and shopping centers." See FHA, *Planning Neighborhoods for Small Houses*, 4.

33 Christopher Tunnard, "America's Super-Cities," *Harper's Magazine* (Aug. 1958): 61.

34 Hal Burton, *The City Fights Back: A Nationwide Survey of What Cities Are Doing to Keep Pace with Traffic, Zoning, Shifting Population, Smoke, Smog and Other Problems* (London: Thames and Hudson, 1954), 148–49; Stephanie Dyer, "Markets in the Meadows: Department Stores and Shopping Centers in the Decentralization of Philadelphia, 1920–1980," *Enterprise and Society* 3 (Dec. 2002): 606–12; Richard Longstreth, *City Center to Regional Mall: Architecture, the Automobile, and Retailing in Los Angeles, 1920–1950* (Cambridge, Mass.: MIT Press, 1997), 215–18, 226–27.

35 For a detailed description of the postwar geographical structure of retail facilities, see Eugene J. Kelley, *Shopping Centers: Locating Controlled Regional Centers* (Saugatuck, Conn.: Eno Foundation for Highway Traffic Control, 1956), 60–65. See also Yehoshua Cohen, *Diffusion of an Innovation in an Urban System: The Spread of Planned Regional Shopping Centers in the United States, 1949–1968* (Chicago: Department of Geography, University of Chicago, 1972), 29–30; and William L. Garrison et al., *Studies of Highway Development and Geographic Change* (Seattle: University of Washington Press, 1959), 39–50.

36 For a contemporary analysis of the degree to which formal location theory in economics, geography, and sociology influenced the decision-making process of developers, see E. J. Kelley, *Shopping Centers*. For recommendations on what to include in a location study, see Victor Gruen and Larry Smith, *Shopping Towns USA: The Planning of Shopping Centers* (New York: Reinhold Publishing Corp., 1960), 30–37; William Applebaum and Saul B. Cohen, "The Dynamics of Store Trading Areas and Market Equilibrium," *Annals of the Association of American Geographers* 51 (Mar. 1961): 73; and William Applebaum, "Guidelines for a Store-Location Strategy Study," *Journal of Marketing* 30 (Oct. 1966): 42–45.

37 Richard Longstreth is the preeminent historian of how retailers integrated parking and other car-friendly features into their site layouts. See especially Longstreth, *City Center to Regional Mall*; and Longstreth, *The Drive-In, the Supermarket, and the Transformation of Commercial Space in Los Angeles, 1914–1941* (Cambridge, Mass.: MIT Press, 2000).

38 Gruen and Smith, *Shopping Towns USA*, 23.

39 Jackson, *Crabgrass Frontier*, 246–71, esp. 263–65.

40 Charles S. LeCraw Jr. and Wilbur S. Smith, *Zoning Applied to Parking* (Saugatuck, Conn.: Eno Foundation for Highway Traffic Control, 1947), 8–10, 23–26; Edward G. Mogren and Wilbur S. Smith, *Zoning and Traffic* (Saugatuck, Conn.: Eno Foundation for Highway Traffic Control, 1952), 25–29. Although Columbus, Ohio, had experimented with a zoning ordinance requiring multifamily dwellings to provide parking for their residents as early as 1923, the first ordinance applied to a nonresidential use did not come until 1939, when Fresno, California, required hotels and hospitals to provide parking. Using zoning to require retailers to provide off-street parking was thus a postwar phenomenon. As early as 1946, the American Society of Planning Officials had drafted an ordinance designed to require retailers outside municipal boundaries to provide off-street parking facilities. See LeCraw and Smith, *Zoning Applied to Parking*, 5–6. For an analysis of the further spread of zoning regulations requiring free off-street parking, see David Witheford, *Zoning, Parking, and Traffic* (Saugatuck, Conn.: Eno Foundation for Transportation, 1972), esp. 21–88; and Robert Boylan, *An Approach to Determining Parking Demand* (Chicago: American Society of Planning Officials, 1971).

41 David R. Levin, *Highway Research Board Bulletin No. 24: Zoning for Parking Facilities; Requirements for Off-Street Automobile Parking Facilities in Zoning and Other Local Ordinances* (Washington, D.C.: Highway Research Board, 1950); Levin, *Highway Research Board Bulletin 99: Parking Requirements in Zoning Ordinances; A Supplement to Bulletin 24* (Washington, D.C.: Highway Research Board, 1955), v.

42 Richard Longstreth, "The Neighborhood Shopping Center in Washington, D. C., 1930–1941," *Journal of the Society of Architectural Historians* 51 (Mar. 1992): 17–19. See also M. Scott, *American City Planning*; Gruen and Smith, *Shopping Towns USA*, 52; and E. J. Kelley, *Shopping Centers*, 5–6.

43 On the relationship between shopping center developers and local governments, see Gordon H. Stedman, "Shopping Centers and Local Government— Collision or Co-operation," *Journal of Retailing* 31 (Summer 1955): 77–87. Some tenants, especially chain stores, still performed their own location studies as a measure of self-protection.

44 E. J. Kelley, *Shopping Centers*, 4–8.

45 Gruen and Smith, *Shopping Towns USA*, 28 (quotation).

46 Y. Cohen, *Diffusion of an Innovation*, 34–39; Thomas Hanchett, "U.S. Tax Policy and the Shopping Center Boom of the 1950s and 1960s," *American Historical Review* 101 (Oct. 1996): 1089–90, 1097. On Southdale and its designer, Victor

Gruen, see M. Jeffrey Hardwick, *Mall Maker: Victor Gruen, Architect of an American Dream* (Philadelphia: University of Pennsylvania Press, 2003).

47 Lizabeth Cohen, "From Town Center to Shopping Center: The Reconfiguration of Community Marketplaces in Postwar America," *American Historical Review* 101 (Oct. 1996): 1050–81, esp. 1052–55. See also Longstreth, *City Center to Regional Mall*, 307–47, esp. 307–9. For a somewhat polemical take on many of these same points, including an analysis of how some of the same principles shaping malls have shaped places like Disney World and Atlantic City, see James Howard Kunstler, *The Geography of Nowhere: The Rise and Decline of America's Man-Made Landscape* (New York: Simon and Schuster, 1993), 109, 119–21, 217–44. On the larger social and political history of which mall development was a part, see Lizabeth Cohen, *A Consumers' Republic: The Politics of Mass Consumption in Postwar America* (New York: Knopf, 2003).

48 Dyer, "Markets in the Meadows" (2002), 611.

49 Robert M. Fogelson, *Downtown: Its Rise and Fall, 1880–1950* (New Haven, Conn.: Yale University Press, 2001), 315, 393–94. For a contemporary study arguing that downtown department stores were purely a product of mass transit systems, and that declining transit coupled with mass adoption of the automobile was likely to shift the balance permanently toward suburban stores, see George Sternlieb, *The Future of the Downtown Department Store* (Cambridge: Joint Center for Urban Studies of the Massachusetts Institute of Technology and Harvard University, 1962).

50 Burton, *City Fights Back*, 149.

51 On the problems of retroactively applying parking requirements to nonconforming land uses downtown, see Mogren and Smith, *Zoning and Traffic*, 87–88.

52 Burton, *City Fights Back*, 67. See also Fogelson, *Downtown*, 307–8; and John A. Jakle and Keith A. Sculle, *Lots of Parking: Land Use in a Car Culture* (Charlottesville: University of Virginia Press, 2004).

53 Automobile Manufacturers Association (hereafter AMA), *Automobile Facts and Figures* (Detroit: AMA, 1951), 31.

54 Quoted in Burton, *City Fights Back*, 79.

55 Ibid., 73–81. See also Donald M. Baker, "Financing Express Highways in Metropolitan Areas," *American City* 61 (Oct. 1946): 93–94; Fogelson, *Downtown*, 275–76; Mark H. Rose, *Interstate: Express Highway Politics, 1939–1989*, rev. ed. (Knoxville: University of Tennessee Press, 1990); Gary Schwartz, *Urban Freeways and the Interstate System* (Los Angeles: University of Southern California, 1976); Bruce E. Seely, *Building the American Highway System: Engineers as Policy Makers* (Philadelphia: Temple University Press, 1987), 193–94; Federal Highway Administration (hereafter FHWA), *America's Highways, 1776–1976: A History of the Federal-Aid Program* (Washington, D.C.: Government Printing Office, 1976), 160; and M. Scott, *American City Planning*, 440. The best overview of the politics of postwar urban highway planning before the Federal-Aid Highway Act of 1956 is Rose, *Interstate*, 55–67.

56 Hanchett, "U.S. Tax Policy," 1082–110; Hayden, *Building Suburbia*, 162–72. Thomas Hanchett has done the pioneering research on this subject, and Dolores Hayden has extended his findings for shopping centers to other forms of greenfield commercial development. See also Clawson, *Suburban Land Conversion*, 42.

57 Hanchett, "U.S. Tax Policy," 1095.

58 Y. Cohen, *Diffusion of an Innovation*, 36.

59 Wilbur Smith and Associates, *Future Highways and Urban Growth* (New Haven, Conn.: Wilbur Smith and Associates, 1961), 21.

60 Hayden, *Building Suburbia*, 162–72. In the late 1960s, the Department of the Treasury became concerned by the lost revenue linked to tax write-offs from accelerated depreciation and began what Hanchett calls "systematic annual calculation" of total write-offs in 1967. The totals were enormous: $750 million in 1967, $800 million in 1968, and $850 million in 1969. See Hanchett, "U.S. Tax Policy," 1103.

61 Parts of this section originally were published in slightly different form as Christopher W. Wells, "Fueling the Boom: Gasoline Taxes, Invisibility, and the Growth of the American Highway Infrastructure, 1919–1956," *Journal of American History* 99 (June 2012): 72–81. Reprinted by permission of the author and publisher.

62 Patterson, *Grand Expectations*, 64; U.S. Bureau of the Census, *Historical Statistics of the United States, Colonial Times to 1957* (Washington, D.C.: Government Printing Office, 1960), Series Q 265–279 State Highway Finances: 1890 to 1957, p. 459.

63 Seely, *Building the American Highway System*, 193–95; FHWA, *America's Highways*, 160–61. Seely notes that the increase of eighty-seven billion vehicle miles traveled between 1947 and 1950 equaled the national total of vehicle miles traveled in 1923. Seely, *Building the American Highway System*, 193.

64 Seely, *Building the American Highway System*, 201–2.

65 National Interregional Highway Committee, *Interregional Highways: Report and Recommendations of the National Interregional Highway Committee* (Washington, D.C.: Government Printing Office, 1944), iii.

66 Ibid., 55. For comparison purposes, the section of technical recommendations for route selection strategies ran for seventeen pages, including four figures, two tables, and four photographs (56–70), while the subheading "Relation to Urban Planning" received just over one page (70–71). Nowhere did the report mention coordination with mass transit planning. On the commission and its report, see also Seely, *Building the American Highway System*, 177–82; and M. H. Rose, *Interstate*, 19–21.

67 Seely, *Building the American Highway System*, 187–91; M. H. Rose, *Interstate*, 23–28; FHWA, *America's Highways*, 152–53.

68 Federal Works Agency, *National System of Interstate Highways: Selected by a Joint Action of the Several State Highway Departments as Modified and Approved by the*

Administrator, Federal Works Agency August 2, 1947 (Washington, D.C.: Government Printing Office, 1947).

69   For a typical case, see Alan A. Altshuler, *The City Planning Process: A Political Analysis* (Ithaca, N.Y.: Cornell University Press, 1965), 17–83.

70   FHWA, *America's Highways*, 156–57, 279–80; Altshuler, *City Planning Process*, 26. On attempts by city planners to tie expressways to bigger redevelopment goals, see M. H. Rose, *Interstate*, 55–67.

71   For an account emphasizing the role of funding structures as they intersected with the traffic-service priorities of state highway departments, see Jeffrey R. Brown, Eric A. Morris, and Brian D. Taylor, "Planning for Cars in Cities: Planners, Engineers, and Freeways in the Twentieth Century," *Journal of the American Planning Association* 75 (Spring 2009): 161–77.

72   David Saint Clair, *The Motorization of American Cities* (New York: Praeger, 1986); Stephen Goddard, *Getting There: The Epic Struggle between Road and Rail in the American Century* (New York: Basic Books, 1994), 120–37; Scott Bottles, *Los Angeles and the Automobile: The Making of the Modern City* (Berkeley: University of California Press, 1987); Bradford Snell, *American Ground Transport: A Proposal for Restructuring the Automobile, Truck, Bus, and Rail Industries* (Washington, D.C.: Government Printing Office, 1974); Glenn Yago, *The Decline of Transit: Urban Transportation in German and U.S. Cities, 1900–1970* (New York: Cambridge University Press, 1984), 58–69; Robert C. Post, *Urban Mass Transit: The Life Story of a Technology* (Westport, Conn.: Greenwood Press, 2007), esp. 149–56; Jim Klein and Martha Olson, *Taken for a Ride* (Harriman, NY: New Day Films, 2008), DVD; Edwin Black, *Internal Combustion: How Corporations and Governments Addicted the World to Oil and Derailed the Alternatives* (New York: St. Martin's Press, 2006); Sy Adler, "The Transformation of the Pacific Electric Railway: Bradford Snell, Roger Rabbit, and the Politics of Transportation in Los Angeles," *Urban Affairs Quarterly* 27 (Sept. 1991): 120–37; Cliff Slater, "General Motors and the Demise of Streetcars," *Transportation Quarterly* 51 (Summer 1997): 45–66; Martha Bianco, "The Decline of Transit: A Corporate Conspiracy or Failure of Public Policy? The Case of Portland, Oregon," *Journal of Policy History* 9, 4 (1997): 450–74.

73   Saint Clair, *Motorization of American Cities*, 8. Mark Foster has argued that in the face of evidence of long-term decline before the formation of National City Lines, the General Motors–led conspiracy should be deemed "largely irrelevant." See Foster, *From Streetcar to Superhighway: American City Planners and Urban Transportation, 1900–1940* (Philadelphia: Temple University Press, 1981), 219n41.

74   Zachary Schrag, "'The Bus Is Young and Honest': Transportation Politics, Technical Choice, and the Motorization of Manhattan Surface Transit, 1919–1936," *Technology and Culture* 41 (Jan. 2000): 51–79; R. C. Post, *Urban Mass Transit*, 156.

75   Saint Clair, *Motorization of American Cities*, 8.

76   FHWA, *America's Highways*, 163.

77 Ibid., 165–70; Seely, *Building the American Highway System*, 204–5.

78 Seely, *Building the American Highway System*, 206–8. The Public Roads Administration (PRA) resumed its former name, the Bureau of Public Roads (BPR), in 1949, before ultimately being renamed the Federal Highway Administration (FHWA) in 1967.

79 Of the many notable works covering the subject, see, for example, FHWA, *America's Highways*, 171–74; M. H. Rose, *Interstate*, esp. 69–94; Seely, *Building the American Highway System*, 213–18; Tom Lewis, *Divided Highways: Building the Interstate Highways, Transforming American Life* (New York: Penguin Books, 1997), 95–123; Saint Clair, *Motorization of American Cities*, 136–70; Helen Leavitt, *Superhighway—Superhoax* (Garden City, N.Y.: Doubleday, 1970), 20–51; Richard O. Davies, *The Age of Asphalt: The Automobile, the Freeway, and the Condition of Metropolitan America* (Philadelphia: J. B. Lippincott, 1975), 16–27; and Rae, *Road and the Car*, 187–94.

80 On the designation of additional urban mileage, see Bureau of Public Roads, *General Location of National System of Interstate Highways, Including All Additional Routes at Urban Areas Designated in September, 1955* (Washington, D.C.: Government Printing Office, 1955). This document, also known as the *Yellow Book*, played a key role in swinging congressional approval of the legislation.

81 FHWA, *America's Highways*, 173.

82 On the politics, see Seely, *Building the American Highway System*, 214–17, 222–23; and M. H. Rose, *Interstate*, 85–117. As construction proceeded, costs swelled and deadlines moved back. According to the final official estimate in 1991, total costs amounted to $128.9 billion, of which the federal government paid $114.3 billion. See FHWA, "Interstate FAQ," n.d., www.fhwa.dot.gov/interstate/faq.htm#question6 (accessed 30 May 2011). On the difficult politics of construction, see Mark H. Rose and Bruce E. Seely, "Getting the Interstate System Built: Road Engineers and the Implementation of Public Policy, 1955–1985," *Journal of Policy History* 2, 1 (1990): 23–55. On later freeway "revolts," see especially Raymond A. Mohl, "Stop the Road: Freeway Revolts in American Cities," *Journal of Urban History* 30 (July 2004): 674–75; and Brian Ladd, *Autophobia: Love and Hate in the Automotive Age* (Chicago: University of Chicago Press, 2008), 97–138. Other sources include Raymond A. Mohl, "The Interstates and the Cities: The U.S. Department of Transportation and the Freeway Revolt, 1966–1973," *Journal of Policy History* 20, 2 (2008): 193–226; Richard O. Baumbach Jr. and William E. Borah, *The Second Battle of New Orleans: A History of the Vieux Carre Riverfront-Expressway Controversy* (Tuscaloosa: University of Alabama Press, 1981); T. Lewis, *Divided Highways*; Patricia Cavanaugh, *Politics and Freeways: Building the Twin Cities Interstate System* (Minneapolis: Center for Transportation Studies, University of Minnesota, and Center for Urban and Regional Affairs, 2006); Raymond A. Mohl, "Urban Expressways and the Racial Restructuring of Postwar American Cities," *Jahrbuch fur Wirtschafts Geschichte* 2 (2001): 89–104; Raymond A. Mohl, *The Interstates and the Cities: Highways, Housing, and the Freeway*

Revolt (Washington, D.C.: Poverty and Race Research Action Council, 2002); Zachary M. Schrag, "The Freeway Fight in Washington, D.C.: The Three Sisters Bridge in Three Administrations," *Journal of Urban History* 30 (July 2004): 648–73; and William Issel, "'Land Values, Human Values, and the Preservation of the City's Treasured Appearance': Environmentalism, Politics, and the San Francisco Freeway Revolt," *Pacific Historical Review* 68 (Nov. 1999): 611–46.

83 On slum clearance and the blighting effects of freeways, see F. James Davis, "The Effects of a Freeway Displacement on Racial Housing Segregation in a Northern City," *Phylon* 26 (Fall 1965): 209–15; B. Drummond Ayres Jr., "'White Roads through Black Bedrooms,'" *New York Times*, 31 Dec. 1967; Kenneth R. Schneider, *Autokind vs. Mankind* (New York: Norton, 1971); FHWA, *Social and Economic Effects of Highways* (Washington, D.C.: Government Printing Office, 1976); Robert Caro, *The Power Broker: Robert Moses and the Fall of New York* (New York: Vintage Books, 1974), esp. 837–94; Rose and Seely, "Getting the Interstate System Built"; Mohl, "Racial Restructuring of Postwar American Cities"; Mohl, "The Interstates and the Cities" (2002); T. Lewis, *Divided Highways*; and Joseph F. C. DiMento, "Stent (or Dagger?) in the Heart of Town: Urban Freeways in Syracuse, 1944–1967," *Journal of Planning History* 8 (May 2009): 133–61. On accelerating trends of declining public transit usage and the residential shift to the suburbs, see Edgar M. Hoover, "Motor Metropolis: Some Observations on Urban Transportation in America," *Journal of Industrial Economics* 13, 3 (June 1965): 179.

84 Joel Garreau, *Edge City: Life on the New Frontier* (New York: Doubleday, 1991). Dolores Hayden has argued that the term "edge nodes" would be more accurate. Hayden, *Building Suburbia*, 154–80.

85 Shane Hamilton, *Trucking Country: The Road to America's Wal-Mart Economy* (Princeton, N.J.: Princeton University Press, 2008), esp. 79–231. For a broader policy history of transportation regulations in the twentieth-century United States, see Mark H. Rose, Bruce Edsall Seely, and Paul F. Barrett, *The Best Transportation System in the World: Railroads, Trucks, Airlines, and American Public Policy in the Twentieth Century* (Columbus: Ohio State University Press, 2006).

86 For a compelling analysis of the central role of taxation in shaping postwar American liberalism, including the ways that liberalism relied upon dedicated funding streams to achieve its economic and social goals, see Julian E. Zelizer, *Taxing America: Wilbur D. Mills, Congress, and the State, 1945–1975* (New York: Cambridge University Press, 1998).

87 Masotti and Hadden, *Urbanization of the Suburbs*. For an interpretation stressing the dispersal of industry during World War II as a driver of postwar suburban housing, see Greg Hise, "Home Building and Industrial Decentralization in Los Angeles: The Roots of the Postwar Urban Region," *Journal of Urban History* 19 (Feb. 1993): 95–125.

88 Jackson, *Crabgrass Frontier*, 267–69.

89 Fogelson, *Downtown*, 194. For an early study of industrial suburbs, see Graham

Romeyn Taylor, *Satellite Cities: A Study of Industrial Suburbs* (New York: D. Appleton and Company, 1915).

90 Leon Moses and Harold F. Williamson, "The Location of Economic Activity in Cities," *American Economic Review 57* (May 1967): 211–22.

91 Clawson, *Suburban Land Conversion*, 40. On the suburbanization of business and industry, see also Rae, *Road and the Car*, 249–74; and Richard Walker and Robert Lewis, "Beyond the Crabgrass Frontier: Industry and the Spread of North American Cities, 1850–1950," *Journal of Historical Geography* 27, 1 (2001): 3–19.

92 Brian J. L. Berry and Yehoshua S. Cohen, "Decentralization of Commerce and Industry: The Restructuring of Metropolitan America," in *Urbanization of the Suburbs*, ed. Masotti and Hadden, 439.

93 Clawson, *Suburban Land Conversion*, 233.

94 Jackson, *Crabgrass Frontier*, 267.

95 AMA, *Facts and Figures* (1961), 3.

96 FHWA, *Highway Statistics: Summary to 1985* (Washington: Government Printing Office, 1987), 25.

97 AMA, *Facts and Figures* (1961), 33.

98 FHWA, *Highway Statistics to 1985*, 229–30.

99 On this point, see especially Owen Gutfreund, *Twentieth-Century Sprawl: How Highways Transformed America* (New York: Oxford University Press, 2004).

100 On these points, see especially Cotten Seiler, *Republic of Drivers: A Cultural History of Automobility in America* (Chicago: University of Chicago Press, 2008); John A. Jakle and Keith A. Sculle, *Motoring: The Highway Experience in America* (Athens: University of Georgia Press, 2008); and Tom McCarthy, *Auto Mania: Cars, Consumers, and the Environment* (New Haven, Conn.: Yale University Press, 2007).

101 The first reports in this series are John B. Lansing and Eva Mueller with Nancy Barth, *Residential Location and Urban Mobility* (Ann Arbor: Survey Research Center, Institute for Social Research, University of Michigan, 1964); John B. Lansing and Nancy Barth, *Residential Location and Urban Mobility: A Multivariate Analysis* (Ann Arbor: Survey Research Center, Institute for Social Research, University of Michigan, 1964); and John B. Lansing, *Residential Location and Urban Mobility: The Second Wave of Interviews* (Ann Arbor: Survey Research Center, Institute for Social Research, University of Michigan, 1966).

102 John B. Lansing and Gary Hendricks, *Automobile Ownership and Residential Density* (Ann Arbor: Survey Research Center, Institute for Social Research, University of Michigan, 1967). On the research and data collection methods, see pp. iii–v. On the relationship between this report and other early research focusing on the relationships between travel behavior and urban form, see especially Levine, *Zoned Out*, 24–29.

103 Lansing and Hendricks, *Automobile Ownership and Residential Density*, 4.

104 Ibid., 10.

105 Ibid., 14.

106 Ibid., 18 (quotation), 14–20.

107 Since at least 1985, data has been collected on household-level vehicle use, but in the two decades after World War II this was not the case, making *Automobile Ownership and Residential Density* one of the pioneering attempts to do so. The data since 1988 supports John Lansing and Gary Hendricks's conclusion that household car use correlates strongly with income, but later studies have not followed their lead in systematically analyzing the relationship between car use and residential density. See U.S. Energy Information Administration, *Household Vehicles Energy Consumption 1994*, www.eia.doe.gov/emeu/rtecs/chapter3.html (accessed Feb. 24, 2010).

108 The authors caution that their conclusions "should be regarded as exploratory," in part due to their relatively small sample size and in part because it was not yet common practice to conduct sample surveys of national populations on this subject, which made it impossible to verify their results against other studies. Precisely because their approach was so rare at this early date, however, their results provide the best statistical window that we have today on the relationship between residential density and vehicle miles traveled during the first two postwar decades, making their results extraordinarily important despite their exploratory nature. See Lansing and Hendricks, *Automobile Ownership and Residential Density*, 22.

109 Ibid., 23–30.

110 Ibid., 26–35.

111 For three examples of this explanation from three different points in time, see President's Research Committee on Social Trends, *Recent Social Trends in the United States: Report of the President's Research Committee on Social Trends* (New York: McGraw-Hill, 1933), 464–65; John B. Rae, *The American Automobile: A Brief History* (Chicago: University of Chicago Press, 1965), 219–21; and Patterson, *Grand Expectations*, 71.

112 On this point, see especially Ladd, *Autophobia*. On the connections between protests against the postwar profusion of suburban tract housing and the rise of the modern environmental movement, see Rome, *Bulldozer in the Countryside*.

EPILOGUE: REACHING FOR THE CAR KEYS

1 Jane Jacobs, *The Death and Life of Great American Cities* (1961; New York: Random House Modern Library, 1993), 457.

2 Lewis Mumford, "The Sky Line: Mother Jacobs' Home Remedies," *New Yorker* 38 (1 Dec. 1962): 150–52.

3 Jacobs, *Death and Life*, 5 (quotation); Jane Jacobs, "Downtown Is for People," *Fortune* 57 (Apr. 1958): 113–40ff.

4 Jacobs, *Death and Life*, 10.

5 Ibid., 455 (first quotation), 482 (second quotation), 457 (final quotation).

6   Ibid., 482.

7   For an in-depth account, see Anthony Flint, *Wrestling with Moses: How Jane Jacobs Took on New York's Master Builder and Transformed the American City* (New York: Random House, 2009). That Jacobs engaged in another difficult-yet-successful battle against the Spadina Expressway in Toronto, where she moved in 1968, attested both to her skill and her doggedness, but both victories were essentially local and did little to change the prevailing practices dominating either city planning or transportation planning. For a recent revisionist account that downgrades Jacobs's role in the anti-Spadina protests from "leading the crusade against Spadina" to "playing a prominent part in the debate," see Richard White, "Jane Jacobs and Toronto, 1968–1978," *Journal of Planning History* 10, 2 (2011): 114–38.

8   Jacobs, *Death and Life*, xii.

9   Ibid., xii.

10   Ibid., xiii–xiv.

11   Ibid., xiv.

12   Although Jacobs's ideas about how to foster the "attrition of cars by cities" gained little following at the time among planners in the United States, they have been very influential more recently among New Urbanists and those developing "traffic-calming" techniques. For a recent overview by a leading "public-space" architect, see Jan Gehl, *Cities for People* (Washington, D.C.: Island Press, 2010).

13   For a trenchant analysis of the idea that "urban sprawl is primarily a product of free markets in land development," see Jonathan Levine, *Zoned Out: Regulation, Markets, and Choices in Transportation and Metropolitan Land Use* (Washington, D.C.: Resources for the Future, 2006). Kenneth T. Jackson, the distinguished historian of American suburbanization, likens the typical car-owning American "to the student away at college. The tuition fee includes nineteen meals per week. The student is free to eat off campus, but they have already paid for cafeteria fare. Essentially, Americans do the same thing. Having already paid for roads through property, sales, or income taxes, they would be foolish not to use them. The only cost remaining is the cost of gasoline, which is negligible." Our tendency, Jackson suggests, is to see those things that are already paid for (whether via government subsidies or required room-and-board charges) as "free." He might also have added that we tend to see competing options for which we must pay extra (whether a meal in a restaurant, or a fare for a ride) as "costly." Like a prepaid college meal plan, government subsidies make something that is actually quite costly appear to be cheap, even as they make other, competing options appear relatively expensive. See Jackson, "Transnational Borderlands: Metropolitan Growth in the United States, Germany, and Japan Since World War II," *German Historical Institute Bulletin* 38 (Spring 2006): 26.

14   Jane Holtz Kay, *Asphalt Nation: How the Automobile Took Over America and How We Can Take it Back* (New York: Crown Publishers, 1997), 82.

15   Donald C. Shoup, *The High Cost of Free Parking* (Chicago: Planners Press, 2005). For a significantly less detailed and more polemical account that also illustrates the difficulties of trying to account for Car Country's externalities, see Stanley I. Hart and Alvin L. Spivak, *The Elephant in the Bedroom: Automobile Dependence and Denial, Impacts on the Economy and Environment* (Pasadena, Calif.: New Paradigm, 1993).

16   U.S. Energy Information Administration, "Annual U.S. Product Supplied of Finished Motor Gasoline," www.eia.gov/dnav/pet/hist/LeafHandler.ashx ?n=PET&s=MGFUPUS1&f=A (accessed 27 June 2011).

SELECTED BIBLIOGRAPHY

ARCHIVAL COLLECTIONS

Benson Ford Research Center, The Henry Ford, Dearborn, Michigan
Bentley Historical Library, University of Michigan, Ann Arbor
Detroit Public Library Automotive History Collection, Detroit, Michigan
Minnesota Historical Society, St. Paul
National Archives and Record Administration, College Park, Maryland
State Historical Society of Wisconsin, Madison

SELECTED SOURCES

Abernathy, William J. *The Productivity Dilemma: Roadblock to Innovation in the Automobile Industry*. Baltimore: Johns Hopkins University Press, 1978.

Addams, Jane. *The Spirit of Youth and the City Streets*. New York: Macmillan Co., 1909.

Adler, Sy. "The Transformation of the Pacific Electric Railway: Bradford Snell, Roger Rabbit, and the Politics of Transportation in Los Angeles." *Urban Affairs Quarterly* 27 (Sept. 1991): 120–37.

Advisory Committee on Planning and Zoning. *The Preparation of Zoning Ordinances: A Guide for Municipal Officials and Others in the Arrangement of Provisions in Zoning Regulations*. Washington, D.C.: Government Printing Office, 1931.

[Agee, James]. "The Great American Roadside." *Fortune* 10 (Sept. 1934): 53–63, 172, 174, 177.

Agee, James, and Walker Evans. *Now Let Us Now Praise Famous Men*. Boston: Houghton Mifflin, 1941.

Albert Russel Erskine Bureau. *A Report on the Street Traffic Control Problem of the City of Boston*. Boston: City of Boston Printing Department, 1928.

———. *A Traffic Control Plan for Kansas City*. Kansas City, Mo.: Chas. E Brown Printing Co., 1930.

———. *Traffic Survey by Public Service Engineer under Direction of Joint Committee on Ordinances with Report and Recommendations*. Providence, R.I.: Oxford Press, 1928.

Allenby, Braden. "Industrial Ecology." In *Inventing for the Environment*, edited by Arthur Molella and Joyce Bedi, 339–72. Cambridge, Mass.: MIT Press, 2003.

Altshuler, Alan A. *The City Planning Process: A Political Analysis*. Ithaca, N.Y.: Cornell University Press, 1965.

American Association for Highway Improvement. *Papers, Addresses, and Resolutions before the American Road Congress in Richmond, Va., Nov. 1911*. Baltimore: Waverly Press, 1912.

American Association of General Passenger and Ticket Agents. *Travelers' Official Railway Guide for the United States, Canada, and Mexico* 32 (Mar. 1900).

American Automobile Association. *Highways Green Book: Third Annual Edition.* Washington, D.C.: American Automobile Association, 1922.

American Bar Association. *Legal History of Conservation of Oil and Gas.* Chicago: American Bar Association, Section of Mineral Law, 1938.

American Petroleum Institute. *Petroleum Facts and Figures.* New York: American Petroleum Institute, 1941.

American Public Works Association. *History of Public Works in the United States, 1776–1976.* Chicago: American Public Works Association, 1976.

Applebaum, William. "Guidelines for a Store-Location Strategy Study." *Journal of Marketing* 30 (Oct. 1966): 42–45.

Applebaum, William, and Saul B. Cohen. "The Dynamics of Store Trading Areas and Market Equilibrium." *Annals of the Association of American Geographers* 51 (Mar. 1961): 73–101.

Arnheim, W. W. "Express Routes Suggested to End Congestion." *Nation's Traffic* 3 (Apr. 1929): 38–40.

Arnold, Horace Lucien, and Fay Leone Faurote. *Ford Methods and the Ford Shops.* New York: Arno Press, 1972. First published 1915 by The Engineering Magazine Co.

Association of Licensed Automobile Manufacturers. *Handbook of Gasoline Automobiles, 1904–1906.* New York: Dover Publications, 1969.

Automobile Manufacturers Association. *Automobile Facts and Figures.* Detroit: Automobile Manufacturers Association, 1930–1941, 1951, 1961, 1971.

Ayres, B. Drummond, Jr. "'White Roads through Black Bedrooms.'" *New York Times,* 31 Dec. 1967.

Baker, Donald M. "Financing Express Highways in Metropolitan Areas." *American City* 61 (Oct. 1946): 93–94.

Baldwin, Peter C. *Domesticating the Street: The Reform of Public Space in Hartford, 1850–1930.* Columbus: Ohio State University Press, 1999.

Barber, A. B. "Making Our Traffic Laws Uniform." In *Planning for City Traffic,* edited by Austin F. MacDonald, 128–33. Philadelphia: American Academy of Political and Social Science, 1927.

Barclay, Hartley W. *Ford Production Methods.* New York: Harper and Brothers, 1936.

Barnett, Gabrielle. "Drive-By Viewing: Visual Consciousness and Forest Preservation in the Automobile Age." *Technology and Culture* 45 (Jan. 2004): 30–54.

Barnett, Joseph. "Safe Side Friction Factors and Superelevation Design." *Proceedings of the Highway Research Board, 16th Annual Meeting* 16 (1936): 69–80.

Barrett, Paul. *The Automobile and Urban Transit: The Formation of Public Policy in Chicago, 1900–1930.* Philadelphia: Temple University Press, 1983.

Barron, Hal S. *Mixed Harvest: The Second Great Transformation in the Rural North, 1870–1930.* Chapel Hill: University of North Carolina Press, 1997.

Barth, Gunther. *City People: The Rise of the Modern City Culture in Nineteenth-Century America.* New York: Oxford University Press, 1980.

Bartholomew, Harland. "Reduction of Street Traffic Congestion by Proper Street Design—How St. Louis Is Meeting Its Problem." In *The Automobile: Its Province and Its Problems*, edited by Clyde L. King, 244–46. Philadelphia: American Academy of Political and Social Science, 1924.

———. *Urban Land Uses: Amounts of Land Used and Needed for Various Purposes by Typical American Cities; An Aid to Scientific Zoning Practice*. Cambridge, Mass.: Harvard University Press, 1932.

Basmajian, Carlton. "Projecting Sprawl? The Atlanta Regional Commission and the 1975 Regional Development Plan of Metropolitan Atlanta." *Journal of Planning History* 9, 2 (2010): 95–121.

Bassett, Edward M. "Zoning and Freeways." *City Planning* 9 (July 1933): 138–39.

Baumbach, Richard O., Jr., and William E. Borah. *The Second Battle of New Orleans: A History of the Vieux Carre Riverfront-Expressway Controversy*. Tuscaloosa: University of Alabama Press, 1981.

Baxandall, Rosalyn, and Elizabeth Ewen. *Picture Windows: How the Suburbs Happened*. New York: Basic Books, 2000.

Belasco, Warren James. *Americans on the Road: From Autocamp to Motel*. Cambridge, Mass.: MIT Press, 1979.

Benesch, Alfred A. "Regulating Street Traffic in Cleveland." *American City* 13 (Sept. 1915): 182–84.

Bennett, Edward H., and William E. Parsons. *Plan of St. Paul*. St. Paul: City Planning Board, 1922.

Bennett, Jesse Merl. *Roadsides: The Front Yard of a Nation*. Boston: Stratford, 1936.

Berger, Michael. *The Devil Wagon in God's Country: The Automobile and Social Change in Rural America, 1893–1929*. Hamden, Conn.: Archon Books, 1979.

Bernick, Michael, and Robert Cervero. *Transit Villages in the 21st Century*. New York: McGraw-Hill, 1997.

Berry, Brian J. L., and Yehoshua S. Cohen. "Decentralization of Commerce and Industry: The Restructuring of Metropolitan America." In *Urbanization of the Suburbs*, edited by Louis Masotti and Jeffrey K. Hadden, 51–78. Beverly Hills: Sage Publications, 1973.

Beveridge, Charles E., and Carolyn F. Hoffman, eds. *The Papers of Frederick Law Olmsted, Supplementary Series*. Vol. 1, *Writings on Public Parks, Parkways, and Park Systems*. Baltimore: Johns Hopkins University Press, 1997.

Bianco, Martha. "The Decline of Transit: A Corporate Conspiracy or Failure of Public Policy? The Case of Portland, Oregon." *Journal of Policy History* 9, 4 (1997): 450–74.

Bibbins, J. Rowland. "Traffic Transportation Planning and Metropolitan Development—The Need of an Adequate Program." In *The Automobile: Its Province and Its Problems*, edited by Clyde L. King, 205–14. Philadelphia: American Academy of Political and Social Science, 1924.

Biggs, Lindy. *The Rational Factory: Architecture, Technology, and Work in America's Age of Mass Production*. Baltimore: Johns Hopkins University Press, 1996.

Bijker, Wiebe E. *Of Bicycles, Bakelites, and Bulbs: Toward a Theory of Sociotechnical Change*. Cambridge, Mass.: MIT Press, 1995.

Bijker, Wiebe E., Thomas P. Hughes, and Trevor Pinch, eds. *The Social Construction of Technological Systems*. Cambridge, Mass.: MIT Press, 1987.

Black, Brian. *Petrolia: The Landscape of America's First Oil Boom*. Baltimore: Johns Hopkins University Press, 2000.

Black, Russell Van Nest. "The Spectacular in City Building." In *Planning for City Traffic*, edited by Austin F. MacDonald, 50–56. Philadelphia: American Academy of Political and Social Science, 1927.

Blanke, David. *Hell on Wheels: The Promise and Peril of America's Car Culture, 1900–1940*. Lawrence: University Press of Kansas, 2007.

———. *Sowing the American Dream: How Consumer Culture Took Root in the Rural Midwest*. Athens: Ohio University Press, 2000.

Boggess, Trent E. "The Customer Can Have Any Color He Wants—So Long As It's Black: A Study of the Materials and Methods Used to Paint Model T Fords during the Black Era." *Vintage Ford* 32, 6 (1997): 26–41.

Boston Chamber of Commerce. *Street Traffic in the City of Boston*. Boston: Boston Chamber of Commerce, 1914.

Bottles, Scott L. *Los Angeles and the Automobile: The Making of the Modern City*. Berkeley: University of California Press, 1991.

Boyce, Earnest. "A Study of Oil-Well Brine Disposal." *Transactions of the Kansas Academy of Science* 38 (28–30 Mar. 1935): 131–37.

Boyer, M. Christine. *Dreaming the Rational City: The Myth of American City Planning*. Cambridge, Mass.: MIT Press, 1983.

Boyer, Paul. *Urban Masses and Moral Order in America, 1820–1920*. Cambridge, Mass.: Harvard University Press, 1978.

Boylan, Robert. *An Approach to Determining Parking Demand*. Chicago: American Society of Planning Officials, 1971.

Brilliant, Ashleigh. *The Great Car Craze: How Southern California Collided with the Automobile in the 1920s*. Santa Barbara: Woodbridge Press, 1989.

Brinkley, Douglas. *Wheels for the World: Henry Ford, His Company, and a Century of Progress*. New York: Viking, 2003.

Brown, Jeffrey R., Eric A. Morris, and Brian D. Taylor. "Planning for Cars in Cities: Planners, Engineers, and Freeways in the Twentieth Century." *Journal of the American Planning Association* 75 (Spring 2009): 161–77.

Brownell, Blaine A. "The Commercial-Civic Elite and City Planning in Atlanta, Memphis, and New Orleans in the 1920s." *Journal of Southern History* 41 (Aug. 1975): 339–68.

———. "A Symbol of Modernity: Attitudes Toward the Automobile in Southern Cities in the 1920s." *American Quarterly* 24 (Mar. 1972): 20–44.

Bruce, A. G. "The Effects of Increased Speed of Vehicles on the Design of Highways." *Public Roads* 10 (Mar. 1929): 11–20.

Bruce, A. G., and R. D. Brown. "The Trend of Highway Design." *Public Roads* 8

(1927): 7–14, 20.

Brunner, Edmund de S., and J. H. Kolb. *Rural Social Trends*. New York: McGraw-Hill, 1933.

Brunner, Edmund de S., and Irving Lorge. *Rural Trends in Depression Years: A Survey of Village-Centered Agricultural Communities, 1930–1936*. New York: Columbia University Press, 1937.

Bryan, Ford R. *Beyond the Model T: The Other Ventures of Henry Ford*. Rev. ed. Detroit: Wayne State University Press, 1997.

Burch, Philip H., Jr. *Highway Revenue and Expenditure Policy in the United States*. New Brunswick, N.J.: Rutgers University Press, 1962.

Burchell, Robert W., George Lowenstein, William R. Dolphin, Catherine C. Galley, Anthony Downs, Samuel Seskin, Katherine Gray Still, and Terry Moore. *Costs of Sprawl: 2000*. Washington, D.C.: Transportation Research Board, 2002.

Burchell, Robert W., Naveed A. Shad, David Listokin, Hilary Phillips, Anthony Downs, Samuel Seskin, Judy S. Davis, Terry Moore, David Helton, and Michelle Gall. *Costs of Sprawl Revisited*. Washington, D.C.: Transportation Research Board, 1998.

Bureau of Public Roads. *General Location of National System of Interstate Highways, Including All Additional Routes at Urban Areas Designated in September, 1955*. Washington, D.C.: Government Printing Office, 1955.

———. *Highway Statistics: Summary to 1945*. Washington, D.C.: Government Printing Office, 1947.

———. *Report of a Study of Highway Traffic and the Highway System of Cook County, Illinois*. Chicago, 1925.

———. *Report of a Survey of Transportation on the State Highways of Pennsylvania*. 1928.

———. *Toll Roads and Free Roads*. Washington, D.C.: Government Printing Office, 1939.

Burgess, Patricia. "Of Swimming Pools and 'Slums': Zoning and Residential Development in Post–World War II Columbus, Ohio." In *Inventing for the Environment*, edited by Arthur Molella and Joyce Bedi, 213–39. Cambridge, Mass.: MIT Press, 2003.

Burnham, Daniel H., and Edward H. Bennett. *Plan of Chicago*. Edited by Charles Moore. 1908. New York: Princeton Architectural Press, 1993.

Burnham, John C. "The Gasoline Tax and the Automobile Revolution." *Mississippi Valley Historical Review* 48 (Dec. 1961): 435–59.

Burrows, Edwin G., and Mike Wallace. *Gotham: A History of New York City to 1898*. New York: Oxford University Press, 1999.

Burton, Hal. *The City Fights Back: A Nationwide Survey of What Cities Are Doing to Keep Pace with Traffic, Zoning, Shifting Population, Smoke, Smog and Other Problems*. London: Thames and Hudson, 1954.

Calder, Lendol. *Financing the American Dream: A Cultural History of Consumer Credit*. Princeton, N.J.: Princeton University Press, 1999.

Calthorpe, Peter. *The Next American Metropolis: Ecology, Community, and the American Dream*. New York: Princeton Architectural Press, 1993.

Campbell, Ballard. "The Good Roads Movement in Wisconsin, 1890–1911." *Wisconsin Magazine of History* 49 (Summer 1966): 273–93.

Caro, Robert A. *The Power Broker: Robert Moses and the Fall of New York.* New York: Vintage Books, 1974.

Carr, Ethan. *Wilderness by Design: Landscape Architecture and the National Park Service.* Lincoln: University of Nebraska Press, 1998.

Casey, Robert. *The Model T: A Centennial History.* Baltimore: Johns Hopkins University Press, 2008.

Cavanaugh, Patricia. *Politics and Freeways: Building the Twin Cities Interstate System.* Minneapolis: Center for Transportation Studies, University of Minnesota, and Center for Urban and Regional Affairs, 2006.

Chambers, William T. "Kilgore, Texas: An Oil Boom Town." *Economic Geography* 9 (Jan. 1933): 72–84.

Chandler, Alfred D., ed. *Giant Enterprise: Ford, General Motors, and the Automobile Industry.* New York: Harcourt, Brace & World, 1964.

———. *The Visible Hand: The Managerial Revolution in American Business.* Cambridge, Mass.: Harvard University Press, 1977.

Chatburn, George R. *Highways and Highway Transportation.* New York: Thomas Y. Crowell Co., 1923.

Checkoway, Barry. "Large Builders, Federal Housing Programs, and Postwar Suburbanization." *International Journal of Urban and Regional Research* 4 (Mar. 1980): 21–45.

Chernow, Ron. *Titan: The Life of John D. Rockefeller, Sr.* New York: Random House, 1998.

Clark, Evans. "How Super-Trust Alters Industry: Vertical and Horizontal Business Combines Illustrate Tendency to Control Output from Raw Material to Consumer." *New York Times,* 14 Feb. 1926.

———. "The Super-Trust Arrives in America: The Far-Spreading Vertical Combination Begins a New Economic Order; It Starts with Raw Material and Knits Processes of Manufacture and Distribution through Railroads, Mills and Sales Agencies." *New York Times,* 13 Dec. 1925.

Clarsen, Georgine. *Eat My Dust: Early Women Motorists.* Baltimore: Johns Hopkins University Press, 2008.

Clawson, Marion. *Suburban Land Conversion in the United States: An Economic and Governmental Process.* Baltimore: Johns Hopkins University Press, 1971.

Clymer, Floyd. *Henry's Wonderful Model T, 1908–1927.* New York: McGraw-Hill, 1955.

Coffey, Frank, and Joseph Layden. *America on Wheels: The First 100 Years, 1896–1996.* Los Angeles: General Publishing Group, 1996.

Cohen, Lizabeth. *A Consumers' Republic: The Politics of Mass Consumption in Postwar America.* New York: Knopf, 2003.

———. "From Town Center to Shopping Center: The Reconfiguration of Community Marketplaces in Postwar America." *American Historical Review* 101 (Oct. 1996): 1050–81.

Cohen, Yehoshua. *Diffusion of an Innovation in an Urban System: The Spread of Planned Regional Shopping Centers in the United States, 1949–1968.* Chicago: Department of Geography, University of Chicago, 1972.

Conkin, Paul K. *A Revolution Down on the Farm: The Transformation of American Agriculture since 1929.* Lexington: University of Kentucky Press, 2008.

Crawford, Finla Goff. *Motor Fuel Taxation in the United States.* Syracuse, N.Y.: F. G. Crawford, 1939.

Cray, Ed. *Chrome Colossus: General Motors and Its Times.* New York: McGraw-Hill, 1980.

Cronon, William. "Kennecott Journey." In *Under an Open Sky: Rethinking America's Western Past,* edited by William Cronon, George A. Miles, and Jay Gitlin, 28–51. New York: W. W. Norton, 1992.

———. *Nature's Metropolis: Chicago and the Great West.* New York: W. W. Norton, 1991.

———. "The Trouble with Wilderness; or, Getting Back to the Wrong Nature." In *Uncommon Ground: Rethinking the Human Place in Nature,* edited by William Cronon, 69–90. New York: W. W. Norton, 1996.

Crosby, Alfred. *Children of the Sun: A History of Humanity's Unappeasable Appetite for Energy.* New York: W. W. Norton, 2006.

Curtiss, W. M. *Use and Value of Highways in Rural New York.* Agricultural Experiment Station Bulletin No. 656. Ithaca, N.Y.: Cornell University Agricultural Experiment Station, 1936.

Cutler, Phoebe. *The Public Landscape of the New Deal.* New Haven, Conn.: Yale University Press, 1985.

Dakelman, Mitchell E., and Neal A. Schorr, *The Pennsylvania Turnpike.* Portsmouth, N.H.: Arcadia Publishing, 2004.

Davies, Pete. *American Road: The Story of an Epic Transcontinental Journey at the Dawn of the Motor Age.* New York: Henry Holt and Co., 2002.

Davies, Richard O. *The Age of Asphalt: The Automobile, the Freeway, and the Condition of Metropolitan America.* Philadelphia: J. B. Lippincott, 1975.

Davis, Charles Henry. *Arguments for and Against National Highways versus Federal Aid.* Washington, D.C.: National Highways Association, 1914.

———. *How National Highways are Necessary to the Automobile.* Washington, D.C.: National Highways Association, 1914.

———. *National Highways to Bring About Good Roads Everywhere.* Washington, D.C.: National Highways Association, 1913.

Davis, F. James. "The Effects of a Freeway Displacement on Racial Housing Segregation in a Northern City." *Phylon* 26 (Fall 1965): 209–15.

Davis, Harmer E., and Richard M. Zettal. "Highway Administration and Finance." In *Highway Engineering Handbook,* edited by Kenneth B. Woods, 1–54. New York: McGraw-Hill, 1960.

Davis, Timothy. "Inventing Nature in Washington, D.C." In *Inventing for the Environment,* edited by Arthur Molella and Joyce Bedi, 31–81. Cambridge, Mass.: MIT Press, 2003.

————. "Mount Vernon Memorial Highway and the Evolution of the American Parkway." Ph.D. diss., University of Texas at Austin, 1997.

————. "'A Pleasant Illusion of Unspoiled Countryside': The American Parkway and the Problematics of an Institutionalized Vernacular." *Perspectives in Vernacular Architecture* 9 (2003): 228–46.

————. "The Rise and Decline of the American Parkway." In *The World beyond the Windshield*, edited by Christof Mauch and Thomas Zeller, 35–58. Athens: Ohio University Press, 2008.

Dean, Warren. *Brazil and the Struggle for Rubber: A Study in Environmental History.* New York: Cambridge University Press, 1987.

Dearing, Charles L. *American Highway Policy.* Washington, D.C.: Brookings Institution, 1941.

Derrick, Peter. *Tunneling to the Future: The Story of the Great Subway Expansion That Saved New York.* New York: New York University Press, 2001.

Detroit Rapid Transit Commission. *General Plan of Rapid Transit and Surface Line System for the City of Detroit.* Detroit: Rapid Transit Commission, 1923.

————. *Proposed Super-Highway Plan for Greater Detroit.* Detroit: Rapid Transit Commission, 1924.

Deutsch, Tracey. *Building a Housewife's Paradise: Gender, Politics, and American Grocery Stores in the Twentieth Century.* Chapel Hill: University of North Carolina Press, 2010.

Diers, John W., and Aaron Isaacs. *Twin Cities by Trolley: The Streetcar Era in Minneapolis and St. Paul.* Minneapolis: University of Minnesota Press, 2007.

DiMento, Joseph F. C. "Stent (or Dagger?) in the Heart of Town: Urban Freeways in Syracuse, 1944–1967." *Journal of Planning History* 8 (May 2009): 133–61.

Dittmar, Hank, and Gloria Ohland, eds. *The New Transit Town: Best Practices in Transit-Oriented Development.* Washington, D.C.: Island Press, 2004.

Dodge, Martin. *Report of the Office of Public Road Inquiries.* Washington, D.C.: Government Printing Office, 1902–1903.

Dosch, Arno. "The Science of Street Traffic." *World's Work* 27 (Feb. 1914): 398–409.

Douglass, Harlan Paul. *The Suburban Trend.* New York: The Century Co., 1925.

Downer, Jay. "Parkways and Super-Highways: Their Comparative Advantages in Inter-Urban Planning." *Official Proceedings of the Annual Convention of the American Society of Municipal Engineers* 36 (1930): 49–52.

Doyle, Jack. *Taken for a Ride: Detroit's Big Three and the Politics of Pollution.* New York: Four Walls Eight Windows, 2000.

Drake, Douglas C. "Herbert Hoover, Ecologist: The Politics of Oil Pollution Control, 1921–1926." *Mid America: An Historical Review* 55 (July 1973): 207–28.

Duany, Andres, Elizabeth Plater-Zyberk, and Jeff Speck. *Suburban Nation: The Rise of Sprawl and the Decline of the American Dream.* New York: North Point Press, 2001.

Dunn, James A., Jr. *Driving Forces: The Automobile, Its Enemies, and the Politics of Mobility.* Washington, D.C.: Brookings Institution Press, 1998.

————. "The Importance of Being Earmarked: Transport Policy and Highway

Finance in Great Britain and the United States." *Comparative Studies in Society and History* 20 (Jan. 1978): 29–53.

Dyer, Stephanie. "Markets in the Meadows: Department Stores and Shopping Centers in the Decentralization of Philadelphia, 1920–1980." Ph.D. diss., University of Pennsylvania, 2000.

———. "Markets in the Meadows: Department Stores and Shopping Centers in the Decentralization of Philadelphia, 1920–1980." *Enterprise and Society* 3 (Dec. 2002): 606–12.

Eichler, Ned. *The Merchant Builders.* Cambridge, Mass.: MIT Press, 1982.

Eliot, Charles W. "The Influence of the Automobile on the Design of Park Roads." *Landscape Architecture* 13 (Oct. 1922): 27–37.

Ellenberg, George B. "Debating Farm Power: Draft Animals, Tractors, and the United States Department of Agriculture." *Agricultural History* 74 (Spring 2000): 545–68.

Elliott, Frederick H. "New Uniform Rules for Street Traffic." *American City* 14 (Feb. 1916): 124.

Eno, William Phelps. *How Traffic Regulation May Be Improved in Town and Country: A Supplement to Simplification of Highway Traffic.* Fairfield, Conn.: Eno Foundation for Highway Traffic Regulation, 1936.

———. *The Science of Highway Traffic Regulation, 1899–1920.* Washington, D.C.: Brentano's, 1920.

———. *The Story of Highway Traffic Control, 1899–1939.* Saugatuck, Conn.: Eno Foundation for Highway Traffic Control, 1939.

———. *Street Traffic Regulation.* New York: Rider and Driver Publishing Co., 1909.

Eno Foundation for Highway Traffic Control. *Zoning Applied to Parking.* Saugatuck, Conn.: Eno Foundation for Highway Traffic Control, 1947.

Epstein, Ralph C. *The Automobile Industry: Its Economic and Commercial Development.* Chicago: A. W. Shaw Co., 1928.

Estey, J. A. "Financing the Sale of Automobiles." In *The Automobile: Its Province and Its Problems,* edited by Clyde L. King, 44–49. Philadelphia: American Academy of Political and Social Science, 1924.

Everett, Frederic E. "Diversion Dangers and Gasoline Tax Evasions." *American Highways* 11 (Jan. 1932): 1–2.

Fairbank, H. S. "Newly Discovered Facts about Our Highway System." Typescript [1938]. Ohio Department of Transportation Library, Columbus.

———. "State-Wide Highway Planning Surveys." *Civil Engineering* 7 (Mar. 1937): 178–81.

Faragher, John Mack. *Sugar Creek: Life on the Illinois Prairie.* New Haven, Conn.: Yale University Press, 1986.

Federal Aid Good Roads Convention. *Proceedings of the Federal Aid Good Roads Convention: Held at Washington, D.C., Jan. 16 and 17, 1912, Called by the American Automobile Association.* Washington, D.C.: American Automobile Association, 1912.

Federal Highway Administration. *America's Highways, 1776–1976: A History of the Federal-Aid Program*. Washington, D.C.: Government Printing Office, 1976.

———. *Highways Statistics: Summary to 1965*. Washington, D.C.: Government Printing Office, 1967.

———. *Highway Statistics: Summary to 1975*. Washington, D.C.: Government Printing Office, 1977.

———. *Highway Statistics: Summary to 1985*. Washington, D.C.: Government Printing Office, 1987.

———. *Social and Economic Effects of Highways*. Washington, D.C.: Government Printing Office, 1976.

Federal Housing Administration. *Planning Neighborhoods for Small Houses*. Washington, D.C.: Federal Housing Administration, 1936.

———. *Successful Subdivisions: Principles of Planning for Economy and Protection against Neighborhood Blight*. Washington, D.C.: Federal Housing Administration, 1940.

———. *Underwriting Manual: Underwriting and Valuation Procedure under Title II of the National Housing Act*. Washington, D.C.: Government Printing Office, 1938.

Federal Works Agency. *National System of Interstate Highways: Selected by a Joint Action of the Several State Highway Departments as Modified and Approved by the Administrator, Federal Works Agency August 2, 1947*. Washington, D.C.: Government Printing Office, 1947.

Feeny, David, Susan Hanna, and Arthur F. McEvoy. "Questioning the Assumptions of the 'Tragedy of the Commons' Model of Fisheries." *Land Economics* 72 (May 1996): 187–205.

Feigon, Sharon, David Hoyt, and Gloria Ohland. "The Atlanta Case Study: Lindbergh City Center." In *The New Transit Town: Best Practices in Transit-Oriented Development*, edited by Hank Dittmar and Gloria Ohland, 176–92. Washington, D.C.: Island Press, 2004.

Fein, Michael R. *Paving the Way: New York Road Building and the American State, 1880–1956*. Lawrence: University Press of Kansas, 2008.

Finch, Christopher. *Highways to Heaven: The AUTO Biography of America*. New York: HarperCollins, 1992.

Finlay, Mark R. *Growing American Rubber: Strategic Plants and the Politics of National Security*. New Brunswick, N.J.: Rutgers University Press, 2009.

Fischer, Claude S., and Glenn R. Carroll. "Telephone and Automobile Diffusion in the United States, 1902–1937." *American Journal of Sociology* 93 (Mar. 1988): 1153–78.

Fishman, Robert. *Bourgeois Utopias: The Rise and Fall of Suburbia*. New York: Basic Books, 1987.

Flink, James J. *America Adopts the Automobile, 1895–1910*. Cambridge, Mass.: MIT Press, 1970.

———. *The Automobile Age*. Cambridge, Mass.: MIT Press, 1988.

———. *The Car Culture*. Cambridge, Mass.: MIT Press, 1975.

———. "Three Stages of American Automobile Consciousness." *American Quarterly* 24 (Oct. 1972): 451–73.

Flint, Anthony. *Wrestling with Moses: How Jane Jacobs Took on New York's Master Builder and Transformed the American City.* New York: Random House, 2009.

Fogelson, Robert M. *Downtown: Its Rise and Fall, 1880–1950.* New Haven, Conn.: Yale University Press, 2001.

———. *The Fragmented Metropolis: Los Angeles, 1850–1930.* Cambridge, Mass.: Harvard University Press, 1967.

Forbes, Kingston. *The Principles of Automobile Body Design: Covering the Fundamentals of Open and Closed Passenger Body Design.* Philadelphia: Ware Bros., 1922.

Ford, Henry. "Arranging to Build 20,000 Runabouts" (letter to the editor). *The Automobile,* 11 Jan. 1906, 107.

———. "Special Automobile Steel." *Harper's Weekly* 51 (16 Mar. 1907): 336G.

Ford, Henry, with the collaboration of Samuel Crowther. *My Life and Work.* Garden City, N.Y.: Doubleday, Page and Co., 1922.

Ford Motor Company. *The Ford Industries: Facts about the Ford Motor Company and Its Subsidiaries.* Detroit: Ford Motor Co., 1924.

Forman, Richard T. T. "Estimate of the Area Affected Ecologically by the Road System in the United States." *Conservation Biology* 14 (Feb. 2000): 31–35.

———. *Land Mosaics: The Ecology of Landscapes and Regions.* New York: Cambridge University Press, 1995.

Forman, Richard T. T., Daniel Sperling, John A. Bissonette, Anthony P. Clevenger, Carol D. Cutshall, Virginia H. Dale, Lenore Fahrig et al. *Road Ecology: Science and Solutions.* Washington, D.C.: Island Press, 2003.

Foster, Mark S. "The Automobile and the City." *Michigan Historical Quarterly* 19 (Fall 1980): 459–71.

———. *From Streetcar to Superhighway: American City Planners and Urban Transportation, 1900–1940.* Philadelphia: Temple University Press, 1982.

———. "In the Face of 'Jim Crow': Prosperous Blacks and Vacations, Travel and Outdoor Leisure, 1890–1945." *Journal of Negro History* 84 (Spring 1999): 130–49.

Fox, John P. "Traffic Regulation in Detroit and Toronto." *American City* 13 (Sept. 1915): 175–79.

Franz, Kathleen. *Tinkering: Consumers Reinvent the Early Automobile.* Philadelphia: University of Pennsylvania Press, 2005.

Free St. Paul Shopping Guide and Street Railway Directory. St. Paul: Ramaley Publishing Co., 1906.

"Freeways and the Rights of Abutting Owners." *Stanford Law Review* 3 (Feb. 1951): 298–311.

Frost, Harwood. *The Art of Roadmaking: Treating of the Various Problems and Operations in the Construction and Maintenance of Roads, Streets, and Pavements.* New York: Engineering News Publishing Co., 1910.

Fuller, Wayne E. "Good Roads and the Rural Free Delivery of Mail." *Mississippi Valley Historical Review* 42 (June 1955): 67–83.

———. *RFD: The Changing Face of Rural America.* Bloomington: Indiana University Press, 1964.

Furnas, J. C. "—And Sudden Death." *Reader's Digest* 47 (Aug. 1935): 21–26.

Garreau, Joel. *Edge City: Life on the New Frontier.* New York: Doubleday, 1991.

Garrison, William L., Brian J. L. Berry, Duane F. Marble, John D. Nystuen, and Richard L. Morrill. *Studies of Highway Development and Geographic Change.* Seattle: University of Washington Press, 1959.

Gartman, David. *Auto Opium: A Social History of American Automobile Design.* New York: Routledge, 1994.

Geddes, Norman Bel. *Magic Motorways.* New York: Random House, 1940.

Gehl, Jan. *Cities for People.* Washington, D.C.: Island Press, 2010.

Gladding, Effie Price. *Across the Continent by the Lincoln Highway.* New York: Brentano's, 1915.

Glenn, Norval D. "Suburbanization in the United States since World War II." In *The Urbanization of the Suburbs,* edited by Louis Masotti and Jeffrey K. Hadden, 51–78. Beverly Hills: Sage Publications, 1973.

Goddard, Stephen. *Getting There: The Epic Struggle between Road and Rail in the American Century.* New York: Basic Books, 1994.

Goodrich, Ernest P. "Zoning and Its Relation to Traffic Congestion." In *Planning for City Traffic,* edited by Austin F. MacDonald, 222–33. Philadelphia: American Academy of Political and Social Science, 1927.

Grandin, Greg. *Fordlandia: The Rise and Fall of Henry Ford's Forgotten Jungle City.* New York: Metropolitan Books, 2009.

Greene, Ann Norton. *Horses at Work: Harnessing Power in Industrial America.* Cambridge, Mass.: Harvard University Press, 2008.

Greenleaf, William. *Monopoly on Wheels: Henry Ford and the Selden Automobile Patent.* Detroit: Wayne State University Press, 1961.

Gruen, Victor, and Larry Smith. *Shopping Towns USA: The Planning of Shopping Centers.* New York: Reinhold Publishing Corp., 1960.

Gudis, Catherine. *Buyways: Billboards, Automobiles, and the American Landscape.* New York: Routledge, 2004.

Gutfreund, Owen D. *Twentieth-Century Sprawl: Highways and the Reshaping of the American Landscape.* New York: Oxford University Press, 2004.

Haar, Charles M., and Jerold S. Kayden, eds. *Zoning and the American Dream: Promises Still to Keep.* Washington, D.C.: American Planning Association Press, 1989.

Hall, George D. "The 'Freeway': A New Thought for Subdividers." *Landscape Architecture* 21 (Jan. 1931): 115–18.

Hall, Peter. *Cities of Tomorrow: An Intellectual History of Urban Planning and Design in the Twentieth Century,* updated ed. Malden, Mass.: Blackwell Publishers, 1996.

Hamilton, Shane. *Trucking Country: The Road to America's Wal-Mart Economy.* Princeton, N.J.: Princeton University Press, 2008.

Hanchett, Thomas W. "Federal Incentives and the Growth of Local Planning, 1941–1948." *Journal of the American Planning Association* 60 (Spring 1994): 197–208.

————. "U.S. Tax Policy and the Shopping Center Boom of the 1950s and 1960s." *American Historical Review* 101 (Oct. 1996): 1081–110.

Hardin, Garrett. "The Tragedy of the Commons." *Science* 162 (13 Dec. 1968): 1243–48.

Hardwick, M. Jeffrey. *Mall Maker: Victor Gruen, Architect of an American Dream.* Philadelphia: University of Pennsylvania Press, 2003.

Hart, Stanley I., and Alvin L. Spivak. *The Elephant in the Bedroom: Automobile Dependence and Denial, Impacts on the Economy and Environment.* Pasadena, Calif.: New Paradigm Books, 1993.

Havlick, David G. *No Place Distant: Roads and Motorized Recreation on America's Public Lands.* Washington, D.C.: Island Press, 2002.

Hawley, Amos. *Human Ecology: A Theory of Community Structure.* New York: Ronald Press, 1950.

Hayden, Dolores. *Building Suburbia: Green Fields and Urban Growth, 1820–2000.* New York: Vintage Books, 2004.

Hays, Samuel P., and Barbara D. Hays. *Beauty, Health, and Permanence: Environmental Politics in the United States, 1955–1985.* New York: Cambridge University Press, 1987.

Heer, Clarence. "Taxation and Public Finance." In *Recent Social Trends in the United States,* edited by President's Research Committee on Social Trends, 1331–90. New York: McGraw-Hill, 1933.

Heimann, Jim. *California Crazy and Beyond: Roadside Vernacular Architecture.* San Francisco: Chronicle Books, 2001.

Heitmann, John. *The Automobile and American Life.* Jefferson, N.C.: McFarland & Co., 2009.

Herlihy, David V. *Bicycle: The History.* New Haven, Conn.: Yale University Press, 2004.

Herrold, George H. "The Parking Problem in St. Paul." *Nation's Traffic* 1 (July 1927): 28–30+.

Hewes, L. I. "Federal Road Building in the National Forests of the West." *Public Roads* 3 (June 1920): 15–28.

Higgens-Evenson, R. Rudy. *The Price of Progress: Public Services, Taxation, and the American Corporate State, 1877 to 1929.* Baltimore: Johns Hopkins University Press, 2003.

Hines, T. S. *Burnham of Chicago: Architect and Planner.* New York: Oxford University Press, 1974.

Hirsch, Arnold R. *Making the Second Ghetto: Race and Housing in Chicago, 1940–1960.* New York: Cambridge University Press, 1983.

Hise, Greg. "Home Building and Industrial Decentralization in Los Angeles: The Roots of the Postwar Urban Region." *Journal of Urban History* 19 (Feb. 1993): 95–125.

Hodges, Henry G. "Financing the Automobile." In *The Automobile: Its Province and Its Problems,* edited by Clyde L. King, 49–57. Philadelphia: American Academy of Political and Social Science, 1924.

Hoffman, Paul G. "The White Line Isn't Enough." *Saturday Evening Post* 210 (26 Mar. 1938): 12–13+.

Hokanson, Drake. *The Lincoln Highway: Main Street across America*. Iowa City: University of Iowa Press, 1988.

Holley, I. B., Jr. "Blacktop: How Asphalt Paving Came to the Urban United States." *Technology and Culture* 44 (Oct. 2003): 703–33.

——. *The Highway Revolution, 1895–1925: How the United States Got Out of the Mud.* Durham: Carolina Academic Press, 2008.

Holt, W. Stull. *The Bureau of Public Roads: Its History, Activities and Organization.* Baltimore: Johns Hopkins University Press, 1923.

Hoover, Edgar M. "Motor Metropolis: Some Observations on Urban Transportation in America." *Journal of Industrial Economics* 13, 3 (June 1965): 177–92.

Horses, Mules and Motor Vehicles. USDA Statistical Bulletin No. 5. Washington, D.C.: Government Printing Office, 1925.

Hounshell, David A. *From the American System to Mass Production, 1800–1932.* Baltimore: Johns Hopkins University Press, 1984.

Hoy, Suellen. *Chasing Dirt: The American Pursuit of Cleanliness.* New York: Oxford University Press, 1995.

Hubbard, Theodora Kimball, and Henry Vincent Hubbard. *Our Cities To-Day and To-Morrow: A Survey of Planning and Zoning Progress in the United States.* Cambridge, Mass.: Harvard University Press, 1929.

Hudson, John C. "Settlement of the American Grassland." In *The Making of the American Landscape*, edited by Michael Conzen, 169–85. Boston: Unwin Hyman, 1990.

Hughes, Thomas P. *American Genesis: A Century of Invention and Technological Enthusiasm, 1870–1970.* Chicago: University of Chicago Press, 1989.

Hugill, Peter J. *The Elite, the Automobile, and the Good Roads Movement in New York: The Development and Transformation of a Technological Complex, 1904–1913.* Discussion Paper Series. Syracuse, N.Y.: Department of Geography, Syracuse University, 1981.

——. "Good Roads and the Automobile in the United States, 1880–1929." *Geographical Review* 72 (July 1982): 327–49.

——. "Technology and Geography in the Emergence of the American Automobile Industry, 1895–1915." In *Roadside America: The Automobile in Design and Culture*, edited by Jan Jennings, 29–39. Ames: Iowa State University Press, 1990.

——. "Technology Diffusion in the World Automobile Industry, 1885–1985." In *The Transfer and Transformation of Ideas and Material Culture*, edited by Peter J. Hugill and D. Bruce Dickson, 110–42. College Station: Texas A&M University Press, 1988.

Hurley, Andrew. *Environmental Inequalities: Class, Race, and Industrial Pollution in Gary, Indiana, 1945–1980.* Chapel Hill: University of North Carolina Press, 1995.

Ickes, Harold. *Back to Work: The Story of PWA.* New York: Macmillan Co., 1935.

Ihlder, John. "The Automobile and Community Planning." In *The Automobile: Its*

Province and Its Problems, edited by Clyde L. King, 199–205. Philadelphia: American Academy of Political and Social Science, 1924.

Ingram, Tammy Leigh. "Dixie Highway: Private Enterprise and State Building in the South." Ph.D. diss., Yale University, 2007.

International Joint Commission of United States and Canada. *Report on the Pollution of Boundary Waters*. Washington, D.C., and Ottawa: International Joint Commission, 1951.

Interrante, Joseph Anthony. "A Moveable Feast: The Automobile and the Spatial Transformation of American Culture, 1890–1940." Ph.D. diss., Harvard University, 1983.

———. "The Road to Autopia: The Automobile and the Spatial Transformation of American Culture." In *The Automobile and American Culture*, edited by David L. Lewis and Laurence Goldstein, 89–104. Ann Arbor: University of Michigan Press, 1980.

———. "You Can't Go to Town in a Bathtub: Automobile Movement and the Reorganization of Rural American Space, 1900–1930." *Radical History Review* 21 (Fall 1979): 151–68.

Issel, William. "'Land Values, Human Values, and the Preservation of the City's Treasured Appearance': Environmentalism, Politics, and the San Francisco Freeway Revolt." *Pacific Historical Review* 68 (Nov. 1999): 611–46.

Jackson, Kenneth T. *Crabgrass Frontier: The Suburbanization of the United States*. New York: Oxford University Press, 1985.

———. "Transnational Borderlands: Metropolitan Growth in the United States, Germany, and Japan Since World War II." *German Historical Institute Bulletin* 38 (Spring 2006): 11–32.

Jacobs, Jane. *The Death and Life of Great American Cities*. 1961. Reprint with foreword by the author, New York: Random House Modern Library, 1993.

———. "Downtown Is for People." *Fortune* 57 (Apr. 1958): 113–40+.

Jakle, John A. "Landscapes Redesigned for the Automobile." In *The Making of the American Landscape*, edited by Michael P. Conzen, 293–310. Boston: Unwin Hyman, 1990.

Jakle, John A. and Keith A. Sculle. *Fast Food: Roadside Restaurants in the Automobile Age*. Baltimore: Johns Hopkins University Press, 1999.

———. *The Gas Station in America*. Baltimore: Johns Hopkins University Press, 1994.

———. *Lots of Parking: Land Use in a Car Culture*. Charlottesville: University of Virginia Press, 2004.

———. *Motoring: The Highway Experience in America*. Athens: University of Georgia Press, 2008.

James, M. H. "The Automobile and Recreation." In *The Automobile: Its Province and Its Problems*, edited by Clyde L. King, 32–34. Philadelphia: American Academy of Political and Social Science, 1924.

Jay, Harry Byron. "The Evolution of Road Location." *Highway Magazine* 20 (Sept. 1929): 227–29.

Jellinek-Mercédès, Guy. *My Father Mr. Mercédès*. Translated by Ruth Hassell. Philadelphia: Chilton Books, 1961.

Jennings, Jan, ed. *Roadside America: The Automobile in Design and Culture*. Ames: Iowa State University Press, 1990.

Johnson, A. E., ed. *American Association of State Highway Officials: A Story of the Beginning, Purposes, Growth, Activities and Achievements of AASHO*. Washington, D.C.: American Association of State Highway Officials, 1965.

Johnson, Paul E. *A Shopkeeper's Millennium: Society and Revivals in Rochester, New York, 1815–1837*. New York: Hill and Wang, 1978.

Joint Committee on Roadside Development. *Roadside Development Part II: Final Report, Subcommittee on Erosion*. Washington, D.C.: Highway Research Board, Apr. 1940.

Judson, William Pierson. *City Roads and Pavements Suited to Cities of Moderate Size*. 2nd revised and enlarged ed. New York: Engineering News Publishing Co., 1902.

Kay, Jane H. *Asphalt Nation: How the Automobile Took Over America and How We Can Take It Back*. New York: Crown Publishers, 1997.

———. *Lost Boston*. Expanded and updated edition. Boston: Houghton Mifflin, 1999.

Kelley, Albert. *The Pavers and the Paved*. New York: D. W. Brown, 1971.

Kelley, Eugene J. *Shopping Centers: Locating Controlled Regional Centers*. Saugatuck, Conn.: Eno Foundation for Highway Traffic Control, 1956.

Kenealy, James L. *Model "T" Ford: Authentic Accessories, 1909–1927*. 3 vols. Seattle: James L. Kenealy, 1976.

Kimes, Beverly Rae, and Henry Austin Clark Jr. *Standard Catalog of American Cars, 1805–1942*. 3rd ed. Iola, Wisc.: Krause Publications, 1996.

King, Clyde L., ed. *The Automobile: Its Province and Its Problems*. Philadelphia: American Academy of Political and Social Science, 1924.

Kingery, Robert. "Highways of the Future." *Transactions of the National Safety Council, 18th Annual Safety Conference* (Sept.–Oct. 1929): 72–75.

Kirsch, David A. *The Electric Vehicle and the Burden of History*. New Brunswick, N.J.: Rutgers University Press, 2000.

Kitman, Jamie Lincoln. "The Secret History of Lead: How Did Lead Get into Gasoline in the First Place? And Why Is Leaded Gas Still Being Sold in the Third World, Eastern Europe and Elsewhere?" *Nation* 270 (20 Mar. 2000): 11–44.

Kline, Ronald. *Consumers in the Country: Technology and Social Change in Rural America*. Baltimore: Johns Hopkins University Press, 2000.

Kline, Ronald, and Trevor Pinch. "Users as Agents of Technological Change: The Social Construction of the Automobile in the Rural United States." *Technology and Culture* 37 (Oct. 1996): 763–95.

Kolb, John, and Edmund de S. Brunner. *A Study of Rural Society*. Boston: Houghton Mifflin Co., 1946.

Kovarik, William. "Henry Ford, Charles Kettering and the 'Fuel of the Future.'" *Automotive History Review* 32 (Spring 1998): 7–27.

Kriebel, David, Joel Tickner, Paul Epstein, John Lemons, Richard Levins, Edward L.

Loechler, Margaret Quinn, Ruthann Rudel, Tedd Schettler, and Machael Stoto. "The Precautionary Principle in Environmental Science." *Environmental Health Perspectives* 109 (Sept. 2001): 871–76.

Krier, James E., and Edmund Ursin. *Pollution and Policy: A Case Essay on California and Federal Experience with Motor Vehicle Air Pollution, 1940–1975*. Berkeley: University of California Press, 1977.

Kruse, Kevin M., and Thomas J. Sugrue, eds. *The New Suburban History*. Chicago: University of Chicago Press, 2006.

Kunstler, James Howard. *The Geography of Nowhere: The Rise and Decline of America's Man-Made Landscape*. New York: Simon and Schuster, 1993.

Lacey, Robert. *Ford: The Men and the Machine*. Boston: Little, Brown and Co., 1986.

Ladd, Brian. *Autophobia: Love and Hate in the Automotive Age*. Chicago: University of Chicago Press, 2008.

Laird, Pamela Walker. "'The Car without a Single Weakness': Early Automobile Advertising." *Technology and Culture* 37 (Oct. 1996): 796–812.

Lansing, John B. *Residential Location and Urban Mobility: The Second Wave of Interviews*. Ann Arbor: Survey Research Center, Institute for Social Research, University of Michigan, 1966.

Lansing, John B., and Nancy Barth. *Residential Location and Urban Mobility: A Multivariate Analysis*. Ann Arbor: Survey Research Center, Institute for Social Research, University of Michigan, 1964.

Lansing, John B., and Gary Hendricks. *Automobile Ownership and Residential Density*. Ann Arbor: Survey Research Center, Institute for Social Research, University of Michigan, 1967.

Lansing, John B., and Eva Mueller, with Nancy Barth. *Residential Location and Urban Mobility*. Ann Arbor: Survey Research Center, Institute for Social Research, University of Michigan, 1964.

Larrabee, Eric. "Six Thousand Houses That Levitt Built." *Harper's Magazine* 197 (Sept. 1948): 79–88.

Laux, James M., Jean-Pierre Bardou, Jean-Jacques Chanaron, and Patrick Fridenson. *The Automobile Revolution: The Impact of an Industry*. Edited and translated by James M. Laux. Chapel Hill: University of North Carolina Press, 1982.

Lavenir, Catherine Bertho. "How the Motor Car Conquered the Road." In *Cultures of Control*, edited by Miriam R. Levin, 113–34. Amsterdam: Harwood Academic Publishers, 2000.

Lavis, Fred. "Highways as Elements of Transportation and Discussion." *Transactions of the American Society of Civil Engineers* 95 (1931): 1021–59.

Leach, Sara Amy. "The Daughters of the American Revolution, Roane F. Byrnes, and the Birth of the Natchez Trace Parkway." In *Looking beyond the Highway: Dixie Roads and Culture*, edited by Claudette Stager and Martha Carver, 99–114. Knoxville: University of Tennessee Press, 2006.

Lears, Jackson. *No Place of Grace: Antimodernism and the Transformation of American Culture, 1880–1920*. New York: Pantheon Books, 1981.

Leavitt, Helen. *Superhighway—Superhoax*. Garden City, N.Y.: Doubleday, 1970.

Leavitt, Judith Walzer. *The Healthiest City: Milwaukee and the Politics of Health Reform*. Madison: University of Wisconsin Press, 1982.

LeCraw, Charles S., Jr., and Wilbur S. Smith. *Zoning Applied to Parking*. Saugatuck, Conn.: Eno Foundation for Highway Traffic Control, 1947.

Levin, David R. *Highway Research Board Bulletin 99: Parking Requirements in Zoning Ordinances; A Supplement to Bulletin 24*. Washington, D.C.: Highway Research Board, 1955.

———. *Highway Research Board Bulletin No. 24: Zoning for Parking Facilities; Requirements for Off-Street Automobile Parking Facilities in Zoning and Other Local Ordinances*. Washington, D.C.: Highway Research Board, 1950.

Levine, Jonathan. *Zoned Out: Regulation, Markets, and Choices in Transportation and Metropolitan Land Use*. Washington, D.C.: Resources for the Future, 2006.

Lewis, David L. *The Public Image of Henry Ford: An American Folk Hero and His Company*. Detroit: Wayne State University Press, 1976.

———. "The Rise and Fall of Old Henry's Northern Empire, Part I." *Cars and Parts* 17 (Dec. 1973): 90–97.

———. "The Rise and Fall of Old Henry's Northern Empire, Part II." *Cars and Parts* 17 (Jan.–Feb. 1974): 100–105.

Lewis, Harold M. "The New York City Motor Traffic Problem." In *The Automobile: Its Province and Its Problems*, edited by Clyde L. King, 214–23. Philadelphia: American Academy of Political and Social Science, 1924.

———. "Routing through Traffic." In *Planning for City Traffic*, edited by Austin F. MacDonald, 19–27. Philadelphia: American Academy of Political and Social Science, 1927.

Lewis, Robert D., ed. *Manufacturing Suburbs: Building Work and Home on the Metropolitan Fringe*. Philadelphia: Temple University Press, 2004.

Lewis, Tom. *Divided Highways: Building the Interstate Highways, Transforming American Life*. New York: Penguin Books, 1997.

Lichtenstein, Alex. "Good Roads and Chain Gangs in the Progressive South: 'The Negro Convict Is a Slave.'" *Journal of Southern History* 59 (Feb. 1993): 85–110.

Liebs, Chester. *Main Street to Miracle Mile: American Roadside Architecture*. Boston: Little, Brown, 1985.

Lincoln, Frederick C. "The Menace of Oil Pollution." *The Auk* 47 (Oct. 1930): 546–50.

Lincoln Highway Association. *The Lincoln Highway: The Story of a Crusade That Made Transportation History*. New York: Dodd, Mead & Co., 1935.

Ling, Peter J. *America and the Automobile: Technology, Reform and Social Change*. New York: Saint Martin's Press, 1990.

Lloyd, M. G. "Uniform Traffic Signs, Signals, and Markings." In *Planning for City Traffic*, edited by Austin F. MacDonald, 121–27. Philadelphia: American Academy of Political and Social Science, 1927.

Loeb, Alan P. "Birth of the Kettering Doctrine: Fordism, Sloanism and the Discovery of Tetraethyl Lead." *Business and Economic History* 24, 1 (1995): 72–87.

Longstreth, Richard. *City Center to Regional Mall: Architecture, the Automobile, and Retailing in Los Angeles, 1920–1950*. Cambridge, Mass.: MIT Press, 1997.

———. "The Diffusion of the Community Shopping Center Concept during the Interwar Decades." *Journal of the Society of Architectural Historians* 56 (Sept. 1997): 268–93.

———. *The Drive-In, the Supermarket, and the Transformation of Commercial Space in Los Angeles, 1914–1941*. Cambridge, Mass.: MIT Press, 1999.

———. "The Neighborhood Shopping Center in Washington, D.C., 1930–1941." *The Journal of the Society of Architectural Historians* 51 (Mar. 1992): 5–34.

Louter, David. *Windshield Wilderness: Cars, Roads, and Nature in Washington's National Parks*. Seattle: University of Washington Press, 2006.

Lundberg, George A., Mirra Komarovsky, and Mary Alice McInerny. *Leisure: A Suburban Study*. New York: Columbia University Press, 1934.

Macauley, Alvan. *City Planning and Automobile Traffic Problems*. Detroit: Packard Motor Car Co., 1925.

MacDonald, Austin F. *Federal Aid: A Study of the American Subsidy System*. New York: Thomas Y. Crowell Co., 1928.

———, ed. *Planning for City Traffic*. Philadelphia: American Academy of Political and Social Science, 1927.

MacDonald, Thomas H. "The Financing of Highways." In *The Automobile: Its Province and Its Problems*, edited by Clyde L. King, 160–68. Philadelphia: American Academy of Political and Social Science, 1924.

———. *Report of the Chief of the Bureau of Public Roads*. Washington, D.C.: Government Printing Office, 1919–1939.

———. "The Trend of Modern Highways." *Motor Transportation* 64 (June 1938): 1134–38.

Mackay, H., and Gareth Gillespie. "Extending the Social Shaping of Technology Approach: Ideology and Appropriation." *Social Studies of Science* 22 (1992): 685–716.

MacKaye, Benton. "The Townless Highway." *New Republic* 62 (12 Mar., 1930): 93–95.

MacKaye, Benton and Lewis Mumford. "Townless Highways for the Motorist: A Proposal for the Automobile Age." *Harper's Magazine* 163 (Aug. 1931): 347–56.

Maher, Neil M. *Nature's New Deal: The Civilian Conservation Corps and the Roots of the American Environmental Movement*. New York: Oxford University Press, 2008.

Makielski, S. J., Jr. *The Politics of Zoning: The New York Experience*. New York: Columbia University Press, 1966.

Marchant, Gary E. "From General Policy to Legal Rule: Aspirations and Limitations of the Precautionary Principle." *Environmental Health Perspectives* 111 (Nov. 2003): 1799–1803.

Marsh, Benjamin Clark. *An Introduction to City Planning: Democracy's Challenge to the American City*. 1909. New York: Arno Press, 1974.

Marsh, Burton W. "Traffic Control." In *Planning for City Traffic*, edited by Austin F. MacDonald, 90–113. Philadelphia: American Academy of Political and Social Science, 1927.

Martin, James W. "The Administration of Gasoline Taxes in the United States." In *State Tax Systems under Changing Technology: The Problem of the Roadways*, edited by Richard E. Gift, 37–52. Lexington: College of Business and Economics of the University of Kentucky, 1980. Originally published in *National Municipal Review* (Oct. 1924).

Mason, Philip P. "The League of American Wheelmen and the Good Roads Movement, 1880–1905." Ph.D. diss., University of Michigan, 1957.

Massen, John A., and Miller McClintock. *Limited Ways: A Plan for the Greater Chicago Traffic Area; A Report to the City Council of the City of Chicago*. 3 vols. Chicago: Committee on Traffic and Public Safety, 1933.

Maxim, Hiram Percy. *Horseless Carriage Days*. New York: Harper & Brothers, 1936.

McCalley, Bruce. *Model T Ford: The Car That Changed the World*. Iola, Wisc.: Krause Publications, 1994.

McCarthy, John J., and Robert Littell. "Three Hundred Thousand Shacks." *Harper's Magazine* 167 (July 1933): 180–88.

McCarthy, Tom. *Auto Mania: Cars, Consumers, and the Environment*. New Haven, Conn.: Yale University Press, 2007.

———. "The Coming Wonder? Foresight and Early Concerns about the Automobile." *Environmental History* 6 (Jan. 2001): 46–74.

———. "Henry Ford, Industrial Ecologist or Industrial Conservationist? Waste Reduction and Recycling at the Rouge." *Michigan Historical Review* 27 (Fall 2001): 53–88.

———. "The Road to Respect: Americans, Automobiles, and the Environment." Ph.D. diss., Yale University, 2001.

McClelland, Linda Flint. *Presenting Nature: The Historic Landscape Design of the National Park Service*. Washington, D.C.: National Park Service, 1993.

McClintock, Miller. *The Greater Chicago Traffic Area: A Preliminary Report on the Major Traffic Facts of the City of Chicago and Surrounding Region*. Chicago: Committee on Traffic and Public Safety, 1932.

———. *Report and Recommendations of the Metropolitan Street Traffic Survey*. Chicago: Chicago Association of Commerce, 1926.

———. *A Report on the Parking and Garage Problem of Washington, D.C.* Washington, D.C.: Automobile Parking Committee of Washington, 1930.

———. *A Report on the Street Traffic Control Problem of San Francisco*. San Francisco: San Francisco Traffic Survey Committee, 1927.

———. *Street Traffic Control*. New York: McGraw-Hill, 1925.

———. *The Street Traffic Control Problem of the City of New Orleans*. New Orleans: New Orleans City Planning and Zoning Commission, 1928.

———. "The Traffic Survey." In *Planning for City Traffic*, edited by Austin F. MacDonald, 8–18. Philadelphia: American Academy of Political and Social Science, 1927.

McConnell, Curt. *Coast to Coast by Automobile: The Pioneering Trips, 1899–1908*. Stanford, Calif.: Stanford University Press, 2000.

McEvoy, Arthur F. *The Fisherman's Problem: Ecology and Law in the California Fisheries.* New York: Cambridge University Press, 1986.

McKenzie, Roderick D. *The Metropolitan Community.* New York: McGraw-Hill, 1933.

McNeill, J. R. *Something New under the Sun: An Environmental History of the Twentieth-Century World.* New York: W. W. Norton, 2000.

McShane, Clay. "American Cities and the Coming of the Automobile, 1870–1910." Ph.D. diss., University of Wisconsin–Madison, 1975.

———. *The Automobile: A Chronology of Its Antecedents, Development, and Impact.* Westport, Conn.: Greenwood Press, 1997.

———. *Down the Asphalt Path: The Automobile and the American City.* New York: Columbia University Press, 1994.

———. "The Origins and Globalization of Traffic Control Signals." *Journal of Urban History* 25 (Mar. 1999): 379–404.

———. "The Politics of Pavements." In *Urban Bosses, Machines, and Progressive Reformers,* edited by Bruce M. Stave and Sondra Astor Stave, 271–96. Malabar, Fla.: Robert E. Krieger Publishing Co., 1984.

———. "Transforming the Use of Urban Space: A Look at the Revolution in Street Pavements, 1880–1924." *Journal of Urban History* 5 (May 1979): 279–307.

———. "Urban Pathways: The Street and Highway, 1900–1940." In *Technology and the Rise of the Networked City in Europe and America,* edited by Joel A. Tarr and Gabriel Dupuy, 67–87. Philadelphia: Temple University Press, 1988.

McShane, Clay, and Joel Tarr. *The Horse in the City: Living Machines in the Nineteenth Century.* Baltimore: Johns Hopkins University Press, 2007.

Meinig, D. W. *The Shaping of America.* Vol. 4, *Global America, 1915–2000.* New Haven, Conn.: Yale University Press, 2004.

Melosi, Martin V. *Coping with Abundance: Energy and Environment in Industrial America.* Philadelphia: Temple University Press, 1984.

———. *Effluent America: Cities, Industry, Energy, and the Environment.* Pittsburgh: University of Pittsburgh Press, 2001.

———. "Environmental Crisis in the City: The Relationship between Industrialization and Urban Pollution." In *Pollution and Reform in American Cities, 1870–1930,* edited by Martin V. Melosi, 3–31. Austin: University of Texas Press, 1980.

———. *Garbage in the Cities: Refuse, Reform, and the Environment, 1880–1980.* College Station: Texas A&M University Press, 1981.

———. *The Sanitary City: Urban Infrastructure in America from Colonial Times to the Present.* Baltimore: Johns Hopkins University Press, 2000.

Merz, Charles. *And Then Came Ford.* Garden City, N.Y.: Doubleday, Doran & Co., 1929.

Meyer, Stephen. *The Five Dollar Day: Labor Management and Social Control in the Ford Motor Company, 1908–1921.* Albany: State University of New York Press, 1981.

Miller, Zane L., and Patricia M. Melvin. *The Urbanization of Modern America: A Brief History.* 2nd ed. New York: Harcourt Brace Jovanovich, 1987.

Minnesota Department of Highways. *1930 Condition Map of Minnesota Trunk Highways.* St. Paul: Minnesota Department of Highways, 1930.

Misa, Thomas J. *A Nation of Steel: The Making of Modern America, 1865–1925.* Baltimore: Johns Hopkins University Press 1995.

Mogren, Edward G., and Wilbur S. Smith. *Zoning and Traffic.* Saugatuck, Conn.: Eno Foundation for Highway Traffic Control, 1952.

Mohl, Raymond A. *The Interstates and the Cities: Highways, Housing, and the Freeway Revolt.* Research Report. Washington, D.C.: Poverty and Race Research Action Council, 2002.

———. "The Interstates and the Cities: The U.S. Department of Transportation and the Freeway Revolt, 1966–1973." *Journal of Policy History* 20, 2 (2008): 193–226.

———. "Making the Second Ghetto in Metropolitan Miami, 1940–1960." *Journal of Urban History* 21 (Mar. 1995): 395–427.

———. "The Second Ghetto Thesis and the Power of History." *Journal of Urban History* 29 (Mar. 2003): 243–56.

———. "Stop the Road: Freeway Revolts in American Cities." *Journal of Urban History* 30 (July 2004): 674–706.

———. "Urban Expressways and the Racial Restructuring of Postwar American Cities." *Jahrbuch fur Wirtschafts Geschichte* 2 (2001): 89–104.

Moline, Norman C. *Mobility and the Small Town, 1900–1930: Transportation Change in Oregon Illinois.* Research Paper No. 132. Chicago: Department of Geography, University of Chicago, 1971.

Moller, Irving C. "Guiding the Traffic Flow." In *Planning for City Traffic,* edited by Austin F. MacDonald, 114–20. Philadelphia: American Academy of Political and Social Science, 1927.

Molotch, Harvey. "The City as a Growth Machine: Toward a Political Economy of Place." *American Journal of Sociology* 82 (Sept. 1976): 309–32.

Monkkonen, Eric H. *America Becomes Urban: The Development of U.S. Cities and Towns, 1780–1980.* Berkeley: University of California Press, 1988.

Moore, John Brewer. "Wanted: More Open Space in Growing Areas." *American City* 71 (Jan. 1956): 94–95.

Moses, Leon, and Harold F. Williamson. "The Location of Economic Activity in Cities." *American Economic Review* 57 (May 1967): 211–22.

"Motor Cars as Consumers." *Literary Digest* 76 (6 Jan. 1923): 62–63.

"Motorists Don't Make Socialists, They Say." *New York Times,* 4 Mar. 1906.

Mowbray, A. Q. *Road to Ruin: A Critical View of the Federal Highway Program.* Philadelphia: J. B. Lippincott, 1968.

Mumford, Lewis. *The Highway and the City.* New York: Mentor Books, 1964.

———. "The Sky Line: Mother Jacobs' Home Remedies." *New Yorker* 38 (1 Dec. 1962): 148–79.

"Municipal Paving: A Symposium." *Annals of the American Academy of Political and Social Science* 29 (May 1907): 559–600.

Nash, Gerald D. *United States Oil Policy: Business and Government in Twentieth Century America.* Pittsburgh: University of Pittsburgh Press, 1968.

Nash, Roderick. *Wilderness and the American Mind*. New Haven, Conn.: Yale University Press, 1982.

National Automobile Chamber of Commerce. *Facts and Figures of the Automobile Industry*. New York: National Automobile Chamber of Commerce, 1920–1934.

National Conference on Street and Highway Safety. *First National Conference on Street and Highway Safety*. Washington, D.C.: U.S. Department of Commerce, 1924.

———. *National Conference on Street and Highway Safety*. Washington, D.C.: U.S. Department of Commerce, 1926.

National Interregional Highway Committee. *Interregional Highways: Report and Recommendations of the National Interregional Highway Committee*. Washington, D.C.: Government Printing Office, 1944.

National Safety Council. *Accident Facts*. Chicago: National Safety Council, 1928.

Nevins, Allan. *Ford*. Vol. 1, *The Times, the Man, the Company, 1915–1933*. New York: Charles Scribner's Sons, 1954.

———. *John D. Rockefeller: The Heroic Age of American Enterprise*. New York: Charles Scribner's Sons, 1941.

Nevins, Allan, and Frank Ernest Hill. *Ford*. Vol. 2, *Expansion and Challenge, 1915–1933*. New York: Charles Scribner's Sons, 1957.

———. *Ford*. Vol. 3, *Decline and Rebirth, 1933–1962*. New York: Charles Scribner's Sons, 1962.

Newcomb, T. P., and R. T. Spurr. *A Technical History of the Motor Car*. Bristol, UK: Adam Hilger, 1989.

Newman, Peter and Jeffrey Kenworthy. *Sustainability and Cities: Overcoming Automobile Dependence*. Washington, D.C.: Island Press, 1999.

Nicolaides, Becky. *My Blue Heaven: Life and Politics in the Working-Class Suburbs of Los Angeles, 1920–1965*. Chicago: University of Chicago Press, 2002.

Norton, Peter D. *Fighting Traffic: The Dawn of the Motor Age in the American City*. Cambridge, Mass.: MIT Press, 2008.

———. "Street Rivals: Jaywalking and the Invention of the Motor Age Street." *Technology and Culture* 48 (Apr. 2007): 331–59.

———. "Americans' Affair of Hate with the Automobile: What the 'Love Affair' Fiction Concealed." In *Automobile: Les cartes du désamour*, edited by Mathieu Flonneau, 93–104. Paris: Descartes and Cie, 2009.

Nye, David E. *Electrifying America: Social Meanings of a New Technology*. Cambridge, Mass.: MIT Press, 1990.

O'Connor, Harvey. *The Empire of Oil*. New York: Monthly Review Press, 1955.

Office of Public Road Inquiry. *Bulletin No. 32: Public-Road Mileage, Revenues, and Expenditures in the United States in 1904*. Washington, D.C.: Government Printing Office, 1907.

———. *Circular No. 36: List of National, State, and Local Road Associations and Kindred Organizations in the United States*. Washington, D.C.: U.S. Department of Agriculture, 1902.

Office of Public Roads. *Bulletin No. 34: Dust Preventatives*. Washington, D.C.: Government Printing Office, 1908.

———. *Bulletin No. 45: Data for Use in Designing Culverts and Short-Span Bridges*. Washington, D.C.: U.S. Department of Agriculture, 1913.

———. *Bulletin No. 48: Repair and Maintenance of Highways*. Washington, D.C.: Government Printing Office, 1913.

———. *Circular No. 47: Tar and Oil for Road Improvement; Report of Progress of Experiments at Jackson, Tenn.* Washington, D.C.: Government Printing Office, 1906.

———. *Circular No. 89: Progress Reports of Experiments with Dust Preventatives*. Washington, D.C.: Government Printing Office, 1908.

———. *Circular No. 90: Progress Reports of Experiments in Dust Prevention, Road Preservation, and Road Construction*. Washington, D.C.: U.S. Department of Agriculture, 1909.

———. *Circular No. 91: Sand-Clay and Earth Roads in the Middle West*. Washington, D.C.: Government Printing Office, 1910.

———. *Circular No. 93: Bitumens and Their Essential Constituents for Road Construction and Maintenance*. Washington, D.C.: Government Printing Office, 1911.

Office of Public Roads and Rural Engineering. *Bulletin No. 390: Public Road Mileage and Revenues in the United States, 1914; A Summary*. Washington, D.C.: Government Printing Office, 1917.

Office of Road Inquiry. *Bulletin No. 1: State Laws Relating to the Management of Roads*. Washington, D.C.: Government Printing Office, 1893.

———. *Bulletin No. 9: State Aid to Road-Building in New Jersey*. Washington, DC: Government Printing Office, 1894.

———. *Bulletin No. 23: Road Conventions in the Southern States and Object-Lesson Roads Constructed under the Supervision of the Office of Public Road Inquiries, with the Cooperation of the Southern Railway*. Washington, D.C.: Government Printing Office, 1902.

———. *Bulletin No. 24: Proceedings of the North Carolina Good Roads Convention*. Washington, D.C.: U.S. Department of Agriculture, 1903.

———. *Bulletin No. 32: Public-Road Mileage, Revenues, and Expenditures in the United States in 1904*. Washington, D.C.: Government Printing Office, 1907.

———. *Circular No. 14: Addresses on Road Improvement*. Washington, D.C.: Government Printing Office, 1894.

———. *Circular No. 16: Highway Taxation: Comparative Results of Labor and Money Systems*. Washington, D.C.: Government Printing Office, 1894.

———. *Circular No. 18: Report of the Committee on Legislation, Adopted by the State Good Roads Convention, October 10 and 11, 1895*. Washington, D.C.: U.S. Department of Agriculture, 1895.

———. *Circular No. 19: Traffic of the Country Roads*. Washington, D.C.: Government Printing Office, 1896.

———. *Circular No. 24: Highway Repairing*. Washington, D.C.: Government Printing Office, 1896.

————. *Circular No. 26: Going into Debt for Good Roads.* Washington, D.C.: Government Printing Office, 1897.

"Oil Pollution and Refinery Wastes." *Sewage Works Journal* 7 (Jan. 1935): 101–15.

Olmstead, Alan L., and Paul W. Rhode. "The Agricultural Mechanization Controversy of the Interwar Years." *Agricultural History* 68 (Summer 1994): 35–53.

————. "Reshaping the Landscape: The Impact and Diffusion of the Tractor in American Agriculture, 1910–1960." *Journal of Economic History* 61 (Sept. 2001): 663–98.

Olmsted, Frederick Law. "How to Organize a City Planning Campaign." *American City* 9 (Oct. 1913): 303–9.

Olmsted, Frederick Law, Harland Bartholomew, and Henry Charles Cheney. *A Major Traffic Street Plan for Los Angeles.* Los Angeles: Major Highways Committee, 1924.

Olney, Martha L. *Buy Now, Pay Later: Advertising, Credit, and Consumer Durables in the 1920s.* Chapel Hill: University of North Carolina Press, 1991.

Ososski, Sidney. "Clearing Our Crowded Streets." *World To-Day* 19 (Aug. 1910): 872–80.

Owen, Wilfred. *A Study in Highway Economics.* Cambridge, Mass.: Phi Beta Kappa Society, 1934.

Owen, Wilfred, and Charles L. Dearing. *Toll Roads and the Problem of Highway Modernization.* Washington, D.C.: Brookings Institution, 1951.

Page, Logan Waller. "Object-Lesson Roads." In *Yearbook of the United States Department of Agriculture, 1906,* 137–50. Washington, D.C.: Government Printing Office, 1907.

————. *Report of the Director of the Office of Public Roads.* Washington, D.C.: Government Printing Office, 1905–1918.

Patterson, James. *Grand Expectations: The United States, 1945–1974.* New York: Oxford University Press, 1996.

Patton, Phil. *Open Road: A Celebration of the American Highway.* New York: Simon and Schuster, 1986.

Pennybacker, J., and L. Boykin. "Federal Aid to Highways." In *Yearbook of the United States Department of Agriculture, 1917,* 127–38. Washington, D.C.: Government Printing Office, 1918.

Phillips, T. Glenn. "The Traffic Problems in Detroit and How They Are Met." In *The Automobile: Its Province and Its Problems,* edited by Clyde L. King, 241–43. Philadelphia: American Academy of Political and Social Science, 1924.

Pollard, W. L., ed. *The Annals of the American Academy of Political and Social Science* 155.Part 2, *Zoning in the United States* (May 1931): 1–227.

Pope, Albert. "Automobiles and Good Roads." *Munsey's* 29 (May 1903): 167–70.

Post, Emily. *By Motor to the Golden Gate.* New York: D. Appleton and Co., 1916.

Potter, Isaac B. *The Gospel of Good Roads: A Letter to the American Farmer.* New York: Evening Post Job Printing House, 1891.

Pratt, Joseph A. "Letting the Grandchildren Do It: Environmental Planning during the Ascent of Oil as a Major Energy Source." *Public Historian* 2 (Summer 1980): 31–41.

———. "The Ascent of Oil: The Transition from Coal to Oil in Early Twentieth Century America." In *Energy Transitions: Long-Term Perspectives*, edited by Lewis Perelman, Gus Giebelhaus, and Michael Yokell, 9–34. Boulder, Colo.: Westview Press, 1981.

President's Research Committee on Social Trends. *Recent Social Trends in the United States: Report of the President's Research Committee on Social Trends*. New York: McGraw-Hill, 1933.

Preston, Howard Lawrence. *Automobile Age Atlanta: The Making of a Southern Metropolis, 1900–1935*. Athens: University of Georgia Press, 1979.

———. *Dirt Roads to Dixie: Accessibility and Modernization in the South, 1885–1935*. Knoxville: University of Tennessee Press, 1991.

Pridmore, Jay, and Jim Hurd. *The American Bicycle*. Osceola, Wisc.: Motorbooks International Publishers, 1995.

Public Roads Administration. *Highway Statistics: Summary to 1945*. Washington, D.C.: Government Printing Office, 1947.

Radde, Bruce. *The Merritt Parkway*. New Haven, Conn.: Yale University Press, 1993.

Rae, John B. *The American Automobile: A Brief History*. Chicago: University of Chicago Press, 1965.

———. *American Automobile Manufacturers: The First Forty Years*. Philadelphia: Chilton Book Co., 1959.

———. *The Road and the Car in American Life*. Cambridge, Mass.: MIT Press, 1971.

Raff, Daniel M. G. "Making Cars and Making Money in the Interwar Automobile Industry: Economies of Scale and Scope and the Manufacturing behind the Marketing." *Business History Review* 65 (Winter 1991): 721–53.

Railroad Commissioners' Map of Minnesota. Chicago: Rand, McNally & Co., 1900.

Raitz, Karl. "American Roads, Roadside America." *Geographical Review* 88 (July 1998): 363–87.

Real Estate Research Corporation of Chicago. *The Costs of Sprawl: Environmental and Economic Costs of Alternative Residential Development Patterns at the Urban Fringe*. 3 vols. Washington, D.C.: Government Printing Office, 1974.

Regional Plan of New York and Its Environs. 2 vols. New York: Regional Plan of New York and Its Environs, 1929–1931.

Register, Richard. *Ecocities: Building Cities in Balance with Nature*. Berkeley: Berkeley Hills Books, 2002.

Reuss, Martin, and Stephen H. Cutliffe, eds. *The Illusory Boundary: Environment and Technology in History*. Charlottesville: University of Virginia Press, 2010.

Reyes, Jessica Wolpaw. *Environmental Policy as Social Policy? The Impact of Childhood Lead Exposure on Crime*. National Bureau of Economic Research Working Paper No. 13097. Cambridge, Mass.: National Bureau of Economic Research, 2007.

"The Road Improvement Fallacy: Cry for Improved Roads as Necessary Condition for the Progress of the Motor Vehicle Industry Ill Founded and Likely to

Lead Construction and Design into Unprofitable Channels." *Motor Age* 1 (1899): 82–83.

Roberts, Paul. *The End of Oil: On the Edge of a Perilous New World*. Boston: Houghton Mifflin, 2004.

Robinson, Charles Mulford. *The Width and Arrangement of Streets: A Study in Town Planning*. New York: Engineering News Publishing Co., 1911.

Rodgers, Daniel T. "In Search of Progressivism." *Reviews in American History* 10 (Dec. 1982): 113–32.

Rome, Adam. *The Bulldozer in the Countryside: Suburban Sprawl and the Rise of American Environmentalism*. New York: Cambridge University Press, 2001.

Rorabaugh, W. J. *The Craft Apprentice: From Franklin to the Machine Age in America*. New York: Oxford University Press, 1986.

Rose, Albert C. "The Highway from the Railroad to the Automobile." In *Highways in Our National Life: A Symposium*, edited by Jean Labatut and Wheaton J. Lane, 77–87. Princeton, N.J.: Princeton University Press, 1950.

Rose, Mark H. *Cities of Light and Heat: Domesticating Gas and Electricity in Urban America*. University Park: Pennsylvania State University Press, 1995.

———. *Interstate: Express Highway Politics, 1939–1989*. Rev. ed. Knoxville: University of Tennessee Press, 1990.

Rose, Mark H., and Bruce E. Seely. "Getting the Interstate System Built: Road Engineers and the Implementation of Public Policy, 1955–1985." *Journal of Policy History* 2, 1 (1990): 23–55.

Rose, Mark H., Bruce Edsall Seely, and Paul F. Barrett. *The Best Transportation System in the World: Railroads, Trucks, Airlines, and American Public Policy in the Twentieth Century*. Columbus: Ohio State University Press, 2006.

Rosen, Christine Meisner. "Industrial Ecology and the Transformation of Corporate Environmental Management: A Business Historian's Perspective." In *Inventing for the Environment*, edited by Arthur Molella and Joyce Bedi, 319–38. Cambridge, Mass.: MIT Press, 2003.

Rosner, David, and Gerald Markowitz. "A 'Gift of God?': The Public Health Controversy over Leaded Gasoline in the 1920s." *American Journal of Public Health* 75 (Apr. 1985): 344–52.

Roth, Matthew W. "Mulholland Highway and the Engineering Culture of Los Angeles in the 1920s." *Technology and Culture* 40 (July 1999): 545–75.

Rothman, Hal. *Devil's Bargains: Tourism in the Twentieth-Century American West*. Lawrence: University of Kansas Press, 1998.

Runte, Alfred. *National Parks: The American Experience*. 2nd ed. Lincoln: University of Nebraska Press, 1987.

Russell, Edmund, James Allison, Thomas Finger, John K. Brown, Brian Balogh, and W. Bernard Carlson. "The Nature of Power: Synthesizing the History of Technology and Environmental History." *Technology and Culture* 52 (Apr. 2011): 246–59.

Rybczynski, Witold. *A Clearing in the Distance: Frederick Law Olmsted and America in the Nineteenth Century*. New York: Scribner, 1999.

Saint Clair, David. *The Motorization of American Cities*. New York: Praeger, 1986.

Sanborn Map Company. *Digital Sanborn Maps, 1867–1970*. Ann Arbor, Mich.: ProQuest UMI, 2001.

Sandweiss, Eric. *St. Louis: The Evolution of an American Urban Landscape*. Philadelphia: Temple University Press, 2001.

Scharff, Virginia. *Taking the Wheel: Women and the Coming of the Motor Age*. New York: Free Press, 1991.

Schatzberg, Eric. "Culture and Technology in the City: Opposition to Mechanized Street Transportation in Late-Nineteenth-Century America." In *Technologies of Power: Essays in Honor of Thomas Parke Hughes and Agatha Chipley Hughes*, edited by Michael Thad Allen and Gabrielle Hecht, 57–94. Cambridge, Mass.: MIT Press, 2001.

Schiffer, Michael Brian, with Tamara C. Butts and Kimberly K. Grimm. *Taking Charge: The Electric Automobile in America*. Washington, D.C.: Smithsonian Institution Press, 1994.

Schmitt, Peter J. *Back to Nature: The Arcadian Myth in Urban America*. Baltimore: Johns Hopkins University Press, 1969.

Schrag, Zachary M. "The Freeway Fight in Washington, D.C.: The Three Sisters Bridge in Three Administrations." *Journal of Urban History* 30 (July 2004): 648–73.

———. "'The Bus Is Young and Honest': Transportation Politics, Technical Choice, and the Motorization of Manhattan Surface Transit, 1919–1936." *Technology and Culture* 41 (Jan. 2000): 51–79.

Schultz, Stanley K. *Constructing Urban Culture: American Cities and City Planning, 1800–1920*. Philadelphia: Temple University Press, 1989.

Schultz, Stanley K., and Clay McShane. "Pollution and Political Reform in Urban America: The Role of Municipal Engineers, 1840–1920." In *Pollution and Reform in American Cities, 1870–1930*, edited by Martin V. Melosi, 155–72. Austin: University of Texas Press, 1980.

———. "To Engineer the Metropolis: Sewers, Sanitation, and City Planning in Late-Nineteenth-Century America." *Journal of American History* 65 (Sept. 1978): 389–411.

Schwantes, Carlos Arnaldo. *Going Places: Transportation Redefines the Twentieth-Century West*. Bloomington: Indiana University Press, 2003.

Schwartz, Gary. "Urban Freeways and the Interstate System." *Southern California Law Review* 49 (March 1976): 406–513.

Scott, James C. *Seeing Like a State: How Certain Schemes to Improve the Human Condition Have Failed*. New Haven, Conn.: Yale University Press, 1998.

Scott, Mel. *American City Planning since 1890: A History Commemorating the 50th Anniversary of the American Institute of Planners*. Berkeley: University of California Press, 1969.

Sears, Stephen W. *The American Heritage History of the Automobile in America*. New York: American Heritage Publishing Co., 1977.

Seely, Bruce E. *Building the American Highway System: Engineers as Policy Makers.* Philadelphia: Temple University Press, 1987.

Seiler, Cotton. *Republic of Drivers: A Cultural History of Automobility in America.* Chicago: University of Chicago Press, 2008.

Sellars, Richard West. *Preserving Nature in the National Parks: A History.* New Haven, Conn.: Yale University Press, 1997.

Seltzer, Lawrence H. *A Financial History of the American Automobile Industry: A Study of the Ways in Which the Leading American Producers of Automobiles Have Met Their Capital Requirements.* Boston: Houghton Mifflin Co., 1928.

Shaffer, Marguerite. *See America First: Tourism and National Identity, 1880–1940.* Washington, D.C.: Smithsonian Institution Press, 2001.

Shah, Sonia. *Crude: The Story of Oil.* New York: Seven Stories Press, 2004.

Sheridan, Lawrence V. "Planning and Re-Planning the Street System." In *Planning for City Traffic,* edited by Austin F. MacDonald, 28–33. Philadelphia: American Academy of Political and Social Science, 1927.

Shoup, Donald C. *The High Cost of Free Parking.* Chicago: Planners Press, 2005.

Silk, Gerald, et al. *The Automobile and Culture.* Los Angeles: Museum of Contemporary Art, 1984.

Simmons, James. *Feathers and Fur on the Turnpike.* Boston: Christopher Publishing House, 1938.

Slater, Cliff. "General Motors and the Demise of Streetcars." *Transportation Quarterly* 51 (Summer 1997): 45–66.

Sloan, Alfred P., Jr. *My Years with General Motors.* Garden City, N.Y.: Doubleday, 1964.

Smith, Robert A. *A Social History of the Bicycle: Its Early Life and Times in America.* New York: American Heritage Press, 1972.

Snell, Bradford. *American Ground Transport: A Proposal for Restructuring the Automobile, Truck, Bus, and Rail Industries.* Washington, D.C.: Government Printing Office, 1974.

Sorensen, Charles E., with Samuel T. Williamson. *My Forty Years with Ford.* New York: W. W. Norton, 1956.

Spellerberg, Ian F. "Ecological Effects of Roads and Traffic: A Literature Review." *Global Ecology and Biogeography Letters* 7 (Sept. 1998): 317–33.

Spellerberg, Ian F. *Ecological Effects of Roads.* Enfield, N.H.: Science Publishers, 2002.

Squire, Latham C., and Howard M. Bassett. "A New Type of Thoroughfare: The 'Freeway.'" *American City* 47 (Nov. 1932): 64–66.

"Standard Oil's Death Factory." *Nation* 119 (26 Nov. 1924): 561–62.

Staudenmaier, J. M. "Recent Trends in the History of Technology." *American Historical Review* 95 (1990): 715–25.

Stedman, Gordon H. "Shopping Centers and Local Government—Collision or Cooperation." *Journal of Retailing* 31 (Summer 1955): 77–87.

Steinbeck, John. *The Grapes of Wrath.* New York: Viking Press, 1939.

Steinberg, Ted. *Down to Earth: Nature's Role in American History.* New York: Oxford University Press, 2002.

Steiner, J. F. "Recreation and Leisure Time Activities." In *Recent Social Trends in the United States*, edited by President's Research Committee on Social Trends, 912–57. New York: McGraw-Hill, 1933.

Sternlieb, George. *The Future of the Downtown Department Store*. Cambridge: Joint Center for Urban Studies of the Massachusetts Institute of Technology and Harvard University, 1962.

Stilgoe, John R. *Borderland: Origins of the American Suburb, 1820–1939*. New Haven, Conn.: Yale University Press, 1988.

———. *The Common Landscape of America, 1580–1845*. New Haven, Conn.: Yale University Press, 1982.

Stine, Jeffrey K., and Joel A. Tarr. "At the Intersection of Histories: Technology and the Environment." *Technology and Culture* 39 (Oct. 1998): 601–40.

Stone, Roy. *Report of the Director of the Office of Road Inquiry*. Washington, D.C.: Government Printing Office, 1893.

Stradling, David. *Smokestacks and Progressives: Environmentalists, Engineers, and Air Quality in America, 1881–1951*. Baltimore: Johns Hopkins University Press, 1999.

Strasser, Susan. *Satisfaction Guaranteed: The Making of the American Mass Market*. Washington: Smithsonian Institution Press, 1989.

———. *Waste and Want: A Social History of Trash*. New York: Henry Holt and Co., 1999.

Strong, Howard. "Regional Planning and Its Relation to the Traffic Problem." In *Planning for City Traffic*, edited by Austin F. MacDonald, 215–21. Philadelphia: American Academy of Political and Social Science, 1927.

Sugrue, Thomas J. *The Origins of the Urban Crisis: Race and Inequality in Postwar Detroit*. Princeton: Princeton University Press, 1996.

Sutter, Paul S. *Driven Wild: How the Fight against Automobiles Launched the Modern Wilderness Movement*. Seattle: University of Washington Press, 2002.

Sutton, S. B., ed. *Civilizing American Cities: A Selection of Frederick Law Olmsted's Writings on City Landscapes*. Cambridge, Mass.: MIT Press, 1971.

Swan, Herbert S. "Our City Thoroughfares: Shall They Be Highways or Garages?" *American City* 27 (Dec. 1922): 496–500.

———. "The Parkway as a Traffic Artery." *American City* 45–46 (Oct.–Nov. 1931): 73–76, 84–86.

Tabott, Casper. "The Personal Labor System of Road Tax." *Good Roads* 1 (Jan. 1892): 38.

Tamminen, Terry. *Lives per Gallon: The True Cost of Our Oil Addiction*. Washington, D.C.: Island Press, 2006.

Tarbell, Ida. *The History of the Standard Oil Company*. 2 vols. New York: S. S. McClure, 1904.

Tarr, Joel A. *Transportation Innovation and Changing Spatial Patterns in Pittsburgh*. Chicago: Public Works Historical Society, 1978.

———. *The Search for the Ultimate Sink: Urban Pollution in Historical Perspective*. Akron, Ohio: University of Akron Press, 1996.

Tarr, Joel A., and Gabriel Dupuy, eds. *Technology and the Rise of the Networked City in Europe and America*. Philadelphia: Temple University Press, 1988.

Tarr, Joel A., James McCurley, and Terry F. Yosie. "The Development and Impact of Urban Wastewater Technology: Changing Concepts of Water Quality Control, 1850–1930." In *Pollution and Reform in American Cities, 1870–1930*, edited by Martin V. Melosi, 59–82. Austin: University of Texas Press, 1980.

Taussig, Hugo Alois. *Retracing the Pioneers: From West to East in an Automobile*. San Francisco: Philopolis Press, 1910.

Taylor, Clarence P. *A Traffic Officer's Training Manual*. Chicago: National Safety Council, 1930.

Taylor, George Rogers. *The Transportation Revolution, 1815–1860*. New York: Rinehart and Co., 1951.

Taylor, Graham Romeyn. *Satellite Cities: A Study of Industrial Suburbs*. New York: D. Appleton and Co., 1915.

Teaford, Jon C. *The Unheralded Triumph: City Government in America, 1870–1900*. Baltimore: Johns Hopkins University Press, 1984.

Tedlow, Richard S. *New and Improved: The Story of Mass Marketing in America*. New York: Basic Books, 1990.

Thompson, Huston. "Distribution of Gasoline and Methods of Price Control." *Annals of the American Academy of Political and Social Science* 116 (Nov. 1924): 89–95.

Tobin, Gary A. "The Bicycle Boom of the 1890s: The Development of Private Transportation and the Birth of the Modern Tourist." *Journal of Popular Culture* 7, 4 (1974): 838–49.

Toll, Seymour I. *Zoned American*. New York: Grossman Publishers, 1969.

Tomes, Nancy. *The Gospel of Germs: Men, Women, and the Microbe in American Life*. Cambridge, Mass.: Harvard University Press, 1999.

Transportation Research Board. *Driving and the Built Environment: The Effects of Compact Development on Motorized Travel, Energy Use, and CO_2 Emissions*. Washington, D.C.: Transportation Research Board, 2009.

Tunnard, Christopher. "America's Super-Cities." *Harper's Magazine* (Aug. 1958): 59–65.

Turrentine, Gordon H. "Petrochemicals Come of Age." *Analysts Journal* 9 (Nov. 1953): 45–50.

Tylor, W. Russell. "Social Factors in Development of Regional Highways." *Roads and Streets* 76 (June 1933): 219–23.

U.S. Bureau of the Census. *Historical Statistics of the United States: Colonial Times to 1957*. Washington, D.C.: Government Printing Office, 1960.

———. *Historical Statistics of the United States: Colonial Times to 1970*. Vol. 2. Washington, D.C.: Government Printing Office, 1975.

———. *Statistical Abstract of the United States: 2003*. Washington, D.C.: Government Printing Office, 2003.

———. *Statistics of Cities Having a Population of 8,000 to 25,000: 1903*. Washington, D.C.: Government Printing Office, 1906.

U.S. Department of Agriculture. *Circular No. 65: Rules and Regulations of the Secretary of Agriculture for Carrying out the Federal Aid Road Act.* Washington, D.C.: Government Printing Office, 1916.

U.S. Department of Commerce. *A City Planning Primer: By the Advisory Committee on City Planning and Zoning.* Washington, D.C.: Government Printing Office, 1928.

———. *A Standard State Zoning Act: Under Which Municipalities May Adopt Zoning Regulations; By the Advisory Committee on Zoning.* Washington, D.C.: Government Printing Office, 1924.

———. *A Zoning Primer: By the Advisory Committee on Zoning.* Washington, D.C.: Government Printing Office, 1922.

U.S. Public Health Service. *Proceedings of a Conference to Determine Whether or Not There Is a Public Health Question in the Manufacture, Distribution, or Use of Tetraethyl Lead in Gasoline.* Public Health Bulletin No. 158. Washington, D.C.: Government Printing Office, 1925.

"Unfit for Modern Motor Traffic." *Fortune* 14 (Aug. 1936): 85–92+.

"Unjust Automobile Laws." *Outing* 46 (1905): 639.

"Up from the Potato Fields." *Time* 56 (3 July 1950): 67–72.

Van Deventer, John H. "Ford Principles and Practice at River Rouge: Links in a Complete Industrial Chain." *Industrial Management* 64 (Sept. 1922): 131–37.

Veasey, James A. "The Law of Oil and Gas." *Michigan Law Review* 18 (Apr. 1920): 445–69.

Volti, Rudi. "Reducing Automobile Emissions in Southern California: The Dance of Public Policies and Technological Fixes." In *Inventing for the Environment*, edited by Arthur Molella and Joyce Bedi, 277–88. Cambridge, Mass.: MIT Press, 2003.

Waldon, Sidney D. "Superhighways and Regional Planning." *Planning Problems of Town, City, and Region* (1927): 150–66.

Walker, Richard, and Robert Lewis. "Beyond the Crabgrass Frontier: Industry and the Spread of North American Cities, 1850–1950." *Journal of Historical Geography* 27, 1 (2001): 3–19.

Wallock, Leonard. "The Myth of the Master Builder: Robert Moses, New York, and the Dynamics of Metropolitan Development since World War II." *Journal of Urban History* 17 (Aug. 1991): 339–62.

Walsh, Margaret. "Gendering Transport History: Retrospect and Prospect." *Journal of Transport History* 23 (Mar. 2002): 1–8.

Waring, George E, Jr. *Street-Cleaning: And the Disposal of a City's Wastes; Methods and Results and the Effect upon Public Health, Public Morals, and Municipal Prosperity.* New York: Doubleday and McClure, 1898.

———. "The Cleaning of a Great City." *McClure's Magazine* 9 (Sept. 1897): 911–24.

Warner, Sam B., Jr. *Streetcar Suburbs: The Process of Growth in Boston, 1870–1900.* Cambridge, Mass.: Harvard University Press, 1962.

Weart, Spencer R. *The Discovery of Global Warming.* Cambridge, Mass.: Harvard University Press, 2003.

Webb, John N. *The Transient Unemployed: A Description and Analysis of the Transient*

Relief Population. Washington, D.C.: Government Printing Office, 1935.

Webb, John N., and Malcolm Brown. *Migrant Families*. Washington, D.C.: Government Printing Office, 1938.

Weir, Margaret. "Planning, Environmentalism, and Urban Poverty: The Political Failure of National Land-Use Planning Legislation, 1970–1975." In *The American Planning Tradition: Culture and Policy*, edited by Robert Fishman, 193–215. Washington, D.C.: Woodrow Wilson Center Press, 2000.

Weiss, Marc. *The Rise of the Community Builders: The American Real Estate Industry and Urban Land Planning*. New York: Columbia University Press, 1987.

Wells, Christopher W. "The Changing Nature of Country Roads: Farmers, Reformers, and the Shifting Uses of Rural Space, 1880–1905." *Agricultural History* 80 (Spring 2006): 143–66.

———. "From Freeway to Parkway: Federal Law, Grassroots Environmental Protest, and the Evolving Design of Interstate-35E in Saint Paul, Minnesota." *Journal of Planning History* 11 (Feb 2012): 8–26.

———. "Fueling the Boom: Gasoline Taxes, Invisibility, and the Growth of the American Highway Infrastructure, 1919–1956." *Journal of American History* 99 (June 2012): 72–81.

———. "La morte del Modello T: Strade pavimentate, auto coperte e tecnologica desueta" [The death of the Model T: Smooth roads, closed cars, and technological maladaptation]. *I Frutti di Demetra* 21 (2009): 63–75.

———. "The Road to the Model T: Culture, Road Conditions, and Innovation at the Dawn of the American Motor Age." *Technology and Culture* 48 (July 2007): 497–523.

Wells, Nelson M. "Landscaping." In *Highway Engineering Handbook*, edited by Kenneth B. Woods, 28.1–28. New York: McGraw-Hill, 1960.

Whisnant, Anne Mitchell. *Super-Scenic Motorway: A Blue Ridge Parkway History*. Chapel Hill: University of North Carolina Press, 2006.

White, E. B. "Farewell, My Lovely!" In *The Second Tree from the Corner*, 32–40. New York: Harper and Row, 1984. Originally published as Lee Strout White, *Farewell to Model T*. New York: G. P. Putnam's Sons, 1936.

———. *One Man's Meat*. New York: Harper and Row, 1938.

White, Leonard D. "Public Administration." In *Recent Social Trends in the United States*, edited by President's Research Committee on Social Trends, 1391–1429. New York: McGraw-Hill, 1933.

White, Richard. "Jane Jacobs and Toronto, 1968–1978." *Journal of Planning History* 10, 2 (2011): 114–38.

White, Roger B. *Home on the Road: The Motor Home in America*. Washington: Smithsonian Institution Press, 2000.

———. "Body by Fisher: The Closed Car Revolution." *Automobile Quarterly* 29, 4 (1991): 46–63.

Whyte, William, ed. *The Exploding Metropolis*. New York: Doubleday, 1958.

Wiebe, Robert H. *The Search for Order, 1877–1920*. New York: Hill and Wang, 1967.

Wiese, Andrew. *Places of Their Own: African American Suburbanization in the Twentieth Century.* Chicago: University of Chicago Press, 2004.

Wik, Reynold M. *Henry Ford and Grass-Roots America.* Ann Arbor: University of Michigan Press, 1972.

Wilbur Smith and Associates. *Future Highways and Urban Growth.* New Haven, Conn.: Wilbur Smith and Associates, 1961.

Wilcox, Delos F. *The American City: A Problem in Democracy.* New York: Macmillan Co., 1904.

Willey, Malcolm M., and Stuart A. Rice. *Communication Agencies and Social Life.* New York: McGraw-Hill, 1933.

Willey, Malcolm M., and Stuart A. Rice. "The Agencies of Communication." In *Recent Social Trends in the United States,* edited by President's Research Committee on Social Trends, 167–217. New York: McGraw-Hill, 1933.

Williams, Raymond. *The Country and the City.* New York: Oxford University Press, 1973.

———. *Problems of Materialism and Culture.* London: NLB, 1980.

Williamson, Harold F., Ralph L. Andreano, Arnold R. Daum, and Gilbert C. Klose. *The American Petroleum Industry.* Vol. 2, *The Age of Energy, 1899–1959.* Evanston, Ill.: Northwestern University Press, 1963.

Williamson, Harold F., and Arnold R. Daum. *The American Petroleum Industry.* Vol. 1, *The Age of Illumination, 1859–1899.* Evanston, Ill.: Northwestern University Press, 1959.

Winner, Langdon. "Upon Opening the Black Box and Finding It Empty: Social Constructivism and the Philosophy of Technology." In *The Technology of Discovery and the Discovery of Technology,* edited by C. Pitt and E. Lugo, 503–19. Blacksburg, Va.: Society for Philosophy and Technology, 1991.

Witheford, David. *Zoning, Parking, and Traffic.* Saugatuck, Conn.: Eno Foundation for Transportation, 1972.

Wolbert, George S., Jr. *U.S. Oil Pipelines: An Examination of How Oil Pipe Lines Operate and the Current Public Policy Issues Concerning Their Ownership.* Washington, D.C.: American Petroleum Institute, 1979.

Woods, Arthur. "Keeping City Traffic Moving." *World's Work* 31 (Apr. 1916): 621–32.

Worley, William S. *J. C. Nichols and the Shaping of Kansas City: Innovation in Planned Residential Communities.* Columbia: University of Missouri Press, 1990.

Yago, Glenn. *The Decline of Transit: Urban Transportation in German and U.S. Cities, 1900–1970.* New York: Cambridge University Press, 1984.

Yergin, Daniel. *The Prize: The Epic Quest for Oil, Money, and Power.* New York: Simon and Schuster, 1991.

Zelizer, Julian E. *Taxing America: Wilbur D. Mills, Congress, and the State, 1945–1975.* New York: Cambridge University Press, 1998.

Zunz, Olivier. *Making America Corporate, 1870–1920.* Chicago: University of Chicago Press, 1990.

INDEX

Note: page numbers in *italics* refer to figures or tables; those followed by "n" indicate endnotes.

A

AAA (Automobile Association of America), 73, 78, 81
AASHO (American Association of State Highway Officials), 132, 186, 216
ABC Rental Plan, 81
accelerated depreciation, 268–69, 371n60
administrative legibility, 331n120
advertising, 50
African American migration, 367n28
Agee, James, 167, 170
agribusiness and long-haul trucking, 276
agriculture, 11–12, 169, 342n70
Alaska-Yukon-Pacific Exposition race (1909), 49–50
American Association of State Highway Officials (AASHO), 132, 186, 216
American Society of Planning Officials, 369n40
Appalachian oil fields, 176
Arnold, Horace Lucien, 318n67
Arroyo Seco Parkway, Los Angeles, 140
arterial roads: in Bartholomew's system, 134–35; buses on, 261; cyclists and, xxx; defined, xxvii–xxviii; ribbon developments along, 262, 275–76; speeding of, 154
asphalt, 76–77, 214
assembly lines, 57–58. *See also* mass production and Fordism
Atlanta, xxi, xxiii–xxiv, 135

attitudes toward cars vs. influence of land-use patterns, xxiii–xxvi
autobahnen, German, 194
Automobile Association of America (AAA), 73, 78, 81
Automobile Club of America, 323n32
automobile clubs: AAA, 73, 78, 81; formation of, 73; pedestrian safety campaigns, 93–94
automobile design: American touring car, 44–45; array of early designs, 40; closed-steel bodies, 210, 218, 359n36; high-wheelers, 45, 114, 312n21; horseless carriage, 40, 311n13; Mercedes-style, 42–44, 48–49, 113; runabouts (gas buggies), 45; smooth roads and effects on interactions with nature, 218–19; stylish, comfort-oriented amenities, 218–19; weather issues and Model T accessories, 51–54; weight-to-power ratio and search for lightweight car, 45–48; wooden body, 210, 239. *See also* Ford Model T
automobile industry: as conglomeration, 204; earliest motor vehicles, 40; growth of (pre-WWI), 37–39; sales trends, 203, 279; scale and scope of production, 203–4. *See also* Ford Motor Company
automobile manufacturing: 1917 peak in production, 61; during and after World War I, 61–62; European, 42–44, 312n18; Ford Model N and economies of scale, 55; market shares, 58; before Model T, 54–55; Model T and Fordism, 55–60. *See also* mass production and Fordism

developers and FHA guidelines, 256–60
distance in streetcar vs. exit-ramp neighborhoods, xxx, *xxxi*. *See also* mobility
and time-distance geography in
interwar period
distributor streets, 96
Dodge, Martin, 26–27, 68, 69
double-decked streets, 102, 135
downtown districts: accessibility of, 167;
parking in, 163, 167; postwar decline
and boosterism, 266–68; streetcar
systems and congestion in, 15–16,
159–60. *See also* street construction
and improvement, urban
draft animals, decline of, 183, 352n52
dragging: improvement of, 77; OPR and,
68, 70; in Sac County, Iowa, 4; split-
log drag, 32
Drake, Edwin L., 175
"drive-in" service windows, 263
Durant, William, 38
"dustless road" technologies, 76–77
dust problem, 75

E

Eagan, MN, xxvi–xxviii, *xxviii*, 292
earth roads, 69–70, 320n9
economies of scale, 55. *See also* mass
production and Fordism
edge cities, 276
efficiency: centralization vs. self-government and, 27; city efficient planners,
96–97; good-roads movement and,
29; Model T, Fordism, and, 57–59;
patronage politics and, 17–18
Eisenhower, Dwight D., 273–74
electric vehicles, 294–95
elevated railways, 23, 338n42
energy. *See* coal; oil and gasoline
engineering. *See* automobile design;
road construction and improvement, rural; road technologies; street

construction and improvement,
urban; traffic engineering
Eno, William Phelps, 92, 100, 136, 140–41
entrance ramps on parkways, 225
environmental and ecological effects: of
Car Country, xxxiii–xxxiv; electric
vehicles and, 294–95; fossil fuel usage
from mechanization, 205; oil and,
178–79, 237; of roads, 213–17
environmental limits: accommodation
to traffic and, 67; cars and roads as
overcoming, xxxiii, 8, 154; desire to
overcome, xxxiii; industrialization
and, 11; rail-based revolution and,
142; as threat to Car Country, 295
epidemics, 17
Ethyl Corporation, 182
Europe, xxiv–xxv, 42–44
exit-ramp neighborhoods: physical layout of, xxvi–xxviii, *xxviii*; streetcar
neighborhoods compared to, xxix–
xxx, *xxxi*
expressways, 270. *See also* freeways
externalities of Car Country, 293–95. *See
also* environmental and ecological
effects

F

farm-to-market roads vs. long-distance
tourist roads, 78–82, 84
Farson, John, 73, 89
fatalities. *See* safety
Faulkner, William, 53
Faurote, Fay Leone, 318n67
Federal-Aid Highway Act (1944), 270–71
Federal-Aid Highway Act (1954), 273
Federal-Aid Highway Act (1956), 254, 274
Federal Aid Road Act (1916), 80–83,
84–85
Federal Highway Act (1921), 129
Federal Housing Administration (FHA),
256–61, 263–64, 365n16, 366n24,

367n30, 368n32

Federal Works Administrator, 271

FHA (Federal Housing Administration), 256–61, 263–64, 365n16, 366n24, 367n30, 368n32

filling stations, 174–75

financing: good-roads movement and, 28, 30–31, 32; Gutfreund on rural roads and, 309n92; interwar insufficiency of, 185; linkage principle, 190–93, 269, 274–75, 276–77; state aid, spread of, 32. *See also* gasoline taxes; taxes

Fisher, Carl Graham, 78, 323n37

Fisher Body Works, 359n40

Five Dollar Day policy (Ford), 59–60, 116

Flink, James, 300n15, 312n20

flush fields, 176

Ford, Henry: on decentralization, 161; economies of scale and, 55; Five Dollar Day policy, 60; forestry and, 208; lightweight car, search for, 47–48; Model T improvements, resistance to, 54; rubber plantations and, 211; on scope of production, 203; "universal car" and, 50, 54; vanadium steel and, 313n26

Fordism. *See* mass production and Fordism

Fordlandia, Brazil, 208, 210–12

Ford Methods and the Ford Shops (Arnold and Faurote), 318n67

Ford Model T, 115; accessories for, 52–54; 316n48; advertising for, 50; auto market and, 49–50; changes in design of, 316n60; closed-body design, 239; demise of, 210; farmer adaptation of, 50; improvements, resistance to, 54; manufacturing, Fordism, and, 54–61; market share, 58; in New York to Seattle race (1909), 49–50; pioneering period, dominance of, 38; price of, 55, 56–57, 314n32, 317n63; production

runs, 55–56, 59; suspension system, 48, 115; as "Universal Car," 50, 54; weight-to-power ratio and, 48

Ford Motor Company: closed-steel bodies, shift to, 210, 359n40; dealership network, 315n39; Five Dollar Day policy, 59–60, 116; Fordlandia rubber plantation in Brazil, 208, 210–12; Highland Park plant, 56, 212–13; Imperial Mine, 358n29; Iron Mountain forestry and lumbering operations, 208–10, 360n41; market share, 58, 61; Model A, 212; Model N (R, S), 47, 55, 314n32; pollution and conservation measures, 206–7; price cuts policy, 56–57; raw materials use, 207–8; replacement parts, 314n39; River Rouge facility, Dearborn, MI, 200, 201; runabouts, 45; vanadium steel and, 313n26; vertical integration by, 204–5, 207–13. *See also* River Rouge Ford facility, Dearborn, MI

forestry operations, Ford, 208–10

Forman, Richard T. T., 360n49

fossil fuels. *See* coal; oil and gasoline

freeways: downtown accessibility and, 267–68; elevated trains compared to, 338n42; initial development of, 140; interstate system, 270–77; Los Angeles, 345n104

French-style vehicles, 42–43

Fresno, CA, 369n40

funding. *See* financing; gasoline taxes; taxes

G

Galamb, Joseph, 47

gasoline. *See* oil and gasoline

gasoline taxes: adequacy questions, 193–94; diversion of funds, 190–91, 191; highway-planning surveys and, 190–93; institution of, 185–86; linkage

I

Imperial Mine, 358n29
income and car ownership, 280, 281, 282
individualism, 341n61
Industrial Revolution, 8–9, 11–13, 111
industries, suburban, 277–78
instant boulevards technique, 139
Institute for Social Research, University of Michigan, 279–80
institutional consolidation, rural, 156–59
Interante, Joseph Anthony, 315n39
interchangeable parts, 56
interest deduction on mortgages, 365n12
International Harvester, 45
interregional highways, 197–98
Interregional Highways (National Interregional Highway Committee), 270, 271
interstate highway system, 270–77
Iron Mountain, Michigan, 208–10, 360n41
isolation, good-roads argument on, 29

J

Jackson, Kenneth T., 377n13
Jacobs, Jane, 288, 289–93
jaywalking, 93, 329n104
Jellinek, Emile, 42
Joint Committee on Roadside Development, 216–17
Joy, Henry B., 323n37

K

Kansas City, 162, 231
Kay, Jane Holtz, 294
kerosene, 175
Kettering, Charles, 181

L

labor productivity, 58–61

landscape architects, 216
land-use patterns. *See specific topics*
LAW (League of American Wheelman), 26
lead in gasoline, 181–83, 351n48
League of American Wheelman (LAW), 26
Leopold, Aldo, 222–23
Levine, Jonathan, 368n31
Levittown developments, 258–59
Levitt & Sons, 258–59
light rail: commuter-rail suburbs and time-distance geography, 147, 147–48; elevated railways, 23; subways, 23–24. *See also* railroads
Lima-Indiana oil fields, 176
Lincoln Highway proposal, 78–79, 323n37
linearity, 143
lines, painted, 101, 102, 130
linkage principle, 190–93, 269, 274–75, 276–77
localism, scientific, 68–72, 97, 320n5
Long Island, New York, 41, 258–59
Longstreth, Richard, 369n37
Los Angeles: Arroyo Seco Parkway, 140; downtown decline, 266; freeway system, 345n104; Miracle Mile, 164; number of automobiles in, 87–88; oil fields, 172; parking ban (1920), 160, 343n89; retail decentralization in, 163–64, 166; smog in, 181; streetcar convergence and downtown congestion, 163; traffic deaths in, 327n80
Los Angeles Traffic Commission, 136
love-affair thesis, xxii, xxiv–xxvi, 297n5
lumbering operations, Ford, 208–10

M

macadam, 14, 41, 65, 75–76, 118
Macalester-Groveland, St. Paul, MN, xxviii–xxx, *xxxi*, *xxxix*, 291–92

National Housing Act (1934), 256
National Industrial Recovery Act
    (NIRA), 181
National Interregional Highway Com-
    mittee, 270
national parks road building, 219–23, 241
National Park-to-Highway Association,
    220
National System of Interstate Highways,
    271–77
natural resources, auto industry demand
    for, 207–8
nature: altered interaction with, xxxiii–
    xxxiv; car design and contact with,
    218–19; mobility and contact with,
    217–18; national forests, 241, 362n71;
    national parks road building, 219–23,
    241; parkways and, 219–20, 223–27;
    reform movements and beliefs about,
    7–8
needs and desires, everyday, xxiii, 299n8
neighborhood, FHA definition of,
    366n24
Nevins, Allan, 313n26
New Deal work-relief programs, 221–22,
    225–26
New York City: civil service, 305n41;
    Committee on Public Thorough-
    fares, 100; dirty streets, 108; dumb-
    bell tenements, 13; Fifth Avenue
    Association, 99; horse manure prob-
    lem, 16; Lower Manhattan Express-
    way (proposed), 292; Manhattan
    Elevated, 23; one-way streets, 100,
    332n135; parkways, 223, 225–26, 242;
    patronage system and reform, 17–18;
    pedestrian fatalities in, 88; pedestri-
    ans, 64, 86, 326n68; police-directed
    traffic, 91; street-cleaning reform, 21;
    street openings, 25; street-widening
    efforts, 99; subway construction, 24;
    traffic control tower, 122; under-street
    systems, 109; Waring and street

cleaning in, 6; wires overhead, 110;
    zoning in, 135
NHUC (National Highway Users Con-
    ference), 190
Nichols, J. C., 162
NIRA (National Industrial Recovery
    Act), 181
Norton, Peter, 297n5, 329n104

O

object-lesson road program, 31, 69–70
Office of Public Road Inquiries (OPRI),
    26–27, 30, 31, 32
Office of Public Roads (OPR), 67–72,
    79–80
Office of Public Roads and Rural Engi-
    neering (OPRRE), 82, 83, 85
Office of Road Inquiry (ORI), 26
offices, suburban, 277
oil and gasoline: coal vs., 177, 184–85,
    236; demand for, 173, 175; discovery
    and extraction, 175–77; draft animal
    decline and, 183, 352n52; environmen-
    tal issues, 178–79, 181, 237; fields, loca-
    tion of, 176; filling stations, 174–75;
    first boom in, 175; kerosene, 175;
    lead as additive, 181–83, 351n48; Los
    Angeles oil fields, 172; petrochemical
    industry emergence, 183–84; pipe-
    lines and distribution of, 178, 236;
    prices, 180, 297n2; refineries, 177, 178,
    179, 215; rule of capture and resource-
    management issues, 179–81; second-
    ary recovery methods, 350n37; service
    station prices and gasoline taxes, 186,
    192. See also gasoline taxes
Oil Code, 181
Oil Pollution Act (1924), 179
Oldsmobile, 45, 46
Olmsted, Frederick Law, Jr., 97, 139
Olmsted, Frederick Law, Sr., 223–24, 225
Omaha, NE, 233

and, 271; Pennsylvania, 198, 217;
postwar, 269
state parks, 222
statute labor system, 18–19, 28
steel: closed-body auto design, 210, 218,
359n36, 359n40; vanadium, 47, 313n26
Steinbeck, John, 342n81
St. Joseph, MO, 25
Stone, Roy, 26, 68, 69, 75
stop signs, 138–39
St. Paul, MN: automobile time-distance
geography in, 151, 152; Macalester-
Groveland, xxvi–xxx, xxviii, xxix,
291–92; number of automobiles in,
87; streetcar time-distance geography
in, 146–47, 147
St. Paul Park, MN: automobile time-
distance geography in, 151–54, 153;
commuter-rail time-distance geography in, 147–48, 149
street and road types and hierarchies:
Bartholomew's system of, 134–35; in
Burnham's Plan of Chicago, 96; in
exit-ramp neighborhoods, xxvii–
xxviii; in streetcar neighborhoods,
xxviii–xxix
streetcar neighborhood pattern, xxviii–
xxx, xxxi, xxxix, 337n34
streetcar systems, electric: buses replacing, 272, 292; congestion from, 15–16,
86–87, 159–60, 163; decline of, 166–67;
horses replaced with, 14–15; motorists
following road patterns of, 337n34;
overhead wires, objections to, 15, 22,
110; teamster confrontations, 328n96;
time-distance geography and, 146–47,
147
street-cleaning movements, 21–22; New
York City, 6
street construction and improvement, urban: before cars, 19–25; city
beautiful movement, 95–96; city
efficient movement and engineering

solutions, 96–99; city planning and
comprehensive plans in interwar
period, 133–35; congestion and,
86–88; double-decked and elaborate
projects, 102, 135; paving and, 98;
pedestrian danger and, 88–90; rural
compared to, 103; widening projects,
98–99, 331n125. See also traffic control
street reform movements. See reform
movements
streets, urban: polluted, 16, 108; power
struggle over, 91; as public space, 13;
trades and markets removed from,
94–95
Street Traffic Regulation (Eno), 92
striping on roads, 101, 102, 130
Strong, William L., 21
subgrades, research on, 215
subsidies: accelerated depreciation as,
268; Federal Aid Road Act (1916),
80–83, 84–85; FHA and, 260; Jacobs
on, 293; for post roads, 81–82; for
streetcars, 167
suburbs and suburbanization: accelerated depreciation and effects on
commercial development, 268–69,
371n60; car ownership and use patterns and, 279–86, 282, 284; causality
question, 285–86; downtown decline
and, 266–69; housing boom and
FHA standards and, 255–61; interstate highway system and, 269–77;
in nineteenth century, 9; offices
and industries and, 277–78; pushed
beyond streetcar zones, 161–62, 232;
retail and shopping centers and,
262–66; "sprawl," 259; time-distance
geography in commuter-rail suburbs,
146–47, 147, 151–54, 153
subways, 23–24
superhighways: BPR report against,
196–98; cost of, 194–95; interstate
system, 271–77; tolls and, 195–96

supermarkets, development of, 165

surveys: citywide traffic surveys, 137; highway-planning surveys and self-supporting issue, 191–93; origin-destination, 271–72

suspension systems, 48, 115

Sutter, Paul P., 321n20

Switzerland, xxi

T

tar binders for macadam, 76, 118, 322n26

tarmac, 76

taxes: accelerated depreciation, 268–69, 371n60; excise, 274; good-roads movement and, 28, 29–30; income, 188; mortgage interest deduction, 365n12; poll, 185; property, 18, 28, 185, 187; statute labor, 18, 185; vehicle, 188, 274. See also gasoline taxes

taxpayer blocks, 164

teamsters vs. streetcars, 328n96

TEL (tetraethyl lead), 181–83

tenement buildings, 10, 13

Tennessee Valley Authority, 217

tetraethyl lead (TEL), 181–83

thermal cracking, 177

Thomas B. Jeffery Company, 45

Thomas Motor Company, 48

thoroughfares, 134–35, 262

time-distance geography. See mobility and time-distance geography in interwar period

timetables, rail, 143–44

time vs. distance, xxx. See also mobility and time-distance geography in interwar period

Title VI, 257

Toll Roads and Free Roads (BPR), 196–98

tolls and toll roads: BPR report against, 196–98; in postwar era, 273; successful toll roads, 198–99; superhighways and, 195–96

tops for automobiles, 315n44

touring car, American, 44–46

tourist cabins, roadside, 169

tourist roads, long-distance: farm-to-market roads vs., 78–82, 84; Lincoln Highway and other proposals, 78–79, 323n37. See also superhighways

Townsend, Charles E., 325n49

traction companies, 14

traffic congestion. See congestion

traffic control: behavior conventions, changing, 90–95, 120; changing use of streets as impetus for, 90; crosswalks and zones of safety, 102; delays and, 88; interwar traffic engineering, 136–41; islands vs. striping, 100–101; lights, 101, 138; mechanical semaphores, 101; one-way streets, 99–100, 138; pedestrian danger and, 88–90; speed limits, 73, 92, 94, 131; stop signs, 138–39; towers, 100, 101, 122; urban congestion and, 86–88; zoning for, 135

traffic courts, 92–93

traffic engineering, 136–39. See also traffic control

traffic-flow maps, 137, 231

traffic jams. See congestion; traffic control

traffic lights, 101, 138

traffic squads, 91

traffic surveys. See surveys

transcontinental superhighway system proposal, 194–98. See also superhighways

transit, public: in Atlanta, xxiii–xxiv; buses replacing streetcars, 272, 292; elevated railways, 23; FHA on, 368n32; land-use patterns and attitudes toward, xxv; in nineteenth century, 9; reform movements and, 22–24; suburbanization and, 261, 272–73; subways, 23–24; traction companies, 14. See also streetcar

systems, electric
transit-oriented development (TOD), 299n11
travel narratives, 52
trolleys. *See* streetcar systems, electric
trucks, motor: agribusiness and long-haul trucking, 276; political economy of agriculture and, 342n70; World War I and growth of, 83–84
turnpikes, 198–99

U

University City, MO, 230
urban centralization, 155
urbanization and spatial transformation, 10
urban street reform. *See* reform movements
utilities: sewers, 16–17, 20, 306n50; street reform and, 22; streets torn up by, 24–25; under-street systems, 109

V

VA (Veterans Administration), 257
vacations, motoring, 41. *See also* national parks road building
vanadium steel, 47, 313n26
Vanderbilt, William K., 41
Vanderbilt Cup, 41
vertical integration by Ford, 204–5, 207–13
Veterans Administration (VA), 257
viaducts, 135

W

wages, 59–61, 116
walking and walkability: distance and, xxx; FHA standards and, 261; in interwar period, 142; Jacobs on, 290–91; motor-age mobility and, 148,
154; opportunities per square mile and, xxv; and small stores, disappearance of, 166; suburban steam-railroad stations and, 9; time-distance and, 146. *See also* pedestrians
Wandersee, John, 313n26
Waring, George E., 6, 21
Washington, D.C., 124
water pollution, 206
weather, 51–53, 218–19
Webb, John, 342n81
weight-to-power dilemma, 46–48
Weir, James, 212
Westchester County, NY, 224
White, E. B., 52, 157, 316n48
"White Wings" street sweepers (New York), 21
Wilderness Society, 223
wildlife deaths, 217, 240
Wills, C. Harold, 313n26
Wilmington, DE, 278
Wilson, Woodrow, 80–81
"windshield wildernesses," 221
Wolf, Bill, 206
wooden body designs, 210, 239
Works Progress Administration, 217, 240
World War I, 61–62, 83

Y

Yard, Robert Sterling, 222–23
Yosemite National Park, 221

Z

zoning: as barrier to densification, 367n31; comprehensive city plans and traffic control with, 135; discrimination with, 162; in New York City, 135; for parking, 263, 369n40; promotional vs. protective, 256; suburbanization and, 260–61; University City, MO, 230

WEYERHAEUSER ENVIRONMENTAL BOOKS